Microsoft® SQL Server® 2008 Integration Services Problem–Design–Solution

Microsoft® SQL Server® 2008 Integration Services
Problem–Design–Solution

Microsoft® SQL Server® 2008 Integration Services
Problem–Design–Solution

Erik Veerman

Jessica M. Moss

Brian Knight

Jay Hackney

WILEY

Wiley Publishing, Inc.

Microsoft® SQL Server® 2008 Integration Services: Problem–Design–Solution
Published by
Wiley Publishing, Inc.
10475 Crosspoint Boulevard
Indianapolis, IN 46256

www.wiley.com

To my family: Amy, Meg, Nate, Kate, and Caleb
—Erik Veerman

About the Authors

Erik Veerman is a Mentor for Solid Quality Mentors, focusing on training, mentoring, and architecting solutions on the SQL Server Business Intelligence (BI) platform. His industry recognition includes Microsoft's Worldwide BI Solution of the Year and *SQL Server Magazine's* Innovator Cup winner. Veerman has designed dozens of BI solutions across a broad business spectrum — telecommunications, marketing, retail, commercial real estate, finance, supply chain, and information technology. His experience with high-volume, multi-terabyte environments and SQL Server 64-bit has enabled clients to scale their Microsoft-based BI solutions for optimal potential. As an expert in on-line analytical processing (OLAP) design, extract, transform, and load (ETL) processing, and dimensional modeling, Veerman is a presenter, author, and instructor. He led the ETL architecture and design for the first production implementation of SQL Server Integration Services (SSIS), and helped to drive the ETL standards and best practices for SSIS on Microsoft's SQL Server 2005 reference initiative, Project REAL. Veerman is also co-author of *Professional SQL Server 2008 Integration Services* (Indianapolis: Wiley, 2008), *Expert SQL Server 2005 Integration Services* (Indianapolis: Wiley, 2006), *Professional SQL Server 2005 Integration Services* (Indianapolis: Wiley, 2007), and lead author for the Microsoft Press SQL Server 2005 and SQL Server 2008 series, focusing on Business Intelligence Development and Implementation. As a resident of Atlanta, Georgia, Veerman participates in the local Atlanta SQL Server User's Group, a Professional Association of SQL Server (PASS) chapter.

Jessica M. Moss (SQL Server MVP) is a well-known practitioner, trainer, author, and speaker for Microsoft SQL Server Business Intelligence (BI). As a Mentor with Solid Quality Mentors, she has created numerous data warehousing solutions for a variety of companies in the retail, Internet, health services, finance, and energy industries, and has delivered training courses on SQL Server Integration Services (SSIS), SQL Server Retail Services (SSRS), and SQL Server Analysis Services (SSAS). While working for a major clothing retailer, Moss participated in the SQL Server 2005 TAP program, where she developed best implementation practices for SSIS. Moss has authored technical content for multiple magazines and Web sites, and has spoken internationally at conferences such as the Professional Association for SQL Server (PASS) Community Summit, SQL Teach International Conference, and the devLink Technical Conference. As a strong proponent of developing user-to-user community relations, Moss organizes meetings for a User Group that discusses different technologies. She also actively participates in local User Groups and code camps in central Virginia. In addition, Moss volunteers her time to help educate people through the PASS organization.

Brian Knight (SQL Server MVP, MCITP, MCSE, MCDBA) is the owner and founder of Pragmatic Works. He is also the co-founder of SQLServerCentral.com and JumpstartTV.com. He runs the local SQL Server Users Group in Jacksonville, Florida (JSSUG). Brian is a contributing columnist for several technical magazines and does regular Webcasts at "Jumpstart TV." He is the author of ten books on the SQL Server technology. Knight has spoken at conferences such as the Professional Association of SQL Server (PASS), SQL Connections, and TechEd, as well as many Code Camps. His blog can be found at www.pragmaticworks.com. Knight lives in Jacksonville, where he loves watching the National Football League Jaguars lose on a regular basis.

About the Authors

Jay Hackney is a mentor and consultant for Solid Quality Mentors, where he helps customers utilize Microsoft technology to build real-world solutions. He has 15 years of development and consulting experience on the Microsoft data platform, and has worked with SQL Server Integration Services (SSIS) since the earliest private beta. Since then, he has used SSIS to deliver data warehousing, extract, transform, and load (ETL), and data migration solutions for many well-known companies, and has presented on SSIS topics at events such as Professional Association for SQL Server (PASS) Summit, Microsoft Tech-Ed, and SQL Server product launches.

 **Rushabh Mehta** is a Mentor for Solid Quality Mentors, and is also the Managing Director for Solid Quality India Pvt. Ltd. Mehta has actively worked with the Microsoft SQL Server and Business Intelligence (BI) platform since 1998. He has developed numerous BI solutions, including predictive-analysis systems, health-care solutions, multi-terabyte financial decision support systems, as well as designing and building an analytical platform to support the Microsoft Windows Azure platform. His experience spans a wide breadth of industrial sectors, including manufacturing, retail, finance, and government, working with clients such as Raymond James Financials, Jackson Hewitt, Publix, the U.S. Department of Veterans Affairs, the U.S. Department of Defense, and Microsoft. Mehta has also developed a number of best practices and standards for implementing BI solutions. He has also developed and delivered advanced training courses on Microsoft BI practices and technologies. An active speaker at a number of large conferences such as the Professional Association for SQL Server (PASS) and TechEd, Mehta also frequently speaks at SQL Server and BI User Groups around the world. Mehta is the Executive Vice President for PASS, the largest global user-driven community for SQL Server professionals.

Credits

Executive Editor
Robert Elliott

Project Editor
Kevin Shafer

Technical Editor
Paul S. Waters

Production Editor
Kathleen Wisor

Copy Editor
Paula Lowell

Editorial Director
Robyn B. Siesky

Editorial Manager
Mary Beth Wakefield

Production Manager
Tim Tate

Vice President and Executive Group Publisher
Richard Swadley

Vice President and Executive Publisher
Barry Pruett

Associate Publisher
Jim Minatel

Proofreader
Scott Klemp, Word One

Indexer
Robert Swanson

Cover Image
©iStockphoto.com/wolv

Acknowledgments

I want to first thank Jessica, Brian, and Jay for adding their valuable expertise and experience to several of the chapters of this book, and sharing their approach and code practices from the SSIS framework, to the dynamic extraction logic, to data cleansing best practices. A big collective thanks to our clients! The unique projects and challenges helped shape and refine this content. I added up the years of experience for all of us, and these pages represent about 50 years of work with data processing and ETL — and that doesn't include late nights and long weekends.

I also want to thank Paul Waters and Rushabh Mehta for their roles in this book as Technical Editor and contributing author, respectively. A big thanks to the Wrox team for their support, hard work, and valuable feedback. And a thanks to you, the reader, because I actually read the Amazon feedback and try to address the constructive criticism in each new work. Hopefully, the diligence has paid off. If so, help us and let the world know!

Last, but not least, thanks to my family for their support. A special thanks to Amy and her encouragement and hard work in so many ways.

— Erik Veerman

As a first-time book author, this acknowledgment holds special meaning to me. I will try to refrain from mentioning everyone I have ever met, and focus on a few special people that truly affected the outcome of this book.

First of all, a huge thank you is due to Erik Veerman, the lead author on this book. He not only convinced me to join this troupe of authors, but also took the time to patiently answer all of my questions about the process. Next, thank you to Jay Hackney, Brian Knight, Rushabh Mehta, Paul Waters, and Wrox for their authoring, technical, and editing contributions. I truly appreciated your support and help.

On a personal note, I would like to thank my friends and family, Mom, Dad, and Lianna, for their never-ending support and patience as I disappeared for days at a time. Finally, a few other people who I would like to recognize for their previous support are Fred Creasy, Georgia Willis, Kathi Walker, and Paul Reynolds — thank you.

— Jessica M. Moss

Thanks to everyone who made this book possible. As always, I owe a huge debt to my wife, Jenn, for putting up with my late nights, and to my children, Colton, Liam, and Camille, for being so patient with their tired dad who has always overextended. Thanks also to the makers of Guinness and other hard liquors for sustaining my ability to keep on writing technical books. Finally, thanks for all the User Group leaders out there who work so hard to help others become proficient in technology. You make a huge difference!

—Brian Knight

I'd like to thank Erik for this opportunity and his hard work on this book.

— Jay Hackney

Contents

Contents

Contents

Contents

Contents

Contents

Contents

Introduction

Our world is a world full of data and, as developers, database administrators (DBAs), or data architects, your job will no doubt require processing data — consolidating data, integrating system data, migrating data, cleansing data, transforming data, or loading data into a data warehouse. This book is about solving problems and building solutions with SQL Server 2008 Integration Services (SSIS). It focuses on the design best practices for the top uses and challenge of SSIS.

In this book, you will learn about how to approach the following kinds of projects, and how to effectively work within SSIS to apply its functionality to these common project requirements and challenges:

- ❑ Designing Extraction Transformation and Loading (ETL) solutions with SSIS to handle file management, data warehouse processing, systems integration, and data cleansing.

- ❑ Resolving common SSIS package deployment and auditing challenges that often get in the way of designing a solid solution.

- ❑ Building an SSIS-based solution that performs well, and can deal with failures or unplanned system outages

As an author team, our vision for this book is very different than the other books on the shelves, which focus mainly on how to use the knobs and buttons in SSIS. Books such as the *Professional Microsoft SQL Server 2008 Integration Services* (Indianapolis: Wiley, 2008) are very valuable to have on your bookshelf for reference and for learning SSIS. But this book is about going to the next level of solution design. Our goal in writing this book was to focus on solving problems, building solutions, and providing design best practices.

In summary, the difference between this SSIS books and all the others out there is that other books simply focus on the product features with little emphasis on solution design. If you go out and buy a new power saw, the manual is going to tell you how to angle the blade, set the right depth, and make a clean cut. But the manual doesn't tell you how to build something. This book shows you how to build the furniture, not just how to use the saw.

To be sure, you must know how to use SSIS before you can build a solution. But going from knowledge to design requires guidance on the right approach, and how to avoid the common pitfalls.

This book empowers you with the confidence, the knowledge, and the understanding to make the right choices in your ETL design that enables easy administration, meets your data processing requirements, and performs well for current and future scalability.

Who This Book Is For

This book is targeted at three primary SSIS users: *data architects, ETL developers, and DBAs responsible for ETL administration and support.*

Because this book focuses on problems and solutions, a base understanding of SSIS is required. A couple of areas of the book walk you through the more advanced features of SSIS, but most of the book builds on top of a foundation of SSIS knowledge and experience. If you have taken an SSIS class, or have read another book and tried out SSIS, or you have built a few packages for various purposes, then that base knowledge will give you enough background for this book. But you should be up for the challenge of learning a new tool in the context of applying it!

The perfect reader of this book is someone who is in the early stages of a new ETL or data integration project (or a redesign project), and is eager to know how to approach the effort with the best practices when designing SSIS packages.

If you are supporting an existing project and must make some changes to aid in administration, deployment, or scalability, then you will also benefit from several of the chapters herein.

What This Book Covers

This book is an expanded, revised, and rewritten version of the *Expert SQL Server 2005 Integration Services* book (Indianapolis: Wiley, 2007). The authors of this book have expanded the coverage to address the current trends in ETL and SSIS, including creating a scaling-out execution model, performing advanced data profiling and cleansing, and handling file management and file processing.

This book also addresses some of the challenges in SSIS surrounding auditing, configurations, and execution management. Two chapters focus on solving these administrative challenges:

❑   Chapter 2 covers building an SSIS package framework, and provides you with an auditing, configuration, and reporting structure that you can use in the packages of your solution.

❑   Chapter 3 also helps you in the area of administration by addressing package deployment and storage. It answers the questions, "Where should I store my packages — in the file system or in SQL Server?" and "What is the best SSIS deployment approach for my environment?" The right answer is that "it depends," and Chapter 3 walks you through all the dependencies, while leading you to the right answer for your environment.

Every ETL or data integration solution involves data extraction of one kind or another. Maybe you're extracting data from flat files, or perhaps your source is coming from an enterprise resource planning (ERP) system, or a line-of-business application. Regardless, you must implement a data extraction methodology that is efficient, reduces the impact on the source, and adequately handles changes and data tracking. Chapter 5 dives into many of the data extraction areas, and even provides you with a dynamic data extraction approach.

Another area that this book covers is data warehouse ETL. In fact, one of the more common uses of SSIS is data warehousing ETL. Chapters 7, 8, and 9 are dedicated to solving the data warehouse ETL challenges all the way from dimension and fact table ETL, to processing cubes in SQL Server Analysis Services (SSAS).

Not to be overlooked, Chapter 11 examines control flow and data flow scripting, and provides examples of common (but complex) challenges that can be solved by scripting, including advanced file management and data processing. Chapter 12 provides performance troubleshooting steps and best practices on data flow design. This chapter also contrasts the right use of SQL commands versus the data flow.

Before you even begin diving into the details of an SSIS-based solution, you must start out on the right foot! Chapter 1 reviews solution architecture, project approach and methodology, package design patterns, the importance of I/O performance, and data element tracking. It answers the question, "Where do I begin and how do I approach an ETL solution?

In all, this book presents a comprehensive picture of SSIS solution challenges and design best practices.

How This Book Is Structured

Before reviewing the chapter organization, let's first note how each chapter is internally structured. Every chapter contains three primary elements — a "Problem" section, a "Design" section, and a "Solution" section. In fact, some chapters are structured with more than one Problem–Design–Solution grouping. Each collection of Problem–Design–Solution addresses the following:

❑ *"Problem"* — Discusses either the current challenges related to the area of focus, or the SSIS-specific problems when trying to design an aspect of the solution.

❑ *"Design"* — Presents the SSIS best practices, or outlines the design aspects and recommendations for a specific solution area.

❑ *"Solution"* — Ties all the aspects of the solution together, and gives either an example solution related to the area, or considers the SSIS solution approach, and factors involved in solving the problem outlined earlier.

This book is generally organized in the way that you would approach a data integration or ETL project. The chapter flow builds on the natural progression that a developer or administrator would go through when designing an SSIS solution.

After beginning with an overview of architecture, the book then moves into putting together the underlying support structure of a solution — the storage, deployment, and management framework. Next, the natural progression is to handle the source data, whether that is in files or extracted from a relational database system (RDBMS), and often requiring a data-cleansing process. Next, the chapters delve into dimension and fact table loading, as well as the cube-processing steps. The final chapters address advanced data handling through scripting, and provide the package availability and performance that many solutions require.

Introduction

The following chapter provides a solution overview and discusses planning:

❑ **Chapter 1,** "SSIS Solution Architecture," addresses the overall solution challenges and planning best practices.

The following chapters examine SSIS administration and the deployment foundation:

❑ **Chapter 2,** "SSIS Management Framework Design," reviews and demonstrates the importance of building an SSIS auditing and execution framework.

❑ **Chapter 3,** "Package Deployment and Storage Decisions," discusses the practices and decisions related to SSIS package deployment and storage.

The following chapters discuss file management and data extraction:

❑ **Chapter 4,** "File Handling and Processing Methods," covers how to deal with different files types, file sources, and file management.

❑ **Chapter 5,** "Data Extraction Best Practices," dives into how to manage data source extractions, including incremental and change data management.

The following chapter discusses data cleansing:

❑ **Chapter 6,** "Data-Cleansing Design," reviews data profiling in SSIS, and how to perform data cleansing of complex and dirty data.

The following chapters cover data warehouse ETL:

❑ **Chapter 7,** "Dimension Table ETL," covers the challenges related to dimension table data changes, and loading for different dimension table types.

❑ **Chapter 8,** "Fact Table ETL," addresses ETL for data warehouse fact table.

❑ **Chapter 9,** "SSAS Processing Architecture," looks at how to handle SSAS cube processing in different ways, based on your processing requirements.

The following chapters examine advanced ETL concepts:

❑ **Chapter 10,** "Implementing Scale-Out ETL Process," looks at how to deal with package reliability, and provides an approach to scaling out an SSIS solution.

❑ **Chapter 11,** "Scripting Design Patterns," presents a few different solution examples geared toward handling advanced data and processing requirements with scripts.

❑ **Chapter 12,** "SSIS Package Scaling," presents troubleshooting steps, and provides best practices for package design with a focus on performance.

The Problem–Design–Solution format and order of the chapters together provide a well thought-out, organized, and systematic approach to SSIS solution design.

What You Need to Use This Book

Following is a breakdown of what you need to use this book:

❏ Since this book is about SQL Server 2008 Integration Services, you will get more out of it if you have the Developer Edition of SQL Server 2008 installed, including the sample applications and the tools.

❏ If you don't have a licensed copy of SQL Server 2008 Developer Edition, you can download a trial version from the Microsoft Web site, `http://download.microsoft.com`. Search for "SQL Server 2008 Evaluation."

❏ The `Adventure Works 2008` samples are required for several of the examples in the chapters. The samples are available on Microsoft Open Source community site, `www.codeplex.com`. Search for "SQL Server 2008 Product Samples."

❏ The source code for the chapters is posted on the Wrox Web site (`www.wrox.com`). See the later section, "Source Code," for directions on how to access to the material. Each chapter has the source code. In addition, a database called `SSIS_PDS` is included in the source code download, and has all the database objects required for the examples.

This book has been written for SQL Server 2008 with SP1 installed (which was released in February 2007).

Conventions

To help you get the most from the text and keep track of what's happening, a number of conventions have been used throughout the book.

> **Boxes like this one hold important, not-to-be forgotten information that is directly relevant to the surrounding text.**

Tips, hints, tricks, and asides to the current discussion are offset and placed in italics like this.

As for styles in the text:

❏ Important new terms and important words are *highlighted* when we introduce them.

❏ Keyboard strokes are shown like this: Ctrl+A.

❏ File names, URLs, and code within the text are shown like this: `persistence.properties`.

❏ Code is presented in the following two ways:

```
In code examples we highlight new and important code with boldfaced text.
The boldface is not used for code that's less important in the present context,
or has been shown before.
```

Source Code

As you work through the examples in this book, you may choose either to type in all the code manually, or use the source code files that accompany the book. All of the source code used in this book is available for download at www.wrox.com. Once at the site, simply locate the book's title (either by using the Search box, or by using one of the title lists), and click the Download Code link on the book's detail page to obtain all the source code for the book.

> Because many books have similar titles, you may find it easiest to search by ISBN; for this book, the ISBN is 978-0-470-52576-0.

Once you download the code, just decompress it with your favorite compression tool. Alternately, you can go to the main Wrox code download page at www.wrox.com/dynamic/books/download .aspx to see the code available for this book and all other Wrox books.

Errata

We make every effort to ensure that there are no errors in the text or in the code. However, no one is perfect, and mistakes do occur. If you find an error in one of our books (such as a spelling mistake or faulty piece of code), we would be very grateful for your feedback. By sending in errata, you may save another reader hours of frustration, and, at the same time, you will be helping us provide even higher-quality information.

To find the errata page for this book, go to www.wrox.com and locate the title using the Search box or one of the title lists. Then, on the book details page, click the Book Errata link. On this page, you can view all errata that has been submitted for this book and posted by Wrox editors. A complete book list including links to each book's errata is also available at www.wrox.com/misc-pages/booklist .shtml.

If you don't spot "your" error on the Book Errata page, go to www.wrox.com/contact/techsupport .shtml and complete the form there to send us the error you have found. We'll check the information and, if appropriate, post a message to the book's errata page and fix the problem in subsequent editions of the book.

p2p.wrox.com

For author and peer discussion, join the P2P forums at p2p.wrox.com. The forums are a Web-based system for you to post messages relating to Wrox books and related technologies, and to interact with other readers and technology users. The forums offer a subscription feature to email you topics of interest of your choosing when new posts are made to the forums. Wrox authors, editors, other industry experts, and your fellow readers are present on these forums.

At http://p2p.wrox.com you will find a number of different forums that will help you not only as you read this book, but also as you develop your own applications. To join the forums, just follow these steps:

1. Go to p2p.wrox.com and click the Register link.

2. Read the terms of use and click Agree.

3. Complete the required information to join, as well as any optional information you wish to provide, and click Submit.

4. You will receive an email with information describing how to verify your account and complete the joining process.

You can read messages in the forums without joining P2P, but to post your own messages, you must join.

Once you join, you can post new messages and respond to messages other users post. You can read messages at any time on the Web. If you would like to have new messages from a particular forum emailed to you, click the "Subscribe to this Forum" icon by the forum name in the forum listing.

For more information about how to use the Wrox P2P, be sure to read the P2P FAQs for answers to questions about how the forum software works, as well as many common questions specific to P2P and Wrox books. To read the FAQs, click the FAQ link on any P2P page.

Microsoft® SQL Server® 2008 Integration Services
Integration Services
Problem–Design–Solution

SSIS Solution Architecture

Imagine that this is the first day of a new internal or client project. You will have responsibility on the data and processing layer of the solution, which involves processing data — a lot of data — from several sources, and then either integrating systems, or maybe consolidating data for reporting. Maybe your background is a developer, or a database administrator (DBA), or a data designer, and you know SSIS fairly well. But now they are calling you the "data and ETL architect."

> ETL is the acronym for Extraction, Transformation, and Loading, which is used to describe the data-processing layer in a data-integration or data warehouse solution.

The project manager approaches you and says that the Vice President of Technology has asked the team to give him an estimate of the infrastructure needed. Furthermore, the business owner wants a high-level overview of how the solution architecture will help the company achieve the business need most efficiently. The project manager also wants your thoughts on the best way to approach the solution, how the development should be coordinated between team members, and how deployment should be handled.

Three meetings are scheduled for tomorrow to address these things, and you've been asked to provide your feedback in those areas.

Where do you start? How should you approach the solution design with SSIS as the main technology? How should all the pieces work together?

This chapter examines how to lay the foundation for successful solutions based on SQL Server Integration Services (SSIS). And, in fact, this whole book is about SSIS solutions to real-world requirements and challenges. It addresses questions such as the following:

❑ What are the problems and issues?

❑ What are the design principles?

❑ How do you put it all together for a complete and successful solution?

Before you dive into the technical challenges of a project, you must first step back and ensure that you are laying the right foundation. Jumping right in is tempting! But resist the urge, because you want to (and need to) set the precedence and patterns for the solution upfront. If you don't, chances are you won't be able to go back and make changes down the road.

As with all chapters in this book, this chapter is organized into the following three major sections:

❑ *"Problem"* — Coordinating and architecting an SSIS solution is not an easy task. The "Problem" section reveals some common challenges and common mistakes when planning and extending your ETL environment.

❑ *"Design"* — The "Design" section in this chapter examines the right approach to a project, and the long-term project aspects that you should set in motion early in a project.

❑ *"Solution"* — In many ways, the remainder of this book provides you with the solutions to make it all work together. This section launches you into the rest of the book, and shows how you can follow the chapters to build or redesign your SSIS solution.

Problem

Data and ETL projects have many challenges. Some challenges relate to data, some to enterprise integration, some to project coordination, and some to general expectations. This section begins by looking at the bigger picture of data within an organization, but then quickly looks at ETL projects and SSIS packages and execution.

Macro Challenge: Enterprise Data Spaghetti

Maybe your SSIS project is only a small solution in a bigger enterprise pond. The problem is that it can still cause a ripple effect when you tie it into your environment. Or, you can have challenges caused by an unwieldy enterprise environment when you try to implement your solution.

Figure 1-1 shows a not-so-nice telephone/electricity pole that illustrates the data nervous system of many organizations.

Figure 1-1

The problem with Figure 1-1 is that this mess didn't happen overnight! It grew into this twisted unorganized process because of poor planning, coordination, and execution. However, be aware that, a lot of the time, a corporation's politics may lead to this type of situation. Departments hire their own technical people and try to go around IT. Systems don't talk to each other nicely. Project pressures (such as time and budget) cause designers to cut corners.

Following are a few reasons why this kind of tangled mess happens in an organization's data processing, and examples of the many problems that this "unorganization" causes:

❑   *Debilitating dependency chains* — The biggest problem is that often systems are built on top of systems on top of systems. The core source data has been connected through so many precedence links that it takes more time and administrative and development overhead. Systems at the source and in the middle of dependencies become un-replaceable because of the amount of effort that switching to a new system would take.

❑ *Unknown and uncontrollable data processing* — The operations that process data are not centralized, and, in many cases, unknown because of department applications that are created without coordination with other applications. Processes run at uncontrolled times, and may impact systems within the processes even during peak times, which affects work efficiency.

❑ *Fragile enterprise changes* — Changes to applications are difficult and costly. They may break processes, or cause data integration or reporting applications to be inaccurate.

❑ *Delayed data access* — Even when the processes are somewhat controlled, the complicated system dependencies cause delays in data availability and nightly overhead processes that often run into mid-morning schedules. When they break, customer perception and employee efficiency are affected.

The "Design" section later in this chapter discusses how to approach your SSIS-based ETL project in the right way, and ensure that you are helping to solve the problem, rather than adding to it.

Micro Challenge: Data-Processing Confusion

Another common problem with data processing is when the logic contained to process data is overly complicated and confusing. Just like the macro enterprise problem, this problem usually is the result of changes over time where logic is modified and appended. It usually comes in one of two ways:

❑ *Runaway stored procedures* — Procedures that run with complicated logic and lots of temporary tables, inserts, updates, and/or deletes can be difficult to manage, and are often inefficient. Supporting the procedures is also very difficult because the logic is difficult to follow, and, many times, the developers or DBAs who wrote the code are unavailable. Overall, this type of process requires a lot of administration and wasted time spent on following and learning the process.

❑ *Unmanageable packages* — SSIS packages can also be designed with difficult-to-follow logic and sometimes complex precedence with hundreds of components used in a single package. These kinds of packages have challenges similar to those of runaway stored procedures, such as troubleshooting and the learning curve required for the process. Figure 1-2 shows the control flow of a package that has too many components to effectively manage. (The SSIS designer is zoomed in at 50 percent to fit on the screen.)

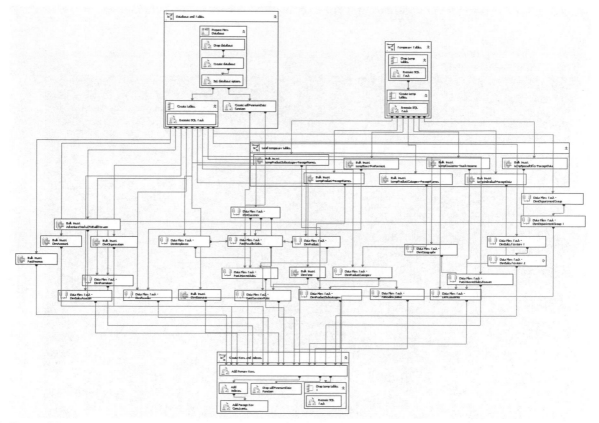

Figure 1-2

The overly complex control flow shown in Figure 1-2 is similar to an overly complex data flow, where too many components are used, thus making the development, troubleshooting, and support difficult to manage. The "Design" section later in this chapter proposes a better approach for SSIS packages called the *modular package approach*.

In summary, both of these types of processes (runaway procedures and unmanageable packages) are very difficult to support, and not suited to team development, error handling, and scalability (all of which are addressed in Chapter 12).

Problems with Execution and Troubleshooting

A couple of other issues that often come up in an ETL or data-integration solution are poor process coordination and difficulty doing root cause analysis. If the "what happened?" question can't be answered quickly and with confidence, then likely there is a problem with the overall solution execution and logging strategy.

Figure 1-3 shows the command-line output of an example SSIS package execution.

```
C:\Windows\system32\cmd.exe                                                    _|□|×
Log:
      Name: User:PipelineComponentTime
      Computer: SOLIDQBI
      Operator: SOLIDQBI\Administrator
      Source Name: Data Flow Task 2
      Source GUID: {67E8F1DE-E882-437C-83CD-058FA560CC09}
      Execution GUID: {CFA98E22-077E-4C5C-B536-3C7C7990A889}
      Message: The component "Fuzzy Grouping" (19) spent 501 milliseconds in Prim
eOutput filling buffers on output "Fuzzy Grouping Output" (21).
      Start Time: 2009-07-28 08:33:41
      End Time: 2009-07-28 08:33:41
End Log
Log:
      Name: User:PipelineComponentTime
      Computer: SOLIDQBI
      Operator: SOLIDQBI\Administrator
      Source Name: Data Flow Task 2
      Source GUID: {67E8F1DE-E882-437C-83CD-058FA560CC09}
      Execution GUID: {CFA98E22-077E-4C5C-B536-3C7C7990A889}
      Message: The component "Aggregate" (56) spent 172 milliseconds in PrimeOutp
ut filling buffers on output "Aggregate Output 1" (58).
      Start Time: 2009-07-28 08:33:41
      End Time: 2009-07-28 08:33:41
End Log
Log:
      Name: User:PipelineComponentTime
      Computer: SOLIDQBI
      Operator: SOLIDQBI\Administrator
      Source Name: Data Flow Task 2
      Source GUID: {67E8F1DE-E882-437C-83CD-058FA560CC09}
      Execution GUID: {CFA98E22-077E-4C5C-B536-3C7C7990A889}
      Message: The component "Sort" (93) spent 375 milliseconds in PrimeOutput fi
lling buffers on output "Sort Output" (95).
      Start Time: 2009-07-28 08:33:41
      End Time: 2009-07-28 08:33:41
End Log
Log:
      Name: User:PipelineComponentTime
      Computer: SOLIDQBI
      Operator: SOLIDQBI\Administrator
      Source Name: Data Flow Task 2
      Source GUID: {67E8F1DE-E882-437C-83CD-058FA560CC09}
      Execution GUID: {CFA98E22-077E-4C5C-B536-3C7C7990A889}
      Message: The component "Sort 1" (130) spent 704 milliseconds in PrimeOutput
 filling buffers on output "Sort Output" (132).
      Start Time: 2009-07-28 08:33:41
      End Time: 2009-07-28 08:33:41
End Log
Log:
      Name: User:PipelineComponentTime
      Computer: SOLIDQBI
      Operator: SOLIDQBI\Administrator
      Source Name: Data Flow Task 2
      Source GUID: {67E8F1DE-E882-437C-83CD-058FA560CC09}
      Execution GUID: {CFA98E22-077E-4C5C-B536-3C7C7990A889}
      Message: The component "Merge Join" (146) spent 125 milliseconds in PrimeOu
tput filling buffers on output "Merge Join Output" (149).
      Start Time: 2009-07-28 08:33:41
      End Time: 2009-07-28 08:33:41
End Log
Log:
      Name: OnInformation
```

Figure 1-3

If you were to consider spending time trying to work through this output when trying to figure out what went wrong, then you should consider implementing a better execution and auditing structure. This includes package execution in your development environment.

If you have just turned on the out-of-the-box SSIS logging and are capturing results to output to a table, it still may not be enough. If you write custom queries every time against the SSIS logging table to figure out what happened, then you also need a better strategy.

Infrastructure Challenges

When designing an SSIS ETL solution, how do you determine the infrastructure components such as server hardware, memory, processor cores, network switches, disk arrays, storage networks, and I/O controllers? Related to that, where should you run your SSIS packages taking into consideration sources, destinations, and other applications, while balancing hardware scalability and location within your network topology?

These questions are not trivial, and the answers depend on a lot of factors, including processing windows, source and destination availability, application impact and availability, network bandwidth, fault-tolerance requirements, and so on.

I/O is usually the biggest bottleneck, and the one most often overlooked. *I/O* (or, more precisely, *disk I/O*) is the throughput that the system can handle on the drive volumes. And this challenge is not just about trying to get the greatest throughput on a single drive. You must consider staging and temporary environments, logging, and current and historical data. And you must balance it all with hardware availability and budget.

The reason disk I/O is so important when considering a data-integration or ETL effort is because of the nature of what you are doing, including the following:

❑ *Bulk operations* — ETL and integration efforts typically process data in bulk, meaning that, when a process is kicked off (hourly, daily, or weekly), data is moved from sources to destinations with some transformation processes in-between. The processes usually move or integrate thousands or millions of records. That can be a lot of data that moves between systems, and it generates a lot of disk activity.

❑ *Source databases* — Processes that are extracting a lot of data from sources incur disk overhead either by the sheer volume of the data, or when complicated queries against large tables require temporary operations that use disks (such as the SQL Server `TempDB`).

❑ *Destination databases* — The nature of relational databases requires that data be stored to disk before a transaction is marked as complete. When inserting or updating a lot of data, the server must wait until the data is committed for the process to be complete.

❑ *Staging databases* — Staging databases and tables are a common intermediate step in an ETL process and can be used for many reasons. Any time that data is landed to a staging database and then extracted from the staging database, it has the overhead of both the insert and the select, which can, at times, be done simultaneously with inserts into the destination database and, therefore, the I/O is compounded.

❑ *File management* — A lot of ETL operations deal with files such as delimited files, XML, EDI, and so on. Large files require file management, archiving, and sometimes processing, and, therefore, incur disk I/O overhead.

The bottom line is that you will most likely have a disk I/O bottleneck in your data-processing operations, and you'll need to plan and manage for that to meet your service level agreements (SLAs) and performance requirements.

Other Challenges

The list of common project challenges can go on and on, but here are a few more:

❑ *Data challenges* — Of course, you will have data challenges in your project anywhere from missing records to dirty data to bad data, and you will need to understand those problems as soon as possible so that you can set the expectations upfront about what can and what cannot be done about them. Although you can do a lot in SSIS (including fuzzy matching), magic is not on the component list — you can't make up data that doesn't exist. Don't overpromise. Be realistic.

❑ *Corporate political challenges* — This book is about solving problems with a technology, namely SSIS. But, because you are trying to solve problems, you are going to be dealing with people. Everyone has an agenda, and a lot of times those agendas will not be in your project's best interest. Watch out for people who are threatened because you are changing the way things are done (even when it is for the better), or because your solution will be replacing one of their legacy applications, or because they are territorial about their "sandbox." You want to fix the enterprise spaghetti shown in Figure 1-1, but don't forget that some people have their tribal knowledge and make their living by keeping the corporate data nervous system tangled.

❑ *Requirement and scope challenges* — Any project has scope creep. Just be careful about how the changes affect the project timeline, and don't leave data validation until the last day. You'll get burned!

Design

Now that you are scared, step back and take a deep breath. Designing an ETL process is doable, and, with the right approach in mind, you can be successful. This section discusses the overall design approach to an SSIS-based solution by examining the following:

❑ Choosing the right tool

❑ Solution architecture

❑ Project planning

❑ Package design patterns

❑ Server and storage hardware

❑ Package execution location

Choosing the Right Tool

This book is about applying SSIS. You are probably reading it because you assume that SSIS is the right tool for the job. That's probably the case. However, be sure to consider what you are doing, and ensure that using SSIS is in line with what you are doing.

Think about all the different types of data-processing needs that you have across your organization:

❑   Data synchronization between systems

❑   Data extraction from enterprise resource planning (ERP) systems

❑   Ad hoc reporting

❑   Replication (both homogeneous and heterogeneous)

❑   PDA data synchronization

❑   Legacy system integration

❑   Data warehouse ETL processing

❑   Vendors and partner data files integration

❑   Line-of-business data processing

❑   Customer and employee directory synchronization

As you may know, when it comes to data processing, a lot of tools are out there. Some are created for specific situations (such as folder synchronizing tools), whereas other tools are designed to perform a variety of functions for different situations. So, the traditional question often posed is which tool can best meet the business and logical requirements to perform the tasks needed?

Consider the host of tools found in the ever-evolving Microsoft toolset. You can use Transact SQL (TSQL) to hand-code a data load, Host Integration Server to communicate with a heterogeneous data source, BizTalk to orchestrate messages in a transactional manner, or SSIS to load data in batches. Each of these tools plays a role in the data world.

Although overlaps exist, each tool has a distinct focus and target purpose. When you become comfortable with a technology, there's always the tendency to want to apply that technology beyond its intended "sweet spot" when another tool would be better for the job. You've no doubt heard the phrase "when you're a hammer, everything looks like a nail." For example, C# developers may want to build an application to do something that SSIS could potentially do in an hour of development time. The challenge everyone faces entails time and capacity. There is no way everyone can be an expert across the board. Therefore, developers and administrators alike should be diligent about performing research on tools and technologies that complement each other, based on different situations.

For example, many organizations use BizTalk for a host of purposes beyond the handling of business-to-business communication and process workflow automation. These same organizations may be perplexed as to why BizTalk doesn't scale to meet the needs of the organization's terabyte data warehousing ETL. The easy answer is that the right tool for bulk Business Intelligence (BI) processing is an ETL tool such as SSIS.

> ### Be Careful About Tool Selection
>
> In some client environments, an ETL tool may be chosen without consideration for the availability of industry skills, support, or even the learning curve. Even though the tool could perform "magic," it usually doesn't come with a pocket magician — just the magic of emptying your corporate wallet. In many cases, thousands of dollars have been spent on an ETL tool that takes too long to master, implement, and support. Beyond the standard functionality questions you should ask about a tool, be sure to also consider the following:
>
> ❑ Your internal skill sets
>
> ❑ The trend of industry use of the tool
>
> ❑ How easy it is to learn
>
> ❑ The ease of supporting the tool

Overall Solution Architecture

The reality is that creating a perfectly efficient enterprise data ecosystem is impossible. But there are certainly levels of efficiency that can be gained when your SSIS solution is planned and implemented thoughtfully. Figure 1-4 contrasts Figure 1-1 by showing a city's central power station, organized and efficient.

Figure 1-4

The tendency when developing a new integration or ETL system is to get it done as quickly as possible. What often happens is that the overall architecture is not integrated well into an organization's environment. Maybe some time is saved (and that is even questionable), but in the end, more time and money will be wasted.

A solution architecture should have several key data-processing objectives. The following apply to SSIS-based solutions, but also relate generically to any data-processing solution architecture:

❑ The solution should coordinate with other data-centric solutions in the enterprise. Do not build a separate data silo, especially if your effort is a data warehouse or data mart — that causes multiple versions and variations of the data.

❑ Source data that is required for the solution must be extracted as close to the source as possible and not plugged at the end of a long dependency chain. (Be sure to follow the previous bullet point).

❑ The solution should have a centralized administration and execution strategy that coordinates with other systems, or follows the practices of other corporate systems. This does not require limiting a scale-out architecture, but simply that the support structures are centralized.

❑ Real-time execution auditing is also needed to know what is happening and what did happen. This information will go a long way in supporting a system. In addition, you should have a way to track data back to the source. This tracking is critical for both data validation and troubleshooting data errors.

❑ The processes must have rollback layers. In other words, if your requirements necessitate a complicated or long process, don't require the whole process to be re-run from the start if the last part breaks. Plan for restarting at interim points after the issues are identified. Doing so also enables you to easily compartmentalize changes in the ETL solution.

These objectives represent the larger picture of an overall solution architecture. Other aspects, of course, are important and situational to what you are building in SSIS. Two common types of data-processing efforts are discussed in the following sections: system integration and data warehouse ETL. These fit well into the SSIS toolset.

Data Integration or Consolidation

One common use of SSIS is to integrate data between systems, or to synchronize data. For example, you may want to create a business-to-business portal site, and you may need the site to interface with the source data on the mainframe. In this case, you may get the data delivered in nightly extracts from the mainframe and load it into your SQL Server table.

Another very common ETL task that DBAs face is receiving files from File Transfer Protocol (FTP) servers (or on network shares) that must be processed and loaded into another system. This type of process involves moving files, and then processing the data, which may involve de-duping (removing duplicates), combining files, cleaning bad data, and so on. Two systems may also need to talk to one another or pass business keys in order for records to be matched between environments.

Figure 1-5 shows an example solution architecture that integrates data between different systems in an enterprise.

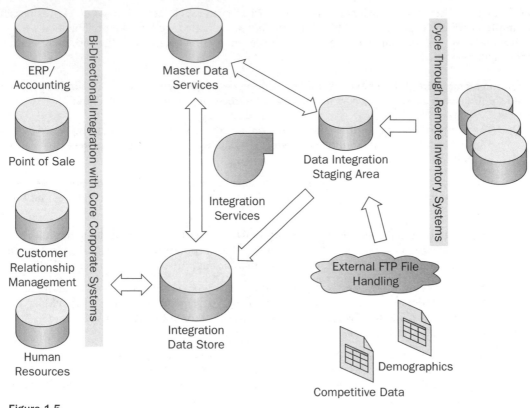

Figure 1-5

In this diagram, data from different systems is integrated. Often, a master data management service (sometimes called *master dimension management*) helps to synchronize entities between systems so that an organization's data relates (for example, so that a customer record from the customer relationship management, or CRM, system can tie into the ERP sales system). This data process contains some aspects that are bidirectional, and other parts that perform extraction and loads. Data staging is used in this example to help integrate the data, and a data store is used to centralize many of the corporate data processes (which helps alleviate the long chains of system dependencies).

Of course, other variations of system integration solutions exist, such as consolidation of different divisional data, especially when companies go through mergers and acquisitions.

Data Warehouse ETL

One of the more common uses of SSIS is for performing data warehouse ETL. Data warehousing focuses on *decision support*, or enabling better decision making through organized accessibility of information. As opposed to a *transactional system* such as a point of sale (POS), Human Resources (HR), or CRM that is designed to allow rapid transactions to capture information data, a data warehouse is tuned for reporting and analysis. Because data warehousing is focused on the extraction, consolidation, and reporting of information to show trending and data summaries, the ETL part of a data warehouse is important and critical.

Processing ETL for data warehousing involves *extracting* data from source systems or files, performing *transformation* logic on the data (to correlate, cleanse, and consolidate), and then *loading* a data warehouse environment (for reporting and analysis). Figure 1-6 shows common data-processing architecture for a data warehouse ETL system.

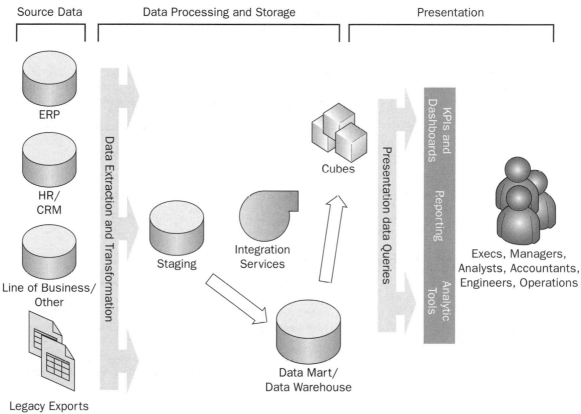

Figure 1-6

For those who are already versed in ETL concepts and practice, you may know that when it comes to developing a data warehouse ETL system, moving from theory to practice often presents the biggest challenge. Did you know that ETL typically takes up between 50 and 70 percent of a data warehousing project? That is quite a daunting statistic. What it means is that even though presenting the data is the end goal and the driving force for business, the largest portion of developing a data warehouse is spent not on the presentation and organization of the data, but rather on the behind-the-scenes processing to get the data ready.

Project Planning and Team Development

This is not a project methodology book, but you should give some thought to your solution approach. Whether your overall objective is system integration or warehouse ETL, you should give consideration to using an agile development methodology. An *agile methodology* is an iterative approach to development. You add features of the solution through smaller development cycles, and refine requirements as the solution progresses.

Agile Benefits

Even if your solution does not involve a user interface (such as a system integration), an agile approach enables you to tackle aspects of the solution in smaller development cycles, and to troubleshoot data issues along the way. Following are some the general benefits of this approach:

- ❏ *Project and task definition* — The agile approach requires definition of the tasks in a project and the prioritization of the tasks, which are set and known by the technology team and the business or project owners. Tasks can change as a better understanding of the requirements is defined.

- ❏ *Scope management* — Given the clear definition of the activities in an iteration, the scope is set, and any deviation is known to the parties involved, and agreed upon. In essence, project communication is clearer for all parties — developer, management, and ownership.

- ❏ *Addressing of issues and obstacles* — Part of the ongoing process involves identifying the areas in the project that can impede progress. These are highlighted and addressed soon in the process.

- ❏ *Roles and responsibility clarity* — Roles are clearly defined and tasks are assigned, which limits the possibility of team members spinning their wheels in the process.

Agile Cautions and Planning

However, you must exercise some caution. Do not use an agile methodology to foster bad architecture practices. In other words, if you are just using the agile approach and you or your developers' ultimate goal is to meet the tasks and deadlines in whatever way possible, you are going to fall into the trap of compounding the problems of your overall data nervous system (that is, those problems outlined in the earlier "Problem" section).

You must ensure that you have an overall solution architecture, and your agile tasks must fit in that plan and support the cause.

Therefore, whatever project methodology you use, be sure to push for an upfront plan and architecture. If you don't, you will likely run into the tyranny-of-the-urgent problem — that means that you will get overwhelmed with the tasks and, as you throw them together, your solution gets out of control, code is messy, and your stress will be compounded over time.

Following are a few things to consider in your development process:

- ❏ Plan for an early-on proof-of-concept, and use the proof-of-concept to iron out your data process architecture.

- ❏ Set your SSIS package and database conventions upfront, including your auditing structure (as discussed in Chapter 2).

❑ Estimate your data volumes in one of the initial development cycles so that you can purchase the right hardware.

❑ Get your server storage ironed out upfront. Be sure to set expectations with the storage group or vendor early on in the process.

❑ Plan out your package storage and deployment plan in one of the initial phases. (Chapter 3 provides an in-depth discussion of this topic).

❑ In every development cycle, be sure to include a data-validation task so that you can have data checkpoints along the way, rather than having one data-validation test at the end (which often leads to changes).

❑ In regard to SSIS data-related solutions, you must plan upfront any initial data load requirements. If you leave out this planning step, you will likely underestimate the overall solution scope.

Data Element Documentation

Not many developers or system architects are fans of documentation — or at least writing documentation. However, it is a necessary task in any data-centric or ETL project.

Again, this book is more about SSIS solutions than project management, but given the importance of tracking data, included here are some recommendations on data-tracking documentation that can help you in your project.

Data documentation is about tracking the source and destination data elements, data profiling, and mapping the data elements to requirements. You must be diligent about these tasks, and keep them up-to-date, because doing so can help you keep control of the data your project uses. Documentation is also useful in future administration and lineage.

The following data-tracking documents should be used above and beyond your usual documentation (requirements, conceptual design, physical design, ETL design, and so on).

Source Data Dictionary, Profile, and Usage

The source data dictionary is about more than just a definition of what the data elements represent. It's also about what the data looks like, and what destination elements it is used in. Planning sessions can then refer to the source dictionary to help validate requirements and data availability.

You should structure this in two sections: entity definitions and element definitions.

Table 1-1 provides some details for entity tracking.

Table 1-1

Item	Description
Table or filename	This names the file or table and any ongoing naming conventions (such as name variations if different systems are involved, or if files have timestamps included).
Source and definition	Describes the source system where the data originates, and general data that the file contains.
Number of initial records and size	If the solution includes an initial data load, this represents the number of records that are included in the initial data, and the size of the file or table.
Number of incremental records and size	For ongoing data loads, this describes how many records are involved in the incremental source data, and the size of the incremental file or table.
Entity usage	How the source table or file is used in the solution.

Table 1-2 provides some details for element tracking.

Table 1-2

Item	Description
Source table or file	The table of the file that the element is sourced from.
Source column or field	Name of the table column of field from the file.
Definition	Describes the usage of the element in the source.
Data profile analysis	An analysis of the data profile — completeness, value variations, dependencies on other elements, key usage, or uniqueness.
Element usage	Lists the destination tables and columns that this source element is used in, which will be important to keep up-to-date.

Destination Data Dictionary, Usage, and Mapping

Tracking the destination elements so that you can use them to understand what the elements are for, where they came from, and how they are used is also important.

The destination dictionary describes the elements, but also describes the mapping from the source. This is invaluable in the ETL process. Again, you should include both an entity mapping and an element mapping description.

Table 1-3 provides some details for entity tracking.

Table 1-3

Item	Description
Table name	This is the destination table name, schema, and database that the table is used in.
Table description	Describes the use of the table in the overall entity-relationship diagram (ERD), and what general records and grain are included in it.
Keys and grain	Lists the primary key and any candidate keys in the table, and the data grain of the table.
Number of initial records	This is the count of the number of expected rows in the table.
Yearly record growth	Estimates the number of additional rows that will be added to the table.
Source entity mapping	Lists the source tables of files that are involved in the population of the table.

Table 1-4 provides some details for element tracking.

Table 1-4

Item	Description
Destination table name	The table and schema that the column is in.
Destination column name	Name of the table column.
Column description	Describes the usage of the column within the source.
Data type description	Describes the expected data types and ranges used in the column.
Usage type	Describes the type of usage for the column, such as a primary key, candidate key, foreign key, auditing column, descriptor column, and so on.
Source mapping	Lists the source fields used to populate the column, and describes the detailed mapping and transformations needed from the source to the data elements in the column. This is crucial for ETL processing.

Just as a review, this discussion only addresses the tracking of data elements, and is supplementary to the overall solution documentation. You may have other related data documentation, or you may choose to include additional items in your documentation (such as partitioning strategy of the destination table, or other pertinent things about the source data availability or data processing).

Package Design Patterns

The way you design your packages is important for the team development, deployment, future changes, ongoing support, and maintenance. In the "Problem" section earlier in this chapter, an example package was shown that had too much logic in a single package. A better approach is available through the use of modular packages and master packages.

Modular Packages

Instead of putting a lot of your data processing in a single package, focus your packages so that the processing logic contained in them is manageable, and the precedence is not overly complicated. This is called *modular package development,* and it provides the following benefits:

❑   *Facilitates team development* — A team of developers can be working on different aspects of the solution at the same time in different SSIS packages. Also, a single modular package is easier to unit test.

❑   *Eases source control and versioning* — Smaller packages are easier to identify in a source control system, and versioning can isolate changes easier.

❑   *Simplifies deployment* — Deploying changes with modular packages allows only the logic groups that change to be deployed.

❑   *Allows multi-use package execution* — A package may be used in multiple execution groups for related package execution, which reduces redundancy.

❑   *Helps identify errors* — When you're troubleshooting, isolating package bugs and failures is easier with smaller packages.

❑   *Enables better auditing and support* — Administration of an ETL solution is easier to track and audit with smaller module packages that are enabled with auditing and logging.

What does a modular package look like? Package designs vary, depending on the solution and requirements. But a good general rule is to keep the components visually manageable in the package designer without requiring a lot of scrolling to find aspects of the solution.

Figure 1-7 shows a package control flow that demonstrates a modular package.

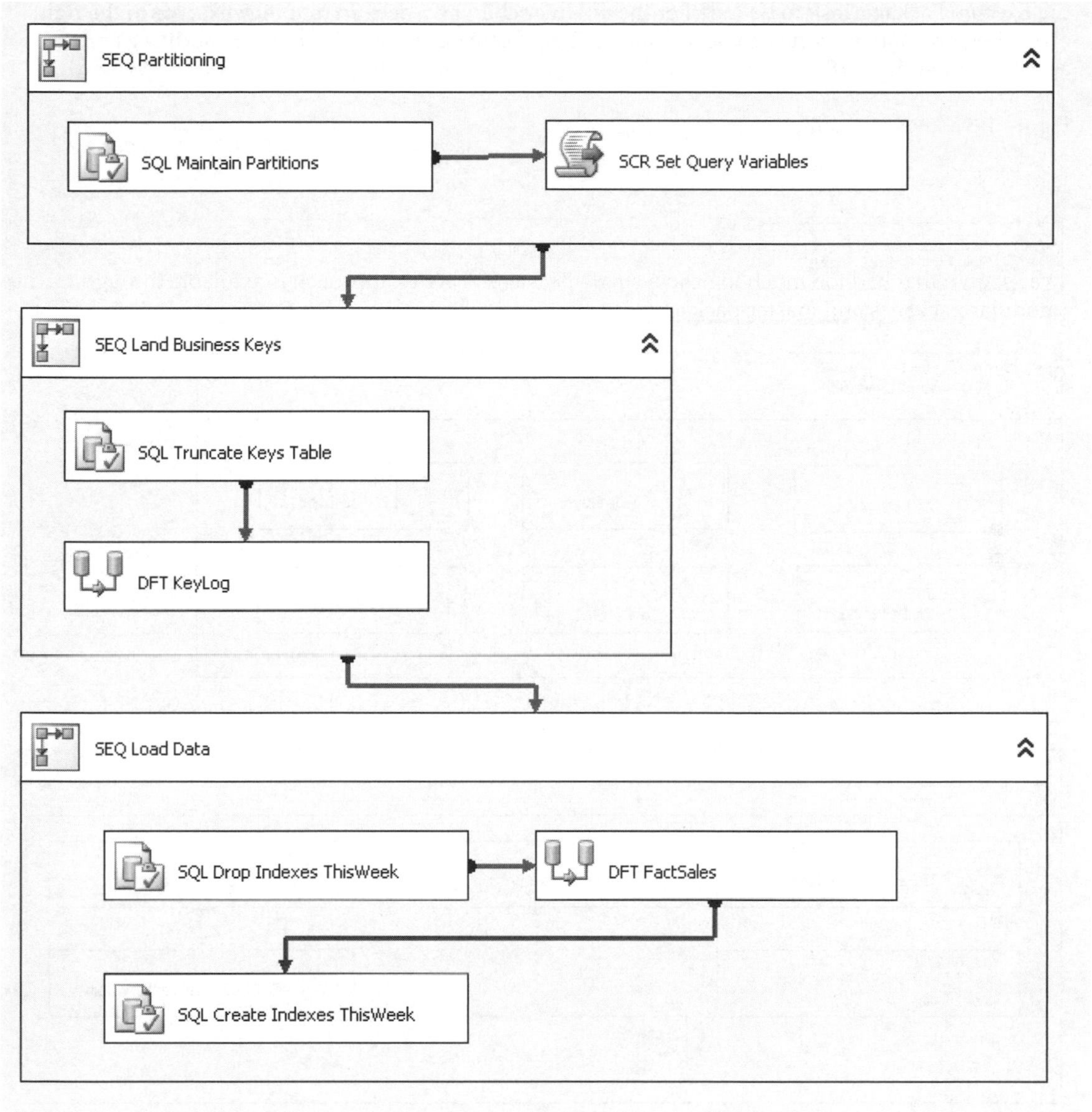

Figure 1-7

In this example, a couple of data flows and a few other tasks support the processing. In all, ten tasks are in the control flow, which is a very manageable group.

Master Packages

The way to still keep your complicated order of data processing (or precedence) is to coordinate the execution of the modular packages through a master package. A *master package* (or *parent package*) uses the Execute Package Task to tie together the modular child packages so that they execute in the right order. Logging and auditing can be included to help facilitate an overall execution auditing and administrative support.

Figure 1-8 shows an example parent package.

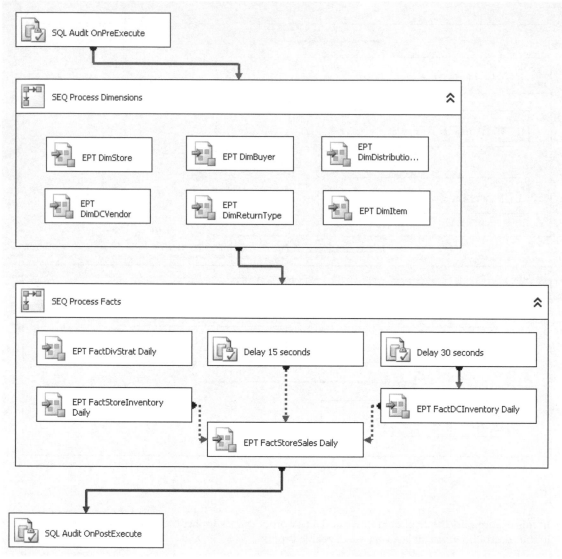

Figure 1-8

Each Execute Package Task ties to a package either stored in the file system, or in the msdb database package store. In many solutions, you will need to execute a set of packages at different times and with different precedence. The master package allows this, and helps implement a rollback and checkpoint system. Chapter 2 provides more coverage of this topic when discussing the building of a package framework.

Server and Storage Hardware

Identifying hardware upfront is a "Catch-22." In other words, you may not know the total scope of your project, or even what to expect from a load standpoint, but you are asked to estimate the hardware requirements for the project.

Server Hardware

Here are some general principles to follow concerning the server hardware:

❑   *64-bit* — You can't really purchase a server these days that is not an x64 processor architecture. This is good news. But be sure that the x64-bit version of Windows Server OS is installed, and that the x64 version of SQL Server 2008 is installed.

❑   *Multicore processors* — The biggest advantage to multicore processors (that is, dual core, quad core, and six core, as of the writing of this book) is that for SQL Server 2008, you are only paying per-socket. If you have a two-CPU quad core, the OS and SQL Server will see eight CPUs, but you are only buying the license for two sockets.

❑   *Memory* — Memory is relatively cheap and very valuable for SSIS. You should use at least 16GB of memory, but preferably 32GB or 64GB, or more, depending on the intensity of your ETL and how much you are utilizing the SSIS data flow.

You are now probably asking, "But how many cores and how many servers should I target?" There is no definitive answer to that question because it is so dependent on your ETL solution complexity, volume, and schedule.

If you must estimate, keep in mind that for a small-scale ETL solution that is dealing with less than 10GB of data (during your ETL), and that is working with a destination database that is less than 1TB, your ETL machine can probably run on a two-socket dual-core or quad-core server with 16GB or 32GB of RAM.

For a medium ETL solution (where your ETL requires execution in a smaller window, and your recurring volumes are larger and/or your destination database is in the multi-terabyte range), consider a quad socket with multicore processors, and at least 32GB of RAM or possibly 64GB with the option to expand.

Larger solutions are really dependent on so many factors, and you should also consider scale-out ETL (which is discussed in Chapter 10). Thus, recommending a general rule — especially if you are building an SSIS server that will run all your enterprise ETL operations — is difficult.

Again, there is so much context that will really drive the hardware requirements, that you must evaluate your situation and customize a recommendation on what you see in your solution.

Development and Test Servers

For mission-critical ETL processes, you must have a test environment that mirrors your production hardware. It will be costly, but consider the cost if you deploy a change that you couldn't test and your server goes down.

If your budget is restricted, and your ETL process is not mission-critical to your business, then your test environment can be a scaled-down version of your production servers or a virtual server. One option to save on cost is to use the same server for both development and testing, and then you may be able to use equivalent hardware. Use different database instances and packages for your testing.

One aspect of setting up test servers that is critical is that the number and naming of your volumes (drive letters) must match between all your environments. In other words, if you have G:, H:, and I: as logical drives on your production server, ensure that your development and test machines have the same logical drives, and the folder structures and databases are the same as well. You don't necessarily need to have the same number of physical drives, but you should partition what you do have into the same logical volumes. Doing so can alleviate a lot of deployment pain.

ETL Collocation

Sharing the source or destination server with your ETL process (called *collocation*) is an option if your source or destination is not impacted by your ETL process. What you must watch out for is the database engine taking all the available RAM on the server, and starving your SSIS process of memory, which can be very debilitating to the ETL.

You can configure the SQL Server memory through the `sp_configure` TSQL statement. You can begin your SSIS processes by limiting the RAM that SQL uses, then run your ETL, and at the end of the ETL process, reset the memory usage on the SQL Server.

SSIS collocation is best for smaller to medium solutions where the ETL only runs nightly or weekly. The next section clarifies the execution location of your environment.

Storage Hardware

As mentioned in the "Problem" section earlier in this chapter, the storage hardware is important because you are performing bulk operations. The more throughputs you can generate with your disk subsystem, the better.

How do you estimate hardware needs? Doing so is very difficult at the start of a solution, but if you can get a gut sense of the record volume and growth, then you can probably do it. A good DBA will be able to help estimate the table sizes by taking the estimated row width, multiplying that number by the expected rows, and then adding some overhead for indexing and growth. (You must consider a lot of factors such as, the SQL Server data page width and free space.)

Disk Volumes and Configuration

Following are some general principles to follow as you try to estimate your disk volumes:

❑ Limit the use of internal server storage, and especially don't put your databases on the boot/system drive (`C:`).

❑ Go with smaller, faster drives, and more of them, rather than bigger and slower drives (except for backups and archive). You can get a lot more throughput for the drives because you can stripe more drives.

❑ Separate your staging and `TempDB` databases on separate drives (even when using a storage area network, or SAN) because, for ETL operations, you will create a bad I/O bottleneck if your source or destinations share the same drives as staging.

❑ Logs should also be on a separate drive because, even if your database is set up as simple recovery (where the log file gets truncated), you will still generate a lot of log activity during ETL operations.

❑ If you estimate your destination database will be 1TB, you will probably need 3–4TB of raw drive space to accommodate for logs, temp, staging, disk striping, redundancy (RAID), and so on. Set this expectation upfront!

Storage Area Network (SAN) Versus Direct Attached Storage (DAS)

Both Storage Area Networks (SANs) and Direct Attached Storage (DAS) have their benefits and drawbacks. SANs come at a higher price, but have the benefit of adding better redundancy, caching, controller throughput, more drives in a stripe, fault tolerance (clusters in different cities), advanced disk mirroring (where a mirror can be split and mounted on other servers), dual read in a mirror (where both drives in a mirror can be read at the same time), and so on.

DAS has the benefit of cost (a fraction of the cost of a SAN), but can also achieve similar throughput (and, in some cases, faster throughput, but without the caching) and easier control of the setup and configuration.

For mission-critical ETL processes and databases, use a SAN. But if your solution doesn't need that high availability, you can consider DAS. Or, you can consider DAS for your staging environment, and SAN for your production databases.

> *This is an SSIS ETL book, so you should consult the current best practices out there for recommendations on drive configuration. However, just remember that ETL generates a lot of I/O in a short amount of time and, therefore, you should watch out for recommendations that are targeted for transactional systems.*

> *A lot of varying and seemingly contradictory recommendations are out there, but each is based on a set of assumptions for different types of data-centric solutions. Be careful to understand those assumptions in your decision.*

The next section is related to hardware, and addresses the question of where you should run your SSIS-based ETL operations.

Package Execution Location

When you are planning out your SSIS solution architecture, you must consider your package execution strategy. Your objective is to leverage the servers and network bandwidth that can handle the impact load from package execution, but without impacting resources that need primary performance. When it comes to where a package should be executed, there is no absolute answer. However, some general principles can direct one architecture design over another.

Package Storage Location Versus Execution Location

When it comes to running a package, a difference exists between where a package is run and where that package is stored. You can store a package as a file and put it in a file system folder, or you can load a package into the msdb system database in SQL Server 2008. Either way, when the package is executed, the storage location is merely where the metadata of that package lives. The package is loaded from that source location through an execution method, and run on the machine where the execution is kicked off. In other words, if you are running a package through the command line or through a job, the package will run on the machine where the command line is called, or the job runs.

Figure 1-9 shows the storage location server on the left and the execution server on the right. The package is executed on the server on the right, even though the package is stored on the server on the left.

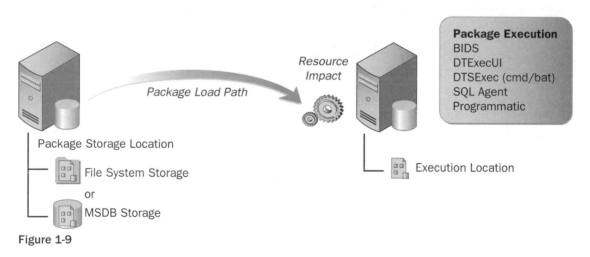

Figure 1-9

Execute SQL Task and Bulk Insert Task Execution

Although a package may be run on any machine with the SSIS service (or, really, that has the SSIS executables and DLLs), this isn't necessarily the place where all the work is being done in the package. For example, if you run an Execute SQL Task in a package and execute the package on a different server than where the Execute SQL Task connection is defined, then the SQL statement is run where the connection is configured, not on the SSIS execution machine. To be sure, the workflow coordination will still be handled on your SSIS execution machine, but the actual SQL code would be run on a different machine.

For the Execute SQL Task and Bulk Insert Task, the SQL code or BCP command is executed on the machine that the connection specifies. This is different from the Data Flow Task, which runs on the machine where the package is executed.

Package Execution and the Data Flow

For your packages that have data flows (which is probably most of your packages), you should understand what happens to the data based on where you execute that package (with the embedded data flow). Additionally, understanding where the data flow execution impact will be dictates where you decide to run your packages.

The *data flow impact* on the package execution server involves the resources needed to manage the data buffers, the data conversion requirements as data is imported from sources, the memory involved in the lookup cache, the temporary memory and processor utilization required for the Sort and Aggregate transformations, and so on. Essentially, any transformation logic contained in the data flows is handled on the server where the package is executed.

The following examples are common configurations for where data is sourced, the destination location, and where packages are executed. Obviously, data flows can be varied and complex with multiple sources and destinations, so this simplification provides the framework with single-source locations and single-destination locations.

Packages Executed on the Source or Destination Servers

The most common example is when a package (that contains a data flow) is executed on either the source or destination server, assuming they are separate.

Figure 1-10 shows the data path and impact on the environment when the package is executed on the machine where the source data is located.

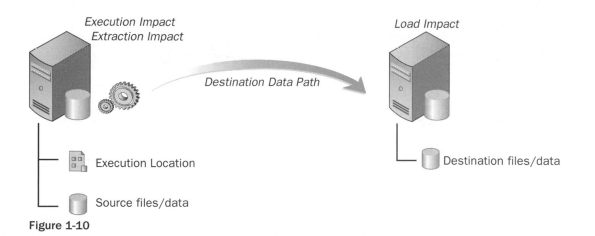

Figure 1-10

The source server will both provide the extracted data and handle the data flow transformation logic, and the destination server will require any data load overhead (such as disk I/O for files, or database inserts or index reorganization).

Following are some of the benefits of this approach:

❑ There is decreased impact on the destination server, where potential users are querying.

❑ Data flow buffers are loaded rapidly, given that the location of the source files and package execution is local and involves no network I/O.

❑ The impact on the destination server is limited, which is useful for destination servers that have 24/7 use, or the SSIS process runs often.

Following are some of the drawbacks of this approach:

❑ The impact on the source server's resources, which may affect applications and users on the source server

❑ Potential reduced performance of the data flow destination adapter and the inability to use the SQL Destination adapter, which requires the package be executed on the same server as the package

Destination Server Package Execution

Similar to the impact of running a package on a source server, running a package on the destination server, as Figure 1-11 demonstrates, has similar benefits and drawbacks, just reversed.

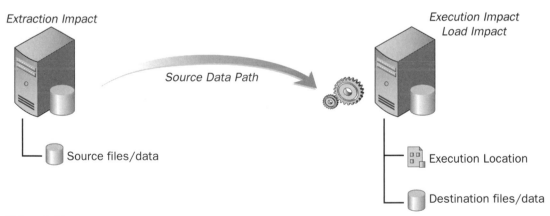

Extraction Impact

Source Data Path

Source files/data

Execution Impact
Load Impact

Execution Location

Destination files/data

Figure 1-11

Following are some of the benefits of executing a package on a destination server:

❑ Limited impact on your source server if it is running other critical tasks

❑ Potential performance benefits for data inserts, especially because the SQL Destination component can now be used

❑ Licensing consolidation if your destination server is also running SQL Server 2008

One drawback of this approach is that it has a heavy impact on the destination server, which may affect users interacting with the destination server.

This approach is very useful if you have users querying and using the destination during the day, and your SSIS processing requirements can be handled through nightly processes.

Standalone SSIS Servers

An alternative execution option is to run your SSIS packages on a second or third server.

In Figure 1-12, an SSIS package is executed on a second server, and, in this diagram, both the source and destination are on the same machine.

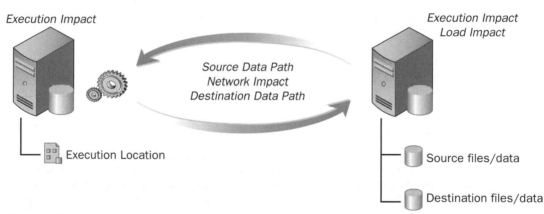

Figure 1-12

As you can see, this scenario is not ideal, because the data would need to travel over the network to the second server, be processed, and then travel back to the same original machine, creating potentially high network utilization, depending on the volume. However, it would reduce the resource impact on the data source and destination server.

Using a standalone SSIS server if your sources and destinations are not on the same physical machines makes more sense. Figure 1-13 highlights this architecture.

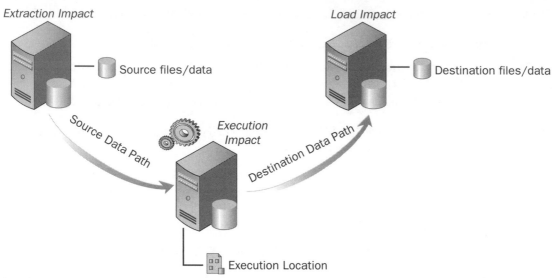

Figure 1-13

In this case, the impact on both the source and destination machines is reduced because the SSIS server would handle the data flow transformation logic. This architecture also provides a viable SSIS application server approach, where the machine can handle all the SSIS processing packages no matter where the data is coming from and going to.

The drawbacks to this approach lie in the capability to optimize the source extraction and destination import, increased network I/O (because the data has to travel over the wire two times), as well as licensing.

Design Review

As you can see, you have a lot to juggle at once when you are planning and building an ETL or data-integration solution. In many cases (such as the infrastructure), all you need to do is set the ball in motion with your IT hardware group. If you are working with a smaller team, you will have more to do, but the discussion in this "Design" section gives you direction to go in, and helps you stay on top of your project. Sometimes you may feel like you are juggling several balls at once, but you'll be better off starting early, rather than trying to juggle ten balls in the middle of the project!

Solution

Now it is time to focus on the SSIS ETL solution. The project is in motion, expectations are set with the stakeholders, and you have laid the foundation to a successful project.

The next step is about designing and implementing your SSIS solution. Just when you think that you have a handle on things, you now have to dive into the details of data and processes! This section launches you into your SSIS design . . .not by providing all the steps in these next few pages, but by giving you the driving directions on where to find your design and solution answers in the rest of this book.

The chapters in this book flow in the natural progression that you may go through when designing your SSIS solution. The next couple chapters provide you with the underlying SSIS support structure for your solution — the storage, deployment, and management framework.

Next, as you delve into the data, you will be dealing with source data, whether in files or extracted from a relational database management system (RDBMS) and often requiring a data-cleansing process. Chapters 4–6 cover files, data extraction, and cleansing.

If your SSIS solution involves data warehouse ETL (which involves dimension and fact table loading, and often cube processing) Chapters 7–9 are for you.

The final chapters address advanced package scalability and availability, advanced scripting for those really complex scenarios, and performance tuning and design best practices.

Setting the Stage: Management and Deployment

One of the very first things you must design is an SSIS package template that integrates with a management and auditing environment. You must do this upfront, because retrofitting your logging and auditing while your packages are being designed is very difficult.

Chapter 2 examines building an SSIS management framework for this purpose. A management framework is about knowing the what, when, and why of when a package executes. Knowing these items is critical for SSIS administration and troubleshooting. Chapter 2 considers how to approach creating package templates, supporting auditing structures, and centralized configurations.

The next design task is also related to management. It is defining your package deployment strategy and your package storage model where you save your packages. Chapter 3 looks at all the surrounding issues and factors involved in choosing the right model for your situation.

Deciding on a deployment and package storage model (the file system or in the msdb system database) is important early on because, as the number and design complexity of your SSIS packages grows (in an organization), so do the challenges related to package deployment and management.

Source Data: Files, Tables, and Data Cleansing

Every ETL or data-integration project involves data. And this data must come from somewhere, either from a file provided or a table (or query). Therefore, you are going to deal with source data in some aspect.

Chapter 4 discusses how to deal with files. Many of the data-integration and processing projects involve working with data files of many kinds, such as delimited files, binary files, image files, Excel files, or XML files. These file types and other types may need to be moved around, modified, copied, or even deleted, and their contents may need to be imported. Chapter 4 walks you through the methods and practices using SSIS to handle file management.

Your project may not involve files, but even if it does, you will more than likely have to extract data from a source database. Chapter 5 examines data extraction. SSIS solutions often have a data-extraction component, which may involve connecting to relational systems like Oracle, DB2, Sybase, MySQL, or TeraData. Chapter 5 considers the best practices for extracting data from various sources, and addresses different extraction requirements (such as optimization, incremental or targeted extraction, change data capture, or data staging), and also addresses common challenges from the various source types, 32-bit or 64-bit platform.

If someone ever tells you that his or her source data is perfect, he or she is lying. Don't believe it! The fact is that data sources are rarely pristine, and often require handling data anomalies, missing data, typographical errors, and just plain bad data. Chapter 6 delves into the practical design steps to handle data cleansing in SSIS using the fuzzy logic, text parsing, and scripting components for data cleansing and text mining. Chapter 6 also demonstrates the use of the SSIS Data Profile Task to better understand the source data that you are dealing with.

Data Warehouse ETL and Cube Processing

The "Design" section of this chapter already reviewed the overall ETL architecture of a data warehouse and BI system. As a background to Chapter 7 (which discusses dimension tables) and Chapter 8 (which discusses fact table ETL), databases designed for data warehousing are created in a structure called a *dimensional model*, which involves two types of tables:

❑   *Dimension tables* hold informational data or attributes that describe entities.

❑   *Fact tables* capture metrics or numeric data that describe quantities, levels, sales, or other statistics.

A data warehouse involves both dimension tables and fact tables. Therefore, your ETL processes need to handle the transformation and loading of dimension tables and fact tables.

Chapter 7 focuses on loading data into data warehouse dimension tables, which requires handling attribute changes, managing business keys, and dealing with surrogate keys. Chapter 7 dives into the best practices for loading different dimension table types, and examines how to optimize the SSIS process to scale to large and complex dimension tables.

Chapter 8 focuses on loading data warehouse fact tables, which often contain millions or billions of rows. Loading data into a fact table requires designing an SSIS package that can scale and also handle the various loading scenarios (such as table partitions, large record updates, and missing keys). Chapter 8 considers the design practices for loading the different types of fact tables.

A data warehouse is often accompanied by a set of cubes. A Microsoft cubing engine, which is a part of SQL Server, is called SQL Server Analysis Services (SSAS). Data warehouse or business intelligence solutions that use SSAS need a data-processing architecture that loads data from the data warehouse or mart into SSAS. Chapter 9 focuses on how to use SSIS to load SSAS data cube structures through the out-of-the-box SSAS processing components, as well as through scripting and the command-line tools. Also included in Chapter 9 is a discussion on how to manage SSAS partitions, and how to deal with incremental data updates.

Advanced ETL: Scripting, High Availability, and Performance

The final three chapters of this book deal with the advanced topics of scripting, high availability, and scaling your package. Chapter 10, for example, dives into how to build a scale-out SSIS solution for high-availability solutions.

One of the most powerful tools within SSIS is the scripting engine. Often, the out-of-the box tasks and transformations cannot handle a unique situation effectively. However, the Script Task and Script component can often be the perfect solution to a complicated problem. Chapter 11 demonstrates examples (both control flow and data flow) where SSIS scripting can solve challenging requirements effectively.

Finally, Chapter 12 addresses the problem of performance and scalability. Data volumes and complexity can sometimes inhibit SSIS package performance. In fact, even SSIS packages designed for simpler requirements can have performance challenges, and if you are dealing with tight data-processing windows, or you want to limit the impact of packages, then scaling and tuning your packages is important. Chapter 12 delves into the best practices for tuning, as well as isolating and resolving performance problems.

Summary

Enterprise environments are often difficult to work in, given the complexities of system dependencies. Even if your organization's data nervous system is limited, or your SSIS project is only a small part of your bigger environment, you must carefully plan how your solution integrates into it. In fact, you should use your ETL project as an opportunity to demonstrate how to build a solution the right way, from the infrastructure, to the processes, to the package design, and management. Approach your project with an overall architecture in mind, be diligent about documenting data elements, plan for the right infrastructure and process execution strategy, and consider solution and data growth as the project is expanded, or more data is loaded or integrated.

When you launch your project in the right direction, the very next thing you should do is implement an SSIS management structure. Chapter 2 examines building an ETL management framework for your packages.

2

SSIS Management Framework Design

Before designing any SSIS packages, you must decide on a number of factors that will affect the design of your packages. These factors include auditing, configurations, and monitoring.

This chapter contains one Problem-Design-Solution. The "Problem" section discusses the issues you will face in trying to manage these factors across developers and departments, and the fact that you can create a standard framework implementation to avoid these issues. The "Design" section discusses in detail how to create a standard SSIS management framework implementation. Finally, the "Solution" section shows how to implement and deploy the framework in SSIS.

Problem

Whether you are creating an extraction, transformation, and loading (ETL) package, a maintenance package, or a simple process workflow, certain requirements are the same for every package. As a developer, you want to decrease your development and maintenance times. The rest of your team also has requirements for the package, which includes the following:

❑   A support person must know how, when, and why a package failed.

❑   A system administrator must see when that package executed and how long it took.

❑   A change control operator must promote the package through environments with as little change as possible.

It comes down to you to put all of these requirements into every package that you create.

Challenges of Not Having a Framework Implementation

You will face many hurdles when coming up with an approach to handle the aforementioned requirements. This section discusses some of the problems you might encounter in order to show you how to avoid them in your final design.

Different Development Methods

The first hurdle you encounter is different packages following different development methods. Having no standard approach (that is, a configuration schema or deployment strategy) makes modifying and maintaining the package after the initial development difficult for either another developer, or maybe even you. To make any changes, the new developer must understand the configuration, logging, and error-handling methods that the original developer used. Only after that understanding can the new developer make modifications, which will result in a longer maintenance cycle.

Using different development methods can also result in confusion about where to make the change. If a new database must be added to the package, should the connection string be added directly to the package? Or should it be included in an external configuration location? If so, should the configuration be stored as a full connection string, or as a server/database combination?

Choosing different development methods will not only cause confusion, it could also result in bad deployments or extended test cycles. In the event that a logging database server name changes, checking that all packages have the new database server name would be necessary. If any packages used text-based logging instead of database logging, the package would either miss the change, or need to be modified separately.

By having packages with different development methods for these base requirements, you'll also end up with an inconsistent problem-solving routine. Each time you start to research an issue on a new package, you'll need to look in an entirely different place than you did the last time you looked at a package. This could lead to missing what should have been an easy solution, and causing general frustration with the state of the packages.

Changing Metadata

Another hurdle you'll face is how to handle changing metadata. This issue was briefly touched upon earlier in this chapter in the discussion of how to store a connection string, but it is not just isolated to databases. Changing metadata could refer to file locations, control variables that indicate whether a section of the package should run, and other numerous facets of a package. The metadata could need to be changed on a regular basis, or more intermittently.

If the metadata change is overarching across all packages, changing, testing, and redeploying every package that contains that metadata would take a lot of effort. A good example of this would be renaming a shared network folder in which multiple packages store files to adhere to new corporate standards. Modifying the variable that contains the shared network folder name in multiple packages would take a long time, and be a good candidate for mistyping just one of the packages and finding the mistake late in the test cycle.

One change that will happen every time you create a package is modifying the name of a server location while moving a package through your environments, from development to quality assurance (QA) to production, or something similar. Every time you need to open and change the package itself, you open yourself up to the possibility of error.

Getting the Right Information to the Right People at the Right Time

The last hurdle to discuss is getting the right information to the right people at the right time. The type of information needed includes (but is not limited to) the following:

❑ The time the package started and ended its execution

❑ Whether the package succeeded or failed

❑ What events occurred during the execution

Depending on your scenario, you may also need to know what variables were modified or who executed the package. If you realize you need this information after the package has already run, you're already too late. You must ensure that all of this information is recorded every time every package runs.

After a package has run and the information has been recorded, you must ensure that other developers or the support staff have access to that information in a readable format. They must also have the capability to go to one centralized location to find that readable information. You don't want to spend your time writing reporting queries off your information when you could be spending it creating more packages!

Reusability

Although SSIS offers a variety of methods out of the box to help assist with these concerns, a few limitations exist to using these standard methods. In general, one issue that arises is that you must set up all the options every time you create a package. Not only does this slow down development time, it also opens up the possibility of a fellow developer mistyping something, or choosing a different method than you have used. These potential problems can make maintaining and supporting the package a nightmare for someone who did not initially create the package.

Framework Implementation

So, how do you overcome all of these issues that happen when developing SSIS packages? You create your own SSIS management framework, of course!

To design an SSIS management framework, you must solve all the previously mentioned issues. The framework must be easy to use, and help improve the SSIS package experience for all parties involved. Several pieces must work together fluidly to create the full framework.

Configuration Management Scheme

The first component, a configuration management scheme, eliminates making any modifications directly to the package, including changes needed to move a package through environments, and adjustments to file or server names. The configuration should manage variable and connection changes to reduce package execution errors caused by wrong information. You want to eliminate storing redundant configuration information, and create the capability to adjust subsets of configurations at a package level, or adjust all configurations at a system level.

Logging and Auditing

The next component provides a way to log events and errors that occur during execution, and to audit package objects during execution. To begin, you record all information in one central location that can be made accessible only through the security needed by your organization. You must keep track of any changes to a package to enable you to determine whether a new package version affected execution times. Speaking of execution times, you also want to record the start and end times of all package executions. To see the hierarchy of what package calls other packages, also include batching information.

The package objects that you want to audit are variables and tasks. You record the start and end times of the tasks with task identification information. Whenever a variable's value changes, you record that change with the new value. All log entries and audit information should be linked together to promote easy querying and investigation into the data.

Template Package

The final component is a template package that all developers will use to start their packages. The components already described in this section should be incorporated into this package to enable you to start developing the logic of the package immediately. Because all logging and configurations are already in place, you don't need to worry about having multiple versions, or accidentally mistyping a value.

Framework Benefits and Value

By implementing a framework, you can overcome the challenges previously discussed. The framework components come together to create an easy-to-use template for all developers to use. This provides a consistent method for logging and configurations. You have a central repository for configurations that can be managed in one location. Development and maintenance times will be much lower with a framework than with having a variety of logging and configuration methods. You are also tracking all the execution and audit information for all packages, providing a transparent look into the system for all members of your team.

Although implementing and deploying the framework has an initial start-up cost, the benefit will greatly outweigh any delays over the long run. Figure 2-1 shows an idea of how the total cost of ownership will actually be lower over time using an SSIS management framework implementation.

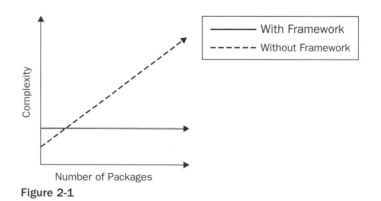

Figure 2-1

To summarize, you need to create an SSIS management framework that promotes standardization, configurations, and centralized monitoring. The overall goal includes reducing development and management time by creating a configuration management schema, logging and auditing mechanism, and a template package.

The following section discusses the design of the SSIS management framework.

Design

As discussed in the "Problem" section, you must create three components in order to build an SSIS management framework. This section takes a further look at the following components:

- Configuration management
- Logging and auditing mechanism
- Template package

These pieces will fit together to create an overall SSIS architecture that can be used for all packages. Figure 2-2 shows a diagram of this architecture.

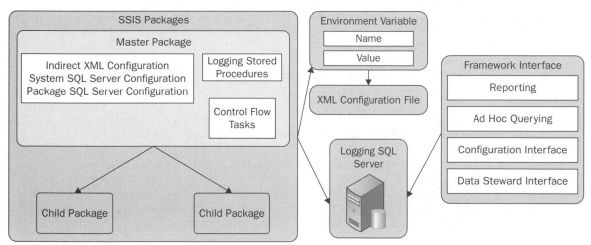

Figure 2-2

To fully appreciate the rest of this chapter, you must understand how package configurations, events, variables, and package execution works. For a more detailed description of these topics, see the book *Professional Microsoft SQL Server 2008 Integration Services* by Brian Knight, Erik Veerman, Grant Dickinson, Douglas Hinson, and Darren Herbold (Indianapolis: Wrox, 2008).

Configuration Management

Often, in an application, you have a piece of data that you would like to change at runtime. This data could be as simple as the value of a variable to change the number of iterations of a loop, or as advanced as an argument that directs a program on which logical flow it should take. By extracting that information out to a different location, you can make modifications to an external source without touching your program. Called *configurations*, these are usually assigned in name-value pairs, where the *name* is what property you want to affect and the *value* is the new piece of data you provide to the program.

Configurations in SSIS are called *package configurations*, and they allow you to set the value of package and task properties, variables, connection managers, and event handlers. You can set the configurations using a SQL Server table, an XML file, an environment variable, a registry entry, or a variable from the calling parent package. Details of all methods are not provided here, as this chapter only uses a few of them for framework implementations.

The following sections describe the overall design that will be used, followed by a closer look at each configuration method, and then wraps up with some things you'll need to consider as you implement your framework.

Overall Design

This configuration design employs a three-pass strategy that contains moving packages through environments and creating configuration levels. By using multiple passes, developers can assign configurations applicable not only at a system level, but also at a package level. Following are the three passes:

❑　An environment variable that points to an XML configuration file that points to a SQL Server database

❑　A SQL Server configuration that is filtered at the system level

❑　A SQL Server configuration that is filtered at the package level

The purpose of the first pass is to tell the SSIS package where to look for its configurations. You obviously can't store that information in the same location as the rest of the configurations because the package would never know where to start! Instead, you use an environment variable configuration to tell the package where to look for the XML configuration file. Then, the XML configuration file will configure the connection string value of a SQL Server connection manager.

The second pass applies the system-level configurations by using the SQL Server connection manager that the XML configuration file just modified to make any necessary run-time changes to the package. The third pass uses the same pattern, but uses a different filter to only apply the package specific configurations.

Environment Variable Configuration

The first thing the SSIS package uses is a system environment variable. Applications typically use environment variables as a configuration avenue. Stored as name-value pairs on the server, environment variables are accessed using the variable name and cannot be moved to a different location.

Because of the nature of environment variables, they make a perfect constant location from which to pull your initial configuration. Having different drive letters or folder structures between servers across environments is common. If you were to use an XML configuration file directly to pull your SQL Server information from, you would have to worry about updating the package when you moved the package between environments. With an environment variable, you can reference the same name in the package, but the value of the variable can be different on each server.

The environment variable should be created once when the server has been designated as part of the SSIS system. Keep in mind, however, that you'll need to add the creation of the environment variable to your Disaster Recovery (DR) procedure in case of a server failure.

XML Configuration File

Now that you understand why you need to use an environment variable configuration, it's time to take a closer look at the XML configuration file. The value of the environment variable points to the location of the XML file, which contains just one configuration. The configuration replaces the connection string of a SQL Server connection manager in the package.

Why can't you just use the connection string of the SQL Server database as the value of the environment variable? The main reason is for flexibility. Because you have an extra layer, you can easily change which SQL Server the packages should use. This may come in handy during your development if you need to work in both your development and QA environments. You can modify the XML configuration file to point to the new server, and your packages will instantly pick up the change, rather than having to modify the environment variable and need to restart your development application. In some organizations, you may need to add multiple databases to the XML configuration file, or other checks that the template package needs. Because the environment variable only allows you to set one property at a time, this is another place where the XML configuration file would be helpful.

If you have multiple SSIS servers per environment, it may behoove you to create a shared network folder to store a single copy of the XML configuration file. In the event that the SQL Server moves to a different server, you will only need to make that corresponding XML configuration file change in one place, rather than on every server.

SQL Server Configuration

The final two configuration passes use SQL Server configurations that utilize the connection manager that the XML configuration just modified. These configurations hold the dynamic values needed to execute the package. The first configuration uses a system-wide filter for all packages. These types of configurations could include connection strings or file share names needed across the organization. The second configuration uses a filter that is specific to the package and includes applicable information.

Essentially, you use SQL Server as your main repository of dynamic information. Because you use a database rather than a text- or system-based configuration method, you can include this database into your normal database maintenance routine. This allows for easy backups, restores, and other maintenance. You will most likely already have a process in place to manage change control and promotions, so this system will easily fall into place. By using SQL Server, you also have the capability to secure your tables and database against any who should not have access. This also applies for encrypting certain values within the data itself, in case you need to configure passwords. Finally, you have an easy method to update and insert multiple records or query for information.

Now that you've set up all of your run-time values, you must record all the execution information of the package.

Logging and Auditing Mechanism

SSIS packages often run automatically in the middle of the night without any assistance on a server. Because no one is there to watch the package, you must record the information of the execution. This recording of package executions and events is known as *logging*, and is an important part of any SSIS architecture.

Although SSIS comes with its own logging mechanism, ferreting out the exact record you desire can often be difficult. For example, not all records contain a critical piece of data: the name of the package. Even though creating queries that work around this shortcoming is possible, wouldn't having that information readily available to you be nice?

To assist in the overall logging design, you can circumvent the standard logging mechanism and create one of your own. This also enables you to add auditing of variable changes and events. You can also record any errors that occur during package execution.

The following sections take a look at what objects are needed to store the data and how the log entries get loaded.

Storage

For this example, you store log entries in a SQL Server database — although modifying the statements to use an alternative relational database management system (RDBMS) should be a trivial task. By using SQL Server, you can use the already-created configuration connection manager to point to your new logging database. Using a database gives a variety of benefits. Similar to configurations, you can back up and restore the database in the event of a server failure or unexpected data wipe. In fact, including this database in your normal database maintenance routine is expected. Additionally, you can easily delete historical log entries by running a simple delete statement filtered on the date column. Finally, this logging database gives you a `queryable` location to get aggregated or detailed information.

Tables

This logging design starts with a set of custom tables. These tables hold the log entries for package execution events, variable values changing, and any errors that occur. These entries also contain information to associate the entry with a package and time of execution.

Now to take a closer look at these tables:

- ❑ `dbo.Package` — This table is where it all starts. This table contains general information, including the package name, who created it, and when it first entered the system.

- ❑ `dbo.PackageVersion` — This table links to the `Package` table to tell an observer when someone modified the package. Each time a change is made to an existing package or a new package is created, a new package version will be created.

- ❑ `dbo.PackageLog` — This table contains the information about the executions of packages. Every execution should have one record in this table. This is where you can find the start and end times of the execution, as well as whether the package succeeded, failed, or is still running.

❑ `dbo.BatchLog` — This table is linked to by the `PackageLog` table. A *batch* consists of all children packages that are called from a master package. Each new master package starts a new batch and a new record in this table. This allows reporting of execution times and statuses at a higher level than the package.

❑ `dbo.PackageErrorLog` — As its name implies, this table stores error information. It also links to the `Package` table and stores the time the error occurred and what task caused the error.

❑ `dbo.PackageTaskLog` — This table records the audit trail of what tasks executed during the execution of a package. It links to the `Package` table, and has start and end times of the tasks' executions. This table completes the three-level drill-down view from batch to package to task.

❑ `dbo.PackageVariableLog` — This table contains the name of the variable, the new value of the variable, and the time that the value changed. It also links to the `Package` table.

Figure 2-3 shows how the tables are related. Later in the "Solution" section of this chapter, you will learn more about the definition and descriptions of the columns.

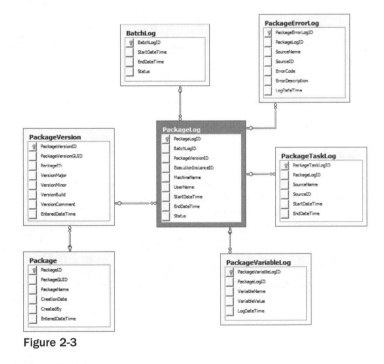

Figure 2-3

Stored Procedures

The next set of objects in the framework contains several management stored procedures, which are the only way to write to the previously mentioned tables. These stored procedures contain the business logic needed to insert and update the log entries. You place the calls to these stored procedures in either the control flow of the package, or the event handlers, depending on the type of event.

Here is a look at each stored procedure individually:

❑   `dbo.LogPackageStart` — This stored procedure records general information about the package, and records an entry associated with the beginning of a package execution. You should place this stored procedure in the control flow preceding any other control flow tasks.

❑   `dbo.LogPackageEnd` — This stored procedure updates the execution of the package and batch to show that the package completed successfully. You should place this stored procedure in the control flow following all other control flow tasks.

❑   `dbo.LogPackageError` — This stored procedure inserts a record into the error table with its associated execution time and error information. This stored procedure also updates the status information in the main tables to show that the execution of the package and batch failed. You should place this stored procedure in the `OnError` event handler, scoped to the package level.

❑   `dbo.LogTaskPreExecute` and `dbo.LogTaskPostExecute` — This pair of stored procedures records the start and end timing information of each of the tasks within the package. You place them in the `OnPreExecute` and `OnPostExecute` event handlers scoped to the package level, respectively.

❑   `dbo.LogVariableValueChanged` — You place this stored procedure in the event handler for `OnVariableValueChanged`, scoped to the package level. It records the variable information into the variable log table.

At this point, you've completed a good portion of the framework design, including your configuration schema and your logging implementation. The final step is putting it all together in a template package for developers to use.

Template Package

The *template package* (the artifact of the management framework that developers must understand) is a normal SSIS package where the framework settings have already been set up for the developer. This feature enables you to jump right into developing the business logic of the package. The package should contain package configurations, connection managers, variables, and logging helpers.

The package configurations should already be configured in the package, which is possible because the configurations should be the same for all packages, and follow the previously described order. This also ensures the connection manager that the XML configuration sets will be available and named properly.

Ideally, all connections that you think you need will be included in the template package, to prevent a developer from worrying about creating the correct configurations for all environments. Developers won't even need to name the connection managers correctly, as they will already be available!

The configuration modifies a variable that matches a connection manager. An expression utilizing the variable then sets the connection manager in the package.

> *In SSIS 2005, using a configuration set that contained connection manager configurations that were not included in the package was possible. As of SSIS 2008 SP1, this action causes an error that fails the execution of the package. To work with this issue, use a configuration to set a variable within the package. You can then use an expression to set the appropriate property on the connection manager.*

The template package includes any system-level variables, including the ones that set the connection managers. One example of a variable used across packages is the number of days to retrieve data from a source system. If all packages must pull data that has been modified in the past 100 days, you would want to create a variable for this value and set it to be configurable, in case it must be changed in the future to 150 days.

The template package should not include any values specific to a particular package. These variables can be included on a case-by-case basis during development.

The package also contains preconfigured tasks that call the management stored procedures. The tasks use the same connection manager that the configuration used. All log entries end up in one central logging entity, as long as the developer uses the provided template.

After the template has been created, you can install it on all developers' machines. They can then add the template package using the project menus within Business Intelligence Development Studio (BIDS). They first need to generate a new package ID, and then they can begin their development.

Implementation Guidelines

Now that you've laid out the design, you can use SQL Server and SSIS to put it in motion. To review, you want to include the following features:

- ❑ Multipass configuration management schema
- ❑ SQL Server tables that contain log events, audit information, and error information
- ❑ Template package that contains a development base

Solution

Now that you understand the problems that you might face and the design to solve those issues, implement the SSIS management framework! This session breaks up the framework into three sections, where each section builds off of the previous implementation.

Configuration Management

To recall the configuration management strategy, you want to start with an environment variable that points you to an XML configuration file. The configuration file modifies a SQL Server connection manager that is used by two more package configurations.

You start by setting up your server. To begin, you must create a system environment variable. You typically create environment variables under your computer's Advanced System Properties window. The environment variable information should be as follows:

```
Variable Name: SSIS_PDS_CONFIG_FILE
Variable Value: C:\SSIS_PDS\CH02 Framework\~CA
SSIS_PDS_Management_Framework.dtsConfig
```

Next, you must create the XML configuration file. You can do so by going into BIDS and creating an XML configuration that will replace the connection string of a connection manager that points to the SSIS_PDS database, or you can use the XML provided in Figure 2-4. Put this XML information into a file named SSIS_PDS_Management_Framework.dtsConfig, and place the file under the directory C:\SSIS_PDS\CH02 Framework.

```xml
<?xml version="1.0" ?>
<DTSConfiguration>
  <DTSConfigurationHeading>
    <DTSConfigurationFileInfo
      GeneratedBy="JMMCONSULTING\Jessica Moss"
      GeneratedFromPackageName="SSIS_PDS_Template"
      GeneratedFromPackageID="{EA3D047E-765D-4A2B-B8C6-
      0D8AA497B699}" GeneratedDate="1/1/2005 12:00:00 AM" />
  </DTSConfigurationHeading>
  <Configuration ConfiguredType="Property"
    Path="\Package.Connections[SSIS_PDS].Properties
    [ConnectionString]" ValueType="String">
    <ConfiguredValue>Data Source=localhost;Initial
      Catalog=SSIS_PDS;Provider=SQLNCLI10.1;Integrated
      Security=SSPI;Auto Translate=False;</ConfiguredValue>
  </Configuration>
</DTSConfiguration>
```

Figure 2-4

Now that you've prepped the server, you can work in SSIS. You want to end up with a set of configurations in a package that will allow you to dynamically configure information from a SQL Server. Figure 2-5 shows what the final product will look like.

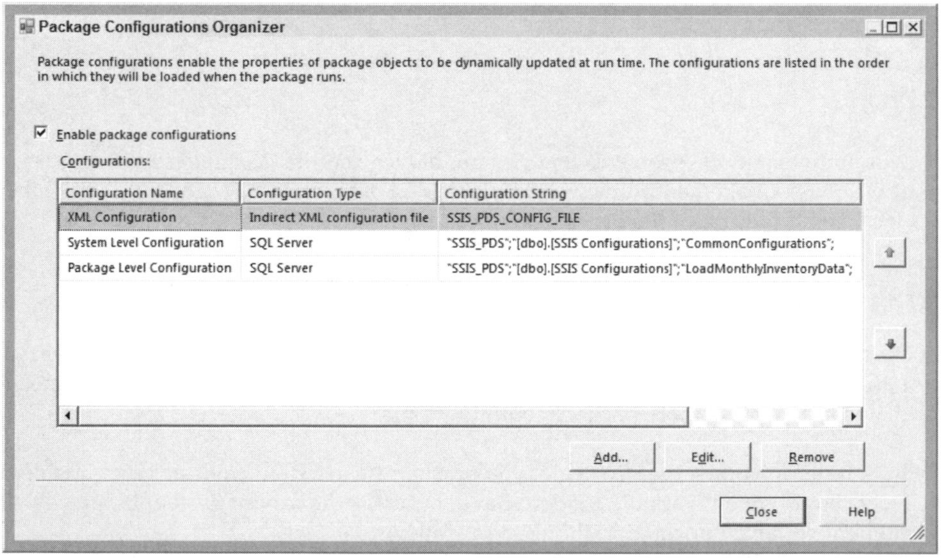

Figure 2-5

Now that you know where you're going, let's walk through the steps to build it by starting with a blank SSIS package, named SSIS_PDS_Template.dtsx. Before setting any configurations, you create the connection to the database where all your configurations and log entries will exist. In this example, the database is named SSIS_PDS. You'll create a standard OLE DB connection to a local server using that database. After you create the SSIS_PDS connection manager, you can set up the package configurations.

You can enter the Package Configurations Organizer by going to the SSIS menu in BIDS, or right-clicking on the design area in the Control Flow and selecting the Package Configurations . . . option. Select the checkbox to enable package configurations and add a configuration of type "XML configuration file." By selecting the second option of "Configuration location is stored in an environment variable," you can create an indirect configuration to use your environment variable. Select SSIS_PDS_CONFIG_FILE from the drop-down list, and you've created your first package configuration.

> **If you don't see** SSIS_PDS_CONFIG_FILE **in the drop-down list, you may need to close and reopen BIDS. Any new environment variables will not be available to open applications. Even if you make a change to an existing environment variable and you already have BIDS open, be sure to close and reopen it to reload the correct value.**

The next configuration is a SQL Server configuration, which uses the SSIS_PDS Connection. When asked to select a Configuration table, choose the New . . . button and click OK to create the configuration table. Or you can use the following code to create the table, and then select the dbo.SSISConfigurations table in the drop-down list.

```
USE [SSIS_PDS]
GO

CREATE TABLE [dbo].[SSIS Configurations]
(
    ConfigurationFilter NVARCHAR(255) NOT NULL,
    ConfiguredValue NVARCHAR(255) NULL,
    PackagePath NVARCHAR(255) NOT NULL,
    ConfiguredValueType NVARCHAR(20) NOT NULL
)
```

You then add a Configuration filter. Because this is the system-level configuration, call the filter CommonConfigurations. Using this filter fetches all configuration entries that match that filter name to adjust the package at runtime. Depending on whether you've created this table before, when you go to the next screen, you may see a dialog window with the message shown in Figure 2-6. If so, choose the Reuse Existing button to prevent overwriting existing configurations. If the next screen asks you to select configurations, select any one property because you must select at least one configuration. It is not important which one, because you will manage configurations directly in the database table you just created.

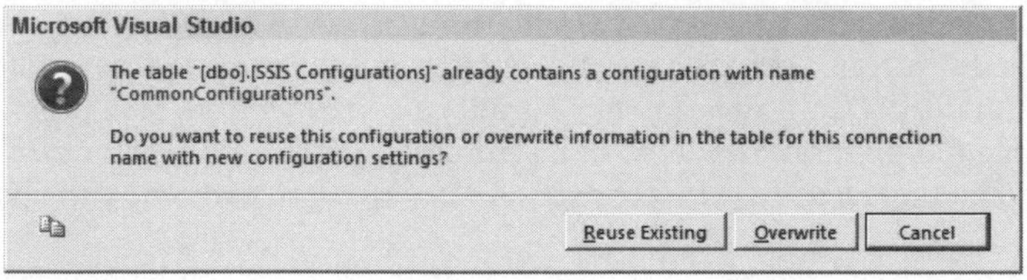

Figure 2-6

You can then add a third SQL Server configuration that will manage the package-specific configurations. The individual developer needs to make this choice, and it is possible that there will be no package-specific configurations at all. If there are, you can follow the same steps as creating the system-level configuration, but instead of using CommonConfigurations as the filter name, use the package name.

> The package configurations discussed must be in this exact order, because each preceding configuration affects the current configuration. If you create the configurations in the wrong order, you can move them up or down by using the arrows on right side of the Package Configurations Organizer.

Creating two levels of SQL Server configurations introduces a layered effect, where the package applies the system-level configurations that use the CommonConfigurations filter first. Next, the package applies the package-level configurations with the package filter, overriding the system-level configurations if needed.

One place where this feature would come in handy is if you have a connection string with server and database information at a company level, but a specific user name and password to use for this particular package. The connection string would get applied for all packages and would not overwrite the username needed for your package. You are also ensuring that no matter what happens at a system level, your package will have the last say in what values it should use.

Up to this point, you've told the package to read the configurations, but you haven't actually created any configurations for the package to read. Here are the steps to configure a connection manager:

1. Add a variable to the package. Every time you want to create a connection manager, you must add a matching variable. With your mouse focused on the Control Flow design area, create a new variable named connAdventureWorksDW2008. Set the data type to String and leave the value as an empty string. Figure 2-7 shows the variable window.

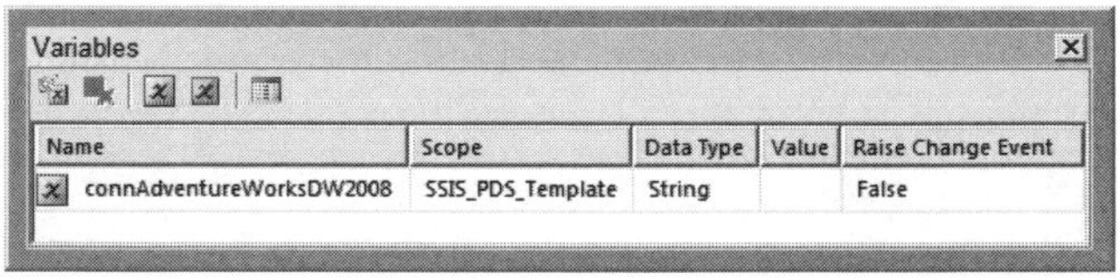

Figure 2-7

2. Now you can add the connection manager directly to the package, which will be an OLE DB connection to the AdventureWorksDW2008 database named the same. On the properties windows of the connection manager, select the ellipses next to the Expressions property. Set the ConnectionString property to @[User::connAdventureWorksDW2008]. Figure 2-8 shows the full Property Expressions Editor window. This property tells the connection manager to use whatever value is in the connAdventureWorksDW2008 variable when the package runs.

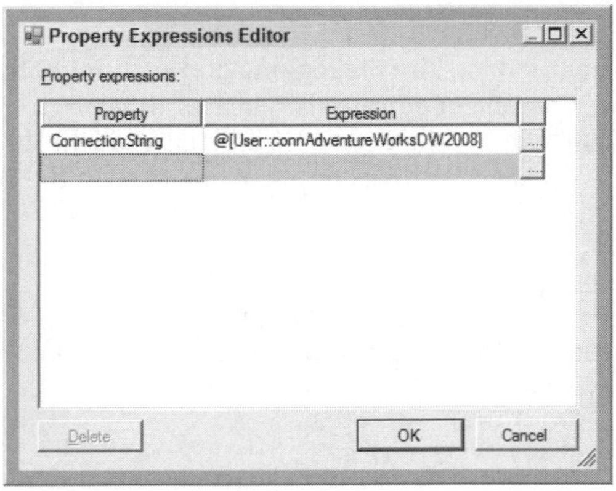

Figure 2-8

3. Last (but certainly not least), you must add a configuration for the variable. You can add this directly into the dbo.SSISConfigurations table by running the following INSERT statement:

```
INSERT INTO [dbo].[SSIS Configurations]
    ([ConfigurationFilter]
    ,[ConfiguredValue]
    ,[PackagePath]
    ,[ConfiguredValueType])
VALUES
    ('CommonConfigurations'
    ,'Data Source=localhost;Initial Catalog=AdventureWorksDW2008;~CA
        Provider=SQLNCLI10.1;Integrated Security=SSPI;'
    ,'\Package.Variables[User::connAdventureWorksDW2008].Properties[Value]'
    ,'String')
```

Any time you need to add a configuration at the system or package level, you must follow the previously described steps to configure a connection manager. You must also run this script on each of your environments, and, at least in the case of connections, the ConfiguredValue field will probably be different on each environment. Fortunately, you only need to do this the first time someone uses that connection or variable. After that time, it will be available for everyone to use, and will be configured automatically, as long as the developer names the variable or connection manager the same as in the database.

You have now successfully set up a package to use package configurations, read configurations from your configuration management system, and use a layered effect to apply the appropriate configurations.

The next section examines the logging of events that happen during package execution.

Logging and Auditing Mechanism

In the "Design" section, you named the objects needed to hold your logging and auditing information. This section looks at the code for creating the objects and adding data, beginning with descriptions of the tables and what data each column contains. Then, the discussion moves on to the stored procedures, and explains the logic used to populate the tables.

Storage and Tables

A number of custom tables are used to store the logging and auditing information. Each of them is examined here in detail, and you can get a script that creates all tables from this book's companion Web site (www.wrox.com). Run that script in the SSIS_PDS database, so the tables will be available when you start working with your SSIS package. As an example of one table in the creation script, the following is the script to create the Package table:

```
CREATE TABLE [dbo].[Package](
    [PackageID] [int] IDENTITY(1,1) NOT NULL,
    [PackageGUID] [uniqueidentifier] NOT NULL,
    [PackageName] [varchar](255) NOT NULL,
    [CreationDate] [datetime] NOT NULL,
    [CreatedBy] [varchar](255) NOT NULL,
    [EnteredDateTime] [datetime] NOT NULL DEFAULT getdate(),
  CONSTRAINT [PK_Package] PRIMARY KEY CLUSTERED (
    [PackageID] ASC
))
GO
```

The Package table contains an IDENTITY field that you use to link to other tables. The PackageGUID, PackageName, CreationDate, and CreatedBy columns come from the package's properties. The EnteredDateTime column will always be set to the date when the record was inserted. Table 2-1 shows the data type information and data from a sample record.

Table 2-1

Column Name	Data Type	Sample Data
PackageID	int	2
PackageGUID	uniqueidentifier	18535AC3-45E2-4A54-B794-D9ADF9892486
PackageName	varchar(255)	SSIS_PDS_LoadMonthlyInventoryData
CreationDate	datetime	2009-05-10 02:23:06.000
CreatedBy	varchar(255)	JMMCONSULTING\Jessica Moss
EnteredDateTime	datetime	2009-05-11 05:06:56.820

Similar to the `Package` table, the `PackageVersion` table consists of an `IDENTITY` column, which, in this case, is used to identify a particular record. It also contains a foreign key to the `Package` table to identify which package has changed. The remaining columns are directly taken from the package's properties, except for `EnteredDateTime`, which records the date the record was inserted. Table 2-2 shows the data type information and sample data.

Table 2-2

Column Name	Data Type	Sample Data
PackageVersionID	int	6
PackageVersionGUID	uniqueidentifier	9A70E554-5B63-4F0E-A76A-D35115E26224
PackageID	int	2
VersionMajor	int	1
VersionMinor	int	0
VersionBuild	int	30
VersionComment	varchar(1000)	Added new data flow to add rowcount
EnteredDateTime	datetime	2009-05-11 05:12:30.950

Although the `Package` and `PackageVersion` tables are updated at package runtime, they contain general information about the state of the packages. The rest of the tables reviewed here are specific to package executions.

The first table is the `BatchLog` table. As previously discussed, batches are created by parent packages. If you have no parent-child package relationships, each package will create its own batch. This table contains an identity to indicate a unique batch, the time the master package started, and the time the master package completed, along with a status field. If any of the children packages failed, or the master package itself failed, the batch will have failed. Table 2-3 lists the data types and sample information for the `BatchLog` table.

Table 2-3

Column Name	Data Type	Sample Data
BatchLogID	int	9
StartDateTime	datetime	2009-05-11 05:31:11.000
EndDateTime	datetime	2009-05-11 05:31:11.000
Status	char(1)	S

The `PackageLog` table is the center of the design. One record in this table constitutes one execution of a package. It links to the `Batch` table to be able to group packages together into a batch. It also links to the `PackageVersion` table, so you know which version of the package is running. The `ExecutionInstanceID`, `MachineName`, `UserName`, `StartDateTime`, and `EndDateTime` columns are provided from the package's properties. Finally, the `Status` column will contain either an 'S' for Success, 'F' for Failure, or 'R' for Running. Table 2-4 shows the data type information and data from a sample record.

Table 2-4

Column Name	Data Type	Sample Data
PackageLogID	int	10
BatchLogID	int	9
PackageVersionID	int	6
ExecutionInstanceID	uniqueidentifier	9C48CFA8-2735-4811-A035-83D74717F95E
MachineName	varchar(64)	JMMCONSULTING
UserName	varchar(64)	JMMCONSULTING\Jessica Moss
StartDateTime	datetime	2009-05-11 05:31:23.000
EndDateTime	datetime	2009-05-11 05:31:36.360
Status	char(1)	S

The `PackageErrorLog` table has a zero-to-many type relationship with the `PackageLog` table. In other words, for every record in the `PackageLog` table, you could have no records in the `PackageErrorLog`, or you could have multiple records. Having records is completely dependent on whether the package threw any error events. If the package did throw an error, this table links to the `PackageLog` table, and includes the `SourceName`, `SourceID`, `ErrorCode`, and `ErrorDescription` from the package's properties. The `LogDateTime` field contains the time that this record was inserted. Table 2-5 shows the data type information and sample data.

Table 2-5

Column Name	Data Type	Sample Data
PackageErrorLogID	int	6
PackageLogID	int	5
SourceName	varchar(64)	SQL Get Data
SourceID	uniqueidentifier	DB9AAD75-8719-4B26-8F88-5E8B6F18B54A
ErrorCode	int	-1073548784
ErrorDescription	varchar(2000)	Executing the query "select cast('abc' as int)" failed with the following error: "Conversion failed when converting the varchar value 'abc' to data type int.". Possible failure reasons: Problems with the query, "ResultSet" property not set correctly, parameters not set correctly, or connection not established correctly.
LogDateTime	datetime	2009-05-11 05:11:06.177

The PackageTaskLog table contains an IDENTITY field to uniquely identify a record and a link to the PackageLog table. The remaining columns come from the task properties within the package. Similar to the PackageErrorLog table, this table can have a zero-to-many type relationship with the PackageLog table, depending on the number of tasks that the package contains. Table 2-6 lists the data type information and sample data for this table.

Table 2-6

Column Name	Data Type	Sample Data
PackageTaskLogID	int	46
PackageLogID	int	9
SourceName	varchar(255)	SQL Update Source System
SourceID	uniqueidentifier	37965000-8AA6-4E13-99DE-D61B5C9FCF40
StartDateTime	datetime	2009-05-11 05:31:13.560
EndDateTime	datetime	2009-05-11 05:31:13.560

The PackageVariableLog table also has a zero-to-many type relationship with the PackageLog table, because it only comes into play if a variable has the Raise Change Event flag set and the variable's value changed. If that situation does happen during the execution of the package, the information will be logged from the package's information with the time that the record was inserted. The PackageVariableLog table also contains an IDENTITY field and the link to the PackageLog table. Table 2-7 shows the data type information and data from a sample record.

Table 2-7

Column Name	Data Type	Sample Data
PackageVariableLogID	int	5
PackageLogID	int	9
VariableName	varchar(255)	rowCount
VariableValue	varchar(max)	2724
LogDateTime	datetime	2009-05-11 05:31:32.010

Stored Procedures

Now take a look at the logic in the stored procedures used to load data into these tables. This discussion of each stored procedure shows the script to create that stored procedure, and then how to execute it from within the package. All creation scripts should be executed in the SSIS_PDS database to give the package access to them.

In passing data between packages, the package needs several variables. To ensure availability later, create these variables now, as shown in Table 2-8.

Table 2-8

Name	Scope	Data Type	Value	Raise Change Event
BatchLogID	SSIS_PDS_Template	Int32	0	False
PackageLogID	SSIS_PDS_Template	Int32	0	False
EndBatchAudit	SSIS_PDS_Template	Boolean	False	False
strVariableValue	OnVariableValue Changed	String	Unable to Convert to String	False

Control Flow Stored Procedures

The control flow calls the `LogPackageStart` and `LogPackageEnd` stored procedures. To run them, you use Execute SQL Tasks in your SSIS package. You should place one Execute SQL Task before all other tasks in the control flow, and the other Execute SQL Task after all other tasks in the control flow, as shown in Figure 2-9.

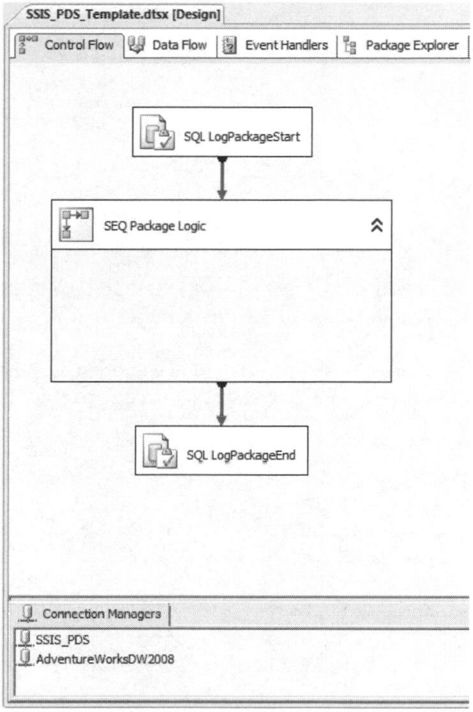

Figure 2-9

The `LogPackageStart` stored procedure contains the most complex logic of the set. Following is the code needed to create the script:

```
CREATE PROCEDURE [dbo].[LogPackageStart]
(    @BatchLogID int
    ,@PackageName varchar(255)
    ,@ExecutionInstanceID uniqueidentifier
    ,@MachineName varchar(64)
    ,@UserName varchar(64)
    ,@StartDatetime datetime
    ,@PackageVersionGUID uniqueidentifier
    ,@VersionMajor int
    ,@VersionMinor int
    ,@VersionBuild int
    ,@VersionComment varchar(1000)
```

```
    ,@PackageGUID uniqueidentifier
    ,@CreationDate datetime
    ,@CreatedBy varchar(255)
)

AS
BEGIN
SET NOCOUNT ON

DECLARE @PackageID int
,@PackageVersionID int
,@PackageLogID int
,@EndBatchAudit bit

/* Initialize Variables */
SELECT @EndBatchAudit = 0

/* Get Package Metadata ID */
IF NOT EXISTS (SELECT 1 FROM dbo.Package WHERE PackageGUID =
    @PackageGUID AND PackageName = @PackageName)
Begin
    INSERT INTO dbo.Package (PackageGUID, PackageName, CreationDate, CreatedBy)
        VALUES (@PackageGUID, @PackageName, @CreationDate, @CreatedBy)
End

SELECT @PackageID = PackageID
    FROM dbo.Package
    WHERE PackageGUID = @PackageGUID
    AND PackageName = @PackageName

/* Get Package Version MetaData ID */
IF NOT EXISTS (SELECT 1 FROM dbo.PackageVersion
    WHERE PackageVersionGUID = @PackageVersionGUID)
Begin
    INSERT INTO dbo.PackageVersion (PackageID, PackageVersionGUID, VersionMajor,
        VersionMinor, VersionBuild, VersionComment)
        VALUES (@PackageID, @PackageVersionGUID, @VersionMajor, @VersionMinor,
            @VersionBuild, @VersionComment)
End
SELECT @PackageVersionID = PackageVersionID
    FROM dbo.PackageVersion
    WHERE PackageVersionGUID = @PackageVersionGUID

/* Get BatchLogID */
IF ISNULL(@BatchLogID,0) = 0
Begin
    INSERT INTO dbo.BatchLog (StartDatetime, [Status])
        VALUES (@StartDatetime, 'R')
    SELECT @BatchLogID = SCOPE_IDENTITY()
    SELECT @EndBatchAudit = 1
End

/* Create PackageLog Record */
```

```
INSERT INTO dbo.PackageLog (BatchLogID, PackageVersionID, ExecutionInstanceID,
    MachineName, UserName, StartDatetime, [Status])
  VALUES(@BatchLogID, @PackageVersionID, @ExecutionInstanceID, @MachineName,
    @UserName, @StartDatetime, 'R')

SELECT @PackageLogID = SCOPE_IDENTITY()

SELECT @BatchLogID as BatchLogID, @PackageLogID as PackageLogID, @EndBatchAudit as
    EndBatchAudit

END
GO
```

It starts by checking to see whether matching entries in the Package and PackageVersion tables exist based on the input arguments. If not, it will create appropriate new entries and store the identity fields to be used in the PackageLog table. Before you get that far, you must check the batch status. If a BatchLogID was passed in, you know you are already part of a batch and do not need to create a new record. If there is no BatchLogID, it will come in as 0, and the stored procedure will create a new record in the BatchLog table. You can then take the BatchLogID along with the PackageVersionID values you just created (and/or retrieved) to insert the start of the execution into the PackageLog table. The statuses for both the BatchLog and PackageLog tables will be set to 'R' for Running.

To execute this stored procedure, set the first Execute SQL Task to use the SSIS_PDS connection manager that you have already manipulated when working with configurations. In the SQLStatement property, enter the following code:

```
exec dbo.LogPackageStart
@BatchLogID = ?
,@PackageName = ?
,@ExecutionInstanceID = ?
,@MachineName = ?
,@UserName = ?
,@StartDatetime = ?
,@PackageVersionGUID = ?
,@VersionMajor = ?
,@VersionMinor = ?
,@VersionBuild = ?
,@VersionComment = ?
,@PackageGUID = ?
,@CreationDate = ?
,@CreatedBy = ?
```

Remember that the last statement of the stored procedure is a SELECT statement that returns information for the package. You must tell the Execute SQL Task to retrieve that data, which you can do by setting the ResultSet property to "Single row." At this time, your Execute SQL Task Editor screen should like Figure 2-10.

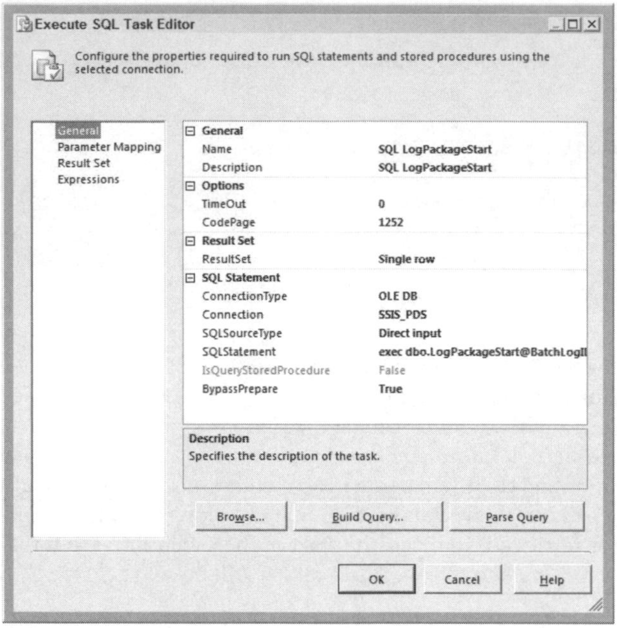

Figure 2-10

Next, you must set the input parameters that the stored procedure needs. On the Parameter Mapping menu, add parameters and fill out the values exactly as shown in Figure 2-11. These variables map to the question marks in your SQLStatement, and must be in the correct order to run successfully.

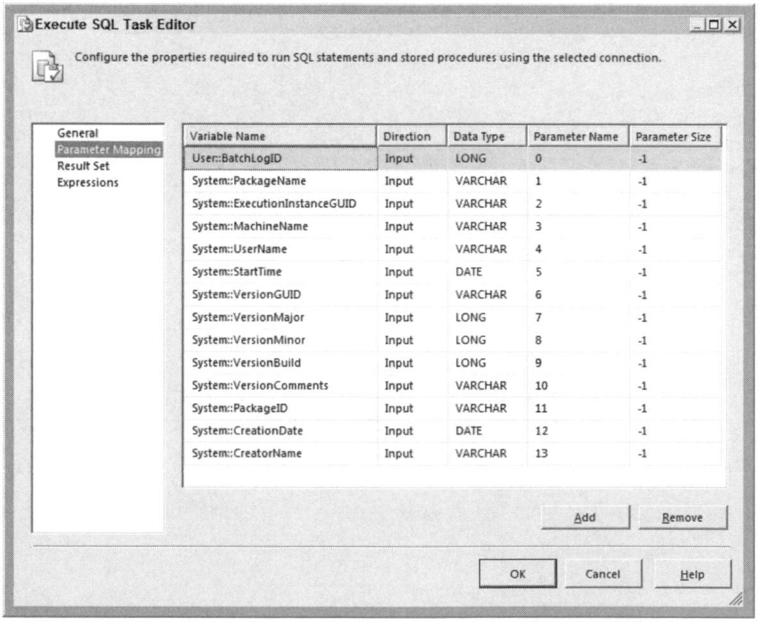

Variable Name	Direction	Data Type	Parameter Name	Parameter Size
User::BatchLogID	Input	LONG	0	-1
System::PackageName	Input	VARCHAR	1	-1
System::ExecutionInstanceGUID	Input	VARCHAR	2	-1
System::MachineName	Input	VARCHAR	3	-1
System::UserName	Input	VARCHAR	4	-1
System::StartTime	Input	DATE	5	-1
System::VersionGUID	Input	VARCHAR	6	-1
System::VersionMajor	Input	LONG	7	-1
System::VersionMinor	Input	LONG	8	-1
System::VersionBuild	Input	LONG	9	-1
System::VersionComments	Input	VARCHAR	10	-1
System::PackageID	Input	VARCHAR	11	-1
System::CreationDate	Input	DATE	12	-1
System::CreatorName	Input	VARCHAR	13	-1

Figure 2-11

To capture the data returned in the ResultSet, you map returned column names to the existing variables in your package on the Result Set menu. Set these values to match Figure 2-12.

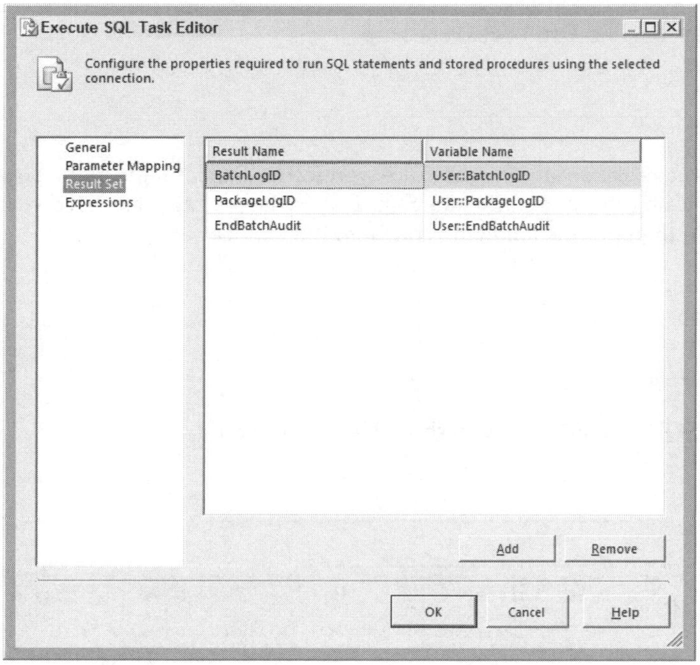

Figure 2-12

The LogPackageEnd stored procedure records the time that the package finished execution, and marks the status as 'S' for success in the PackageLog table. If the EndBatchAudit flag is flipped, it also marks the batch status to 'S' and records the time in the BatchLog table. If an error occurred during the package and batch, this stored procedure will not be called, and those columns will be updated by the next stored procedure to be reviewed, LogPackageError. The creation script contains this logic:

```
CREATE PROCEDURE [dbo].[LogPackageEnd]
(    @PackageLogID int
    ,@BatchLogID int
    ,@EndBatchAudit bit
)

AS
BEGIN
    SET NOCOUNT ON
    UPDATE dbo.PackageLog
        SET Status = 'S'
        , EndDatetime = getdate()
        WHERE PackageLogID = @PackageLogID
```

```
        IF @EndBatchAudit = 1
        Begin
            UPDATE dbo.BatchLog
            SET Status = 'S'
            , EndDatetime = getdate()
            WHERE BatchLogID = @BatchLogID
        End
END
GO
```

To set up the `LogPackageEnd` stored procedure, you follow similar logic to the `LogPackageStart` stored procedure. Using the second Execute SQL Task in the package, you set the connection to `SSIS_PDS`. You can then put the following code into the `SQLStatement`:

```
exec dbo.LogPackageEnd
@PackageLogID = ?
,@BatchLogID = ?
,@EndBatchAudit = ?
```

The final Execute SQL Task Editor screen should like Figure 2-13.

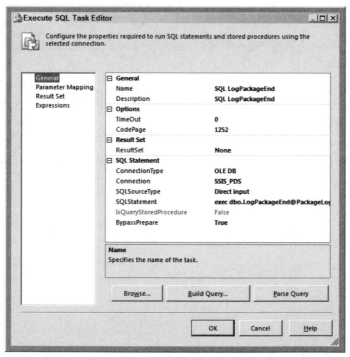

Figure 2-13

This stored procedure doesn't return any information, so you do not need to set a ResultSet. The only setup you have left is on the Parameter Mapping menu. Set the values to look like Figure 2-14.

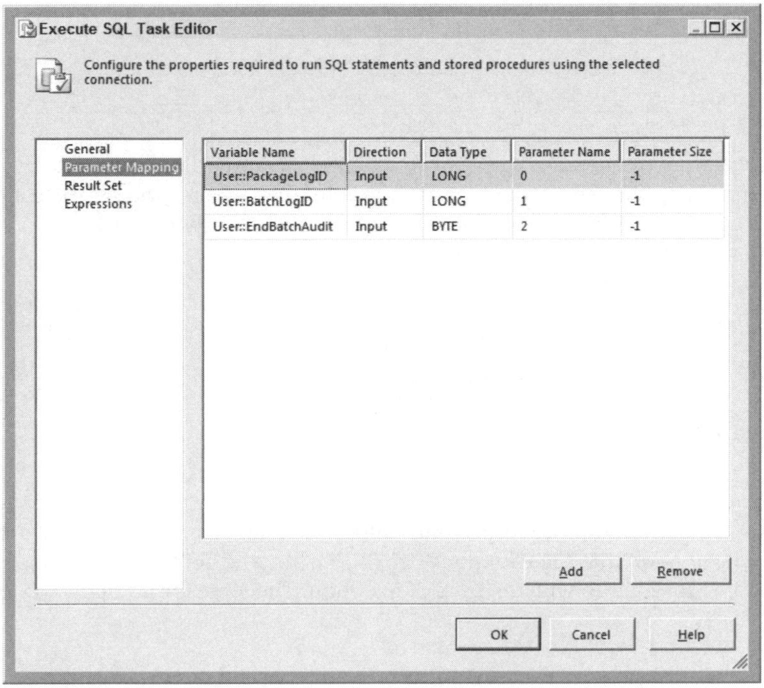

Figure 2-14

Event Handler Stored Procedures

This section takes a look at the stored procedures called when an event happens. If an event handler is created for an event, every time the event occurs, the event handler code executes. You can use the same types of tasks that you used in the control flow, including Execute SQL Tasks and Script Tasks. Following are the stored procedures that fall under this category:

- ❏ LogPackageError
- ❏ LogTaskPreExecute
- ❏ LogTaskPostExecute
- ❏ LogTaskVariableValueChanged

To work with the event handlers, you want to click on the Event Handlers tab across the top of the package. All the information you need should be scoped at a package level, so ensure that the Executable drop-down list shows the package name. You select the event that you desire in the "Event handler" drop-down list. As you work with each new event, you must create the design area. If you see the message shown in Figure 2-15, click the link to open the design area that is similar to the control flow. If, at any time, you decide that you do not want that event handler anymore, click the Delete button next to the "Event handler" drop-down list.

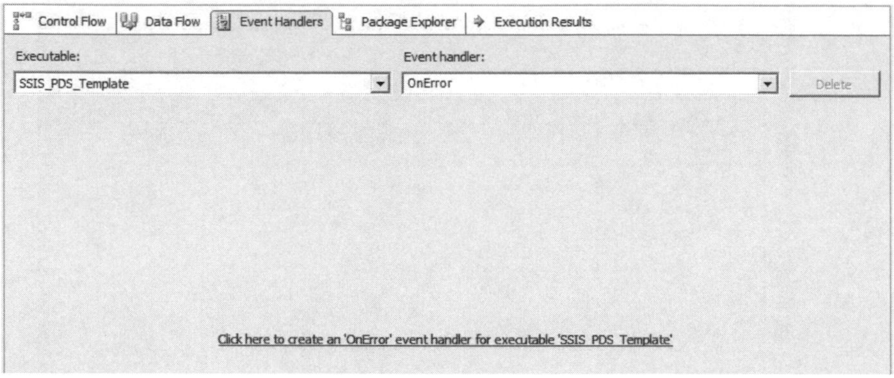

Figure 2-15

The `LogPackageError` stored procedure is only called when an error has occurred. In that case, you insert the error information into the `PackageErrorLog` table, and set the `PackageLog` and `BatchLog` tables' statuses to 'F' for Failure with the time of insertion. The logic for `LogPackageError` is as follows:

```
CREATE PROCEDURE [dbo].[LogPackageError]
(     @PackageLogID int
    ,@BatchLogID int
    ,@SourceName varchar(64)
    ,@SourceID uniqueidentifier
    ,@ErrorCode int
    ,@ErrorDescription varchar(2000)
    ,@EndBatchAudit bit
)

AS
BEGIN
    SET NOCOUNT ON
    INSERT INTO dbo.PackageErrorLog (PackageLogID, SourceName, SourceID,
        ErrorCode, ErrorDescription, LogDateTime)
    VALUES (@PackageLogID, @SourceName, @SourceID, @ErrorCode,
        @ErrorDescription, getdate())

    UPDATE dbo.PackageLog
        SET Status = 'F'
            , EndDatetime = getdate()
        WHERE PackageLogID = @PackageLogID
```

```
        IF @EndBatchAudit = 1
        Begin
        UPDATE dbo.BatchLog
            SET Status = 'F'
            , EndDatetime = getdate()
            WHERE BatchLogID = @BatchLogID
        End
    END
    GO
```

This stored procedure will also be run through an Execute SQL Task, but is located on the OnError event handler, scoped at the package level. The Executable field should have the package name selected, and the "Event handler" field should have OnError selected. This tab should look like Figure 2-16.

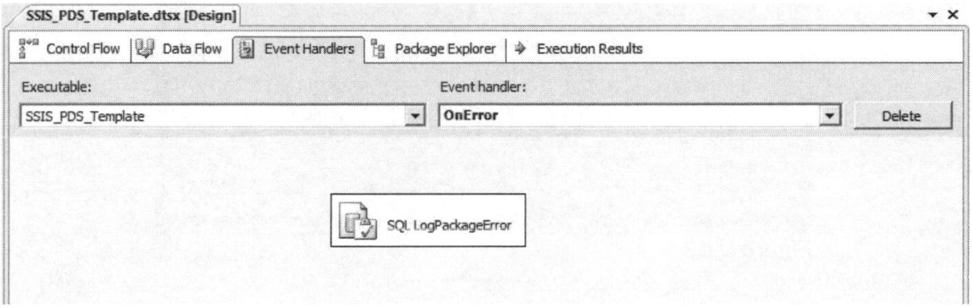

Figure 2-16

In the Execute SQL Task's properties, you must set the Connection to use SSIS_PDS connection manager. You can then set the SQLStatement to use the following code:

```
exec dbo.LogPackageError
@PackageLogID = ?
,@BatchLogID = ?
,@SourceName = ?
,@SourceID = ?
,@ErrorCode = ?
,@ErrorDescription = ?
,@EndBatchAudit = ?
```

Because the stored procedure doesn't return any data, you can leave the ResultSet field set to the value of None. After you complete those steps, the Execute SQL Task's Editor screen should look like Figure 2-17.

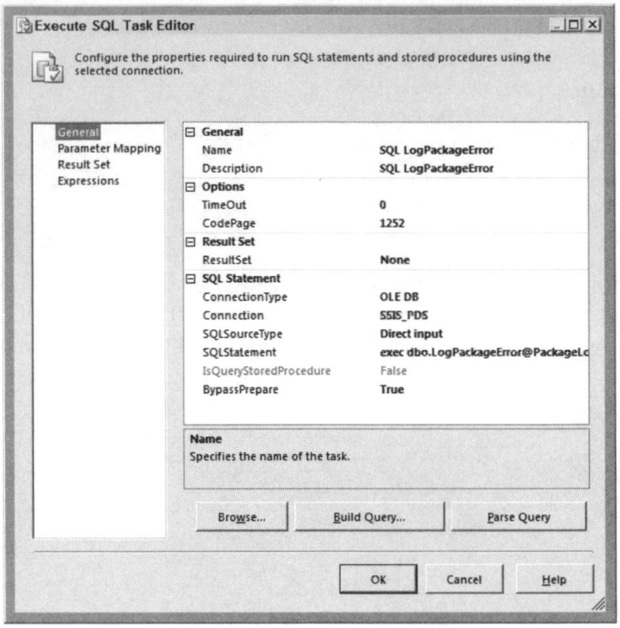

Execute SQL Task Editor

Configure the properties required to run SQL statements and stored procedures using the selected connection.

General
Parameter Mapping
Result Set
Expressions

General	
Name	SQL LogPackageError
Description	SQL LogPackageError
Options	
TimeOut	0
CodePage	1252
Result Set	
ResultSet	None
SQL Statement	
ConnectionType	OLE DB
Connection	SSIS_PDS
SQLSourceType	Direct input
SQLStatement	exec dbo.LogPackageError@PackageLo
IsQueryStoredProcedure	False
BypassPrepare	True

Name
Specifies the name of the task.

Browse...   Build Query...   Parse Query

OK   Cancel   Help

Figure 2-17

You then set up your input parameters in similar fashion to the `LogPackageEnd` Execute SQL Task. Figure 2-18 shows the mappings that you need to make on the Parameter Mapping menu.

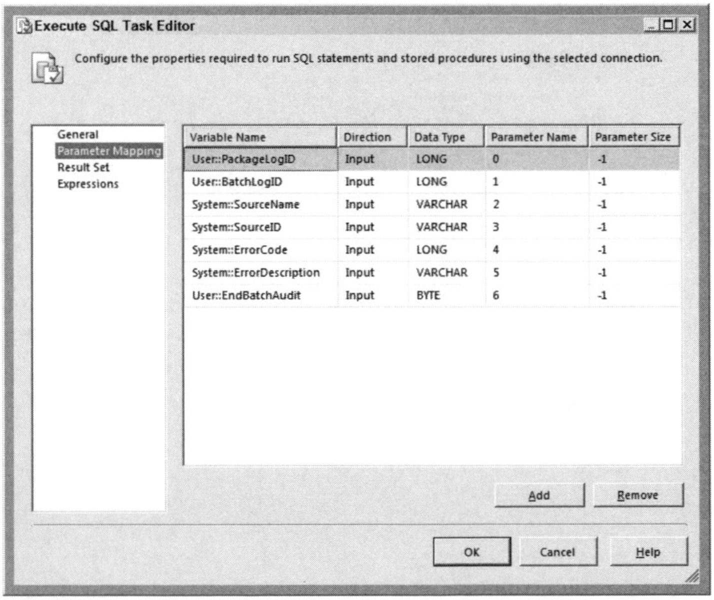

Execute SQL Task Editor

Configure the properties required to run SQL statements and stored procedures using the selected connection.

General
Parameter Mapping
Result Set
Expressions

Variable Name	Direction	Data Type	Parameter Name	Parameter Size
User::PackageLogID	Input	LONG	0	-1
User::BatchLogID	Input	LONG	1	-1
System::SourceName	Input	VARCHAR	2	-1
System::SourceID	Input	VARCHAR	3	-1
System::ErrorCode	Input	LONG	4	-1
System::ErrorDescription	Input	VARCHAR	5	-1
User::EndBatchAudit	Input	BYTE	6	-1

Add   Remove

OK   Cancel   Help

Figure 2-18

The LogTaskPreExecute stored procedure executes every time a new task starts running. As long as the task is not the PreExecute event of the package container, or the auditing Control Flow tasks, the stored procedure will simply insert information into the PackageTaskLog table. Following is the logic in the creation script:

```
CREATE PROCEDURE [dbo].[LogTaskPreExecute]
(    @PackageLogID int
    ,@SourceName varchar(64)
    ,@SourceID uniqueidentifier
    ,@PackageID uniqueidentifier
)

AS
BEGIN
    SET NOCOUNT ON
    IF @PackageID <> @SourceID
        AND @SourceName <> 'SQL LogPackageStart'
        AND @SourceName <> 'SQL LogPackageEnd'
        INSERT INTO dbo.PackageTaskLog (PackageLogID, SourceName, SourceID,
            StartDateTime)
        VALUES (@PackageLogID, @SourceName, @SourceID, getdate())
END
GO
```

The location of the LogTaskPreExecute stored procedure is in the OnPreExecute event handler. It should be scoped at the package level. Drag over an Execute SQL Task to the design window, and set the connection to use SSIS_PDS. Put the following code in the SQLStatement field:

```
exec dbo.LogTaskPreExecute
@PackageLogID = ?
,@SourceName = ?
,@SourceID = ?
,@PackageID = ?
```

At this time, the Execute SQL Task Editor screen should look like Figure 2-19.

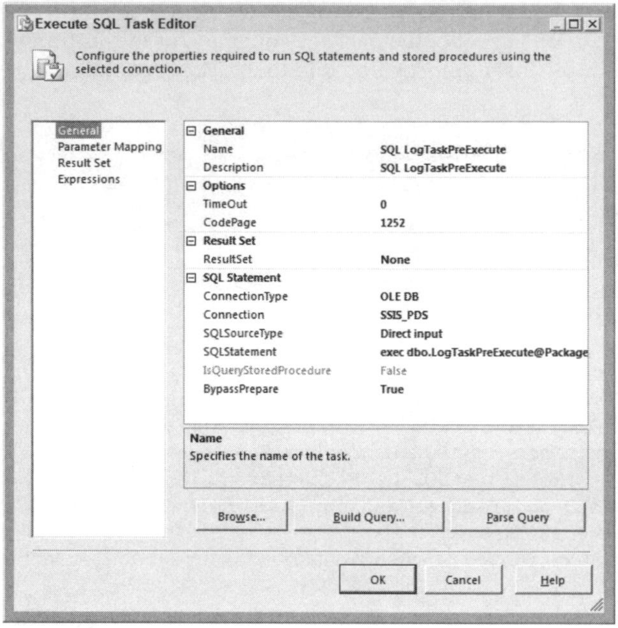

Figure 2-19

You then configure your input parameters on the Parameter Mapping menu. Set them up to look like Figure 2-20.

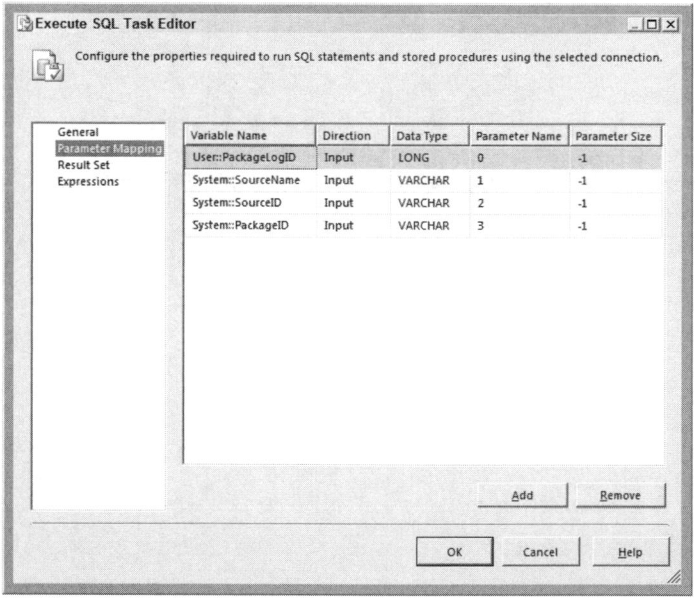

Figure 2-20

The LogTaskPostExecute stored procedure will update the record just inserted by the LogTaskPreExecute stored procedure with the time that the task completed. Following is the logic used:

```
CREATE PROCEDURE [dbo].[LogTaskPostExecute]
(    @PackageLogID int
    ,@SourceID uniqueidentifier
    ,@PackageID uniqueidentifier
)

AS
BEGIN
    SET NOCOUNT ON
    IF @PackageID <> @SourceID
        UPDATE dbo.PackageTaskLog
            SET EndDateTime = getdate()
            WHERE PackageLogID = @PackageLogID AND SourceID = @SourceID
                AND EndDateTime is null
END
GO
```

This stored procedure acts exactly the same as the LogTaskPreExecute stored procedure, except that its Execute SQL Task will be on the OnPostExecute event handler. In the Execute SQL Task's Editor screen, set the connection to SSIS_PDS, and add the following code to the SQLStatement field:

```
exec dbo.LogTaskPostExecute
@PackageLogID = ?
,@SourceID = ?
,@PackageID = ?
```

The Execute SQL Task Editor should match Figure 2-21.

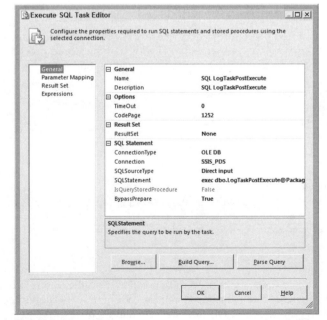

Figure 2-21

65

You are not returning any information, so you do not need to modify anything on the Result Set menu, but you do need to set up your input arguments. Modify the Parameter Mapping menu to look like Figure 2-22.

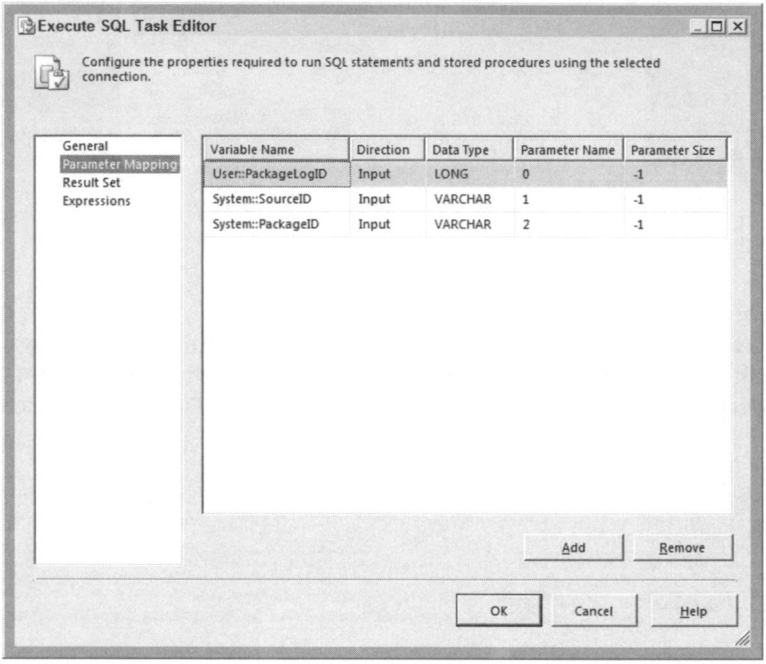

Figure 2-22

The final event handler stored procedure is LogVariableValueChanged. This procedure acts slightly differently than the others you have seen thus far. The logic of the stored procedure is straightforward, in that it just inserts a record into the PackageVariableLog table. Following is the insertion logic:

```
CREATE PROCEDURE [dbo].[LogVariableValueChanged]
(    @PackageLogID     int
    ,@VariableName          varchar(255)
    ,@VariableValue          varchar(max)
)
AS
BEGIN
    SET NOCOUNT ON
    INSERT INTO dbo.PackageVariableLog(PackageLogID, VariableName,
        VariableValue, LogDateTime)
    VALUES (@PackageLogID, @VariableName, @VariableValue, getdate())
END
GO
```

The LogVariableValueChanged stored procedure is called from the OnVariableValueChanged event handler, scoped to the package level. For this stored procedure to work, you must add an additional task, a Script Task, before the Execute SQL Task, as shown in Figure 2-23.

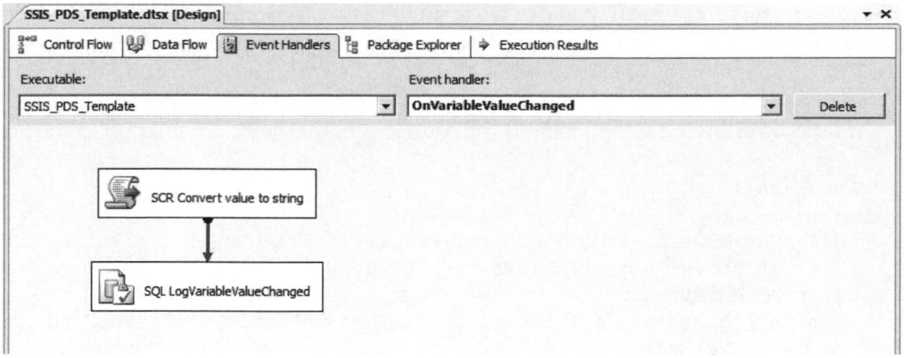

Figure 2-23

The `LogVariableValueChanged` stored procedure inserts the value of the variable after it changes into the `PackageVariableLog` table. Because the variable could be of many different data types, converting the value to a string is important. In your Script Task, select your language of choice in the `ScriptLanguage` field. Starting with SSIS 2008, you have a choice of either Microsoft Visual Basic 2008 or Microsoft Visual C# 2008. Use Microsoft Visual Basic for this example.

In the `ReadOnlyVariables` field, select the `System::VariableValue` option, and in the `ReadWriteVariables` field, select the `User::strVariableValue` option. These options give the script the appropriate access to those variables. Figure 2-24 shows the completed Script Task Editor screen.

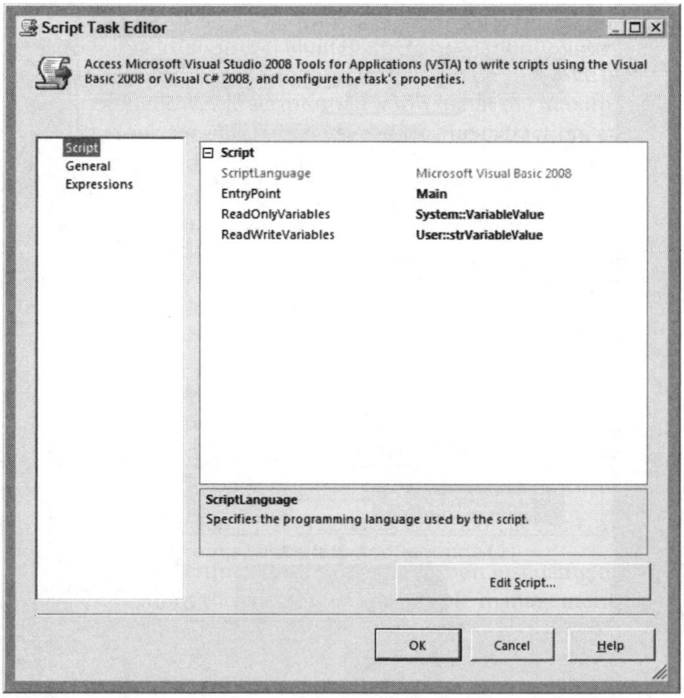

Figure 2-24

After the Script screen is configured, you can work on the actual script by clicking the Edit Script button. When variables are accessed from within the package, they are returned as an object, so you can easily use the .ToString function to convert all types of data. If the .ToString function does not work, you will catch the exception that occurs and record the value "Unable to Convert to String:" with the reason why it failed. Following is the Visual Basic code to replace the Main function in the Script Task:

```
Public Sub Main()
    Try
        Dim sVarValue As String = Dts.Variables("VariableValue").Value.ToString
        Dts.Variables("strVariableValue").Value = sVarValue
    Catch ex As Exception
        Dts.Variables("strVariableValue").Value = "Unable to Convert to String: " _
            & ex.Message
    End Try

    Dts.TaskResult = ScriptResults.Success
End Sub
```

Connect the Execute SQL Task to the Script Task. It should only execute if the Script Task succeeds, so ensure that a green precedence constraint is between the two tasks. Now set up the Execute SQL Task to use the SSIS_PDS connection, and put the following code into the SQLStatement property:

```
exec dbo.LogVariableValueChanged
@PackageLogID = ?
,@VariableName = ?
,@VariableValue = ?
```

After it has been configured, the Execute SQL Task Editor screen should look like Figure 2-25.

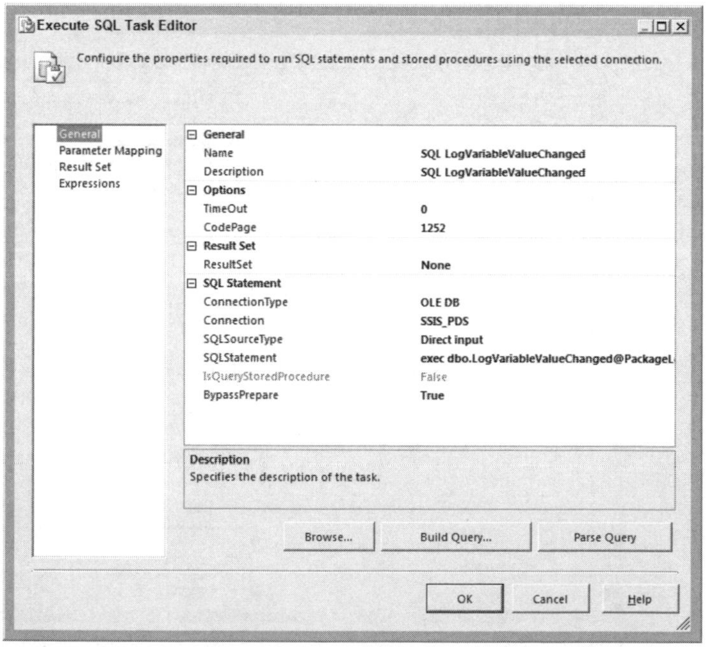

Figure 2-25

The last step is to set up the variables to be used in the Parameter Mapping menu. Map them to look like Figure 2-26.

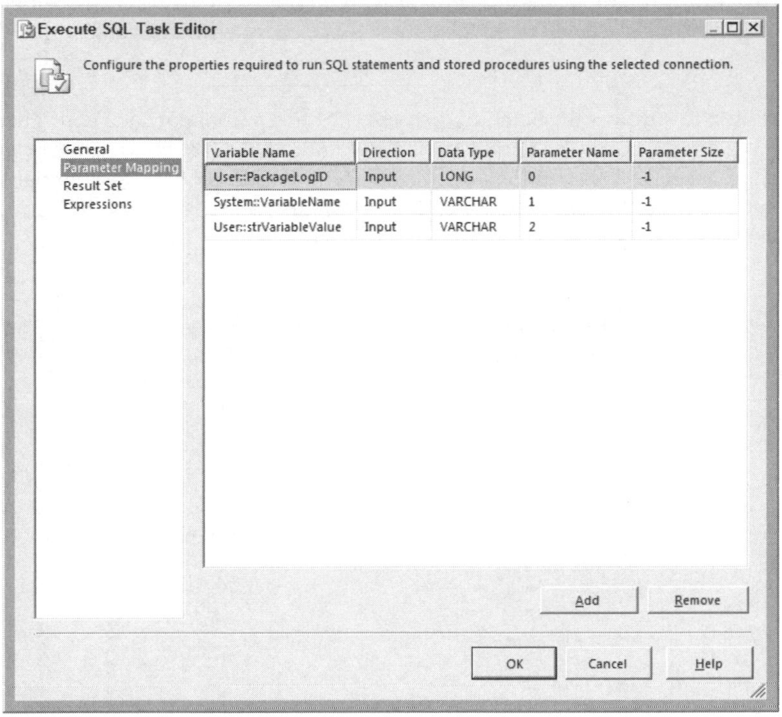

Figure 2-26

You've set up all the code and stored procedures needed to implement logging and auditing. The next section takes a look at the culmination of all your efforts: the template package.

Template Package

When it comes to creating your template package, you've already seen most of what needs to occur. You will need to develop and then install your template package for your fellow developers to use.

Development

Follow the configuration design exactly for the environment variable, XML configuration, and first SQL Server configuration. Do not include the second SQL Server package configuration, because developers will create it on a per-package basis.

The next step is to add as many connection managers and variables that you can imagine your developers might use. This step enables you to control the values that are configurable up front. Also add those entries to the SSISConfigurations table. If anyone comes to you with new configurations after you've distributed the template, you'll need to modify the template and redistribute it again. The more you can do up front, the easier your life will be down the road.

You also need to follow all steps listed for the logging and auditing portion. You may not need to include all variables in the audit trail of values changing. If you do not want a variable included, do nothing to it. If you do want it to be included, you need to set the "Raise event when variable value changes" property on the variable to `True`.

Another step needed to support the batching process is to add a final package configuration of type Parent Package Variable. Choose the Parent Variable of `BatchLogID` to configure the Value of the current `BatchLogID`. The final screen should look like Figure 2-27. This Parent Package Variable passes the `BatchLogID` from the parent package to the child package to ensure that the children know they should be in the same batch.

Figure 2-27

Set the security of the package as the final step in the template package. Although you may have reasons to choose otherwise, the most common framework value used is `DontSaveSensitive`. Because you pass all information in from the SQL Server configuration at either a system-wide or package-specific level, you get that sensitive information from the database, and do not need to keep it in the package. Whichever method you decide to use, now is the time to set that property.

Installation

After you've developed the template package, you must install it on all developer's machines. Copy the package to the `%ProgramFiles%\Microsoft Visual Studio 9.0\Common7\IDE\PrivateAssemblies\ProjectItems\DataTransformationProject\DataTransformationItems` directory.

The `%ProgramFiles%` directory is an environment variable that redirects you to the proper drive for your `Program Files` folder (and would typically resolve to `C:\Program Files`).

When the file is copied into each developer's template folder, the developer can use the template by right-clicking the project and selecting Add ⇨ New Item. Then, the developer selects the filename for the template. A new package will be created that is an exact duplicate of the one created earlier.

The problem with this newly created package being exactly like the original package is that the new package has the same `ID` and `Name` as its parent. This same predicament occurs when you copy and paste a package to clone a package in Solution Explorer. This feature becomes an issue when you have multiple packages logging to the same database. The logging determines whether this package is entirely new based on a new name or new ID.

You can easily fix the problem by generating a new `PackageID` in BIDS. You can do so by going to the Properties window for the package and selecting <Generate New ID> for the `ID` property. You can also do it with the `dtutil.exe` utility by using the `-I` switch. You can also modify the `Name` property to match the name you chose for the package.

Other Considerations

You must keep a few other considerations in mind as you're implementing your SSIS management framework. They are not necessary to have a complete management framework, but may provide different amounts of value to different organizations.

Customizations

Although this chapter has introduced a standard SSIS management framework, you may want to customize your framework. Following are a couple of variations you may include:

❑ Batch logic modifications

❑ Multiple environments on a server

One way to customize your framework is to modify the batching logic. The standard framework includes the parent-child package batch, where all packages are called from a parent that already has a batch ID fall under the same batch. You can modify the logic in the `LogPackageStart` stored procedure to pull batch information based on different logic. One reason you may want to do so is for a long-running package that you don't want to call from a master package. You could have it run separately, and pull the current batch ID at that time to use.

The framework is built on the idea that all packages on a server will want to pull the same configuration information. In the scenario where you have multiple environments on one server, you'll need to modify this logic somewhat. You have the option to only run certain environments during certain times and modifying the XML configuration at that time. You could also have multiple environment variables on the server where there is one per environment. The package would know which one to use, based on a variable passed in through the command-line executable.

Other variations may be needed based on your organization.

ETL Process Framework

Starting with Chapter 7, you will learn how to develop ETL packages, whose core purpose is to move data. If you are creating many ETL packages, creating an ETL process framework may be beneficial to your organization. This framework would track the metadata of the data flow, including from where the data came, any manipulations needed, and the destination of the data, along with execution statuses and states.

You do not track this type of data in the SSIS management framework because it is a different focus area. This management framework helps to configure and monitor SSIS, no matter the purpose of the package.

Process Owner

Having one person (or small group) that owns the framework is important. The implementation works best if this person doesn't report to the developers using the framework. This person is responsible for controlling the rules governing the framework process, including deployments and modifications. This person needs to maintain the configuration database, and make any needed modifications to the SSIS template. This person needs to mediate any conflicting needs, and respond timely to requests. This person will also most likely be the person training new developers (or groups) on how to work with the framework.

Reporting

Rather than training your developers and support team in understanding the logging tables, you can create queries or reports for them to use that will enable them to monitor their packages. Following is an example of a very simple query that returns the execution times of all packages with the most recent runs at the top of the list:

```
select pkg.PackageName
      ,convert(time,pkglog.EndDateTime - pkglog.StartDateTime) as DurationSeconds
      ,pkglog.Status
from dbo.PackageLog pkglog
join dbo.PackageVersion pkgvers on pkglog.PackageVersionID=pkgvers.PackageVersionID
join dbo.Package pkg on pkgvers.PackageID=pkg.PackageID
order by pkglog.StartDateTime desc
```

Summary

As has been discussed in this chapter, you will initially face a number of problems when developing packages. By utilizing an SSIS management framework, you can avoid these issues and increase your developer throughput. The framework described here is a starting point, with variations referenced throughout. If an addition is not described, it still may be the most appropriate for your organization and should be included.

The first step any organization should take is to put an SSIS management framework in place. Following that, you should decide on a set of standards, including how to deploy, store, and scale your packages.

Chapters 3 and 10 explore these topics. With the combination of the framework and these standards, you are fully armed to develop the task and/or data manipulation logic needed in your package.

3

Package Deployment
and Storage Decisions

In Chapter 2, you learned about creating an SSIS management framework to support configurations, error handling, and logging. This chapter continues the standardization of your SSIS environment with a discussion of the many factors that feed the decisions of how to deploy and where to store your packages.

This chapter contains "Problem," "Design," and "Solution" sections that walk you through the questions you must ask to determine your deployment and storage methods. The "Problem" section discusses the questions you must answer when determining these methods. The "Design" section then walks you through the different choices that you could use, and the "Solution" section shows the decision-making process.

Problem

As the number and design complexity of SSIS packages grows in an organization, so do the challenges related to package deployment. Addressing this situation first involves deciding on the right package storage model, and also choosing the method for deployment. These decisions could vary by the organization, application, and environment that you are working in.

Somewhere in the project lifecycle of implementing an SSIS solution, you will realize that you can't continue to execute packages though Business Intelligence Development Studio (BIDS), and that you will actually need to put your packages on a server. Where you store these packages and how you get them to that location is a decision that you should not take lightly. Here are some of the overall issues you will face when choosing a solution:

❑   Do you need to have a standard process?

❑   How does your environment affect your decision?

❑   What application factors should you consider?

Standardization

Most enterprise environments rely on consistent and reproducible patterns in development to keep cost down and deployments predictable. Whether your environment is an enterprise-sized company or a smaller company, you want minimal work to move your solution through development, quality control, and production. These standard approaches make your developers' and production control operators' lives easier.

Standardization also comes into play for storage and deployment methods. Having all departments use the same methods to make operations engineers' jobs simpler is typical. The system will also be easier to maintain and better suited for disaster-recovery scenarios. Adding new servers into the system will use the same setup approach, reducing the setup overhead.

Using the same storage method for all applications can prevent your "re-creating the wheel" each time a new application comes online. You can point your developers to existing solutions, as well as to documentation that explains the "standard" approach. You can also ensure that you know where all packages live to help with your backup solution.

Deploying your packages in the same way will also assist your organization. Not only will you have a tried-and-true method for new applications, you will also reduce the risk for migration mistakes. Some of the deployment methods can even be written to be executed at the click of a button. Overall, having a standard approach for both your storage and deployment methods will help you out in the long run.

Environment

Most organizations have multiple environments for SSIS packages that serve different purposes. For example, you could have a development environment where developers have complete control of packages and execution times. You could also have a quality control environment where business users could validate new changes. Finally, all organizations have a production environment where the final set of packages run for public consumption. There could be anywhere from two to five different environments in your organization.

Each environment has a separate set of requirements, including security access, server locations, and backup schedules. Because your decisions for storage and deployment are based on this type of information, you could end up with different methods per environment. If developers have complete access to the development environment, then allowing them to manually deploy their packages would be an easy deployment method. Then, they can redeploy as many times as they need to. On production, you definitely would not want your developers to have the same kind of access!

This concept leans toward disagreeing with the previous discussion about standardization. Having different environments does affect being able to have a standard approach. Even if you can't have standard methods between environments, try to keep the approach as consistent as possible.

Application

At the highest level, an organization will create standards to be used across an organization. Each environment's methods could vary from the standards, based on some of the previously discussed logic. Finally, each individual application could utilize a different combination of deployment and storage methods.

A number of factors could affect your application's storage and deployment, including security, backup model, and types of packages. Even if the rest of your company is using SQL Server storage for their SSIS packages, you may choose file system storage if your specific application stores all of its data in a different database management system. Also, if your team differs from other departments in that you have limited access to the SQL Servers, you may decide to use a deployment manifest file rather than a manual package deployment.

Determining which methods to use can be a difficult, but necessary, task. Figuring out the best approach based on these factors is what the rest of this chapter covers.

Desired Implementation

Deciding on the correct way to store your SSIS packages and the best way to deploy the packages can be a trying affair. Many debates exist as to which methods are the best, but the decision is really dependent on many factors.

Although SSIS provides a number of different storage and deployment methods to give you the most flexibility, all of the options can be a little overwhelming in the beginning. Using the flow charts and advice in this chapter, you can determite the different methods that are available, and which you should use under what circumstances. This chapter provides straightforward guidance to help you make your decision.

Design

The "Problem" section of this chapter explained what deployment and storage means in terms of SSIS packages, and described the importance of creating standard methods for you or your developers to use. In this section you take a look at the different options available in SSIS. The discussion begins with the locations where you can store your SSIS packages, and then goes into the deployment methods for getting the packages into that storage location.

Storage Methods

SSIS provides two locations where you can store your packages: the file system and SQL Server. The following sections give you a look at how that information is stored, and a look individually at each of those methods.

SSIS Service

When you deploy your packages, they are stored into what is called the *SSIS Package Store*. The Package Store, in some cases, will actually physically store the package, as in the `msdb` database option. Or, in the case, of the file system, the Package Store just keeps a pointer to a specific top-level directory, and enumerates through the packages stored underneath that directory. To connect to the Package Store, the SSIS Service must be running. This service is called SQL Server Integration Services 10.0, or `MsDtsServer100`. Only one instance of the service exists per machine, or per set of clustered machines.

You can configure the SSIS Service in the Services applet in Control Panel ⇨ Administrative Tools ⇨ Services. Double-click on the SQL Server Integration Services 10.0 item. As you can see, the service is set to automatically start by default, and starts under the `NetworkService` account.

Although you can store, execute, and stop packages without the service, the service makes running packages more manageable. For example, anyone who wants to interrogate the service can find out which packages are running. It can also aid in the importing and exporting of packages into the Package Store. One last great use for the service is to enable you to handle centralized management, enumeration, and monitoring of your packages throughout your enterprise.

The `MsDtsServer100` service is configured through an XML file that is located, by default, in the following path:

```
C:\Program Files\Microsoft SQL Server\100\DTS\Binn\MsDtsSrvr.ini.xml
```

This path will vary if your SSIS server is set up to be a cluster. By default, the XML file should look like the following:

```
<?xml version="1.0" encoding="utf-8"?>
<DtsServiceConfiguration xmlns:xsd="http://www.w3.org/2001/XMLSchema"
    xmlns:xsi="http://www.w3.org/2001/XMLSchema-instance">
  <StopExecutingPackagesOnShutdown>true</StopExecutingPackagesOnShutdown>
  <TopLevelFolders>
    <Folder xsi:type="SqlServerFolder">
      <Name>MSDB</Name>
      <ServerName>.</ServerName>
    </Folder>
    <Folder xsi:type="FileSystemFolder">
      <Name>File System</Name>
      <StorePath>..\Packages</StorePath>
    </Folder>
  </TopLevelFolders>
</DtsServiceConfiguration>
```

There really isn't a lot to configure in this file, but it has some interesting uses.

The first configuration line tells the packages how to react if the service is stopped. By default, packages that the service runs will stop upon a service stop or failure. You could also configure the packages to continue to run after the service stops until they complete by changing the `StopExecutingPackagesOnShutDown` property to `False`, as shown here:

```
<StopExecutingPackagesOnShutdown>false</StopExecutingPackagesOnShutdown>
```

The next configuration sections are the most important. They specify which paths and servers the `MsDtsServer100` service will read from. Whenever the service starts, it reads this file to determine where the packages are stored. In the default file is a single entry for a SQL Server that looks like the following `SqlServerFolder` example:

```
<Folder xsi:type="SqlServerFolder">
  <Name>MSDB</Name>
  <ServerName>.</ServerName>
</Folder>
```

The `<Name>` line represents how the name will appear in Management Studio for this set of packages. The `<ServerName>` line represents where the connection will point to. There is a problem if your SQL Server is on a named instance where this file will still point to the default non-named instance (`.`). If you do have a named instance, simply replace the period with your instance name.

The next section shows you where your `File System` packages will be stored. The `<StorePath>` shows the folder from which all packages will be enumerated. The default path is `C:\Program Files\ Microsoft SQL Server\100\DTS\Packages`, which is represented as `..\Packages` in the following default configuration. The `..` part of the statement navigates one directory below the SSIS Service file, and `\Packages` then traverses into the `Packages` folder.

```
<Folder xsi:type="FileSystemFolder">
  <Name>File System</Name>
  <StorePath>..\Packages</StorePath>
</Folder>
```

Everything in the `Packages` folder and below will be enumerated. You can create subdirectories under this folder and they will immediately show up in Management Studio. Each time you make a change to the `MsDtsSrvr.ini.xml` file, you must stop and start the `MsDtsServer100` service in order for the changes to take effect.

File System Storage

The first way to store your SSIS packages is directly in the file system. SSIS packages are just XML files and can be stored as any other file on a shared file share, or a locked-down and secure directory. If you put the file in the location that is in the `StorePath` property in the `MsDtsSrvr.ini.xml` file, you will have access to information about the package and its execution through Management Studio.

To view the package information, open Management Studio, select the Connect drop-down box in the Object Explorer window, and select Integration Services. When you connect, all the different stores that are available for you to explore appears.

A connection to that store isn't made until you expand one of the folders, as shown with the `File System` store in Figure 3-1. At that point, you may experience a timeout if you're trying to connect to an `msdb` database that isn't online, or when the server is offline. Otherwise, when you expand the folder, a list of folders and packages that are stored in that particular store appears.

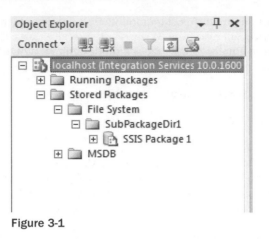

Figure 3-1

You can also access all the packages that are running under the Running Packages folder. From there, you can stop packages that are running too long by right-clicking the package and selecting Stop, as shown in Figure 3-2. This option is available for packages that are stored on the file server as long as they are located in the folder designated by the StorePath property in the MsDtsSrvr.ini.xml file.

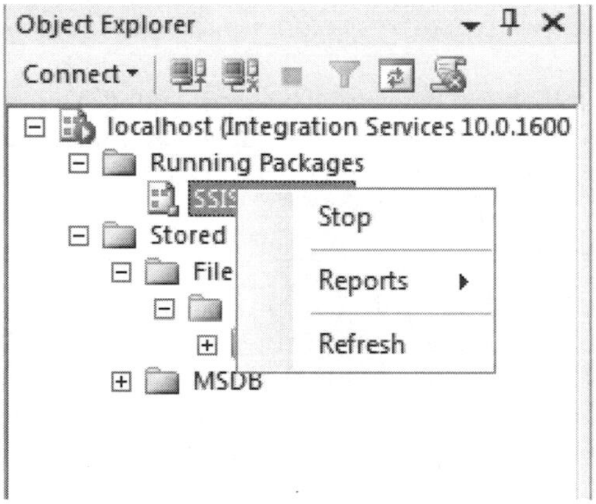

Figure 3-2

The package name shown in this report is the package name from the package properties in BIDS. If your package's filename is Package1.dtsx, but the package name in properties is called FileWatcher, then FileWatcher will show in this window, not Package1.dtsx. Because of this discrepancy, keeping your package's name in synch with the file is very important. Otherwise, finding and managing your packages can become quite complex.

SQL Server Storage

The second option for storing SSIS packages is in SQL Server, in the msdb database. The packages are stored in a table named dbo.sysssispackages, which contains the package XML, along with version and security information for each package.

If you don't have access to export an SSIS package, but you have read-only access to the msdb database, you can retrieve the XML for the SSIS package by running the following SQL statement:

```
select package = cast(cast(packagedata as varbinary(max)) as xml)
from dbo.sysssispackages
```

To manage the packages that you have imported to the SQL Server, you follow the same steps to connect to Management Studio as you did for the file system storage. Instead of looking under the File System folder, you look under the MSDB folder for the available packages. Figure 3-3 shows a view of these packages.

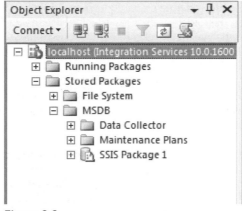

Figure 3-3

The following shows you the pros and cons of each method together to allow a comparison of both storage methods.

Storage Comparison

As discussed earlier, you can store your packages in two places: on the file system or in the msdb database. Each storage option has its own pros and cons, and which option you choose will be based on what is more important to you.

These pros and cons are examined in more depth in this section, but to summarize, the Table 3-1 provides a high-level idea of which storage option is best based on what functionality you're most interested in. Just because a given storage option is not checked does not mean that it doesn't have that functionality. The ones checked are simply most optimized for the given functionality.

Table 3-1

Functionality	Best in File System	Best in msdb
Security		X
Backup and recovery		X
Deployment	X	
Troubleshooting	X	
Availability	X	
Execution speed	X	X

If security concerns you greatly, you may want to consider placing your packages in the msdb database. To secure your packages on the file system, you could have multiple layers of security by using the NT File System (NTFS) security on the folder on the file system where the packages are located. You could also then place a password on the packages to keep users who may have administrator rights to your machine from executing the package. This does add extra complexity to your package deployments in some cases.

If you store your packages in the msdb database, you can assign package roles to each package to designate who can see or execute the package. The packages can also be encrypted in the msdb database, which strengthens your security even more.

Backup and recovery is simpler when you store your packages in the msdb database. If you were to store your packages in the msdb database, then you must only wrap the msdb database into your regular maintenance plan to back up all the packages. As packages are added, they are wrapped into the maintenance plan. The problem with this feature is that you can't restore a single package using this mechanism. You would have to restore all the packages to a point in time, and that would also restore the jobs and history.

The other backup option is a file system backup, which would just use your favorite backup software to back up the folders and files. If you use this method, you must rely on your Backup Operator to do the backup for you, which makes some people uneasy. - In case you need to utilize your backups, you could restore individual packages to a point in time. In reality, you can just redeploy the packages from Source Safe if you can't retrieve a backup file.

File system storage is much simpler, but less sophisticated. You use file system storage by copying packages into the directory for the Package Store. You can create subdirectories under the parent directory to subdivide it easily. You can also copy over a single package easily as well, in case you need to make a package change. To import packages into the Package Store using the msdb database, you must use Management Studio (or the DTUtil.exe command-line tool) and import them package by package.

Along the same lines as deployment is troubleshooting. If something were to go bump in the night, and you wanted to see whether the packages in production were the same release as the packages you thought you had deployed, you must only copy the files down to your machine, and perform a comparison using Source Safe (or another similar tool). If the files were stored in the `msdb` database, you would have to right-click each package in Management Studio and select Export. If the same packages were stored in the file system, you must only copy the files to your machine, or open BIDS on the remote machine.

Availability of your packages is always at the top of the list for DBAs. If you were to store the packages in the `msdb` database and the database engine were to go down, the packages would be unavailable. If they were stored in the file system, then your packages would be available for execution. Of course, if the database engine is down, then probably one of your key data sources would also be down at the same time.

The good news is no matter what storage option you choose, the performance will be the same. As you can see, each storage option has many pros and cons, and neither wins overwhelmingly. Now take a look at the deployment methods.

Deployment Methods

SSIS provides several different methods for deploying packages to either the file system or SQL Server. This section takes a look at the following three methods:

❑ SSIS Deployment Wizard

❑ Manual deployment of packages

❑ DTUtil scripting

SSIS Deployment Wizard

In SSIS, you can create a deployment utility that helps a user install your project of packages and any dependencies (such as configuration files). This deployment utility is similar to creating a program like InstallShield, and is perfect for times when you want to pass a set of packages to a customer or a production DBA who may not know how to install SSIS packages the manual way. When you create a deployment utility, all the files that are necessary to install the project are copied into a centralized directory, and an .SSISDeploymentManifest file is created for the installer to run, which opens the Package Installation Wizard.

To create a deployment utility, simply right-click the project in BIDS and select Properties. In the Property Pages dialog box, go to the Deployment Utility page and change the CreateDeploymentUtility property to True, as shown in Figure 3-4. This is set to False by default. The AllowConfigurationChanges property is a useful setting as well, and when set to True, will prompt the installer to see whether he or she would like to change any settings that may be exposed via a configuration file at installation time. The DeploymentOutputPath property shows you where the deployment utility will be outputted to underneath the project folder.

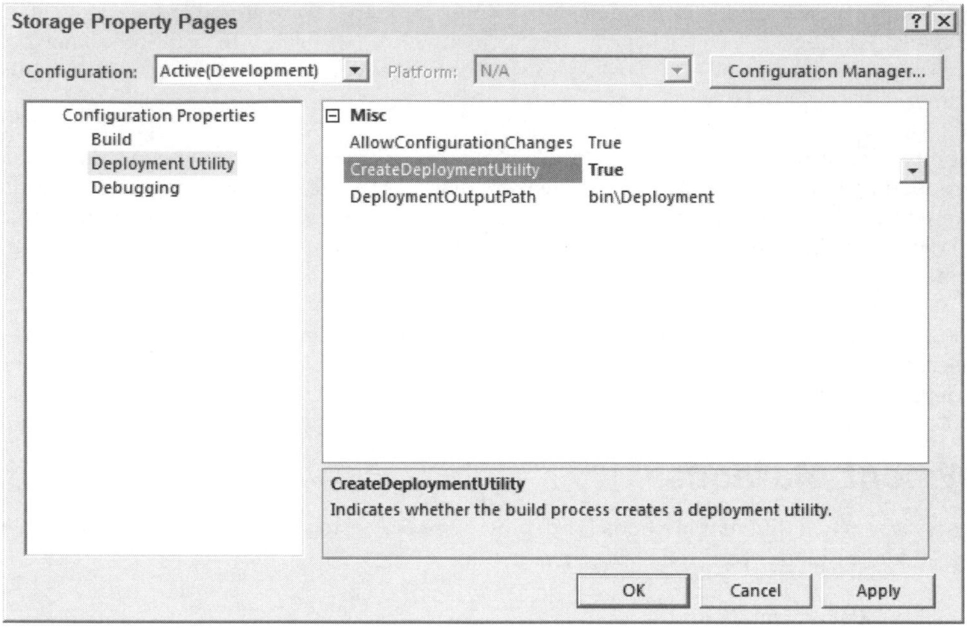

Figure 3-4

Next, under the Build menu, select Build *<Project Name>*, where *<Project Name>* represents your project's name. This option opens and builds each package. If any errors exist in the package, then you will see them at this point. As it builds the project, the wizard outputs each package into the \bin\ deployment directory under your project's folder.

Now that you have created a deployment .SSISDeploymentManifest file, you're now ready to send the entire contents of the \bin\deployment folder to the installation person. The installation person must copy the contents of the folder to the server he or she wants to deploy to, and double-click the .SSISDeploymentManifest file. The installer could also run it remotely, but running it on the same server as the target deployment server to simplify the installation is preferred.

After skipping over the introduction screen, you are asked where you want to deploy the packages, as shown in Figure 3-5. You can either choose a "File system deployment" or a "SQL Server deployment." A "File system deployment" just copies the files to a directory on the server. A "SQL Server deployment" stores the packages in the msdb database on the target server. You can also have the wizard validate each package after you install the package. This step ensures that the package that was delivered to you is valid on your machine, including the data sources and configurations.

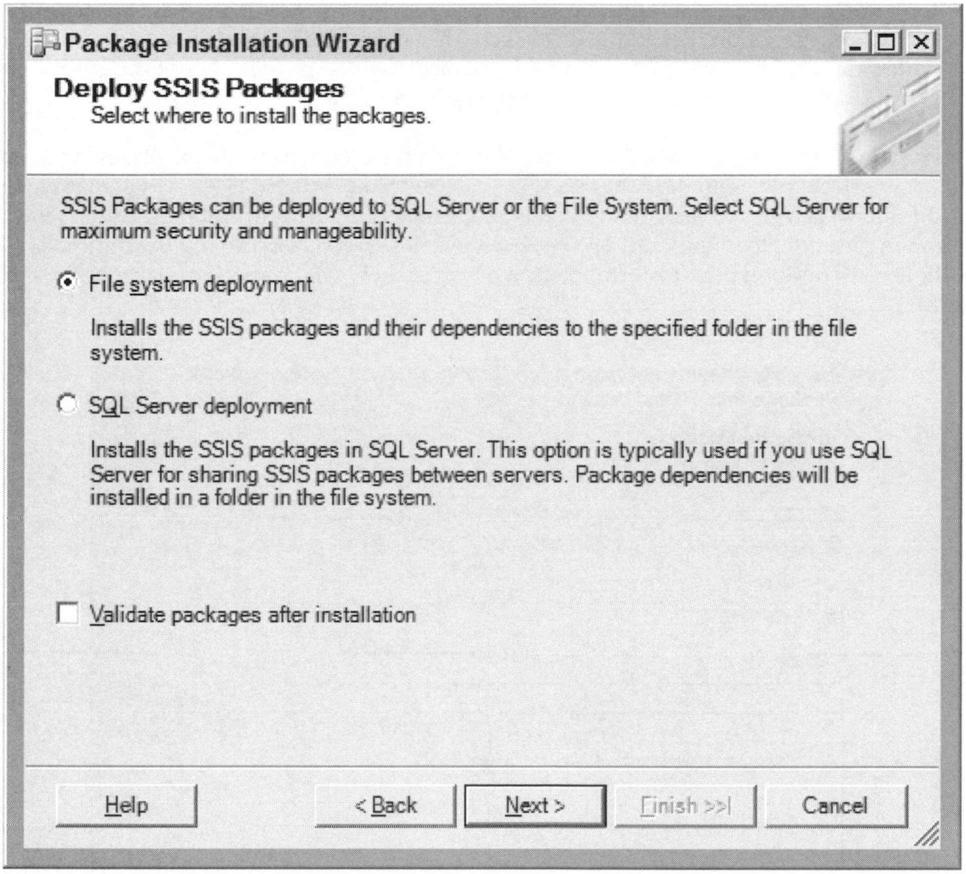

Figure 3-5

If you're following this example, select "SQL Server deployment" and click Next. The next screen prompts you for the SQL Server 2008 machine to which you want to deploy the packages. You cannot deploy SSIS packages to SQL Server 2000 or SQL Server 2005. If you select a "File system deployment," the next screen prompts you for the file path to which you want the packages to be deployed. The last option in the "SQL Server deployment" screen is to specify whether you want to rely on SQL Server for protecting the package by encrypting the package. This option is preferred, and it automatically changes the ProtectionLevel package property to ServerStorage as it installs each package.

Even though you have selected a "SQL Server deployment," you may still have files that you must deploy, such as configuration files and `readme` files. The next screen prompts you for where you want to put these files. Generally, they'll go under a folder named after the project under the `C:\Program Files\Microsoft SQL Server\100\DTS\Packages\` path.

Click Next to install the packages in the Package Store on the server. After the packages are installed, if the developer selected `True` to the `AllowConfigurationChanges` in BIDS (shown earlier in Figure 3-4), then an additional screen appears, giving you (as an installer) a chance to edit the values in the configuration file at deployment time. Figure 3-6 shows this screen. You can use the drop-down box to see multiple configuration files. Unfortunately, it does not show which specific packages these files are tied to.

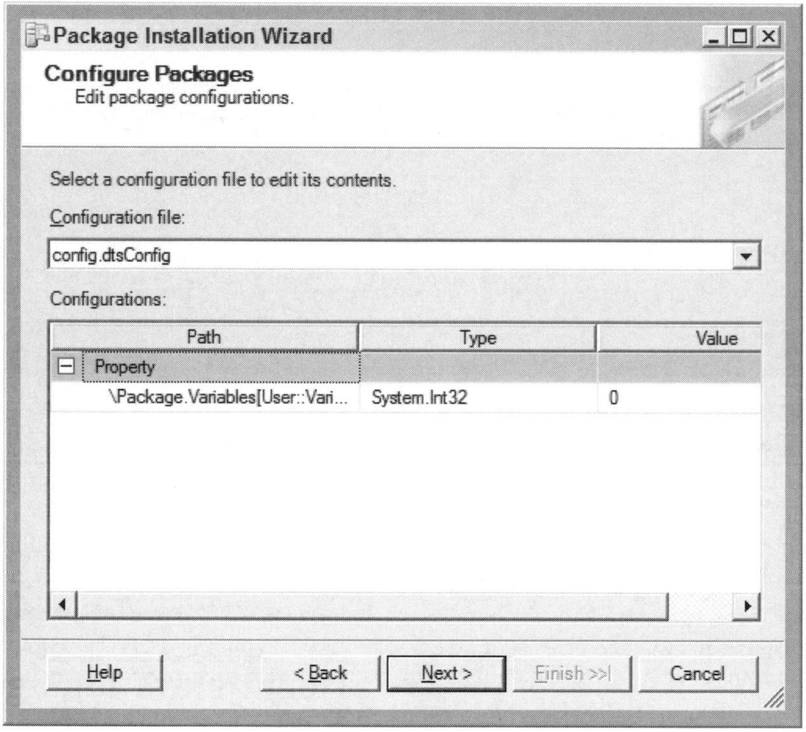

Figure 3-6

The only other additional screen you would see is a pop-up dialog box if there were a user password on any package.

After the packages have been deployed, they are validated, as shown in Figure 3-7. Any problems appear in the Packages Validation screen, and you can redeploy after correcting the problem. The last screen is a summary screen to complete the wizard.

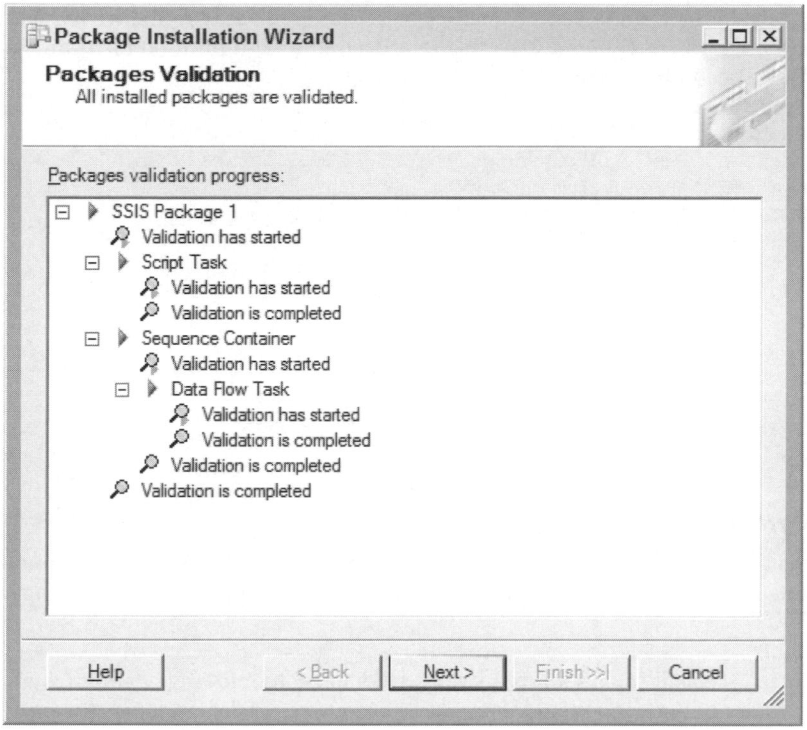

Figure 3-7

The wizard is a great way to deploy packages in bulk. If you want to deploy a package in Management Studio (which is examined in the next section), you have to do it one package at a time. The file system, however, is much easier. With this method of storage, you can just copy the files into a specific directory, and they'll be seen from Management Studio.

The main thing to remember about the deployment utility is that using it deploys every package and dependency. You may not want to deploy this many packages at once all the time. You can edit the .SSISDeploymentManifest file in a text editor to remove any extra files you do not want to migrate. Some developers find that creating a project in the same project solution that contains a subset of the packages that they want to deploy is useful, if the deployment utility is too aggressive for them.

If you did want to edit the .SSISDeploymentManifest XML file before sending the folder to a client, you could just remove one of the <Package> lines, as shown in the following XML example. You can also see, in the header of the XML file, who created the deployment tool for you, and when. This information is useful for tracking down to whom you should ask questions later if the project doesn't install appropriately. If you do not want to deploy a configuration file with the wizard, you can remove or comment out the `<ConfigurationFile>` line to prevent the configuration file from overwriting the older one that may already be on the server:

```xml
<?xml version="1.0"?>
<DTSDeploymentManifest GeneratedBy="JMMCONSULTING\Jessica Moss"
      GeneratedFromProjectName="Storage" GeneratedDate="2009-07-28T16:
      06:39.5776464-04:00" AllowConfigurationChanges="true">
  <Package>SSIS Package 1.dtsx</Package>
  <Package>SSIS Package 2.dtsx</Package>
<!--  <Package>SSIS Package 3.dtsx</Package> -->
  <Package>SSIS Package 4.dtsx</Package>
  <Package>SSIS Package 5.dtsx</Package>
  <Package>SSIS Package 6.dtsx</Package>
  <Package>SSIS Package 7.dtsx</Package>
  <ConfigurationFile>config.dtsConfig</ConfigurationFile>
</DTSDeploymentManifest>
```

Manual Deployment of Packages

The next deployment option is to manually deploy your packages to the SQL Server. You can only use this option for one package at a time. The package loads into either the file system storage or the SQL Server storage.

Manual deployment is exactly as it sounds, in that a DBA must go into Management Studio to perform the deployment. He or she connects to the Integration Services Service and views the packages available. Right-clicking on either the `File System` folder or the `MSDB` folder results in an option called Import Package, as shown in Figure 3-8.

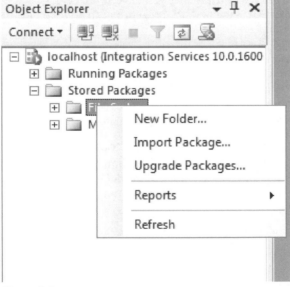

Figure 3-8

Selecting the Import Package menu option opens a dialog window similar to the one shown in Figure 3-9. In this window, you can select where the package is coming from. If it is SQL Server, you select the desired server, and if it is file system, you choose the path of the package. You can also change the "Protection level" property to specify what type of security you want applied to the package. This is the place where you could set the option to enable server storage security, which would use the database security model.

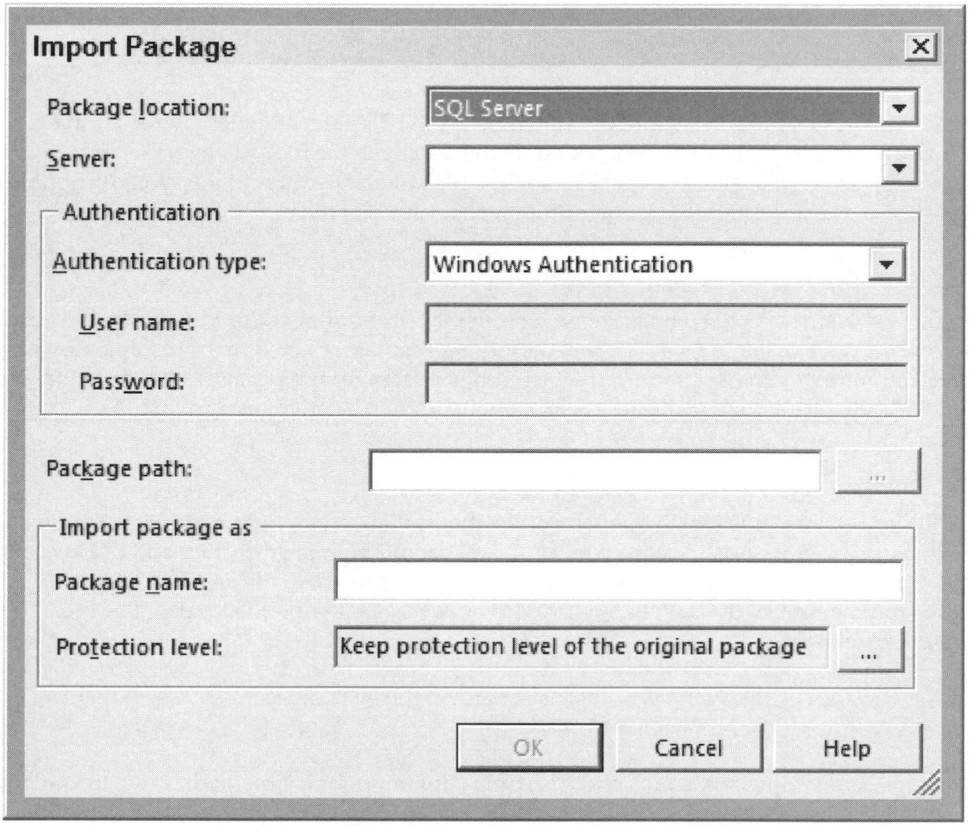

Figure 3-9

You cannot use the server storage security option when deploying to the `File System` folder. If you try to do so, the error message shown in Figure 3-10 appears.

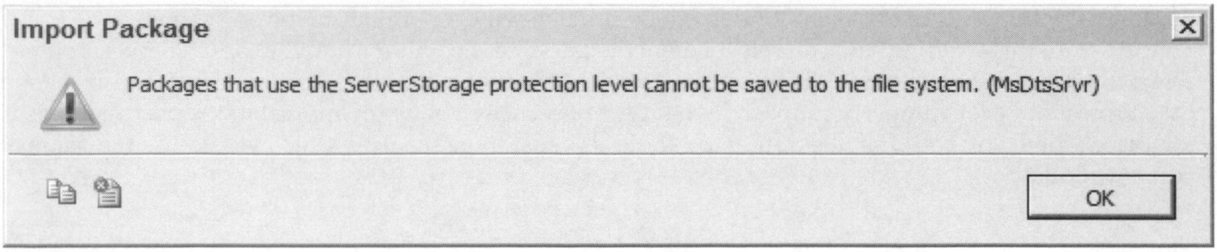

Figure 3-10

Another technique that falls under a manual deployment is simply to copy the packages over by using a command such as XCOPY. This method is often used for .NET application deployments, and is a simple solution that your developers will understand. If you deploy to the file system, no record exists in SQL Server that contains metadata about packages in the file system. Because of this, you can simply copy the packages into a directory, and the Package Store will be aware of them.

DTUtil Scripting

One of the best undiscovered command-line tools in the SSIS administrator kit is DTUtil.exe. This tool is also good for developers as well. The tool performs a number of functions, including moving packages, renumbering the PackageID, re-encrypting a package, and digitally signing a package. To see everything this tool can do, type the following command from a command prompt:

```
DTUtil.exe /?
```

Essentially, you can use this tool to do many of the things that you do in Management Studio and, to a lesser extent, BIDS. You can also create a batch file to loop through the directory and deploy every package in the directory. The batch file will loop through every .dtsx file and execute DTUtil.exe, storing the packages from the C:\SSIS_PDS\CH03 Storage folder on the local SQL Server. The batch file would look like this:

```
for %f in ("C:\SSIS_PDS\CH03 Storage\*.dtsx") do dtutil.exe /File "%f" /DestServer
    localhost /copy SQL;"%~nf"
```

Now that you know some of the pros and cons of the different storage methods, how do you determine which method is best for your organization? That's what is examined in the following "Solution" section.

Solution

Now that you understand each of the storage and deployment options discussed previously in the "Design" section, take a look at a solution for determining which methods you should use. Keep in mind the discussion in the "Problem" section earlier in this chapter, where you learned that multiple methods may be necessary for your organization. You must take many considerations into account for both storage and deployment. The following section takes a look at each of the considerations and maps it to the appropriate method.

Storage Methodology

As discussed in the "Design" section, you can store SSIS packages in two locations: file system and SQL Server. Although both methods have their merits, determining the correct location is dependent on your organization's unique needs. In this section you combine your needs with a set of questions to find the ideal storage method for you.

This discussion addresses all the necessary questions in more detail later, but first, let's take a look at the overall approach you will employ. Figure 3-11 shows a flowchart with questions that you must answer when trying to determine your storage method.

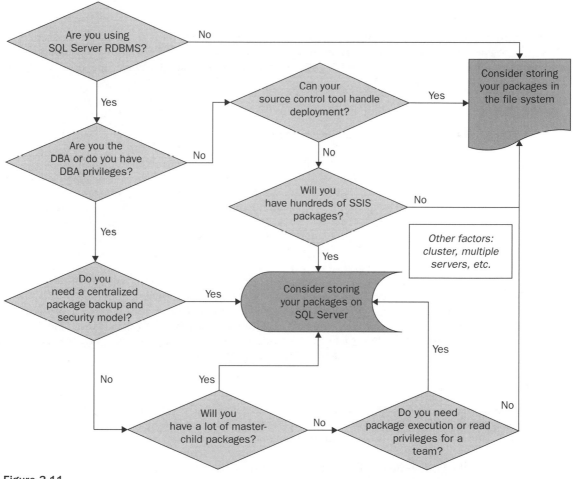

Figure 3-11

The flowchart starts in the top-left corner with the first question, "Are you using SQL Server RDBMS?" If the answer is "Yes," you follow the arrow down to the next question. Alternatively, if the answer is "No," you follow the arrow to the right. The cycle continues until you reach a block that contains either "Consider storing your packages in the file system" or "Consider storing your packages on SQL Server." Each question is associated with an underlying organizational scenario or business need. Let's discuss each of the following considerations in more detail:

❑ Existing infrastructure

❑ Security

❑ Package makeup

Existing Infrastructure

The existing systems in your organization directly affect how you work with your SSIS packages. Deciding to add SSIS packages to your stack of other products, servers, and development techniques should not propagate an entirely new set of rules. This category encapsulates two of the questions from the flowchart shown in Figure 3-11:

❑ Are you using SQL Server RDBMS?

❑ Can your source control tool handle deployment?

Let's start by looking at whether you are already using SQL Server as your relational database management system (RDBMS). One of the beauties of SSIS is being able to move data from any source to any destination, not only SQL Server. If your organization uses packages in this fashion, installing a SQL Server that would just be used for package storage would add extra setup and maintenance overhead. If that is the case, your best option is to store your packages on the file system. If you do already use SQL Server in your organization, you shouldn't automatically use SQL Server storage, because there are more considerations to cover.

You must also consider the second question under this category, which concerns source control. Although it specifies source control, this actually could refer to any continuous integration product that supports automatic builds and deployments. If you use one of these tools in your deployment process, but don't have a high level of permission, you'll want to consider keeping your packages on the file system so that they can be moved over using a `copy` command. If you don't use one of these tools, you'll have to ask further questions to determine the correct places for your package.

Security

The next category of questions to consider falls under security, including the security that the people deploying and using the packages will have, as well as the existing model the organization uses. Following are the questions on the flowchart that fall under this category:

❑ Are you the DBA or do you have DBA privileges?

❑ Do you need a centralized package backup and security model?

❑ Do you need package execution or read privileges for a team?

To begin, you'll want to evaluate who will be working with these packages. Let's jump ahead for just a minute to discuss deployment practices. If you are not the database administrator (DBA) or have similar privileges, then you need to use an alternative method to access the SQL Server to deploy your packages. To bring that back to the storage question, rather than worry about the alternative, you may want to consider file system storage to remove this issue entirely.

You must also question whether you need to have a centralized backup and security model. Hopefully, your answer is "Of course!" But the question is a little more in-depth than just having a backup and security model. The idea here is whether you should include that very important functionality with something you already have in place. For example, if you already use SQL Server as the location for your application databases, you have a backup and security model in place for those applications. If you want your SSIS packages to be included in that centralized system, you may want to store your packages on the SQL Server.

This advice is a double-edged sword, however. The counter example is that if you have a backup system in place for your files, using the file system storage may make more sense. Finally, you must decide whether your team members will need to execute or read the packages. These privileges may be necessary in the event of a package failure if your team handles support duties. Allowing your team members to see and execute the package will be more easily handled through SQL Server. Storing the packages on the file system will entail additional security to allow the users access to the executable to run the packages.

Package Makeup

The last category of questions deals with the SSIS packages that you will be creating. Both the type and number of packages could affect your storage decisions, so you must answer the following two questions from the flowchart:

❑   Will you have hundreds of SSIS packages?

❑   Will you have a lot of master-child packages?

The number of packages is important because of maintenance. Seeing what packages are available is easier through the SQL Server interface. If you are going to have hundreds of packages, seeing them in SQL Server would probably be easier.

The second question deals with master-child packages. A *master-child package* is a concept that utilizes the Execute Package Task within SSIS. One package, known as the *master*, will call a second package, the *child*. If you use SQL Server to store both the master and children packages, the connection will find the correct package based on the Integration Services server name. Conversely, when using file storage, you must specify the exact location of the package and possibly make it configurable to support any change of the directory structure.

Back to the Flowchart

Now that you understand each of the questions, revisit the flowchart in Figure 3-11. If you follow the flow of the questions, you can see that certain questions are not always asked. For example, if you are not using a SQL Server RDBMS, you are automatically routed to use the file system without being asked whether you need a centralized backup and security model, or whether you have hundreds of SSIS packages. This routing is based on a priority of the business needs in which people tend to consider the questions, your needs may vary.

You want to consider some other factors as well, including clustering and multiple servers. If you are trying to scale out your deployment, see Chapter 12 for more insight into having multiple servers.

Deployment Methodology

Now that you understand where you should store the packages, let's examine how to get them there. As you probably could have guessed, determining how to deploy your packages depends on where the packages are stored. You also use another set of questions to determine your business needs. Let's take a look at all of that now.

As previously discussed in the "Design" section of this chapter, many deployment methods exist. But there are also fewer posed questions than in the storage flow. Figure 3-12 shows a flowchart to explain the methodology.

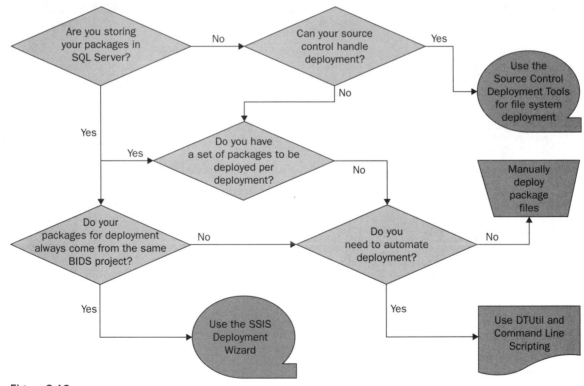

Figure 3-12

Similar to using the storage flowchart, you start your questions in the top-left corner of the flow and continue until you reach a block that contains a deployment method. The types of questions fall into the following categories:

- ❑ Storage method
- ❑ Existing infrastructure
- ❑ Deployment needs

Storage Method

The most important factor when determining what deployment method to use is where you are going to put your packages! The "Are you storing your packages in SQL Server?" question on the flowchart will point you in the correct direction, based on whether you are using the file system or SQL Server storage.

Existing Infrastructure

Similar to the storage methodology, the next category concerns the systems surrounding your SSIS packages. Using the same deployment process as other applications is ideal. Doing so increases supportability, as well as decreases the amount of time to set up the system. Following are the two questions from the flowchart that reference an existing infrastructure:

- ❑ Can your source control handle deployment?
- ❑ Do you need to automate deployment?

The next thing you'll want to look at is your source control system. In association with the similar storage question, this system could refer to any deployment tool. If the tool handles deployments, you can absolutely use it instead of the deployment option typically used for SSIS. This option was not covered in the "Design" section earlier in this chapter because it is dependent on your specific deployment tool.

Also, you must decide whether you want to automate your deployment. This decision could depend on whether you already have a process for deployment automation, for either other applications or the database application for which your SSIS packages were created. If the database application (for example, a data warehouse) uses automatic deployments, you will want to include your SSIS packages in the process. This factor will move you toward using the DTUtil.exe executable for deploying your packages.

Deployment Needs

The last category you must think about is the deployment process. Not specific to any system or infrastructure, your company policy or applications rules will determine how the deployment happens. Two questions on the flowchart fall into this category:

- ❑ Do your packages for deployment always come from the same BIDS project?
- ❑ Do you have a set of packages to be deployed per deployment?

The BIDS project contains multiple SSIS packages. If you have all packages that should be deployed together in one project, using the SSIS Deployment Wizard will make doing so very simple. On the other hand, if your packages are spread out over multiple projects, creating a deployment manifest for each project will be more difficult, and you would be better off using a script or manual deployment.

You must also be concerned with the number of SSIS packages that must be deployed at a single time. If you have a set of packages (anything more than a few packages), you want to consider different deployment methods than if you only have a few. This question then directs you to continue down the flow to find the final deployment method.

Back to the Flowchart

Each category discussed here has questions that affect the final outcome of the deployment method. Take a look at the flowchart in Figure 3-12 again. Along with the general priority that was just discussed, you can see the full priority of considerations, starting with the storage method and trickling down. By following the flow, you end up with the development method that is best suited for you.

Total Methodology

At this point, you must consider several factors when deciding on a storage and development methodology. The two methods are tied together, and if one method changes because of some new piece of information, you should re-evaluate the other method.

As you walk through the flowcharts to decide on your methods, keep in mind that these flowcharts are guidelines. If something you already have in place that would make you lean toward a different storage or deployment option than what seems to be the apparent choice from following the flowchart, by all means, use it! The point of these flowcharts and this solution is to explore all the different questions that you should investigate before making your final decision.

Summary

This chapter discussed the different storage and deployment options for SSIS. You learned about the pros and cons of all options, and the best way to determine which methods you should use in your organization. Before taking the plunge into developing SSIS packages, take the time to make educated and thoughtful decisions concerning these options. After you've discovered your organizational, application, and infrastructure needs, you are then ready to start creating, storing, and deploying your packages.

Chapter 4 starts off the development of SSIS packages by looking at different ways to handle and process files.

File-Handling and Processing Methods

SSIS has many powerful capabilities for handling and processing files. They might be data files from which information needs to be extracted. They might be signal files that are used to coordinate a process between two systems. They might simply be regular document files that need some administrative management. SSIS has features that can be helpful in all of these scenarios.

This chapter examines common file-handling tasks, and how you can accomplish those tasks with SSIS. The common file-handling tasks addressed in this chapter include the following:

- ❑ Finding files by name or other qualification criteria
- ❑ Looping through those files and manipulating them individually
- ❑ Performing simple file system operations
- ❑ Transferring files between servers
- ❑ Receiving notification that a new file has been created

This chapter is structured into the following three sections related to the problem, design, and solution of ETL extraction processes using SSIS:

- ❑ The "Problem" section elaborates on some of the common file system tasks listed previously. This section is general to ETL, and is not directly related to SSIS implementation details.
- ❑ The "Design" section picks up where the "Problem" section leaves off, and discusses how to approach the common file tasks using SSIS.
- ❑ The "Solution" section is dedicated to an example for merging multiple files together.

Problem

Many data-management tasks involve manipulating files. A file must be transferred from another server, an import process must find candidate files, and, after import, they must be moved elsewhere or deleted. These tasks are also generic enough to be needed in cases beyond data management. File-handling operations have been around for almost as long as operating systems have.

Simple File Operations

Simple file operations are the most common types of operations, consisting of copying, moving, renaming, or deleting files. The same operations usually also apply to containing organizational structures such as folders or directories. These operations are fundamental aspects of all mainstream operating systems.

Remote File Operations

Remote file operations are similar to the simple operations previously mentioned, but involve another server, perhaps even one using a different operating system. If the local and remote operating systems are compatible, and the network between them is capable of carrying a file-system protocol, then there is probably not a difference from the simple operations. However, if the remote server was designed decades earlier, or is located on the other side of the planet, then things get more challenging.

File Transfer Protocol (FTP) is the most common solution to these types of problems. It was first introduced in 1971. Thus, it has been adopted by almost all operating systems, and is often used as a lowest common denominator between systems. The Internet has its roots back during the same timeframe, so FTP is also a good choice for Internet-connected systems. FTP allows execution of the simple file operations, including copying files between the two servers.

Other methods exist, and have some merits, but few are as easy or prevalent as FTP.

File Criteria

Files are usually identified by a set of criteria, often by the name (or a portion thereof), or the extension. Sometimes they are identified by other file system attributes such an archival flag, or a modification date. Sometimes in a file import scenario, the import process just looks in a particular folder and attempts to import any files that it contains.

File Iteration

Usually, after the file criteria have been applied to identify one or more candidate files, you then want to do something with these files. Depending on the operation, you might be able to operate on multiple files at once. In these cases, the operation itself will usually accept the criteria directly. Often, though, the operation only supports certain types of criteria, such as a search pattern for the name attribute.

If the operation you want to execute doesn't work on multiple files, or doesn't support the criteria you need to apply, then you'll need to iterate through the candidate files yourself, and perform the operations individually. A loop construct is usually helpful for this task.

File Notification

Finally, if your process must respond quickly when a file is ready, you may want to design a process that stops and waits for a file to appear before continuing. Your process may need to do something with the file, or simply just wait for it as part of coordination with another process. Files have been used as primitive locking and notification mechanisms since the early days of computing.

Design

This section discusses how to perform most common file-handling tasks with SSIS.

File System Task

The File System Task provides functionality to perform simple file-system operations in the SSIS control flow. Figure 4-1 shows the configuration screen of the File System Task. The configuration is very simple with Destination Connection, Operation, and Source Connection sections. The opened drop-down in Figure 4-1 shows the available operations.

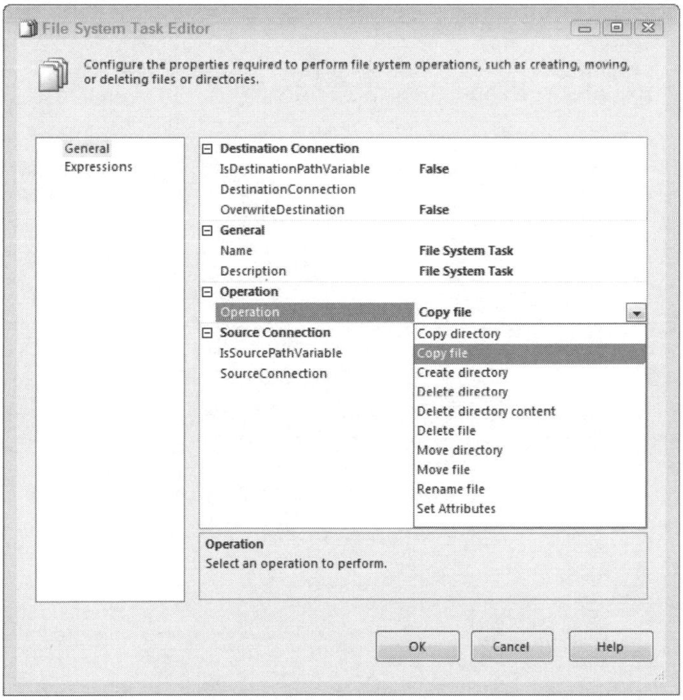

Figure 4-1

Source and Destination Connection

The Source Connection and Destination Connection properties of the File System Task define the information needed to complete the selected operation. You can specify the values for these properties either by a File Connection as shown in Figure 4-2, or through variables. The `IsDestinationPath Variable` and `IsSourcePathVariable` properties shown in Figure 4-1 determine whether a connection or a variable is used.

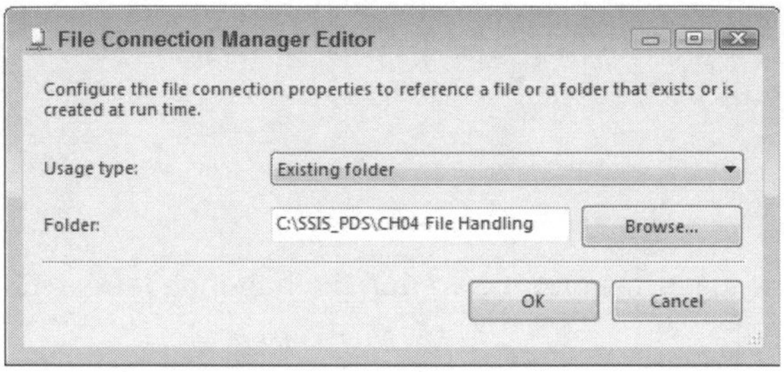

Figure 4-2

Both the variable and the File Connection methods can be manipulated through expressions for dynamic information at runtime.

Depending on the selected operation, the Destination Connection section may disappear from Figure 4-1. For example, a destination is irrelevant for a delete operation.

Attributes

If you select the Set Attributes operation, then an additional Attributes section appears, as shown in Figure 4-3.

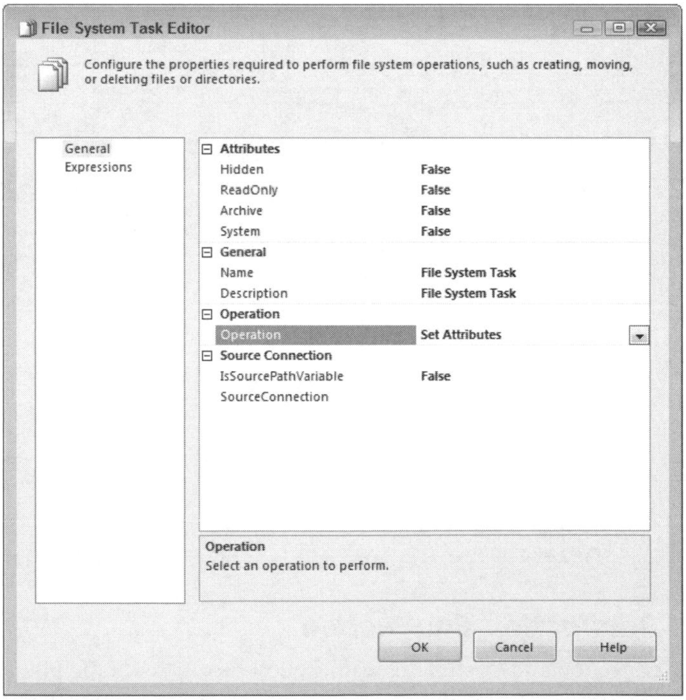

Figure 4-3

Although the File System Task allows you to set attributes as shown in Figure 4-3, there isn't a direct way in SSIS to read those same attributes. Of course, you can use the Script Task to do this job. Chapter 11 provides an example of using a script to access the `Archive` attribute of a file.

Other Windows file properties exist and can also be manipulated through a script, including the following:

❏ Size

❏ Date Modified

❏ Date Created

❏ Date Accessed

❏ Author

❏ Title

❏ File Version

Overwriting the Destination

If you refer to Figure 4-1, you can see that the Destination Connection has an extra property for `OverwriteDestination`. It simply tells the File System Task to overwrite any file specified by the destination connection that already exists. Otherwise, if the file already exists, the task will fail.

Multiple Files

The File System Task can only operate on one file at a time. Wildcard characters that could identify multiple files are not allowed. This feature is a departure from the corresponding OS-level commands that do allow the wildcards. To operate on multiple files, you place the File System Task inside a Foreach Loop container discussed later in this section.

FTP Task

The FTP Task is designed to transfer files between systems using FTP. FTP is a standardized series of commands and responses that define the communication between client and server software for the purpose of facilitating file transfers. The SSIS FTP Task represents the client side of the protocol. The software implementing the server side will depend on the remote operating system.

As shown in Figure 4-4, the FTP Task supports more operations than just transferring files.

Figure 4-4

The FTP Task is very similar to the File System Task. Instead of having direction-neutral source and destination connections, the file transfer has a clear direction relative to the client. The FTP Task Editor therefore uses "local" and "remote" to represent each end of the transfer.

The IsTransferAscii property informs the FTP client whether the file being transferred is binary so that the file can be correctly encoded. This encoding is most important when transferring a binary file because certain byte sequences in the file might be interpreted to have unintended ASCII meanings (such as "end of file").

FTP Connection

The primary differences between the configuration of the File System Task and the FTP Task is that a server is involved and, thus, you must specify an FTP Connection on the General page. Figure 4-5 shows the FTP Connection configuration.

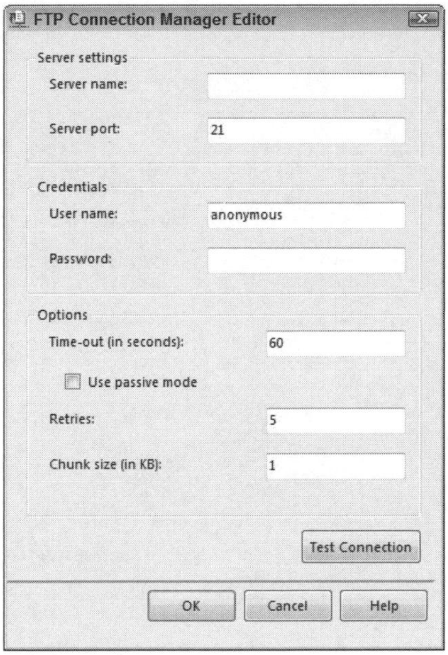

Figure 4-5

The administrator of the FTP server should provide the server settings and credentials if they are not known.

Passive FTP is a method to deal with the common problem where the FTP client is behind a firewall or Network Address Translation (NAT) device. FTP uses two connections:

❑   A control connection for commands

❑   A data connection for the actual file transfer

Active (normal) FTP functions by the server initiating the data connection to a private port on the client. A firewall won't allow this. When in passive mode, the client initiates both connections to the server. For passive mode to work, the server must be configured to support it.

HTTP

The specification for the ubiquitous Hypertext Transfer Protocol (HTTP) has much the same capability as FTP, although it is primarily used only by browsers for retrieving files. Given the vast amount of information available on the Internet, having a way to retrieve this information by HTTP is occasionally necessary. SSIS goes about halfway in helping you do so with the HTTP Connection Manager, as shown in Figure 4-6.

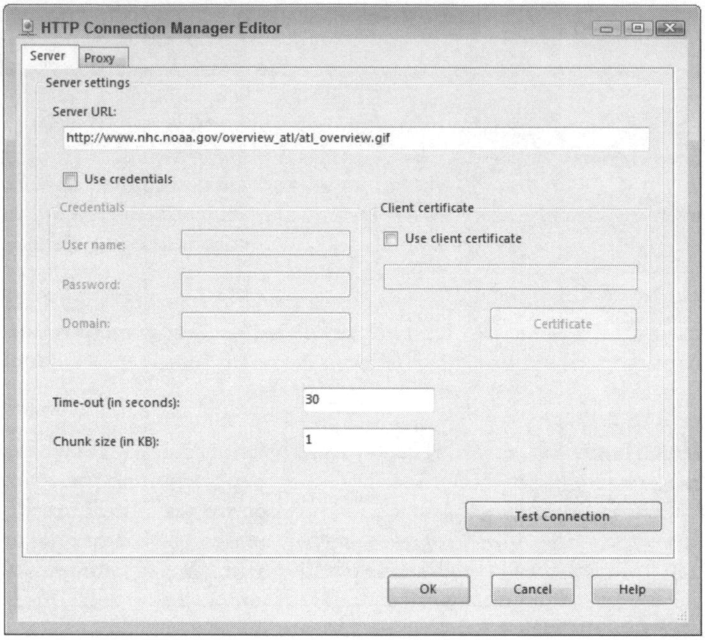

Figure 4-6

You just have to finish it off with a tiny bit of script. The script references the HTTP Connection mentioned previously, calls the `DownloadFile` method, and provides a local filename, as shown here:

```
Dim httpConnection As HttpClientConnection
Dim temp As Object
temp = Dts.Connections("HTTP Connection Manager")
    .AcquireConnection(Nothing)
httpConnection = New HttpClientConnection(temp)
httpConnection.DownloadFile("C:\SSIS_PDS\Atlantic.gif", True)
```

Foreach Loop

If you ever used the predecessor to SSIS, you probably got very excited when you learned that SSIS offered built-in looping capability. Loops add a lot of power to a process workflow. Of interest in this chapter is the Foreach Loop, particularly because it is able to loop over each file in a folder. The Foreach Loop has many enumerators, of which the File enumerator is just one.

Figure 4-7 shows the configuration page of the Foreach Loop with the File enumerator selected. You specify a folder, a file pattern (which can include wildcards), and what part of each filename you want to retrieve. Of course, you can control all of these by expressions.

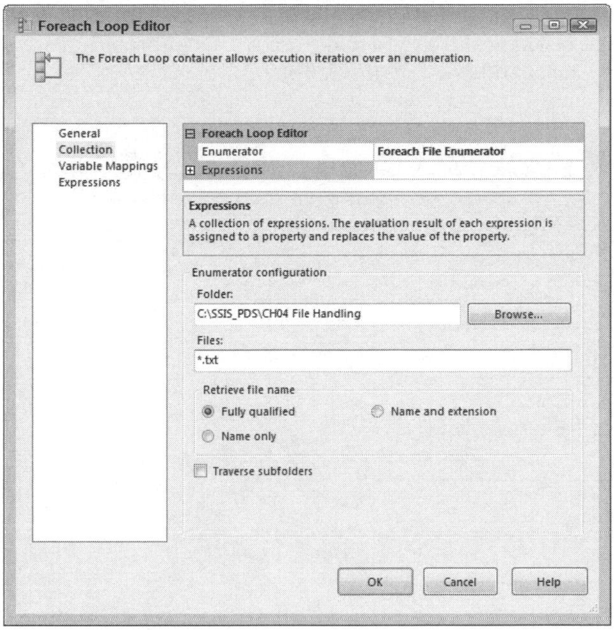

Figure 4-7

The requested portion of each qualifying file is placed in a variable, as shown on the Variable Mappings page displayed in Figure 4-8.

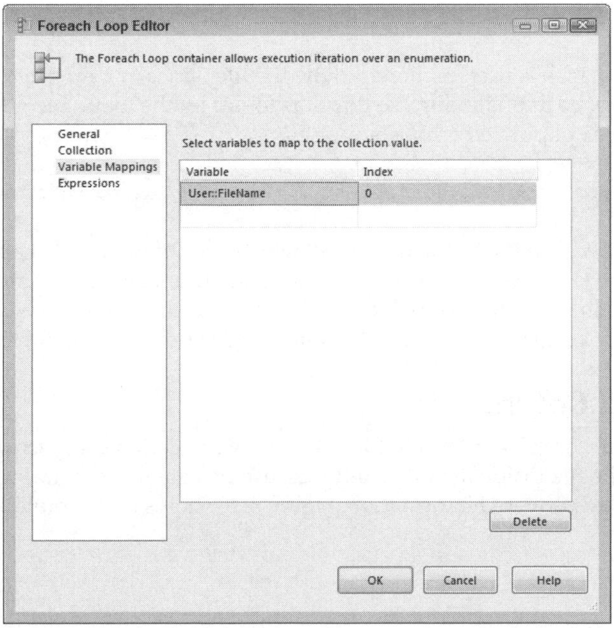

Figure 4-8

The variable containing the filename is then available to any tasks inside a Foreach Loop container, as shown in Figure 4-9. The tasks most likely to make use of this information are the File System Task, the FTP Task, the Data Flow Task, and possibly the Script Task.

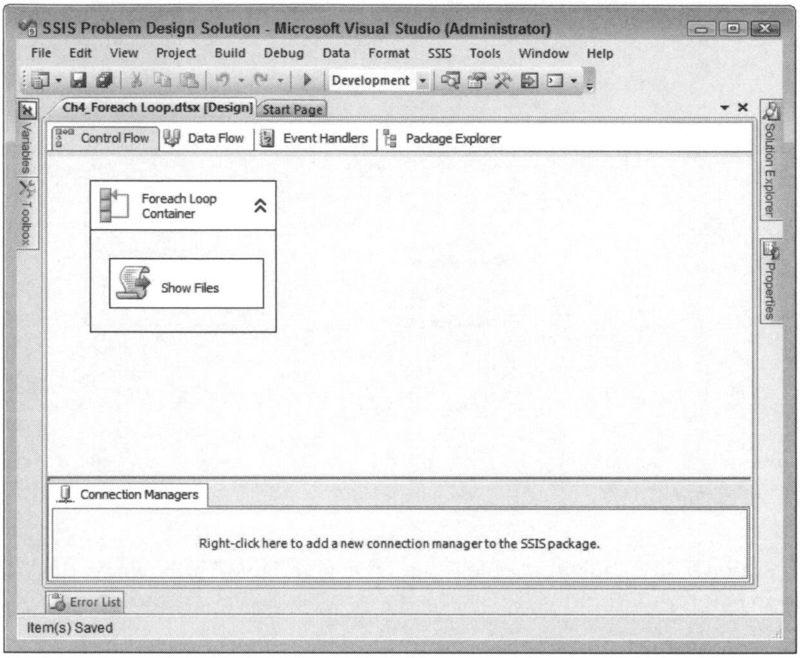

Figure 4-9

In Figure 4-9, the Script Task is used to merely show the filenames in a message box on the screen. The task is executed once for each qualifying file that was found by the loop. Each time the script executes, the `FileName` variable is populated with a new value.

```
MessageBox.Show(Dts.Variables("FileName").Value.ToString)
```

As mentioned earlier, because the Foreach Loop allows the use of wildcards to select multiple files, but the File System Task does not, you can use the two together to achieve File System Task functionality for multiple files. The variable that the Foreach Loop populates with a filename would be used either directly, or through an expression to specify the source and/or destination for the File System Task.

Applying Advanced Criteria

If you must apply more complex criteria to file selection, you need to use a script. The most obvious way to do so is to inspect the file inside the loop, and then use precedence constraints to manipulate the workflow based on the discovered information. Figure 4-10 shows an example.

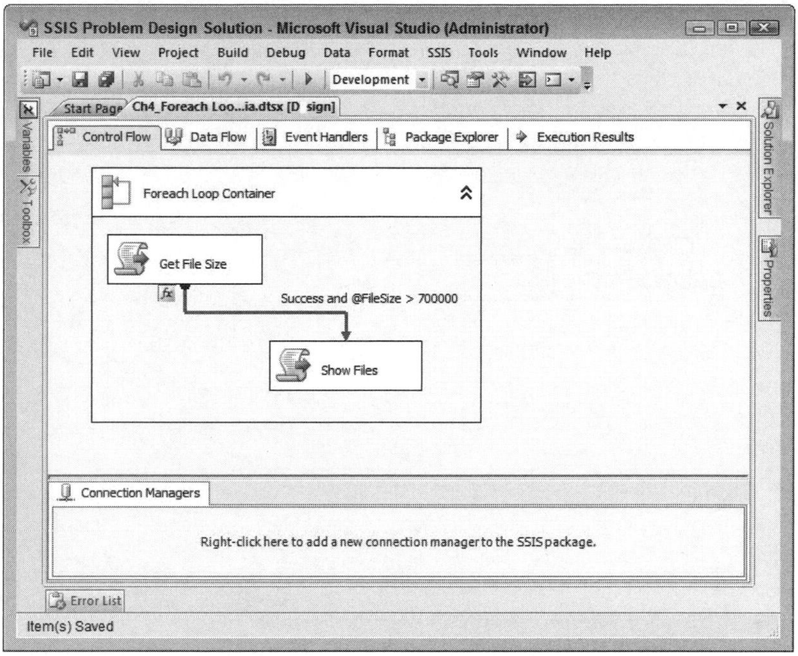

Figure 4-10

The simple script used to get the file size is shown here. The expression used in the precedence constraint is visible in Figure 4-10. When this package runs, only text files larger than 700,000 bytes make it to the Show Files script.

```
Dim info As FileInfo
info = New FileInfo(Dts.Variables("FileName").Value.ToString)
Dts.Variables("FileSize").Value = info.Length
```

Depending on the ratio between the number of files that the loop will qualify and the number that meets your additional criteria, applying the criteria before the loop instead of after it may make more sense. To do so, you would use a script to create a list of files, and then use a different enumerator of the Foreach Loop to iterate through them.

This strategy is the same one you would use if you needed to loop through the files in a sorted order. Experience indicates that the Foreach Loop automatically sorts the files by name in ascending order, but if you need something different, or if it is important, you'll want to do it yourself to make sure.

Figure 4-11 shows a modified control flow that loops through the files in descending order by name.

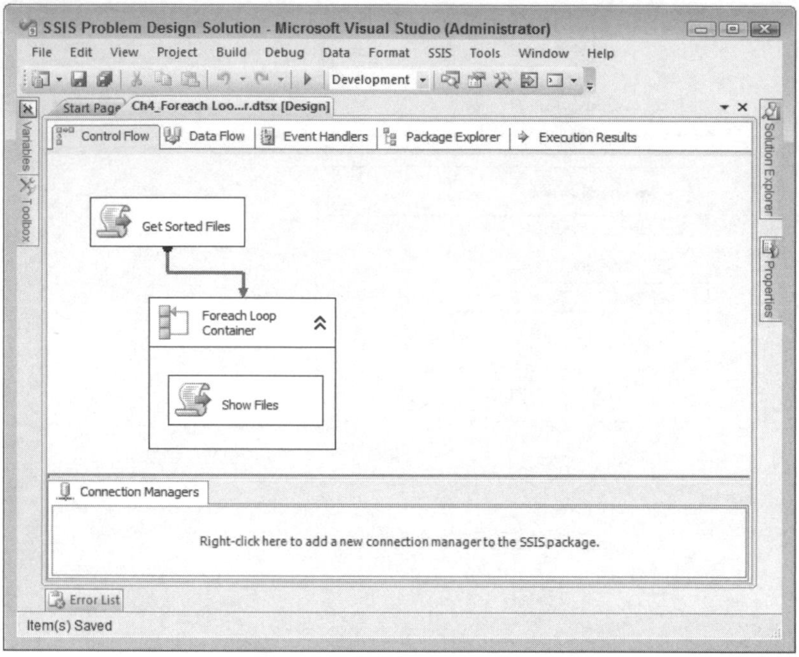

Figure 4-11

The following code shows how the script in Figure 4-11 retrieves the list of files into an array, sorts the array, and then reverses the order. The sorted array is then placed in an SSIS variable. The data type of this variable is Object.

```
Dim Filenames As String() = IO.Directory.GetFiles( _
    "C:\SSIS_PDS\CH04 File Handling", _
    "*.txt")
Array.Sort(Filenames)
Array.Reverse(Filenames)

Dts.Variables("FileNames").Value = Filenames
```

The Foreach Loop then needs just a slight change to make it iterate through the items in the sorted array, instead of files in a folder. Figure 4-12 shows the new enumerator configuration.

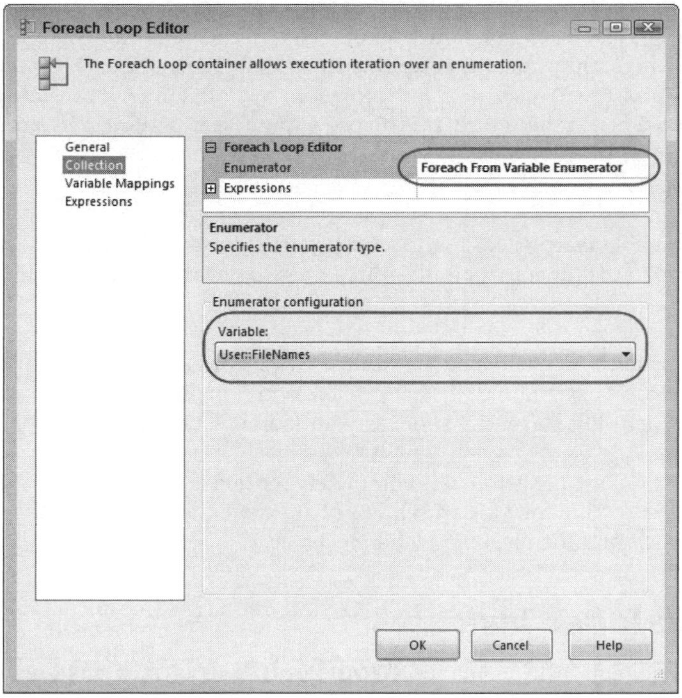

Figure 4-12

File Watcher Task

The most common use case for an SSIS package that handles files is for it to be run manually or executed on a schedule. The package then operates on whatever files exist when it executes. There are very valid cases, however, for a package that executes before the file exists, and then waits for the file before continuing. These cases include the following:

❑ *Fast response* — This is a case when the package must process the file immediately after it is dropped.

❑ *Coordination* — This is a case when the package is using the existence of files to communicate with another process.

❑ *Large files* — This is a case when a large file is being written to by another process, and there may be a period of time when the file appears to exist, but is not complete.

In all the cases, having the package running, but asleep, until a complete file appears is advantageous.

The SQL Server community has produced an excellent solution to this need in the form of the File Watcher Task by SQLIS.com.

For something as static as a book to make a reference to something as dynamic as the Internet is always risky. As of this writing, the File Watcher Task is located at www .sqlis.com/post/file-watcher-task.aspx, but, of course, it can't be guaranteed that it will be there in the future. It is a very popular component, and shouldn't be difficult to find.

You can configure the File Watcher Task with a folder, file pattern (wildcards accepted), and a timeout. The task will wait up to the timeout for a file with a name matching the pattern to be created or modified.

Of course, you can usually get a job done in multiple ways. For example, you could use a For Loop to repeatedly check for the existence of a file, or another condition. Just ensure that you also have a Script Task inside the loop that calls Thread.Sleep, or your loop will hog the processor.

Preventing the detection of a file before it is completely written is often done by using a different name. If your SSIS process is looking for a file with a .txt extension, then the file can be created with another extension such as .tmp, and then renamed when it is ready.

WMI Event Watcher Task

The Windows Management Instrumentation (WMI) Event Watcher Task provided with SSIS is designed to wait for WMI event notifications from the operating system. Among the many events provided by WMI is file creation. The File Watcher Task discussed previously likely implements WMI internally to receive file event notifications. So, why is the WMI Event Watcher at the bottom of this discussion instead of the top? Frankly, the Internet forums are full of posts by people who can't get the WMI Event Watcher to work the way they want it to. That is not to say that it doesn't work, just that it isn't easy.

If you need your SSIS package to wait until processor utilization is below a certain threshold, the WMI Event Watcher Task is probably the best way to get that done. But if you're waiting for files to appear, you're probably better off with the File Watcher Task.

Solution

Data files that SSIS must import are often generated as scheduled exports from legacy systems. The possibility exists for the job exporting the data to get out of synchronization with the SSIS process that consumes them. Sometimes, mainframe jobs get run at odd times because of end-of-month processing. Sometimes, the SSIS process experiences an error and isn't fixed before the next export.

To guard against this synchronization problem, the exported filenames should have timestamps in their names to prevent them from being overwritten before they are imported. The SSIS process should also be designed so that, if multiple exports exist, they are read in the correct order, and do not duplicate data.

Of course, many ways exist for importing multiple files. The example in this section demonstrates one way by creating a file preprocessor. It reads all the available input files and merges them into a single output file that contains only the most recent data.

The sample data for this example is three files representing daily exports of a table. The example uses a technique discussed earlier in this chapter to sort the input files in descending order by date. Then, the rows of each input file will be sorted by the primary key and compared against the output file. Only rows from each input file with previously unseen primary keys will be added to the output file. The result is a single output file that only contains the most recent version of each row. Figure 4-13 shows the package control flow.

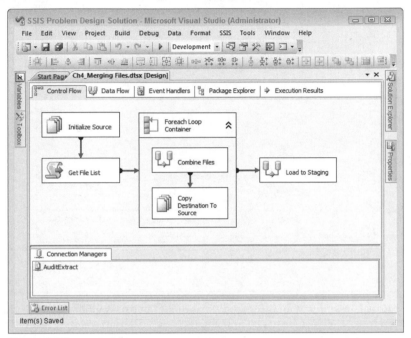

Figure 4-13

The example uses Raw files to maintain the set of rows for the output file between iterations of the input files. *Raw files* are binary files that SSIS can use to save rows from a data flow to the disk, and then read them back at another point.

Because the output file will need to be continually read to compare it to each input file, two copies are used. One is the destination file that is written onto each input file iteration. The other is a copy of the destination file from the previous iteration, which is read back for comparison to the next file. In this way, the output file is continually read and written to as the input files are processed.

As shown in Figure 4-13, the Raw file copy from destination to source occurs after the Combine Files data flow. The source copy, therefore, must be initialized before the first input file is processed. You do so with a simple copy operation of the File System Task configured as shown in Figure 4-14. A blank or "dummy" Raw file is copied over the source Raw file.

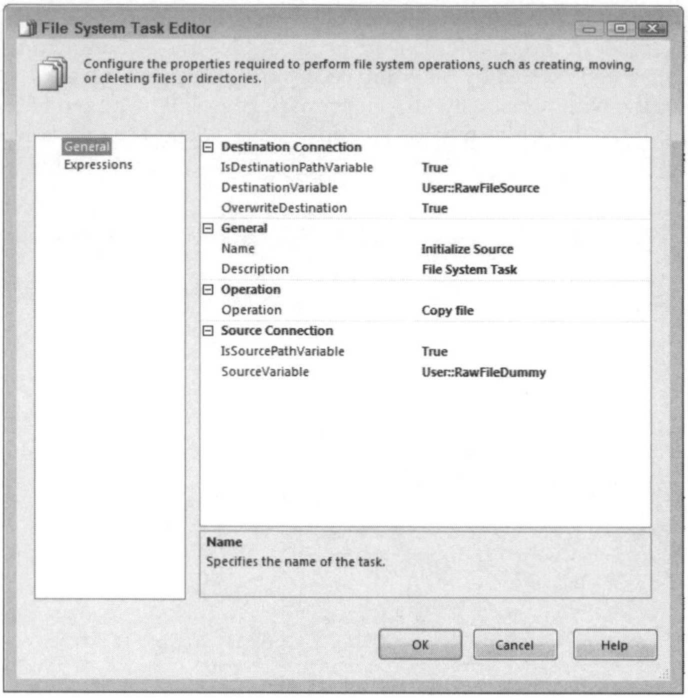

Figure 4-14

> Because Raw files contain an internal definition of the row metadata even if they contain no rows, they can be tricky to manage. In some situations they can become corrupt if an SSIS process dies while writing to one. Having a "dummy" on hand for quick replacement is usually a good idea. You can create a dummy Raw file with a regular data flow containing a conditional split that eliminates all the rows to create an empty Raw file.

Following output file initialization, the Get File List script task creates an array of input filenames sorted in descending order. The files were generated with the export date in the filename, so sorting them by name effectively sorts them by date as well. The script for sorting the filenames was shown earlier in this chapter in the "Design" section, so only the input and output parameters are shown in Figure 4-15.

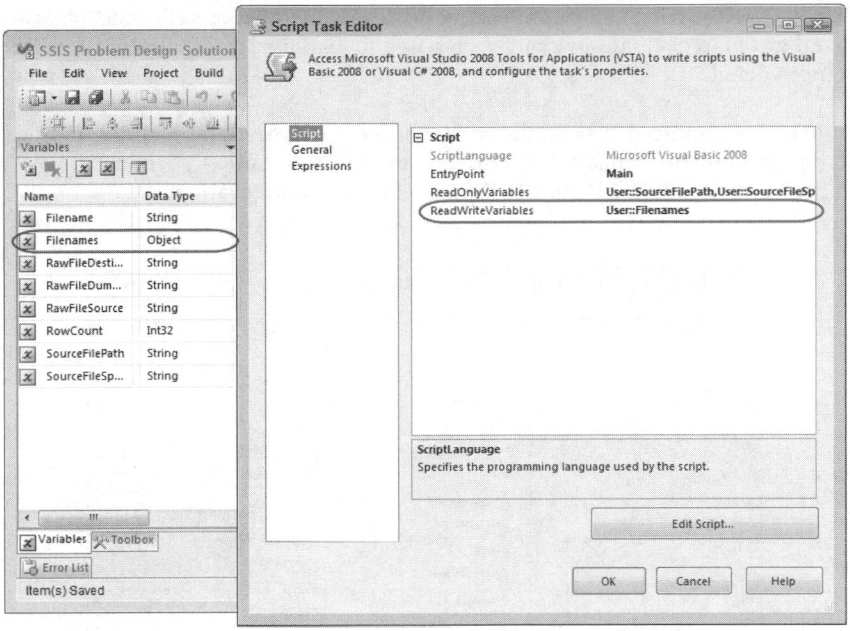

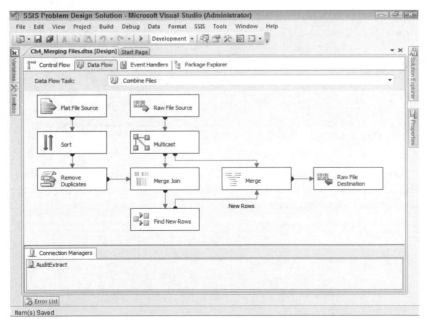

Figure 4-15

The example now loops through each input file in the array. Figure 4-12 shows an example configuration of a Foreach Loop iterating through an array variable. Figure 4-16 shows the Combine Files data flow.

Figure 4-16

The Flat File Source is the current input file being processed by the loop. The Audit Extract connection manager is configured to evaluate an expression based to load the loop's current file. Chapter 5 discusses this topic in more detail.

If the input file isn't guaranteed to be in the correct order, it will need to be sorted. In this example, the rows should be sorted by the primary key, and then by row timestamp in descending order, because you want to find the newest row first. Figure 4-17 shows the sort configuration.

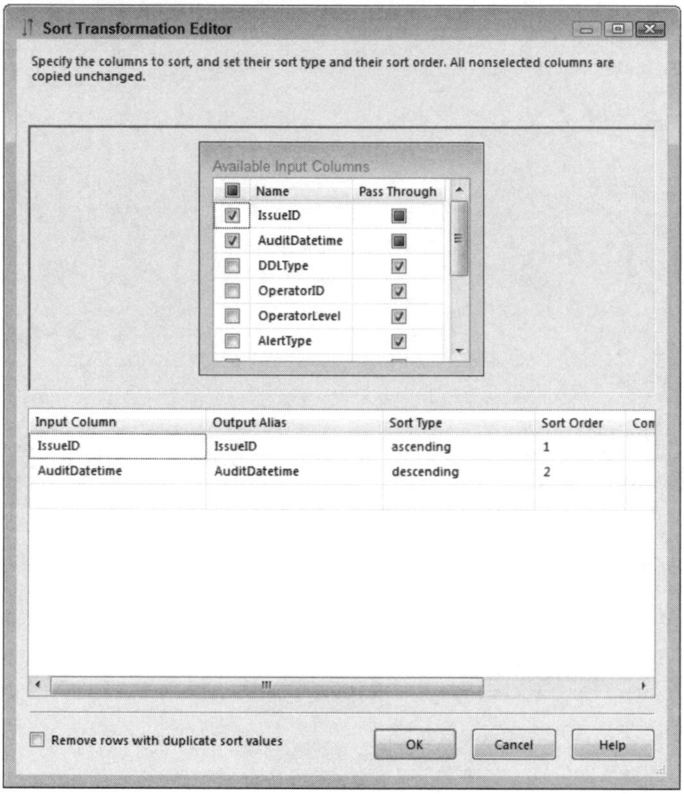

Figure 4-17

Because only the newest row for each primary key is needed, you next use a script as an exclusion filter to pass only the first occurrence of each primary key. You do so by simply setting the ExclusionGroup property on the script's output to 1, as shown in Figure 4-18.

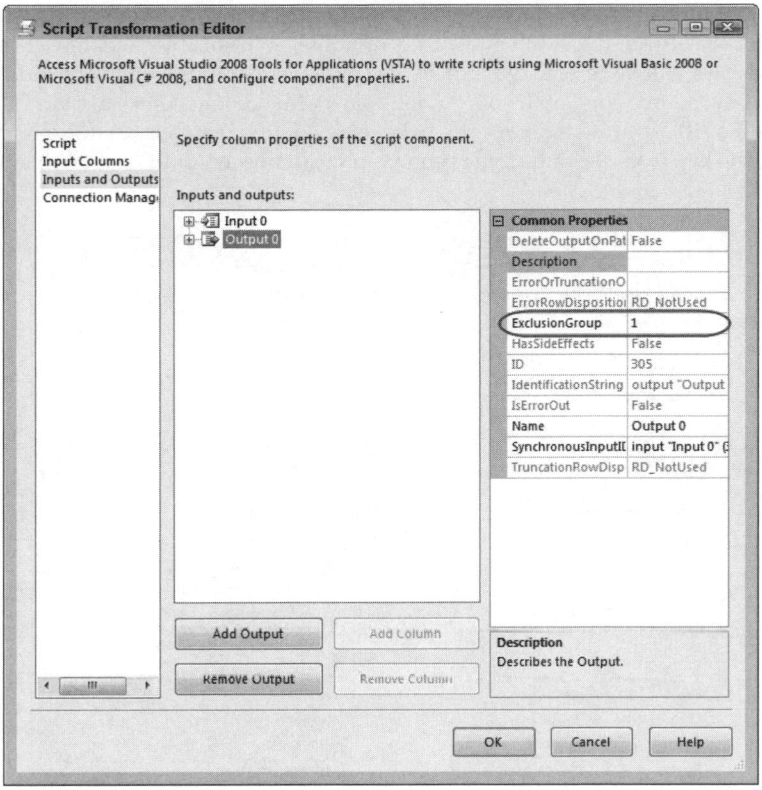

Figure 4-18

With the ExclusionGroup set, the script can simply compare the current primary key column to a saved copy of the last one. Rows will only be sent to the output if the keys are different. Following is the script:

```
Dim LastIssueID As Integer = 0

Public Overrides Sub Input0_ProcessInputRow(ByVal Row As Input0Buffer)

    If Row.IssueID <> LastIssueID Then
        If LastIssueID <> 0 Then
            Row.DirectRowToOutput0()
        End If
        LastIssueID = Row.IssueID
    End If

End Sub
```

Now, the latest row for each key of the input file is ready to be compared to the rows that have already been qualified for the output file. If this is the first input file, no prior rows will have been qualified and, therefore, all file rows will be recognized as new. The package makes the determination by comparing the input file against the source copy of the output file using a Merge Join component in "left outer" mode. The input file is the left input, so those rows will be retained if no match is found from the output file. If a match is found, the key from the output file is brought into a new column, as shown in Figure 4-19.

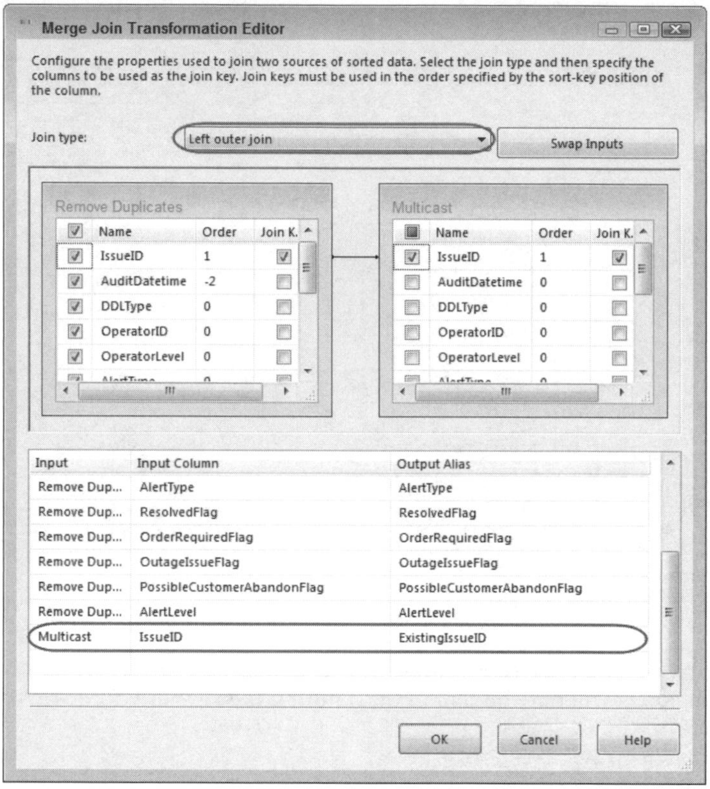

Figure 4-19

Note that the Merge Join and Merge components are both used in this data flow on the rows from the Raw File Source. Both of these components require their inputs to be sorted. The input file was sorted by the Sort component and, therefore, all output file is sorted, too, but a Raw file doesn't record this information. Instead, the IsSorted indicator was set manually via the advanced editor for the Raw File Source.

In the next step after the join, any rows where the new column has a value are dropped using a Conditional Split component. In this way, only the rows from the input file that have a key that doesn't already exist in the output are carried forward. Figure 4-20 shows the configuration of the Conditional Split.

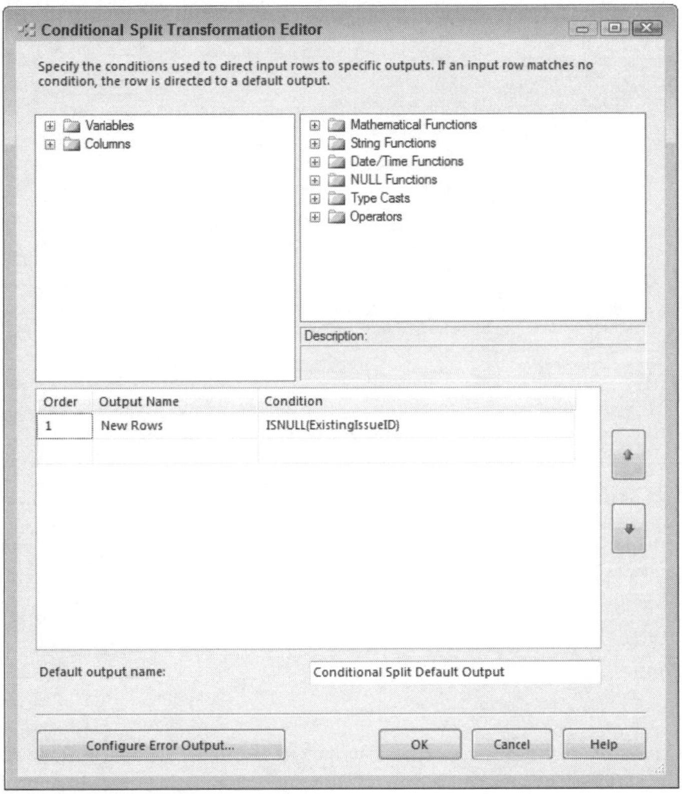

Figure 4-20

Finally, the new rows from the input file are merged with the existing output rows from the source Raw file and written to the destination Raw file.

Back in the control flow, a File System Task is used to copy the destination Raw file over the source Raw file, as shown in Figure 4-21. The loop executes as many more times as necessary to process all the input files.

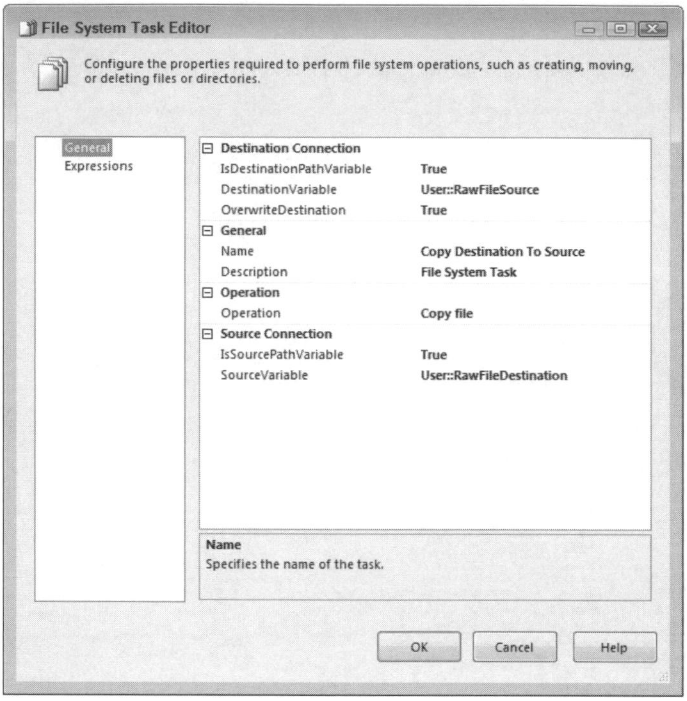

Figure 4-21

After the loop is finished executing, the output rows exist in the destination Raw file. From here, they can be moved wherever necessary, perhaps into a staging database, or possibly back into a text file with the same format.

After the input files have been merged, archiving them is a good idea in case they're needed later. Chapter 11 provides an example for archiving files.

Summary

This chapter covered many SSIS features used to facilitate a variety of file-related operations. These capabilities make SSIS very useful for general management and administration activities. Of course, these types of tasks also go hand-in-hand with more traditional data-loading activities.

Chapter 5 begins a series of chapters related to extraction, transformation, and loading (ETL) of data. Chapter 5 starts off the series by focusing on extracting data from source systems or files.

Data Extraction Best Practices

A natural first discussion point for ETL is the extraction, the *E* in ETL. This chapter applies the concepts of data extraction using SSIS. ETL applies to a broad spectrum of applications beyond just data warehousing and data integration. Therefore, the discussion of this topic includes both generalized extraction concepts and data warehouse–specific concepts.

Data extraction is the process of moving data off of a source system, potentially to a staging environment, or into the transformation phase of the ETL. Figure 5-1 shows the extraction process separated out on the left. An extraction process may pull data from a variety of sources, including files or database systems, as this figure highlights.

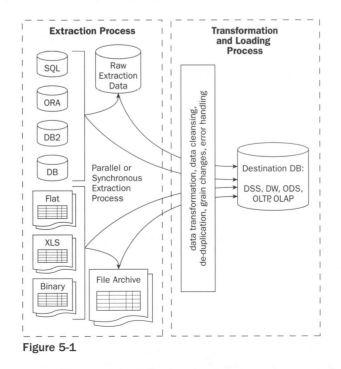

Figure 5-1

Following are a few common objectives of data extraction:

❑ Consistency in how data is extracted across source systems

❑ Performance of the extraction

❑ Minimal impact on the source to avoid contention with critical source processes

❑ Flexibility to handle source system changes

❑ The capability to target only new or changed records

This chapter is structured into three sections related to the Problem-Design-Solution of ETL extraction processes using SSIS:

❑ The "Problem" section elaborates on some of the ETL extraction objectives listed earlier. This section is general to ETL, and is not directly related to SSIS implementation details.

❑ The "Design" section picks up where the "Problem" section leaves off, and deals with how to apply the general ETL principles using SSIS.

❑ The "Solution" section provides an example of extracting data from multiple sources by a single package using metadata. This is a very effective strategy to limit the number of packages required for the extraction phase of an ETL process.

Problem

Extraction of source data is arguably the most important part of an ETL process, because everything afterward depends on its success. It is also of great interest to almost everyone with any involvement with the project:

❑ *End users* want to know where the data they're looking at came from, and that it is current and accurate.

❑ *Developers and administrators* frequently must trace data through the extraction process to the source systems in order to diagnose problems.

❑ *Source system owners* are usually concerned about loads being placed on their systems by the extraction process.

A good extraction process will seldom make you a hero, but a bad one can certainly hurt your chances for "Person of the Year."

Extraction Data Criteria

Deciding what data to extract from the source system is not always easy. Whether the destination is a data warehouse or integration with some other system, extracting all the data available from the source will rarely be necessary. You want to be sure to extract the minimal data elements needed in order to satisfy your requirements, but you should keep in mind some other considerations:

❑ *Context* — The data you extract will likely be kept in your staging database for validation and user drill-through reporting purposes. There likely is some extra information from the source system that isn't strictly required, but could improve the meaningfulness of the extracted data.

❑ *Future Use* — If destination requirements change in the future, you'll look very smart if you have already been extracting the needed data and have it in your staging database. Predicting what extra data might be needed someday can be tricky, but if you can make reasonable guesses and have the space to spare in your staging database, it could pay off big later.

Source System Impact

A good ETL process will be kind to its source systems. For these sources to be heavily loaded transactional systems, and maybe a legacy mainframe system to boot, is not uncommon. The added impact of a selfish ETL process could potentially bring a delicate source to its knees, along with all of its users.

Here are some general principles for creating an extraction process with minimal impact on the source system:

❑ *Bring the data over from the source with minimal transformations* — Don't use expressions or functions that execute on the source system. The less the source system has to think about your query, the better. The exception is if the source data uses a data type that your extraction process doesn't understand. In this case, you may need to cast the data to another type.

❑ *Only extract the columns that you'll use* — Don't ask the source system for 50 columns and then only use 10. Asking for some extra data as discussed previously is okay because you'll be doing something with it, but retrieving columns that have no purpose whatsoever is not good.

❑ *Keep selection criteria simple* — You may need to find a balance between the cost of transferring extra rows, and the cost of filtering them out in the extraction query. Functions or expressions that must think about every single row in the source table would not be good. There may be a significant difference between `OrderDate+5 > Today()` versus `OrderDate > Today()-5`.

❑ *Don't use joins* — This may fall under selection criteria, but it warrants its own bullet. Unless the join is beneficial to reducing the overall extraction cost, it should probably be avoided. Instead of joining from Orders to Products to get the product name, it is better to extract Orders and Products separately.

Some of these principles are subjective in nature, and may have different implications for different source systems. Performance tuning is sometimes as much art as a science, and a little trial and error may be in order. Your mileage may vary.

Incremental Extraction

One of the best ways to be nice to the source system (and it's good for your process, too) is to only extract changed data. This way, you aren't wasting I/O bandwidth and processor cycles on data that hasn't changed since the last time you extracted it. This method is called *incremental extraction*, because you are getting the data from the source in cumulative pieces.

Here are a few of the many ways that you may be able to identify changed source records:

❑ *Use a modified date or created date column from a database source* — These are called *change identifier* columns. In fact, many transactional systems already have change identifier columns that can be used for an incremental extraction. This is probably the most common approach to incremental extraction. Note that a creation date is only valuable if the rows are never updated.

❑ *Use an auto-incrementing change identifier* — If the source system doesn't have a modified date or created date, there may be an auto-incrementing column acting as a change identifier, which increases every time a row change happens. To be useful the incrementing value must be scoped to the table, not the row (that is, no duplicates).

❑ *Use an audit table* — Some source systems already have or allow a trigger (or similar mechanism) to capture the changes to an audit table. An audit table may track keys for that source table, or the details of the change. However, this approach involves overhead, because triggers are expensive.

❑ *Log-based auditing* — Some database servers provide a log reader-based mechanism to automatically track changes in a similar way to the trigger-based mechanism, but with a much lower overhead. These log-based systems are often called *Change Data Capture (CDC) features*, and in order to take advantage of them, you need a source system that supports these features.

Deleted Rows

If the source system allows rows to be deleted, and if that information will be important to the destination (sometimes it isn't), then the fact that a row was deleted must be represented somehow in order for incremental extraction to work. Doing so can be difficult using the change identifier extraction method because, if the row is deleted, the change identifier will be, too. Following are a couple of scenarios where deleted rows work with incremental extraction:

❑ When a "delete" is really just an update to a flag that hides the record from an application

❑ When an audit mechanism records that the row was deleted

Sometimes, more creative solutions can be found. But, if the source system doesn't provide a facility to identify the changed and deleted rows, then all rows must be extracted. The change detection then takes place farther along in the ETL process through comparison with existing data.

> **Understanding the nature of the source data if your extraction process will depend on if it is critical. If you design a process that assumes a modification date will be maintained, or rows will only ever be inserted and never updated or deleted, you had best be sure those requirements are cast in stone. If a bulk load, or a maintenance operation, or even Joe Programmer sometimes bends these rules, your data warehouse will eventually become inaccurate, and inaccuracy is death to data warehouses.**

Staging Database

After you have extracted the source data from the source system, you need a place to put it. Depending on your requirements, you might be able to go directly to the target database, but a staging database is highly recommended. Traditionally, a staging database is one where you perform data cleansing. With today's tools that are capable of performing many data cleansing tasks while the data is "in flight," staging databases are less of a requirement, but can still be beneficial.

The benefits of a staging database may include the following:

❑ *Data lineage* — As discussed in the next section, the primary value of a staging database is as a place where the data lineage can be tracked. Data lineage is very helpful for data validation.

❑ *Restartability* — By saving the extracted data to a staging database as an intermediate step before performing any loading, the data is safe in case of a load failure, and won't need to be re-extracted.

❑ *Source alternative* — A staging database could be handy as an alternative to the source system if that system has limitations.

❑ *Archive* — If you choose to do so, the staging database can be designed to function as an archive to track history on the source system. This could allow a full reload of the data warehouse, including history, if it should ever become corrupted.

❑ *Performance* — Some types of cleansing and transformation operations are best performed by the database engine, rather than the ETL tool. For example, a database engine can usually sort and perform aggregation functions faster and with less memory.

Of course, some downsides exist to using a staging database that may negate some of the benefits just described. Using an intermediary database necessarily involves disks, which may increase storage requirements and decrease performance. Initial development costs may well be higher, but a well-designed staging database will probably pay for itself in the long run.

Data Lineage and Metadata

Data lineage is a part of the metadata tracking in an ETL process associated with mapping data back to the source data points. But, before considering an approach to data lineage tracking, it is important to understand metadata in general.

Metadata is the data about the data. For ETL, it's the integrated tracking mechanism for the process and the core data. Metadata is very important for ETL and data warehousing — not just for administrators to understand what data got loaded, but also for system developers to validate data sources, for data administrators to find out what happened when failures occur, and for users to be confident in the data they are looking at. In fact, the latter may be the most important, because if the users do not trust the data, then their adoption of the solution will be slow going. Tracking data lineage is directly related to knowing where each data point came from, not just what system or table or file, but knowing which source row(s) they came from.

File Sources

It is very common for the source data of an ETL process to be at least partially made up of files.

Text file exports are often the easiest way to deal with mainframe source data. That way, a mainframe programmer has the responsibility of writing the extract, and the ETL developer doesn't have to worry about finicky or esoteric database connectivity. Mainframe programmers also often have access to methods to create incremental extracts that wouldn't otherwise be available.

Chapter 4 discusses several file-handling methods and scenarios that directly apply to extracting data from file sources:

❑ *File transfer* — Often, files are "pushed" from the source system. Sometimes, however, the ETL must use FTP or some other type of file-transfer method in order to retrieve them from a remote server.

❑ *File coordination* — Coordination is usually needed between the various processes, because a transfer could be attempted before the file is finished being written, or read before it is finished being transferred.

❑ *File archive* — There are also file archival considerations. What if you need to reload the warehouse and need a history of old files? Depending on the nature of the file, you may be able to just use the latest one. But, if not, you may find yourself in a pickle, because you aren't in control of the export. Maybe keeping those files in an archive would be a good idea.

Design

This section examines how to apply the general ETL principles you have learned about by using SSIS.

Package Connections and Source Adapters

The data flow sources in SSIS provide the capability to connect to most standard data repositories for which you have an OLE DB provider or Open Database Connectivity (ODBC) driver. SSIS also provides specialized sources for file types, including text, Excel, and XML formats.

Most database products will have either an OLE DB provider or ODBC driver available that SSIS can use. Many of the common database products are covered through the installation of the Windows operating system or SQL Server, but others may only be available from the database vendors or third parties.

Package Connections

Data flow components use separate objects at the package level to define the connection and facilitate connectivity to file, flat file, and OLE DB sources. All data flow sources (except the Raw adapter) leverage these package connections to extract data. As a review, the Connection Manager window appears at the bottom of the control flow and data flow, and right-clicking in the window allows a new connection to be created, as shown in Figure 5-2.

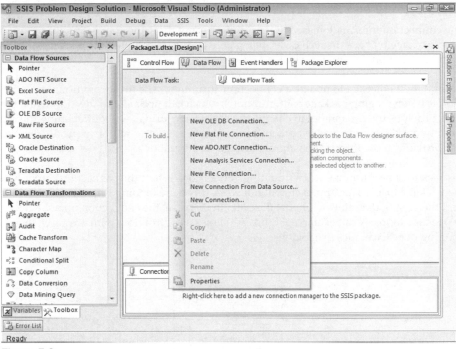

Figure 5-2

Creating a connection is the first step in extracting data, and the second step is typically to create a new Data Flow Task (in the same package) that will contain the source adapter (which references the connection). The next section examines some of the different package adapters, but also be aware that when you create a new source adapter in the data flow, new connections can typically be created automatically right inside the specific adapter's editor.

A data source created within an SSIS project (and viewable in the Solution Explorer window in BIDS) can be linked to and shared among packages. When using a Data Source in this manner, be aware that these shared Data Source connections are only updated in the designer, meaning that when you modify the project Data Source, you must open up all the packages that share that Data Source. Then the linked connection can be updated with the new connection string. When you deploy packages from your development environment and run the package outside BIDS, the connection will no longer be shared among other packages, or updated by the Data Source. Instead, you should use a package configuration to update connections and to share connection strings.

Updating Connections with Property Expressions

Often, the connection information used at design time is not the same connection information that a production package will use. In such cases, being able to dynamically tell the package at runtime what connection information it should use instead is useful.

Three general methods exist to update a connection at runtime. The most common way to update a connection is by leveraging package configurations, which can update a connection when the package loads. This provides the capabilities to change the connection strings without opening the package, such as for moving packages from a development server to a test server, and onto a production server. Chapter 2 provides more information about package configurations.

The drawback to configurations when updating connections is that the connection can only be updated when the package loads. This approach will not work if you are looping through identical files in a folder and then using data flow to import the data. In this case, the connection must be updated every time the package loops. As an example, Figure 5-3 shows a control flow with a Foreach loop container that is looping over Excel files in a folder.

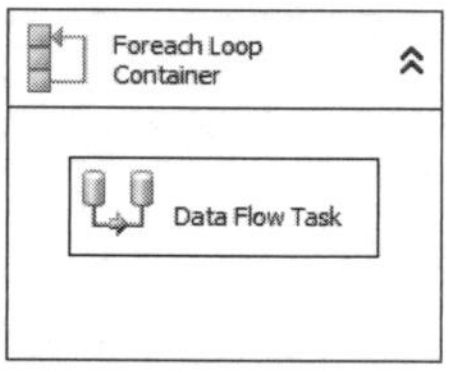

Figure 5-3

The Excel connection must be updated for every file. So, for this situation, a configuration will not work, because connections are only applied when the package loads. Instead, a property expression is utilized. The Foreach loop is updating a package variable called `FileName` every time the container loops, which can easily be used to update the connection. Property Expressions can be found in the sliding property grid window under the property called `Expressions`. Figure 5-4 shows the `Expressions` property selected on the Excel Connection Manager connection.

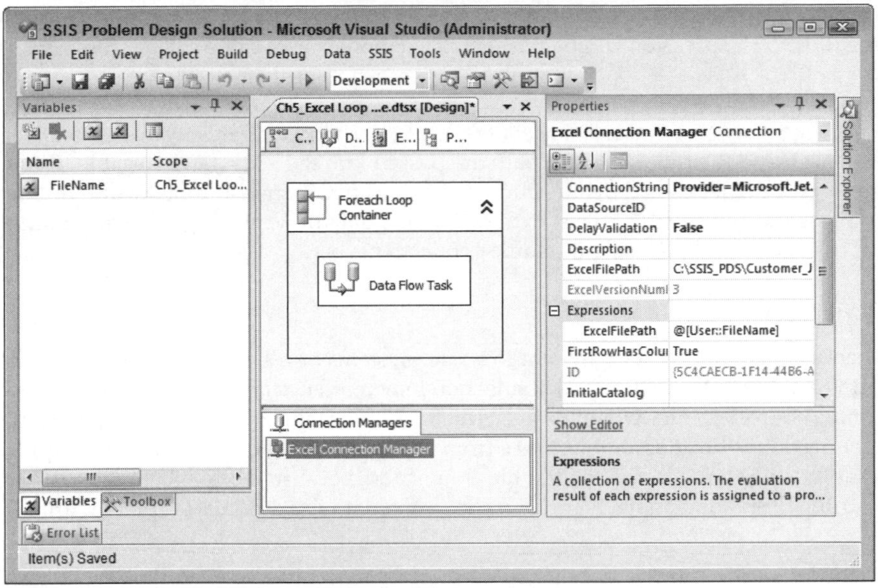

Figure 5-4

To open the Property Expressions Editor, click the plus symbol to the left of the Expressions property name, and then click the ellipses on the right side of the property when it appears. A window opens, allowing several properties of the connection to be updated by an expression. For the purpose of this example, the ExcelFilePath property is selected from the drop-down list, and the expression @[User::FileName] is selected, as Figure 5-5 shows.

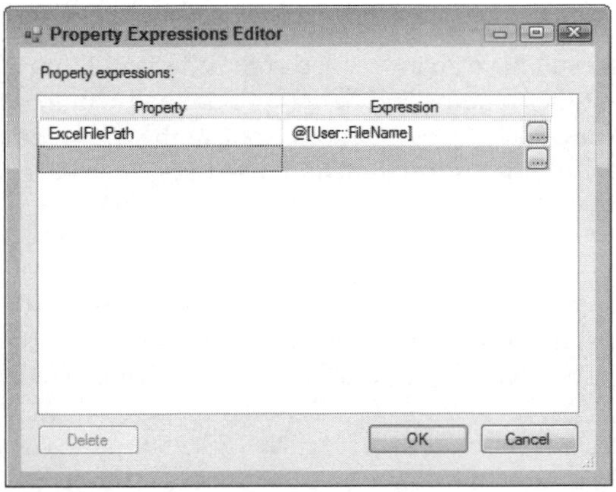

Figure 5-5

In this case, the expression itself is only referencing a package variable. But property expressions can leverage the full SSIS Expression language. To create a more complicated expression, click the ellipse next to @[User::FileName] to open the full SSIS Expression Builder window.

When the package shown in Figure 5-4 executes, the Foreach loop iterates through every file in the designated folder, and the full name and path are passed into the FileName variable. When the data flow runs and the adapter calls the connection, the connection is then automatically updated by the property expression, and the right file is extracted in the data flow, making the extraction flexible to handle multiple sources while using the same connection.

Source Adapters

Although connections in the package point to source systems or files, the adapters are the objects that define what is extracted. For example, a connection may reference an Oracle database or SQL Server database, and a source adapter would define which specific table (or view or query) to extract data from. For Excel connections, the adapter references from which worksheet and data range to pull, and for flat files, the adapter simply references the flat file connection, because the connection already defines the columns and file format metadata. Figure 5-6 shows the data flow source adapters within the data flow toolbox.

Figure 5-6

It's only the raw file that doesn't have an associated connection, and that is because the file itself already contains all the details about the columns and data types defined within. *Professional Microsoft SQL Server 2008 Integration Services* (Wiley, 2008) takes a detailed look at the source adapters in Chapter 5. Therefore, this section simply summarizes this information and discusses some best practices around the adapters.

Flat-File Source

Flat files are a very common extraction source. This is because many source systems will push data to flat files (for various reasons) that can then be consumed by another process (such as SSIS) in a loosely coupled manner. The flat-file source adapter is a powerful mechanism to bring data into the data flow.

Flat files come in many different structures and formats. SSIS supports delimited, fixed-width, and ragged-right, where the last column may have an undetermined number of characters. Even delimited flat files may have different column delimiters and different text qualifiers, and these can be set in the advanced properties of the connection.

Two important features of the flat-file source give the adapter extra flexibility and great performance. First of all, the flat-file adapter supports various code page formats. Figure 5-7 shows the General tab of the Flat File Connection Manager Editor, with the "Code page" drop-down selected.

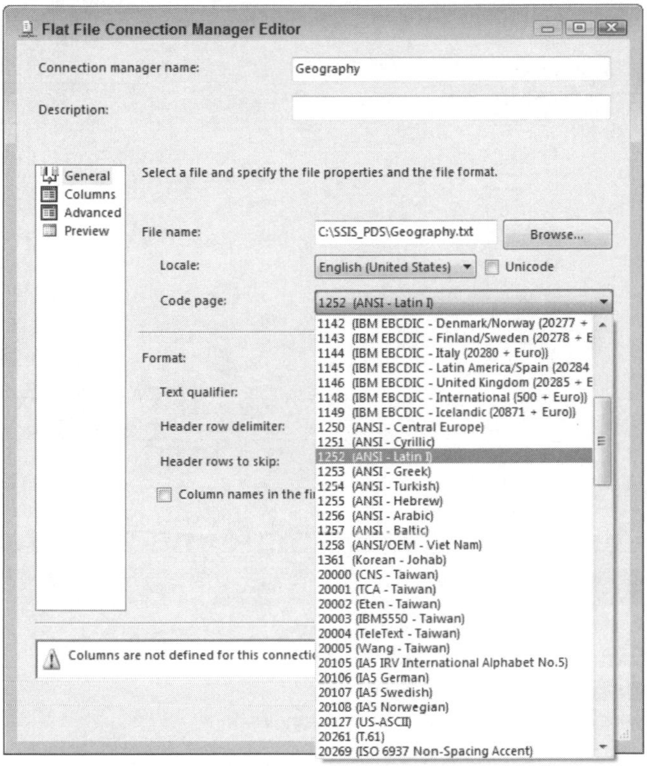

Figure 5-7

The most common code page, of course, is ANSI 1252 – Latin 1. But beyond that, you may have files generated from legacy systems or applications, such as sources with double-byte characters, IBM EBCDIC files, or even other language-specific code pages.

Second, a little-known property of the flat-file adapter is the FastParse property available for date, time, and integer source columns, as Figure 5-8 shows.

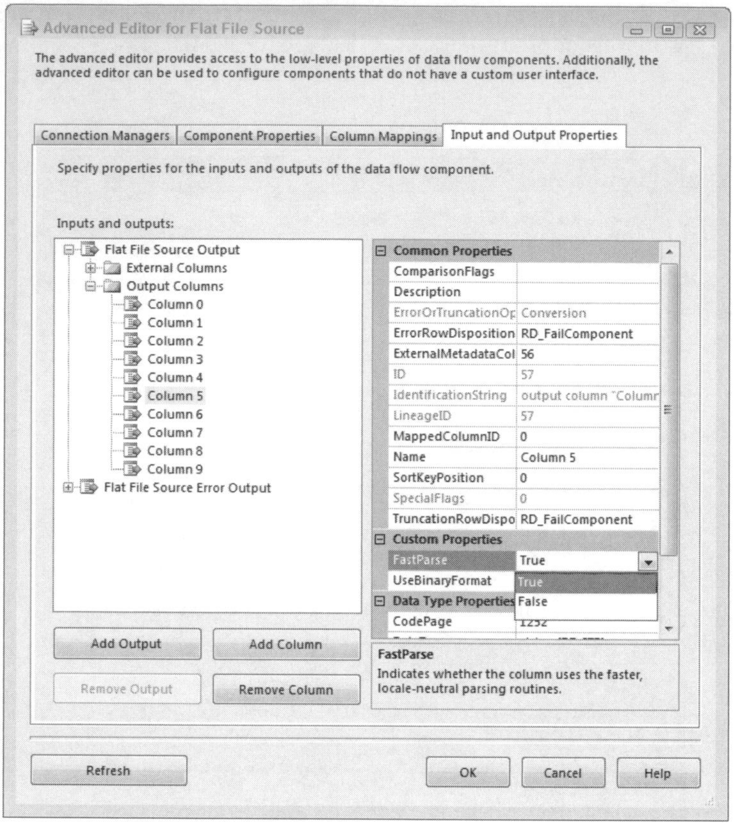

Figure 5-8

The `FastParse` property of output columns (found in the Advanced Editor, "Input and Output Properties" tab) reduces the conversion overhead of each column as it is imported into the data flow buffers, and overall gives generous performance benefits. By using the Fast Parse option, you are giving up the capability to translate the value to the local specific data, and you are forced to have date columns formatted in YYYYMMDD or YYYY-MM-DD format. But, if you are dealing with large flat files, you will want to work through these limitations to take advantage of the setting. In essence, you are telling the connection that the data can be trusted in the source column to be in a standard format.

OLE DB Source

The OLE DB source adapter provides the most flexibility, because it allows several mechanisms to customize the source query, including parameterization and variable bound queries, which are both covered later in this chapter in the section, "Incremental Data Extraction."

When using the OLE DB source adapter to connect to SQL Server, leverage the SQL Native Client (SQLNCI), because it is the best choice for SQL Server sources, offering very fast extraction.

In addition, you can use OS-based Microsoft Data Access Component (MDAC) providers. Download updates for the generic providers at www.microsoft.com/data. These providers have been detached from SQL Server, and are included with the operating system install.

Excel Source

With the release of Service Pack 2 (SP2), there are now two providers to access Excel (or Access). The first version (now legacy) supports Excel 97–2005 and is merely a modified version of the JET provider (the OLE DB provider for connectivity to Access and Excel). New to SP2 is the latest provider for Office 2007 Excel and Access. This provider, called Microsoft ACE OLEDB 12.0, overcomes the 255-character limit when extracting cells.

Both have a limitation in that they are only supported in a 32-bit execution mode (no native 64-bit). This doesn't mean that you cannot extract data from Excel on a 64-bit system; it just means that you must run the package in 32-bit mode, which will be a little more inefficient. (On 64-bit servers, both 64-bit and 32-bit versions of DTExec are installed to handle 64-bit compatibility issues.)

You can create an Excel connection in the data flow simply by using the Excel Source in the Data Flow Source adapter list, as shown earlier in Figure 5-6. The Excel source adapter interface allows a new Excel connection to be generated, which includes the Excel file path property, shown in Figure 5-9.

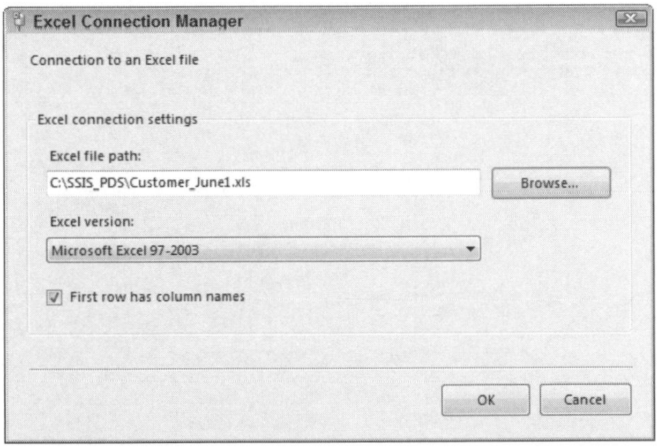

Figure 5-9

The Excel connection references the Excel file, and the data flow adapter for the Excel connection then allows a specific worksheet to be selected.

One thing that may cause you issues when extracting from Excel sources is that all the text columns are pulled back as Unicode (DT_WSTR) data types in SSIS. Even if you try to modify the advanced input and output properties of these columns, the adapter will not accept a change to these types. Therefore, another approach is required to maintain any native string (DT_STR) types.

To change the data type of your columns, you must use the Data Convert transformation, and add new columns for each Unicode column that needs conversion back to native strings. The initial data flow looks like Figure 5-10.

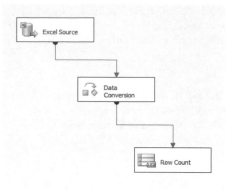

Figure 5-10

When looking at the details of the conversion (see Figure 5-11), notice that the Data Conversion transformation is changing several of the data types from DT_WSTR to DT_STR, because, in many cases, your destinations may be non-Unicode. When converting to non-Unicode, you must specify the code page. Doing so is required to prevent destination errors.

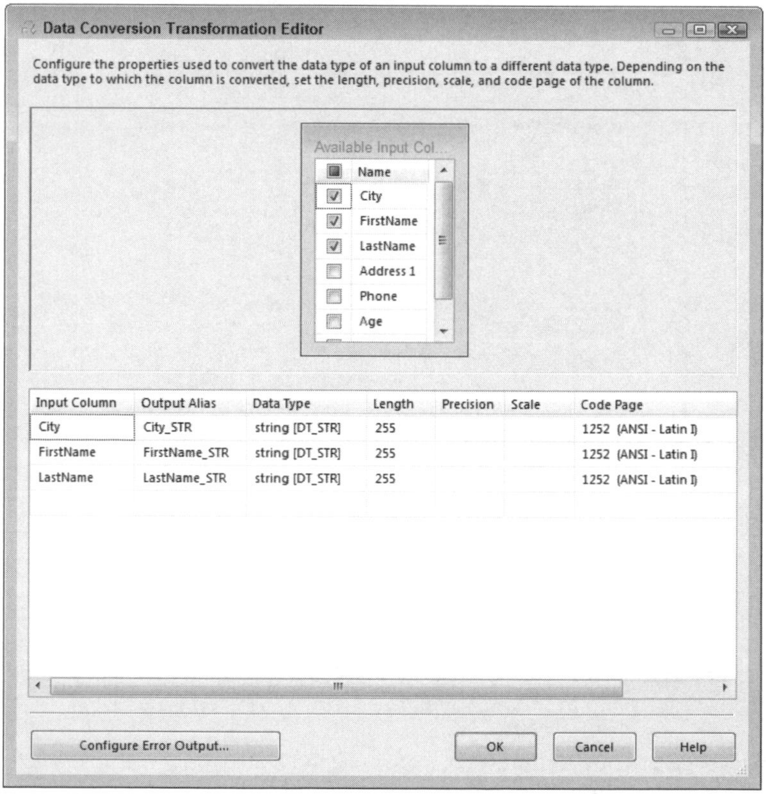

Figure 5-11

Any time you need to change the data type of a pipeline column, SSIS requires a new column to be added to the buffers, because the data type of an existing column cannot be changed in place. Therefore, new columns are added to the pipeline with adjusted data types. The extra columns make the rows wider and the buffers less efficient.

XML Source

Pulling XML data into the data flow may be valuable if you have large XML files that you must import into a database. By nature, XML files have the overhead of tags, which makes their file sizes larger, so XML files are not often used as a bulk data transfer means. Instead, delimited files are more common because they can be created, transferred, and read faster. Smaller data sets or business-to-business (B2B) integration is more commonly XML-based. However, you may have to deal with XML as a source if the data comes from another department, or from a vendor that supplies the data in this way.

The XML Source adapter enables you to import XML data into the data flow. The "Data access mode" property enables you to point to XML data in a few different ways:

❑ *XML file location*, when a hard-coded path to the XML file can be entered

❑ *XML file from variable*, if the path and filename pointing to the XML file is located in a variable

❑ *XML data from variable*, if the XML you are importing is embedded in a text variable

If you have an XML Schema Definition (XSD), then you can enter it right in the "XSD location" property, or you can generate one right from the editor. The XML Source will present multiple outputs, depending on the schema. In some ways, the output acts like a conditional split, where multiple outputs are possible, and you must select the output when connecting it with the next transformation or destination.

One final note is that you should go to the Advanced Editor and modify the input columns to be the right data type and length, because the XML source assigns every output column as a Unicode string (DT_WSTR) of length 255.

Oracle and Teradata

For SSIS 2008 Enterprise and Developer editions, Microsoft has provided specialized adapters for Oracle and Teradata by Attunity. These adapters facilitate high data-loading performance with SSIS 2008 and recent versions of those databases. Both source and destination adapters are provided to allow data movement in either direction. They are available for download from Microsoft's Download Center at www.microsoft.com/downloads, and easily located by a search for "Attunity."

Incremental Data Extraction

Incremental data extraction is the process of targeting modified records and new records, and then tracking the last completed extraction. For example, as you process rows, you might track the last modified datetime value or last identifier for the rows that you've pulled. Then, the next time you extract from the same source system, you start where you left off, rather than extracting the entire source data set.

Incremental Extraction Using a Change Identifier Value

If your source tables contain a change identifier value (such as a last modified `datetime`), or you are able to make small changes to your source tables to allow this, then the process in SSIS will involve three steps:

1. Targeting the changed records by making the source query dynamic. This process involves package variables and two methods in the data flow adapters.

2. Retrieving the incremental extraction values and updating package variables.

3. Capturing the last or maximum value of the change identifier value, so that the value can be tracked and used for the next extraction.

In addition to reviewing some standard approaches to handling this common scenario, this discussion examines an alternative approach if your source system is SQL Server. This approach does involve adding a column to the source tables. However, it doesn't require a table trigger or application logic to update the column value, and, therefore, can add some significant benefits without the overhead common to change identifiers. This approach involves using the SQL Server `rowversion` data type, and is discussed after the three aforementioned steps are examined.

> *The SQL Server* `timestamp` *data type was renamed* `rowversion` *in SQL Server 2008 to clarify its usage and avoid a conflict with a different data type of the same name in the SQL language standard.*

Targeting Change Records through Dynamic Source Queries

The core requirement when attempting to only pull a selected subset of data from a source is the capability to make the query change based on parameters. In the case of an incremental identifier value (such as last modified date), the goal would be to target the source table for the extraction by filtering on the last modified date. Using SSIS, a couple approaches are possible that use properties of the source adapter:

❑   Using an OLE DB source adapter may allow a parameterized query, where the query can reference package variables to filter the query.

❑   The OLE DB adapter also allows the source table name or query to be embedded into a package variable. The adapter can then point to the package variable and use its value as the source text of the query.

OLE DB Parameterized Source Query

The OLE DB source provider can use parameters to modify extraction queries at runtime. Using this functionality involves setting the source adapter "Data access mode" property to "SQL command," and then using the parameterized method of the adapter to define the parts of the statement that should be based on the parameters. Figure 5-12 shows the OLE DB Source Editor with a parameterized query.

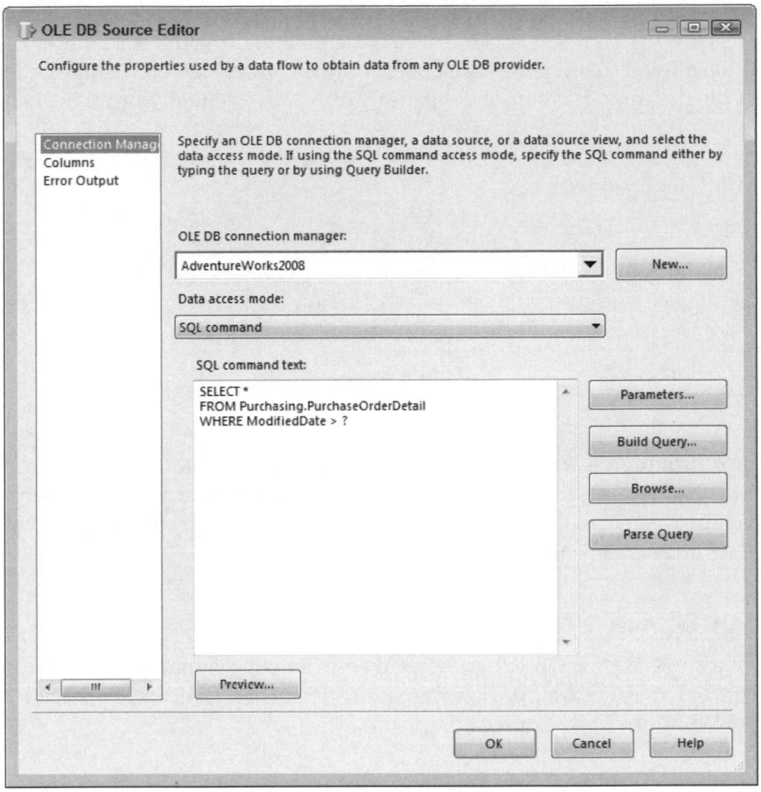

Figure 5-12

The second requirement of the parameterized query is to map the parameters to package variables, which is done using the Parameters button on the same screen. This example simply maps a package variable called `vdtLastModifiedDatetime` to the first parameter, as Figure 5-13 shows.

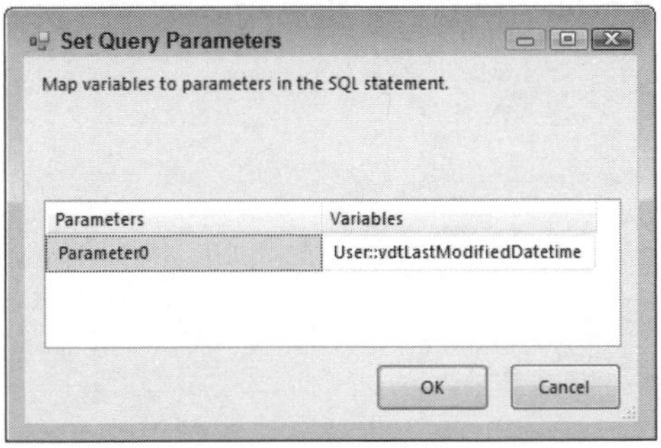

Figure 5-13

OLE DB parameters are 0 based, which means that the first ? in order is defined as the 0 parameter, the second ? in order is the 1 parameter, and so forth. Note that when you use parameterized queries, the statement cannot be parsed (using the Parse Query button) or previewed (using the Preview button). Therefore, to test the parameterization, the data flow must be executed. Figure 5-14 shows the executed data flow.

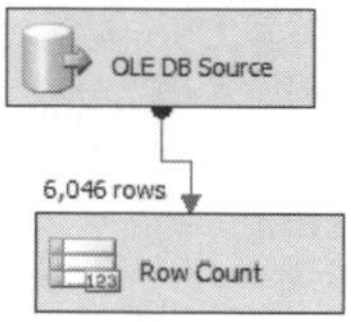

Figure 5-14

A Row Count transformation is merely used as a development technique — a dummy destination to build and test the source adapter. The vdtLastModifiedDatetime variable has been defaulted to '1/1/2004', which caused 6,046 rows out of the 8,845 rows to be extracted. The next section discusses how to both update and retrieve the right variable value.

Variable Bound SQL Source

One major drawback to the OLE DB parameterized source query is that many of the non-SQL Server OLE DB source providers do not support parameterization. Therefore, an alternative approach is needed that is also supported by the same source adapter.

The OLE DB provider also allows a source query to be based on the contents of a package variable. This is different from the parameterized source query in that the entire SQL statement is entered into the variable, rather than just the filter values. To exemplify, a string variable has been added to a package called vsExtractionSQL, and it contains the following SQL code:

```
SELECT *
FROM Purchasing.PurchaseOrderDetail
WHERE ModifiedDate > '1/1/2004'
```

The OLE DB source adapter is defined with the "Data access mode" property set to "SQL command from variable," and the "Variable name" property set to User::vsExtractionSQL, as shown in Figure 5-15.

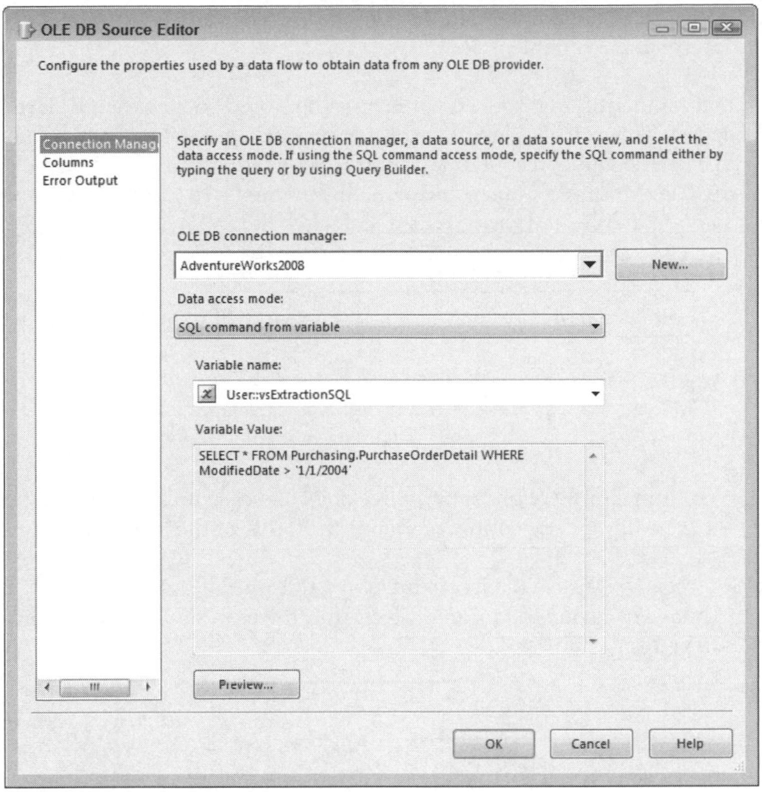

Figure 5-15

Alternatively, if the variable only contained the name of the table or view, you could select the "Table name or view name" variable option in the "Data access mode" property. However, by only selecting a view or a table, you would not be able to filter the rows on the source.

Unlike the OLE DB parameterized statement, using this variable-bound feature, the parsing and previewing feature in the editor works, and when this data flow is executed, the results are identical to Figure 5-14, shown previously. The next section reviews how to update the variables.

Retrieving Incremental Identifier Values and Updating Package Variables

The first step showed how to enable the data flow to be able to run a targeted extraction, and this section reviews how to update the package variables that drive the targeted extraction. Both the OLE DB parameterized approach and the variable-bound source approach need variable values updated in order to extract the correct batch of data.

As an example, let's first update the vdtLastModifiedDatetime column, which is the only variable update that the OLE DB parameterized approach requires. Second, let's look at a couple of methods to update the `vsExtractionSQL` variable with the right `datetime` value from the `vdtLastModifiedDatetime` variable.

The current incremental identifying column value must be stored so that each ETL run can use a new value for the extraction. This can be done in various ways (such as keeping it in a file), but the most common way is to store the value in a database control table that contains only the extraction information. For the Last Modified Date example, a table named `cfgIncrementalExtraction` has been created with two fields with one entry row, which looks like the following:

SourceTable	LastModifiedDatetime
PurchaseOrderDetails	1/1/2004

The `SourceTable` column simply defines the source object, in case multiple configuration entries are made. The `LastModifiedDatetime` column contains the value of the last successful extraction.

Therefore, the first step is to retrieve the last extraction value and update the `vdtLastModifiedDatetime` column variable. To do this, the easiest way is to use an Execute SQL Task. Figure 5-16 shows the editor of an Execute SQL Task.

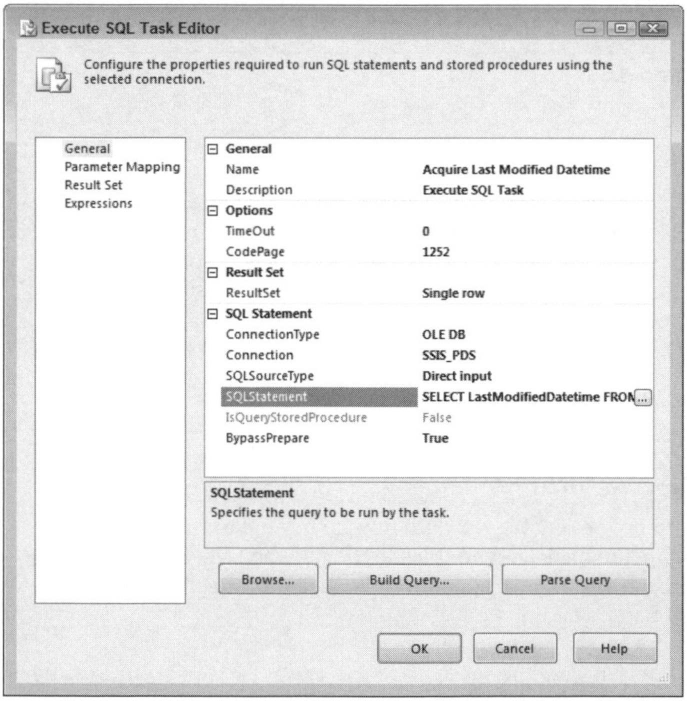

Figure 5-16

The SQLStatement executes the following query against the table defined previously:

```
SELECT LastModifiedDatetime
FROM cfgIncrementalExtraction
WHERE SourceTable = 'PurchaseOrderDetail'
```

The statement returns a single row where the resulting columns must update the variable. The ResultSet property of the task shown in Figure 5-17 has been set to "Single row," and on the Result Set page of the editor, the LastModifiedDatetime column is mapped to the vdtLastModifiedDatetime variable, as Figure 5-17 highlights.

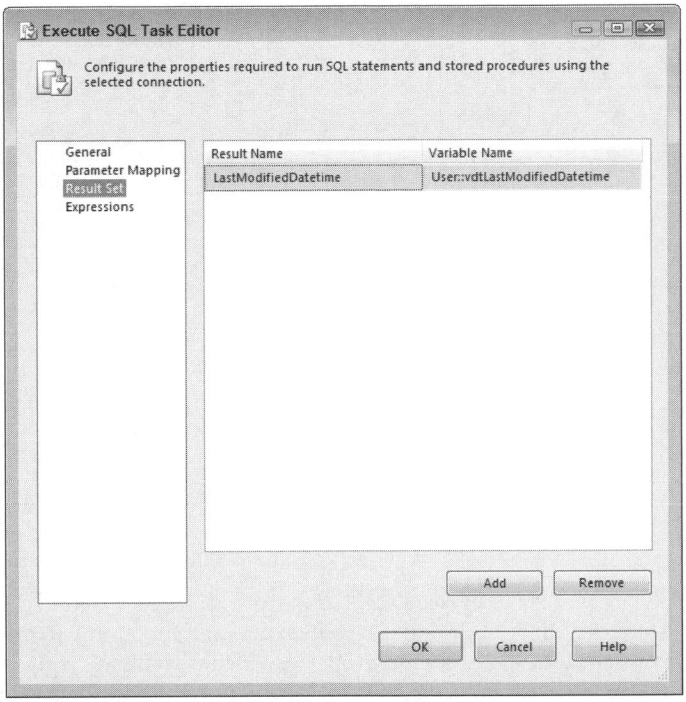

Figure 5-17

As an alternative approach, you could use the SQL logic to acquire the value that then could be embedded into a stored procedure and an output variable.

For the variable-bound source adapter method, a second step is required to update the vsExtractionSQL value for the variable-bound source adapter. In fact, two SSIS methods are available. The first is to have the variable updated by an expression, and the second is to use a Script Task to perform the update.

Variables have a little-known property called `EvaluateAsExpression`, which, by default, is set to `False`. When it is set to `True`, then an expression can be written that is evaluated any time the variable is read. Figure 5-18 shows that the `EvaluateAsExpression` property is viewable in the Properties pane, when the variable is selected in the Variables pane.

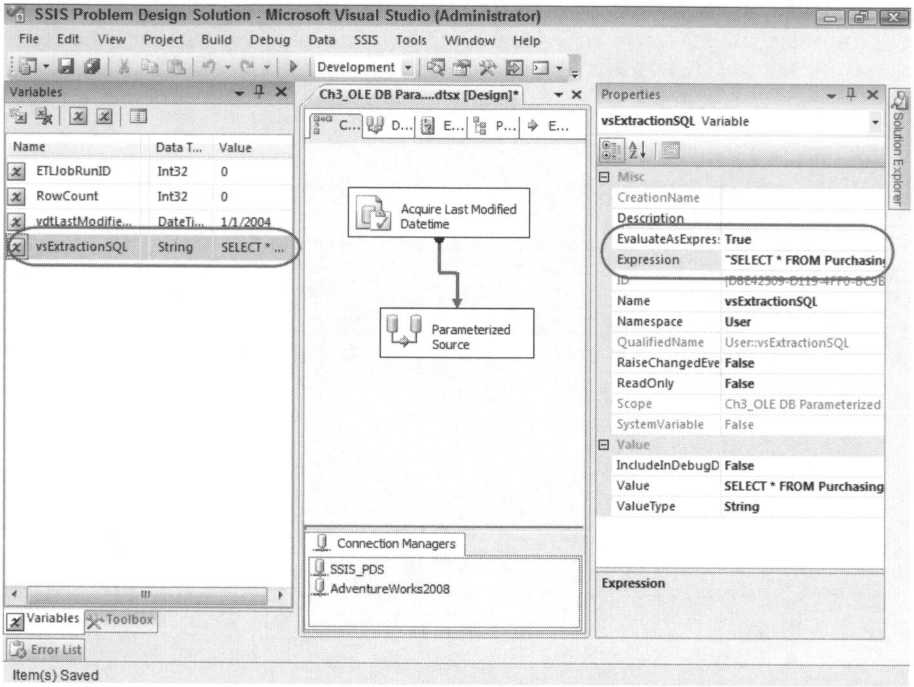

Figure 5-18

Since the release of SQL Server 2005 Service Pack 1, the expression can be entered into an expression editor, allowing the statement to be built with the SSIS expression functions. To invoke the Expression Builder dialog box, you select the `Expression` property, which is right below the `EvaluateAsExpression` property. Figure 5-19 shows the editor with the expression that builds the SQL statement added.

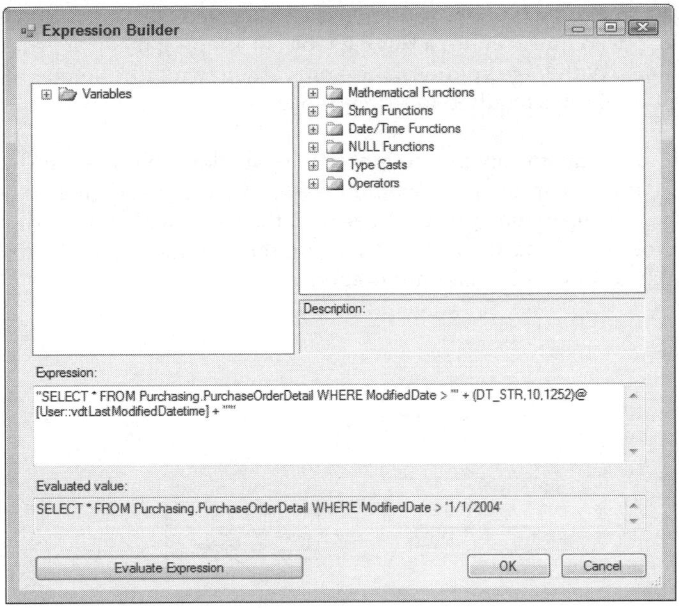

Figure 5-19

In this case, the expression updates the SQL statement by using the vdtLastModifiedDatetime value to update the string.

```
"SELECT * FROM Purchasing.PurchaseOrderDetail
WHERE ModifiedDate > '" + (DT_STR, 10, 1252) @[User::vdtLastModifiedDatetime] + "'"
```

The expression editor also allows the expression to be evaluated for accuracy and functionality.

One drawback of the EvaluateAsExpression feature of variables is that the property is difficult to find. Therefore, you may want to use a Script Task to manually update the value of the variable. To do so, ensure that the Script Task has the vdtLastModifiedDatetime entered in the ReadOnlyVariables list and the vsExtractionSQL in the ReadWriteVariables list. The script code that you would enter under the Public Sub Main() looks like this:

```
Dts.Variables("vsExtractionSQL").Value = _
  "SELECT * FROM Purchasing.PurchaseOrderDetail WHERE ModifiedDate > '" _
  + Dts.Variables("vdtLastModifiedDatetime").Value.ToString + "'"
```

When put together, the control flow would include the Execute SQL Task, an optional Script Task, and a Data Flow Task, as the control flow in Figure 5-18 demonstrated earlier.

Capturing the Maximum Change Identifier Value

So far, when dealing with incremental extractions, you have seen how to dynamically update the source query based on the value of a variable, which was updated from the value stored in a control table. The final part of targeting database records is to capture the final change identifier value so that it can be used for the next extraction.

A couple choices exist to handle this job. You can use an Execute SQL Task to run a SQL MAX operation on the destination table. This requires either a staging table, or keeping the change identifier column in the dimension or fact tables. With large volumes, this approach may require some time and resource overhead if the number of rows required to scan is too large.

A better approach is to handle the operation right in the data flow. In other words, you can use the Aggregate transformation to capture the maximum value. But can the aggregate be done at the same time as the rest of the transformation process? Yes, with the use of a Multicast, the rows can be sent to an Aggregate, while at the same time, the rows are flowing through the rest of the data flow operations. Figure 5-20 shows a data flow with this configuration.

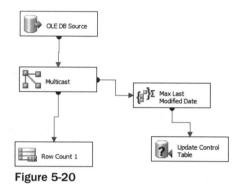

Figure 5-20

On the left side of the Multicast output, the rows are simply sent to a Row Count transformation. Once again, the Row Count transformation serves as a dummy destination for illustration purposes and, in reality, would be replaced by the actual data loading code. On the right side of the multicast, the rows are sent to an Aggregate transformation, configured to capture the maximum value of the ModifiedDate coming from the source. Figure 5-21 shows the Aggregate Transformation Editor.

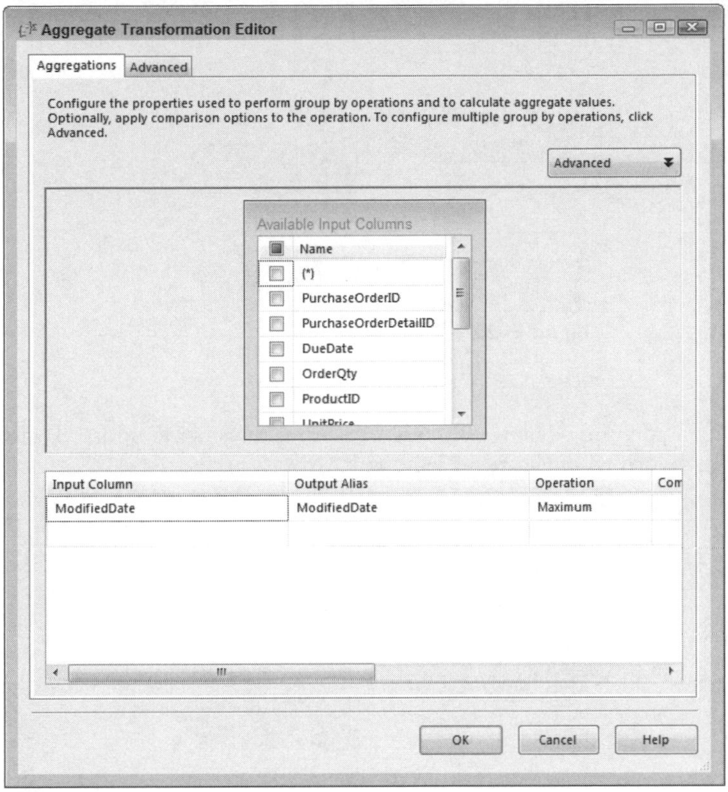

Figure 5-21

Notice that there are no group-by columns in the Aggregate, which means that the maximum value of the ModifiedDate will be captured across the source data set. Because of this, only one row from the Aggregate will be sent downstream.

The next transformation used is an OLE DB Command transformation, which is updating the control table with the following statement:

```
UPDATE cfgIncrementalExtraction
SET LastModifiedDatetime = ISNULL(?, LastModifiedDatetime)
WHERE SourceTable = 'PurchaseOrderDetail'
```

The parameter (?) is mapped to the single-row Modified Date output of the aggregate. This UPDATE statement only executes when given the single-row Aggregate output. Also, it's important to note that an ISNULL is used to trap for NULLs in the parameter. This is because the Aggregate will produce a single-row NULL output even if there are no input rows from the source, because there are no group-by columns. This is expected, and without the ISNULL, the control table would be incorrectly updated with a NULL and affect the next run.

Figure 5-22 shows the data flow results when the extraction package is run in its entirety.

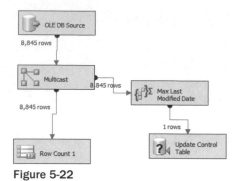

Figure 5-22

If the package is run again immediately, without any source rows being updated, then given the logic, the data flow results return what Figure 5-23 shows.

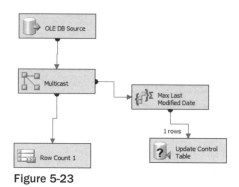

Figure 5-23

As expected, no rows were extracted because the last run captured and tracked the maximum Modified Date, and there were, therefore, no rows left to pull.

You must be careful when using `datetime` change indicators. If the source change indicator data type includes partial seconds, it must be handled carefully, because the SSIS data type will drop the partial second. This means the saved change indicator will be less than what was actually extracted, and the next extraction will pull some of the same records.

One possible solution is to increment the change indicator to the next second, and then look for records that are greater than or equal to that value. There is still then the possibility that more records arrived later during the same second, are less than the saved changed indicator, and so are never extracted. This scenario should be far less likely to happen, though.

Incremental Extraction from SQL Server without a Trigger

Before looking at how to use SSIS to perform incremental extraction on text files and other sources (that is, sources that don't contain a change identification value), take a look at one other option that exists for table extractions from SQL Server.

If you're using SQL Server as your source, then you may be able to perform an incremental extraction, even though you don't have an explicit column that helps identify changes. SQL Server provides a `rowversion` data type that is automatically updated when a row is added or updated, without requiring a trigger.

In a nutshell, you can use the `rowversion` in SSIS to perform incremental extraction. In fact, the `rowversion` is used by SQL Server for internal row checking for things like replication. Each table can have only one `rowversion` column, and when you add it to the table, you are really just exposing it in the table for another use. To leverage this, SSIS requires converting the binary column so that it is useable.

To demonstrate the `rowversion` data type, the `Sales.Customer` AdventureWorks source table has been altered with a new `rowversion` column, using the following T-SQL code:

```
USE AdventureWorks2008
GO
ALTER TABLE Sales.Customer ADD
    CustomerRowVersion rowversion NOT NULL
```

In addition, a new row and column have been added to the control table. The new row contains the `Sales.Customer` source table column value, and a new `varchar` column has been added to capture the converted conversion number value of the binary `rowversion` value.

The difference between the `datetime` example reviewed earlier in this chapter and the `rowversion` being reviewed here is that the source query is also handling the conversion of the `rowversion` from binary to integer. Besides the normal columns being pulled, the `SELECT` statement includes the conversion and adjusted filter, with the following code:

```
SELECT *,
  CONVERT(BIGINT,CustomerRowVersion) as CustomerRowVersion_Int64
FROM sales.customer
WHERE CONVERT(BIGINT,CustomerRowVersion) > ?
```

Figure 5-24 shows the completed data flow for the first time that the process is run.

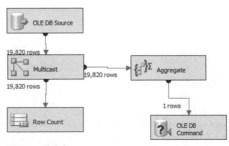

Figure 5-24

As expected, when this package is run immediately a second time, no rows are extracted, as Figure 5-25 shows.

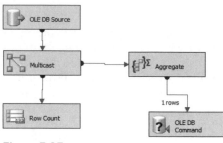

Figure 5-25

Because a trigger already exists on the Sales.Customer table (to illustrate this rowversion use) the trigger should be dropped. Next, the following updates are performed on the table:

```
USE AdventureWorks2008
GO

UPDATE Sales.Customer
SET TerritoryID = 6
WHERE CustomerID = 13

UPDATE Sales.Customer
SET TerritoryID = 4
WHERE CustomerID = 26
```

Then the package is run another time, with the data flow output shown in Figure 5-26.

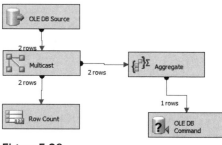

Figure 5-26

The two updated rows have been sent out. As you can see, this method gives you a nice way to handle incremental extraction from a SQL source without requiring application changes or a table trigger. Yes, it does require the addition of an 8-byte column in the source, but the incremental extraction benefits may outweigh the additional table width.

Change Data Capture

If you have a source such as SQL Server 2008 Enterprise that supports Change Data Capture (CDC), then you are in luck. CDC is a feature that is perfectly suited to retrieving the incremental changes that a data table has undergone since the last extraction.

Implementation details vary between database products, but SQL Server 2008 CDC is very easy to use, and puts very little stress on the server. Once enabled, CDC tracks changes to the table through the transaction log, and writes them to an automatically generated shadow table with the same schema. The writes to the shadow table occur when the server is not busy, or can be driven by a schedule or on demand.

The shadow table has some extra columns that enable you to find out information about the change, such as the following:

❑   The log sequence number (LSN) of the change's transaction

❑   The sequence of the change within that transaction

❑   The type of operation (insert, update, or delete) that modified the row

❑   The columns that were modified during an update

You can simply query the shadow table like a normal table. Additionally, several stored procedures and functions are available to help. These functions can do the following:

❑   Translate a `datetime` to an LSN.

❑   Return the changes that occurred between two LSNs.

❑   Compute the net change of the modified rows. For example, an insert and multiple updates would be consolidated into a single insert with the latest column values.

With knowledge of these three functions and a little help from Books Online, you should be able to apply the concepts in this section to create a very efficient extraction process. For more information about CDC, see *Professional Microsoft SQL Server 2008 Integration Services* (Indianapolis: Wiley, 2008). Chapter 11 of that book has an example of an SSIS ETL process using CDC.

Using SSIS to Handle All Aspects of an Incremental Extraction

Ideally, every source would have a method to capture only the new and changed records (and even deletes). But, unfortunately, not every source has this capability, especially when dealing with flat files as your source. Therefore, this section looks at how to handle flat-file sources and database tables that do not have change identifier values.

Flat Files that Contain Change Identifier Values

It is very possible that you may have a flat-file source that contains a `LastModifiedDate` or similar column in the file (and the file contains both changed and non-changed rows from the last extraction). However, because of the nature of flat files, the data flow source adapter cannot issue a query against the file.

You can actually handle this scenario very easily in SSIS, with the use of a Conditional Split transformation as the first step in the data flow. Because you cannot use the `vdtLastModifiedDate` variable in the source, what you can do instead is use the Conditional Split to filter the rows immediately as they are pulled into the pipeline from the file. Figure 5-27 shows the modified data flow.

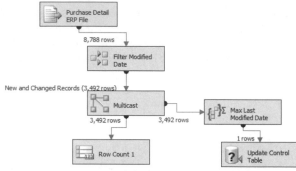

Figure 5-27

The source adapter for the flat file is simply configured for the current structure of the delimited file. The Conditional Split checks the value of the Modified Date column for every row, and only allows rows through that are greater than the last incremental extraction value. Figure 5-28 shows the Conditional Split Transformation Editor.

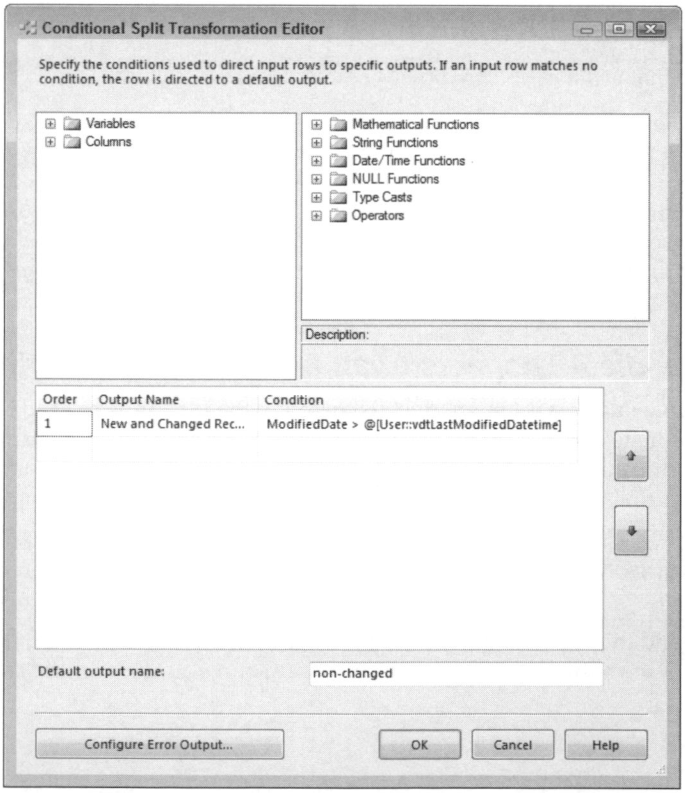

Figure 5-28

Rows that do not meet the criteria would usually go out the default output. But, as you can see in the data flow in Figure 5-28, the default output (named non-changed) is not being used. Therefore, the non-changed rows are discarded by the pipeline.

Notice in the data flow that the next identifier value is captured using a Multicast and Aggregate just like the dynamic query examples in the previous section. Also, not shown is the control flow that uses the same approach as before with an Execute SQL Task to update the vdtLastModifiedDate variable.

Sources Without Change Identifier Values

Finally, you may have a situation where your source just doesn't have a change identifier value at all. In these cases, you will either need to use the data flow to determine which records are changed, or land the entire source to a temporary table and rely on the database to compare the records.

Focusing on the data flow approach, to handle this scenario, the source must be correlated with the destination, and based on the comparison, records must be identified as new or changed and, in some cases, deleted.

A common theme throughout the book is how to do data correlation in the data flow to compare sources with destinations. The straightforward approaches are to use the Lookup or Merge Join transformations to perform the data association. The Lookup can identify matches with the output path, and non-matches with the error row output. The Merge Join requires a Conditional Split to determine matches and non-matches.

In the following example, a flat-file source contains sales data, but does not indicate whether the sale had previously been added to the destination table. To identify whether the sale had been added previously, the source data is merged with the destination table, which, in this case, is the sales fact table within AdventureWorksDW. Figure 5-29 shows the first several steps of the data flow that performs the data association and comparison.

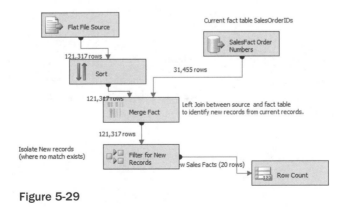

Figure 5-29

The Merge Join component requires both of its inputs to be sorted by the same keys. The data from the flat-file source is sorted on the `SalesOrderID`, which is also contained in the fact table. On the right side of the Merge Join, an OLE DB source adapter is used, which pulls the existing `SalesOrderID` from the existing fact tables, pre-sorted with an `Order By` clause. The OLE DB source adapter does not interpret the SQL statement and, therefore, does not know the data is sorted. It must be told that the output is sorted and the column sort order, using the Advanced Editor configuration, as shown in Figure 5-30. Figure 5-31 shows the Merge Join configured as a left outer join.

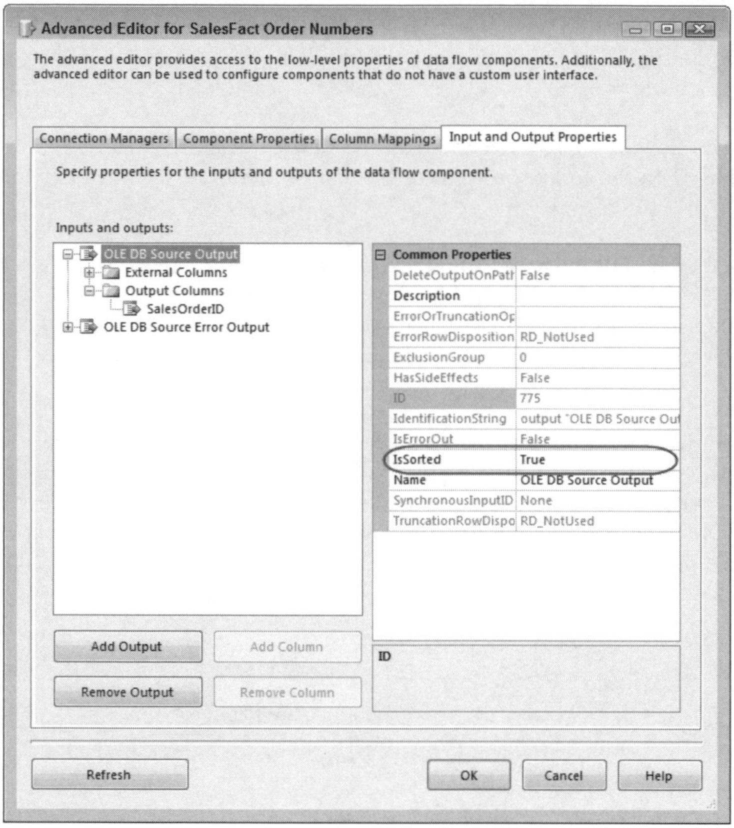

Figure 5-30

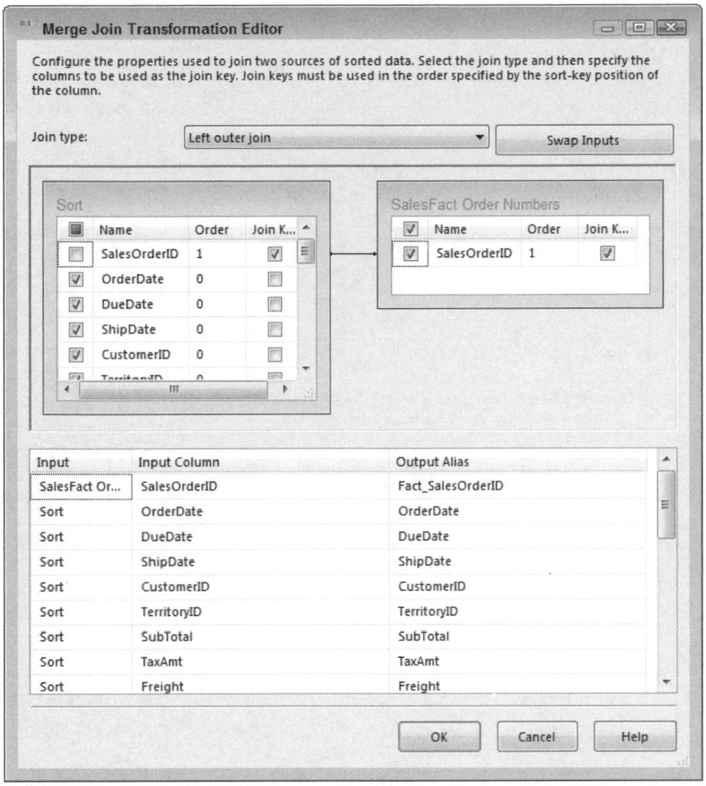

Figure 5-31

To identify new records to add to the destination, the left outer join allows both matches and non-matches from the source to the destination to flow through the transformation. The `SalesOrderID` from the destination is aliased as `Fact_SalesOrderID` to differentiate the value in the Conditional Split transformation. Figure 5-32 highlights the Conditional Split, which performs the filter of records by checking for `NULL`s in the `Fact_SalesOrderID`.

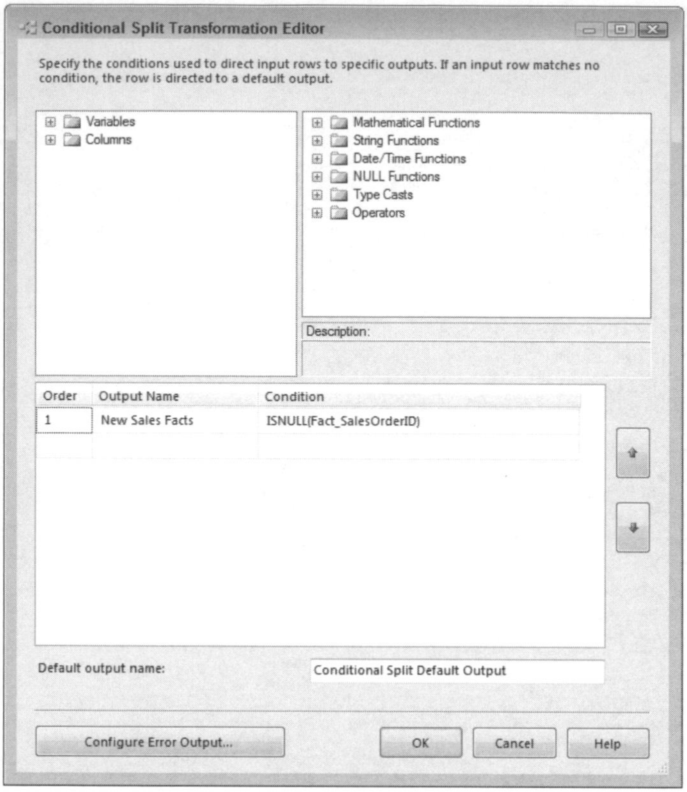

Figure 5-32

If a NULL exists in the Fact_SalesOrderID, it means that the source record is new to the fact table, and, therefore, should be allowed through the transformation process to be added to the fact table. Otherwise, the record already exists, and, in this example, is ignored by the Conditional Split because the default output is not used.

This approach and similar approaches with the Lookup transformation allow incremental data extraction by using SSIS data flow components to filter out rows early in the process.

Data Staging Method

Data staging provides a valuable mechanism for data archiving and data validation. In some cases, a data warehouse may only be using a portion of the source data provided. However, at some later date, this information may become valuable to extend the solution. Having raw staged data can allow reloading and data validation.

When dealing with flat files generated or pushed from a source, the flat file itself can be the archive mechanism. At times, however, having your raw source data persisted into a database for tracking or validating with queries may be valuable. In these cases, when you need to stage the data with SSIS, you can take one of two approaches.

The data can be landed to the staging/archive table in one data flow, and a second data flow can then extract the data from the staged data back into the data flow for further processing. This approach would look like Figure 5-33, with the control flow and data flows, shown side by side.

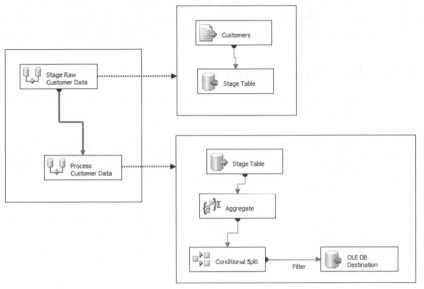

Figure 5-33

The second approach is to handle both the staging and the transformation logic within the same data flow by using a Multicast transformation. Figure 5-34 shows the same process handled in this approach.

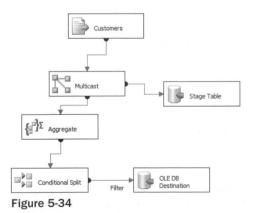

Figure 5-34

Both have their advantages and disadvantages. The second approach scales a lot better when you're dealing with large amounts of data. The reason is twofold. First, the staging process is handled in parallel with the transformation process, but also, the disk I/O is reduced in half because the staging table is only written to, as opposed to written to and then extracted from again.

However, if the transformation process fails, then the staging process will also stop. In the first approach, if the transformation process failed, the staged data would already be in the archive table, and then the data flow containing the transformation logic could be restarted after the data issue resolved.

Tracking Data Lineage Identifiers

As with other requirements, you can handle data lineage several ways in SSIS. The most common way is to add an auto-incrementing number to the data flow that maps data points back to their sources.

If you are staging raw data, the raw data can be leveraged by sending this lineage number to the staged data and also to the destination tables. With raw staging tables, instead of having to track back to a source system, which may be volatile, you are able to go back to the raw staging database and see what the data was at the point in time it was extracted.

To do this, add a lineage sequence identifier to the data flow right after the extraction so that it could then flow to both the stage table as well as the primary transformation processes. A simple Script component can handle the incrementing identifier. Figure 5-35 shows an extraction data flow that was presented earlier. This time, a Script component has been added after the extraction.

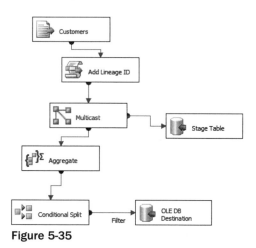

Figure 5-35

To configure the Script component to output a sequence lineage number, you must add a new output column to the Script component output properties. Figure 5-36 shows the Inputs and Outputs properties page, where a new integer column called CustomerLineageID has been added as an output column.

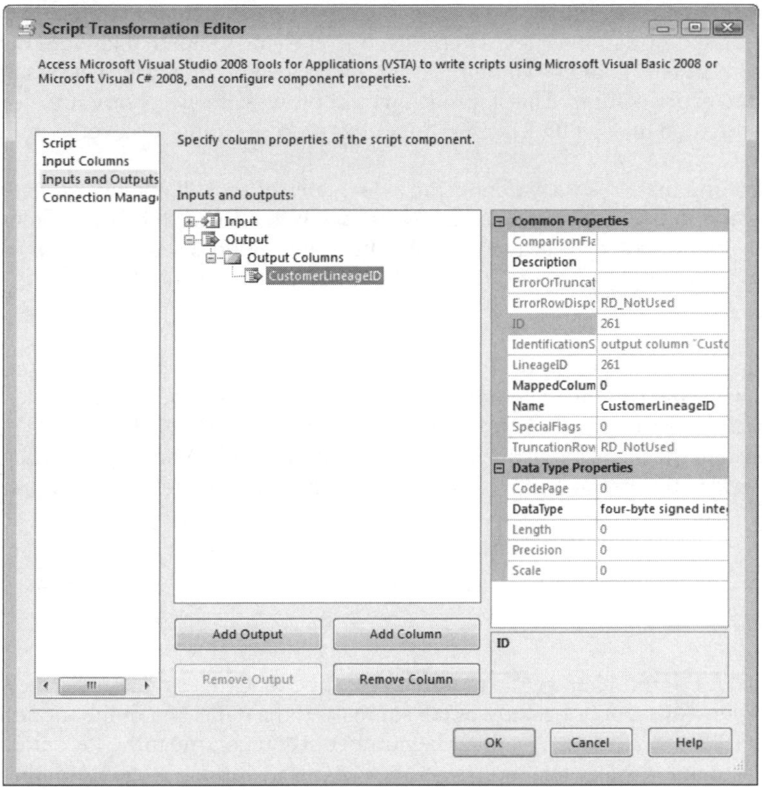

Figure 5-36

The script itself is very straightforward. For every row, the lineage is output and then the value is increased by 1 for the next row. The following code handles this lineage:

```
Public Class ScriptMain
    Inherits UserComponent
    Private CustomerLineageID As Integer = 1

    Public Overrides Sub Input_ProcessInputRow(ByVal Row As InputBuffer)

        Row.CustomerLineageID = Me.CustomerLineageID
        Me.CustomerLineageID = Me.CustomerLineageID + 1

    End Sub

End Class
```

With this sequence lineage approach, the added Customer Lineage ID would flow to both the raw staging table and the destination tables. Alternatively, if the entire source data does not need to be staged, then the lineage ID could be landed to a staging table with only the business keys from the source, rather than every column. This approach would provide the necessary link between the source keys and the destination lineage ID. The SSIS data flow process would look very similar.

It's worth mentioning that, in data warehousing, a fact table often will contain a *degenerate dimension* — or a granular-level number that is an attribute of the fact. But, instead of being broken out into a separate dimension table, it is stored in the fact table itself. Often, this value is seen as a business key of the fact records. It is also a type of data lineage, because the discrete values can relate back directly to the source system.

When the lineage ID is stored in the destination tables, the next step is to put a trigger or action in the destination database that can then reference the source data that is either stored in the raw staging environment, or links directly to the source. Tracking data lineage allows better data validation, but when you can enable the users to see the link between source and destination themselves by building that functionality into the application, you are ahead of the game. To get there requires adding it to your SSIS-based ETL.

Solution

As you've seen so far in this chapter, the requirements for data extraction are relatively simple, but can vary quite a bit, depending on the nature of the source and the data. The number of different extraction patterns in your ETL is usually far less than the number of sources, meaning the same pattern is reused many times. This makes the extraction phase of the ETL very conducive to automation. This last section of this chapter provides an example of creating a metadata-driven extraction process.

Metadata-Driven Extraction Example

A small ETL process might have 5–10 sources. Between 10 and 100 sources would probably be considered medium-sized. Large ones could potentially have any number.

A well-structured, modular, ETL process will have one package for each of the import sources. If the principles shown in this chapter are observed, each extraction package will have at its heart a very simple data flow with no transformations, and the control flow will likely have some framework-related tasks such as described in Chapter 2. These packages will be largely indistinguishable from one another without opening the components of the data flow and examining the source queries or destination tables.

Creating all those packages and setting the source and destination components is a lot of boring, tedious work. Now imagine that your medium- or large-sized ETL needs a new feature that requires a framework change to every package. All those nice packages are now a management liability.

Imagine instead that the source and destination information were contained in a database and the extraction process was performed by a single package. A framework change only affects one extraction package. A source data change only affects metadata, and no extraction packages have to be changed.

The following example was made as simple as possible to clearly demonstrate the idea. A real implementation would probably require additional features and more work to make it robust enough for a production environment.

Metadata Tables

Figure 5-37 shows the metadata tables used in the example.

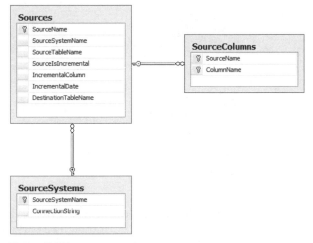

Figure 5-37

A quick perusal of the available columns should give you an idea of where the example is headed. There is a connection string for each source system and a list of columns for each source table. For each source table, there are columns with incremental extraction information and a destination table name. The example uses this information to connect to the source system, and get the specified columns for rows with change indicators since the previous extraction.

Control Flow

The control flow of the package is very simple, as shown in Figure 5-38.

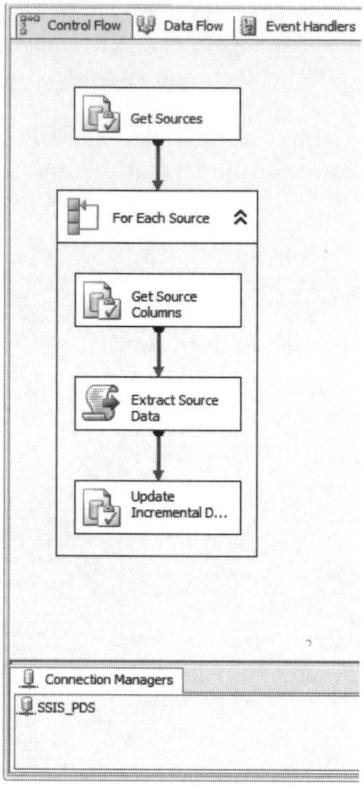

Figure 5-38

A quick glance should show you that the package gets a list of sources and loops through them, executing a query to get the columns for each, and then executing a script to do the extraction. The loop finishes with another query to update the incremental date. It should be fairly obvious that the Extract Source Data script is doing most of the work here.

There is one ADO.NET connection to the staging database where the metadata and destination tables are assumed to be located. The ADO.NET connection manager typically doesn't perform as well as the OLE DB, but it has some convenient features that make the example simpler.

Looping through the Sources

First, the Get Sources Task executes the following SQL statement and stores the full result set in the Sources object variable, as shown in Figure 5-39 and Figure 5-40.

```
SELECT
    a.SourceName,
    a.SourceTableName,
    a.SourceIsIncremental,
    a.IncrementalColumnName,
    a.IncrementalDate,
```

```
        a.DestinationTableName,
        b.ConnectionString
FROM
        dbo.Sources a
        INNER JOIN dbo.SourceSystems b
            ON a.SourceSystemName = b.SourceSystemName
```

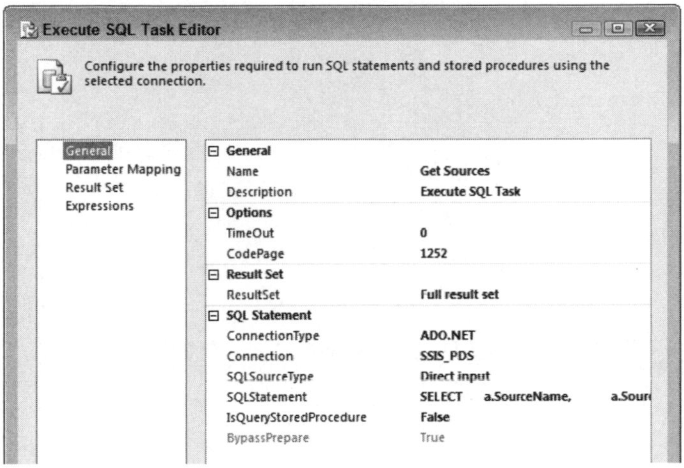

Figure 5-39

Figure 5-40

Then, the Foreach Loop is used to iterate through each row of the Sources variable and split the columns into separate variables, as shown in Figure 5-41 and Figure 5-42.

159

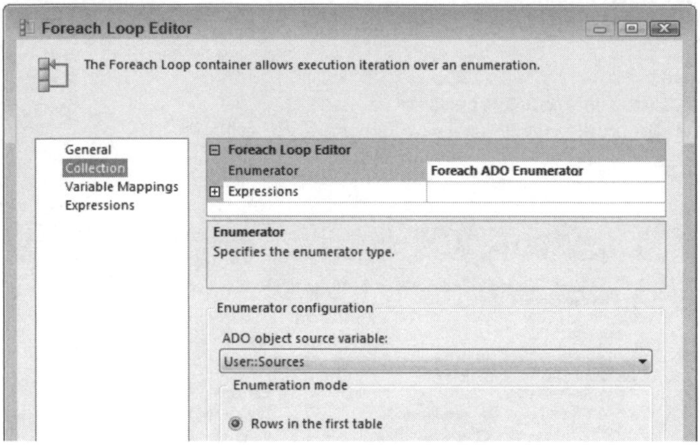

Figure 5-41

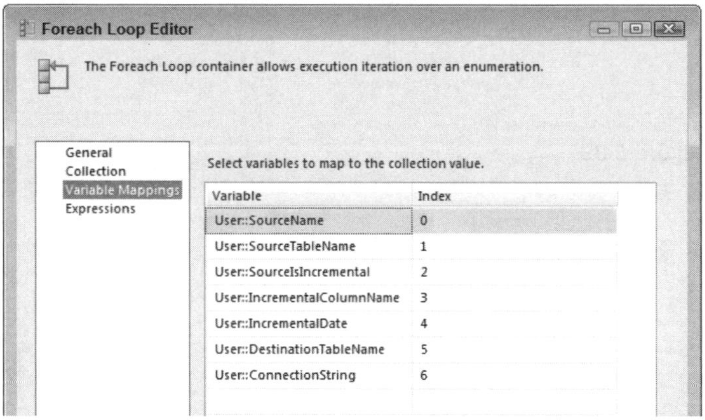

Figure 5-42

Inside the Sources Loop

First, the Get Source Columns Task executes the following query and puts the full result set in the SourceColumns object variable. The query is parameterized to get the columns related to the loop's current source. The query parameter is mapped from the SourceName metadata column via the SourceName package variable, as shown in Figure 5-43.

```
SELECT
      ColumnName
FROM
      SourceColumns
WHERE
      SourceName = @SourceName
```

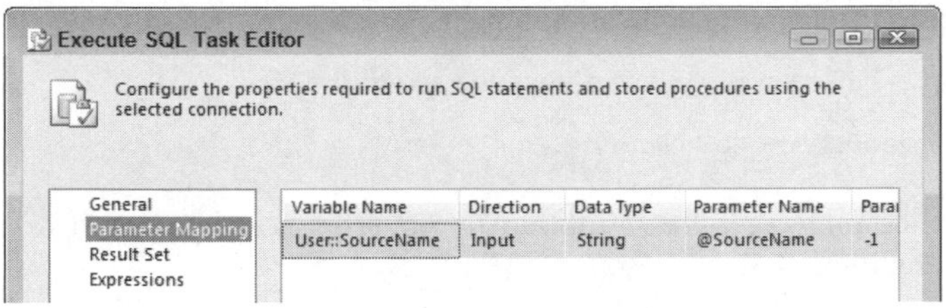

Figure 5-43

Then, the Extract Source Data Task is executed. Most of the variables are passed in as read-only, as shown in Figure 5-44, but a new variable named `IncrementalDateMax` is read-write. The script populates this variable with the maximum value found in the change indicator column identified by the `IncrementalColumnName` metadata column. The next section goes into more detail about the script.

Figure 5-44

Finally, the following statement is executed to update the metadata with the maximum change indicator value that was extracted. This value will then be used for the next extraction to only get new rows.

```
UPDATE
      Sources
SET
      IncrementalDate = @IncrementalDateMax
WHERE
      SourceName = @SourceName
```

The Script

This section is for those who aren't squeamish about looking at code. The previous section should be sufficient for explaining what the example does. This section shows how it does it.

The script has five major sections:

❑ Read the variables passed into the script.

❑ Open the source and destination connections.

❑   Get the maximum change indicator value from the source table.

❑   Get the rows between the old and new change indicators.

❑   Close the connections and clean up.

Several .NET libraries are used in the script that are not referenced by default. To make things clearer, they are added to the references at the top.

```
Imports System.Collections.Generic
Imports System.Data.SqlClient
Imports System.Data.OleDb
Imports System.Text
```

The rest of the code exists in a single block or subroutine. Every Script Task contains a `Public Sub Main()` that is the entry point for execution, and the example's code can be placed there for simplicity. Chapter 11 contains more information about creating control flow scripts.

Read Variables

Several control flow variables contain information about the source being extracted. For clarity of the code in following sections, these are all copied into script variables. Strictly speaking, this section isn't necessary, because the control flow variables can be referenced in-line. There might be a slight performance improvement when using script variables for control flow variables that are referenced multiple times.

```
Dim SourceTableName As String _
    = Dts.Variables("SourceTableName").Value.ToString
Dim SourceIsIncremental As Boolean _
    = CBool(Dts.Variables("SourceIsIncremental").Value)
Dim IncrementalColumnName As String _
    = Dts.Variables("IncrementalColumnName").Value.ToString
Dim IncrementalDate As DateTime _
    = CDate(Dts.Variables("IncrementalDate").Value)
Dim ConnectionString As String _
    = Dts.Variables("ConnectionString").Value.ToString
Dim DestinationTableName As String _
    = Dts.Variables("DestinationTableName").Value.ToString
```

Next, the list of source columns is converted from the control flow's ADO.NET dataset into a friendlier list. Again, this is not really necessary, but hopefully makes the code more readable.

```
Dim dt As DataTable = CType(Dts.Variables("SourceColumns").Value, _
    DataSet).Tables(0)
Dim SourceColumns As List(Of String) = New List(Of String)
For Each dr As DataRow In dt.Rows
    SourceColumns.Add(dr(0))
Next
```

Open Connections

The connections are now ready to be opened. An `OleDbConnection` is used for the source because the database provider is not assumed. This connection should work for any OLE DB database. The source connection string is coming from the metadata.

The destination is assumed to be the SQL Server staging database, and the connection information is taken from the connection manager of the package.

```
' open source
Dim SourceConn As OleDbConnection = _
    New OleDbConnection(ConnectionString)
SourceConn.Open()

' open destination
Dim BulkConn As SqlConnection = _
    New SqlConnection(Dts.Connections("SSIS_PDS").ConnectionString)
BulkConn.Open()
```

Next, a `SqlBulkCopy` object is created on the destination connection. It must be told the name of the destination table and a mapping between the source and destination column names. This allows the example to bulk-load data from the source directly into the destination. Not only is bulk-loading much faster than loading each row individually, but using `SqlBulkCopy` makes the code simpler, too.

```
' create bulkcopy
Dim BulkCopy As SqlBulkCopy = New SqlBulkCopy(BulkConn)
BulkCopy.DestinationTableName = DestinationTableName
For Each ColumnName As String In SourceColumns
    BulkCopy.ColumnMappings.Add( _
        New SqlBulkCopyColumnMapping(ColumnName, ColumnName))
Next
```

Get Max Change Indicator

Now a query is generated against the source table to get the maximum value of the change indicator. This isn't exactly ideal, but as you'll see coming up, the script doesn't have an opportunity to inspect the rows as they are extracted. Somehow, the script must know what the maximum value is, so it asks prior to the extraction. It could also ask the staging database *after* the extraction, and perhaps that makes more sense, but requires that the change identifier be extracted, which this way does not.

The value is placed in the read-write control flow variable so that this value can be written back to the metadata when the script is finished.

```
' build sql statement to get max incremental value
Dim sql1 As String = "SELECT MAX(" + IncrementalColumnName + _
    ") FROM " + SourceTableName

' execute
Dim cmd1 As OleDbCommand = SourceConn.CreateCommand()
cmd1.CommandText = sql1
cmd1.CommandType = CommandType.Text
Dim IncrementalDateMax As DateTime = CDate(cmd1.ExecuteScalar())
IncrementalDateMax = IncrementalDateMax.AddSeconds(1)

' set variable with new value
Dts.Variables("IncrementalDateMax").Value = IncrementalDateMax
```

Extract Changed Source Rows

The change indicator value passed in from the control flow and the maximum value retrieved from the source are now used to construct an extraction query. Using a simple conditional statement to see whether the two change indicators are different, and, thus, skip the extract, would probably be worthwhile.

You might need to adjust the syntax of the generated query depending on the source system. Though intended to be generic, the example was still written for a SQL Server source.

```
' build sql extract statement
Dim sql2 As New Text.StringBuilder
Dim FirstColumn As Boolean = True

sql2.Append("SELECT ")
For Each ColumnName As String In SourceColumns
    If Not FirstColumn Then
        sql2.Append(",")
    Else
        FirstColumn = False
    End If
    sql2.Append("[" + ColumnName + "]")
Next
sql2.Append(" FROM [" + SourceTableName + "]")
If SourceIsIncremental Then
    sql2.Append(" WHERE [" + IncrementalColumnName + "] > '" + _
        IncrementalDate.ToString + "'")
    sql2.Append(" AND  [" + IncrementalColumnName + "] < '" + _
        IncrementalDateMax.ToString + "'")
End If
```

Next, the extraction query is executed and the results are received in a fast `DataReader` object. This object is then passed directly to the `SqlBulkCopy` object and it does the rest. It doesn't get any easier than that!

```
' execute statement
Dim cmd2 As OleDbCommand = SourceConn.CreateCommand()
cmd2.CommandText = sql2.ToString
cmd2.CommandType = CommandType.Text
Dim rdr As OleDbDataReader = cmd2.ExecuteReader()

' insert rows
BulkCopy.WriteToServer(rdr)
```

Close Connections

Assuming that the script didn't hit any errors by this point, the extraction is done and it is time to clean up. The database connections must be closed and the script must return a result back to the control flow.

```
' close source
rdr.Close()
SourceConn.Close()
```

```
' close destination
BulkCopy.Close()
BulkConn.Close()

Dts.TaskResult = ScriptResults.Success
```

Summary

SSIS includes the capability to connect to a wide variety of sources with functionality to make the extraction process scalable and flexible, including many ways to target and filter source data. Data extraction requirements are sometimes unique, and will require variations on the examples and design patterns presented here. For example, you may need to combine some of the incremental extraction approaches with dynamic connections and data lineage tracking. But even given the wide variety of requirements you may run into, SSIS provides the functionality to handle many extraction scenarios.

This chapter covered the extraction of source data from source systems into a staging database, the first step of an ETL process. Chapter 6 focuses on cleansing data, followed by several chapters related to loading a data warehouse.

6

Data-Cleansing Design

At some point in your career, you've probably been told that a given file should always be clean, and there's no reason to spend time working on procedures to protect yourself from a problem. Inevitably, the impossible happens, and that previously perfect file has a problem, causing you to wake up at two o'clock in the morning to correct the production problem. If this has ever happened to you, or if you're trying to not fall victim to this scenario, then this chapter is for you.

In the classic Problem-Design-Solution pattern, this chapter teaches you how to protect your package from breakages from future data problems, and provides new patterns for exploring every realm of data cleansing prior to loading or updating the data. Here's what you can expect in this chapter:

❑ *"Problem"* — The "Problem" section answers the question, "How clean is my data?" The discussion shows how to determine the answer to this question by employing the built-in functionality of the Data Profiling Task.

❑ *"Design"* — After the file or data set is in the pipeline, you may need to protect yourself from unexpected conditions prior to loading the data. In the "Design" section of this chapter, you learn about the methods for using the Script transform to either cleanse or direct bad data elsewhere. You also see how to use the Fuzzy Grouping and Lookup transforms to match the data on non-exact means. Finally, you find out how to cleanse a single file that has two different types of data in the file.

❑ *"Solution"* — The "Solution" section of this chapter explores many of these features by examining an end-to-end example that cleanses data.

Problem

As consultants, the authors of this book have been told many times by customers that the data in a given table is pristine, and not to worry about the table's data quality, only to be later hurt by the assumption of good data. This assumption can add extra time and cost to a project that a client may not have expected. The Data Profiling Task enables you to scan your data to prove that your assumptions about your data are correct. You can use it to determine potentially severe problems (such as the percentage of your data that is NULL), or use it for analytical exploration of your data (such as to determine candidate columns for primary keys).

Suppose that you run a company that exchanges data with partners daily, and you can only import data that reaches a given quality margin. For example, if a given column has NULLs in it, you want to reject the imported data prior to loading it. Not checking the file prior to import could cause the database administrator (DBA) or quality control person to spend additional time later cleansing the data by hand. This process is a fairly trivial check to perform with the Data Profiling Task.

To perform a data quality check with the Data Profiling Task, you must first load the data into a table, because it only supports the ADO.NET connection manager. After it's loaded, you can profile the data in the table and output the results of your profile to an XML file, or to a variable that holds the XML data. Then, you can manually review the results using the Data Profile Viewer, or use an XML Task with an XPath operation to parse the profile results to make a decision on whether to load the data automatically.

An issue you may have with the task is its performance. It performs some queries that are quite extensive, and the more profiling that you perform and the more rows that are included, the slower the response time may be. Later in this section, you learn more about which profile options may require more time.

In this example, you create a package that profiles the DimCustomer table in the AdventureWorksDW2008 database. You use the profile results to determine whether you have a problem in the table.

To configure the task, first create an ADO.Net connection manager that connects you to the AdventureWorksDW2008 database, and then follow these steps:

1. After you've created the Data Profile Task, the fastest way to configure it is to open its editor and click Quick Profile. Point the ADO.NET connection to the newly created connection manager, and then use the Table or View option to select DimCustomer, as shown in Figure 6-1.

2. Select each of the boxes as shown in the figure and click OK. The Profile Request page appears, where you can do more advanced configuration of the task. This will be examined much more in a moment, but let's start with the basics.

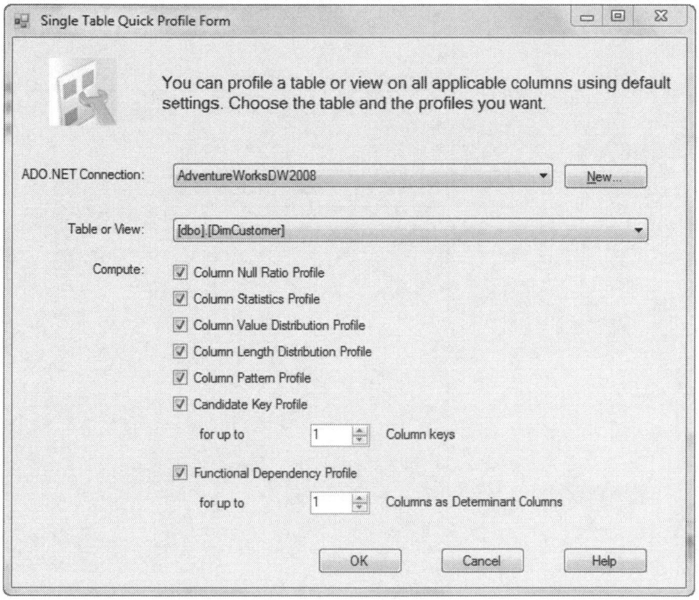

Figure 6-1

3. Go to the General page and configure where you want to write the output of this profile. The easiest output is an XML file that you can later use to review manually, but you could also write the XML output to a variable that could be read with the XML Task. For the purpose of this example, write the output to an XML file somewhere on your machine by changing the Destination drop-down box to a new connection manager.

4. After you have finished configuring this tab, click OK and run the package. Running the package may take a minute, because the queries the task is running are quite intense.

5. When the package completes, open the Data Profile Viewer under the Microsoft SQL Server 2008 ⇨ Integration Services program menu, and open the XML file you just created.

To see the output of the profile that the Data Profile Task generated, you drill into the individual tables, as shown in Figure 6-2.

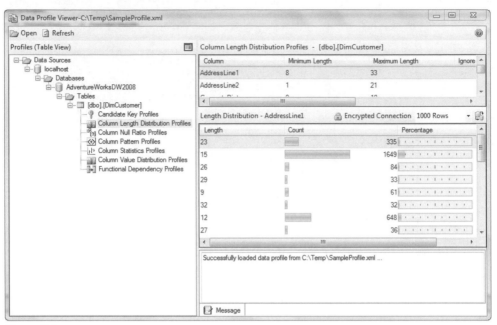

Figure 6-2

As you can see in Figure 6-2, you can select one of the profile types under the DimCustomer table and see details about the table. Your Data Profiling Task potentially could have profiled multiple tables, outputting the results into a single XML file. For example, if you were to select the Column Length Distribution profile, you would see how wide a given column is. In Figure 6-2, you can see that 335 rows are 23 characters wide for AddressLine1. You can also double-click on the length of 23 to see the specific 335 rows that are that wide if you have access to the data. Those rows are not stored inside the XML file. Instead, double-clicking re-runs a query to your SQL Server.

The Quick Profile option rapidly configures the Data Profiling Task with the common profile requests that you may want. You can manually adjust each of these profile requests after the configuration, or you can create new ones by selecting the type of request from the Profile Request drop-down box. The next few sections discuss what each of these profile requests can accomplish.

Candidate Key Profiles

The Candidate Key Profile Request (see Figure 6-3) finds the most appropriate primary key for your table. This is based on uniqueness of a given column (including the value of NULL as a value). You can make this request across a given set of columns, or for all columns at the same time. By limiting the list of columns, you can speed up the execution of the request.

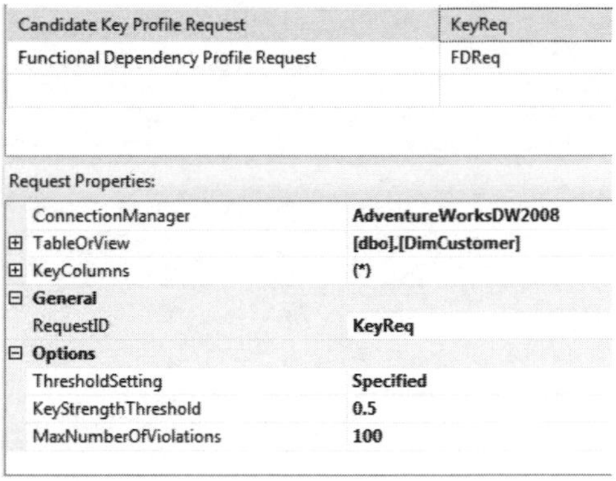

Candidate Key Profile Request	KeyReq
Functional Dependency Profile Request	FDReq

Request Properties:	
ConnectionManager	**AdventureWorksDW2008**
⊞ TableOrView	**[dbo].[DimCustomer]**
⊞ KeyColumns	(*)
⊟ **General**	
RequestID	**KeyReq**
⊟ **Options**	
ThresholdSetting	**Specified**
KeyStrengthThreshold	0.5
MaxNumberOfViolations	100

Figure 6-3

The default setting for the KeyStrengthThreshold property is .95, which states that the candidate primary key must be at least 95 percent unique. By adjusting that setting to 0.5 (as shown in Figure 6-3) and re-running the task, you'll notice that, in the Profile Viewer shown in Figure 6-4, AddressLine1 now appears as a potential key, but it's only 69 percent unique.

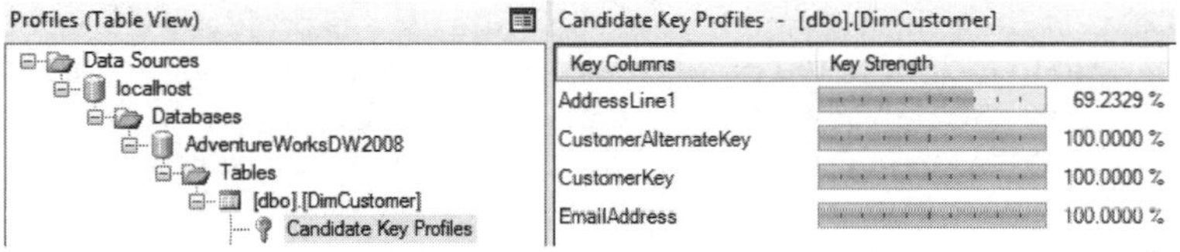

Profiles (Table View)

- Data Sources
  - localhost
    - Databases
      - AdventureWorksDW2008
        - Tables
          - [dbo].[DimCustomer]
            - Candidate Key Profiles

Candidate Key Profiles - [dbo].[DimCustomer]

Key Columns	Key Strength	
AddressLine1		69.2329 %
CustomerAlternateKey		100.0000 %
CustomerKey		100.0000 %
EmailAddress		100.0000 %

Figure 6-4

Column Length Distribution Profiles

The Column Length Distribution Profile Request (see Figure 6-5) visually shows you how long the values in your table are. It's a close relative to the Column Statistics Profile Request, but represents the data in a different way. For each column, you can see the minimum and maximum length. By selecting a given column, you can see the breakdown of how many rows fit each length. In the Data Profiling Task, you can tell the task to ignore leading and trailing spaces.

Column	Minimum Length	Maximum Length
EmailAddress	22	33
EnglishEducation	9	19

Length Distribution - EnglishEducation   1000 Rows

Length	Count	Percentage
15		8253
9		5356
19		1581
11		3294

[EnglishEducation]'s Length = 19

AddressLine1	AddressLine2	BirthDate	CommuteDistance	Custom
2596 Franklin Ca...		12/23/1945	1-2 Milea	AW000
636 Vine Hill Way		2/22/1947	1-2 Miles	AW000

Figure 6-5

Column Null Ratio Profiles

The Column Null Ratio Profile Request is one of the easiest-to-configure profile requests. It simply reviews the table's data to determine the percentage and number of NULLs in your table, as shown in Figure 6-6. The Data Profiling Task has nothing to configure for this profiler request, other than the columns that you want to include in the profile. Like the other requests, you can double-click on a given column name in the Data Profile Viewer and see the rows that are NULL below the column list. This feature is perfect for a data warehouse load where you expect data for each column.

Column	Null Count	Null Percentage
GeographyKey	0	
HouseOwnerFlag	0	
LastName	0	
MaritalStatus	0	
MiddleName	7830	
NameStyle	0	

Figure 6-6

Column Pattern Profiles

One of the most detailed profile types is the Column Pattern Profile. This type of Profile finds patterns in your data and shows you whether any trends exist. For example, a profile with the pattern of \d-\d Miles (as shown in Figure 6-7) has a digit (\d) twice with a hyphen between the two numbers, and the word Miles after that. The output uses regular expressions to symbolize your data.

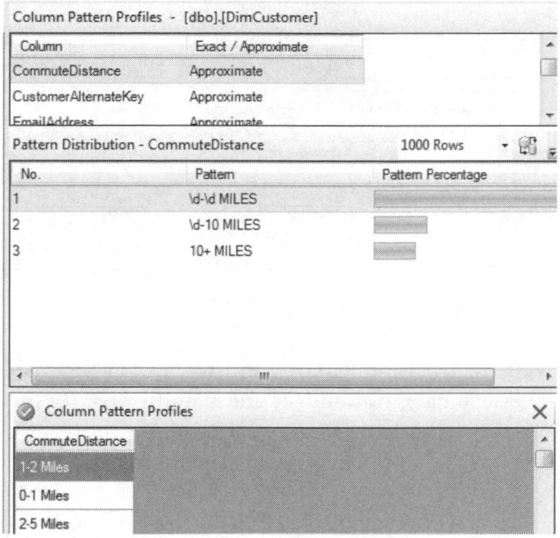

Figure 6-7

You can tweak how many patterns can be returned at a maximum in the Data Profiling Task. You can also tweak what represents a new word with the Delimiters option in the task. Additionally, you can change other settings such as case sensitivity.

Column Statistics Profiles

The best profile to help you tune your physical data structure is the Column Statistics Profile. With this profile (shown in Figure 6-8), you can determine how long your columns should be, based on the data patterns you presently have. The output shows the minimum, maximum, and average (mean) data values.

Column	Minimum	Maximum	Mean
BirthDate	8/13/1910 12:0...	12/26/1980 12:...	
CustomerKey	11000	29483	20241.5
DateFirstPurchase	7/1/2001 12:00:...	7/31/2004 12:0...	
GeographyKey	2	654	257.95628651807
NumberCarsOwned	0	4	1.50270504219...
NumberChildrenAtHo...	0	5	1.00405756329...
TotalChildren	0	5	1.8443518718892
YearlyIncome	10000.0000	170000.0000	57305.7779701...

Figure 6-8

Column Value Distribution Profiles

The Column Value Distribution Profile (see Figure 6-9) shows you the district values for a given column. With this profile, you can find outliers in your data.

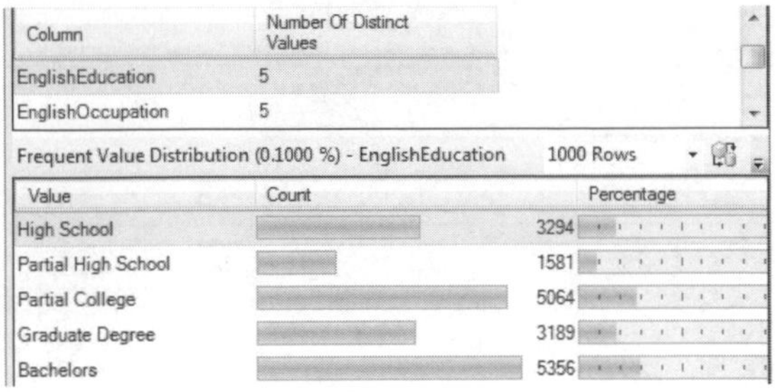

Figure 6-9

By default, the value must represent 0.1 percent of your overall values to show in the list. An e-mail address column in the `Customer` table would never show in this list. If you want to see more discrete values, or have an even more restrictive set of values, you can set the `FrequentValueThreshold` property in the Data Profiling Task to a new percentage, or set the `ValueDistributionOption` to `AllValues`.

Functional Dependency Profiles

A final interesting type of profiling is a Functional Dependency Profile, as shown in Figure 6-10. In this profile, you can determine the loose or tight relationships between the various data elements in your profiled table. For example, in Figure 6-10, you can see that a direct correlation exists between certain first names and a person's gender. As with any name, there are also exceptions, and those are also highlighted in the Profile Viewer.

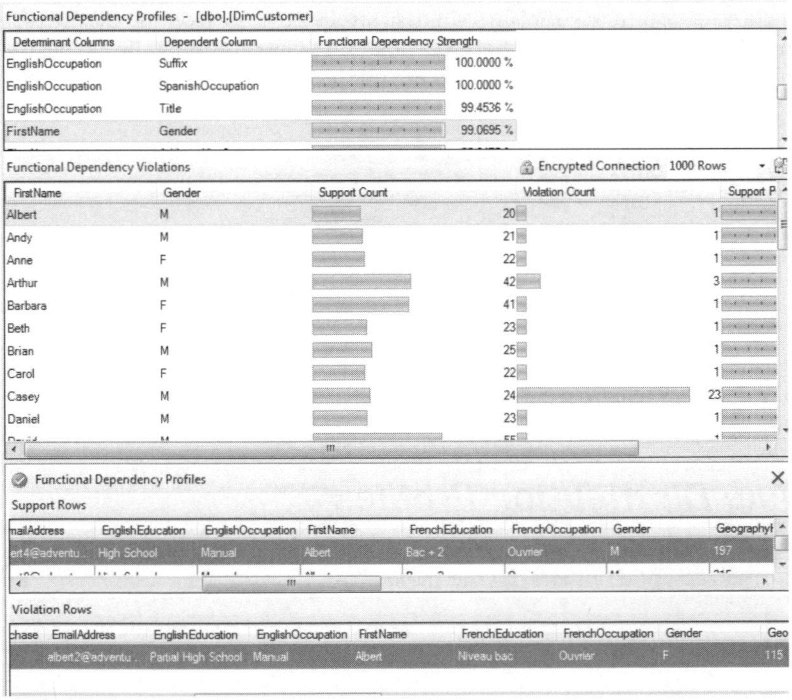

Figure 6-10

Design

Even with the best profiling of your data, bad data will get through your defenses, and you must plan for how to handle the data internally in the data flow. This "Design" section shows you how to use more advanced transforms to scrub your data prior to insertion or acceptance by your destination.

The primary out-of-the-box transform to do this job is the Script transform, which Chapter 11 covers extensively. The other transform that you can use for scrubbing are Fuzzy Grouping and Fuzzy Lookup, which help with data duplication. You'll also see how to take a single file that represents a header and detail data, and load it with SSIS.

Using the Script Transform for Data Scrubbing

The Script transform can handle many scenarios that aren't handled with the out-of-the-box transform. For example, you can use this transform to determine whether a column contains a valid date. If it doesn't meet your criteria, SSIS can remove the row, or change the date to an in-range value. You can also use the transform to remove invalid characters such as Unicode values or unneeded non-alphanumeric values that may be in your text file. You can see this transform in a simple example by downloading CatalogExtract.txt (a comma-delimited file with quoted identifiers) from the Wrox Web site (www.wrox.com). Create a new Data Flow Task in a new package, and connect a new Flat-file Source that points to the CatalogExtract.txt file) to a Script transform.

In the Script transform, select the SellStartDate and ProductNumber as ReadWrite values going into the script in the Input Columns page. In the "Input and Outputs" page under Output 0, add a new output column called SuspectRowFlag, and set it to a Boolean data type.

Go back to the Script page, and set the language to Microsoft Visual Basic 2008. Then, click Edit Script to modify the script. To determine whether a given column is a date, use the IsDate function and pass in Row.SellStartDate.

The following code sets the SellStartDate column to 1/1/2009 if the column has invalid data inside of it for a particular row. The Script transform also creates a new column called SuspectRowFlag and sets it to True if the date is invalid, letting an operator know that this row has had suspect data in it. To fully accomplish this first piece of logic, use the following code inside the ProcessInputRow function, which will run once for each row going through the transform.

```
Public Overrides Sub Input0_ProcessInputRow(ByVal Row As Input0Buffer)

    If IsDate(Row.SellStartDate) = False Then
        Row.SuspectRowFlag = True
        Row.SellStartDate = "1/1/2099"

    Else
        Row.SuspectRowFlag = False
    End If

End Sub

End Class
```

The next problem to solve is having the system remove any non-numeric characters. To do any type of pattern matching like this, you can use *regular expressions* (also referred to *RegEx*). Regular expressions enable you to look for any pattern in data, and replace the invalid characters or validate the data. In SSIS, you can design packages that use RegEx to validate that the e-mail address pattern is valid, and flag those rows or remove/replace invalid characters.

> *More variations of regular expression exist than can be counted, and you can quickly find some great Web sites are out there to guide in you in the creation of these regular expressions.*

To start the Script transform, import `System.Text.RegularExpressions` namespace. You can do this by placing the following simple line with the other `Imports` calls:

```
Imports System.Text.RegularExpressions
```

Next, in the `ProcessInputRow` subroutine, add the following chunk of code. The `Row.ProductNumber_IsNull` statement validates that the data coming in is not `NULL` or blank prior to running the RegEx code.

```
If Row.ProductNumber_IsNull = False Or Row.ProductNumber <> "" Then
    Dim pattern As String = String.Empty
    Dim r As Regex = Nothing
    pattern = "[^0-9]"
    r = New Regex(pattern, RegexOptions.Compiled)
    Row.ProductNumber = Regex.Replace(Row.ProductNumber, pattern, "")
End If
```

You can see in the previous code that the pattern is currently set to `[^0-9]`. The `^` symbol means that numbers are the only acceptable values going in. If you only want alphanumeric characters, you could set this pattern to `[^a-zA-Z0-9]`. If you remove the `^`, it means these are the only characters that are unacceptable and should be removed. `Row.ProductNumber` shows you the column that you're setting in the Script transform.

Following is the entire code that incorporates both examples into the same script:

```
Imports System
Imports System.Data
Imports System.Math
Imports Microsoft.SqlServer.Dts.Pipeline.Wrapper
Imports Microsoft.SqlServer.Dts.Runtime.Wrapper
Imports System.Text.RegularExpressions

<Microsoft.SqlServer.Dts.Pipeline.SSISScriptComponentEntryPointAttribute> _
<CLSCompliant(False)> _
Public Class ScriptMain
    Inherits UserComponent

    Public Overrides Sub Input0_ProcessInputRow(ByVal Row As Input0Buffer)

        If IsDate(Row.SellStartDate) = False Then
            Row.SuspectRowFlag = True
            Row.SellStartDate = "1/1/2099"
```

```
        Else
            Row.SuspectRowFlag = False
        End If

        If Row.ProductNumber_IsNull = False Or Row.ProductNumber <> "" Then
            Dim pattern As String = String.Empty
            Dim r As Regex = Nothing
            pattern = "[^0-9]"
            r = New Regex(pattern, RegexOptions.Compiled)
            Row.ProductNumber = Regex.Replace(Row.ProductNumber, pattern, "")
        End If
    End Sub
End Class
```

Using the Fuzzy Grouping Transform to De-duplicate Data

In project after project, the authors of this book have encountered mainframe systems that, over decades of operation, have let duplicate data get into their tables or files. Often, this happens because an application is poorly engineered and makes adding a new row to a database easier than using an existing valid row. Other times, it may be because of company acquisitions, where the company may have a shared customer base after the merger. In these cases, you can use the Fuzzy Grouping transform to take one or more data streams and de-duplicate the data.

The transform (which is only available in Enterprise Edition) takes an input of data and can de-duplicate the data similar to a soundex routine in .NET languages. But this transform is much more powerful than what you could develop quickly by hand. It comes close to replicating software for which you may pay tens or hundreds of thousands of dollars.

Let's walk through a quick example by loading a small file of leads that the sales department has purchased. In this file, FuzzyGroupingExample.txt (which you can download from www.wrox.com), you can see what to the naked eye appears to be some simple duplication of customers. If this sales department were going to market to this list, then customer Brian Knight would likely receive four brochures, quadrupling the marketing expense.

```
CustomerID,FirstName,LastName,Address
1,Brian,Knight,123 Main Street
2,Brian,Night,123 Main Sreet
3,Bryan,Knight,123 Main Street
4,Brain,Knight,123 Main street
5,Denny,Lee,124 Main Street
```

For this example, follow these steps:

1. Create a new package with a connection manager that points to a Flat-file Connection Manager that uses the FuzzyGroupingExample.txt file.

2. Create a Data Flow Task and drag a Flat-file Source over into that data flow. Configure the Flat-file Source to pull data from your previously created Flat-file Connection Manager.

3. Now comes the fun part. Connect the Flat-file Connection Manager to a Fuzzy Grouping transform and double-click it to configure it. A Fuzzy Grouping transform requires an OLE DB

Connection Manager for you to stage the data into. You can create the connection manager in the Connection Manager tab of the Fuzzy Grouping Transformation Editor.

4. In the Columns page shown in Figure 6-11, select the columns that you want to send into the transform for de-duplication. For this example, select all the columns except the `CustomerID` column, which will just be passed through.

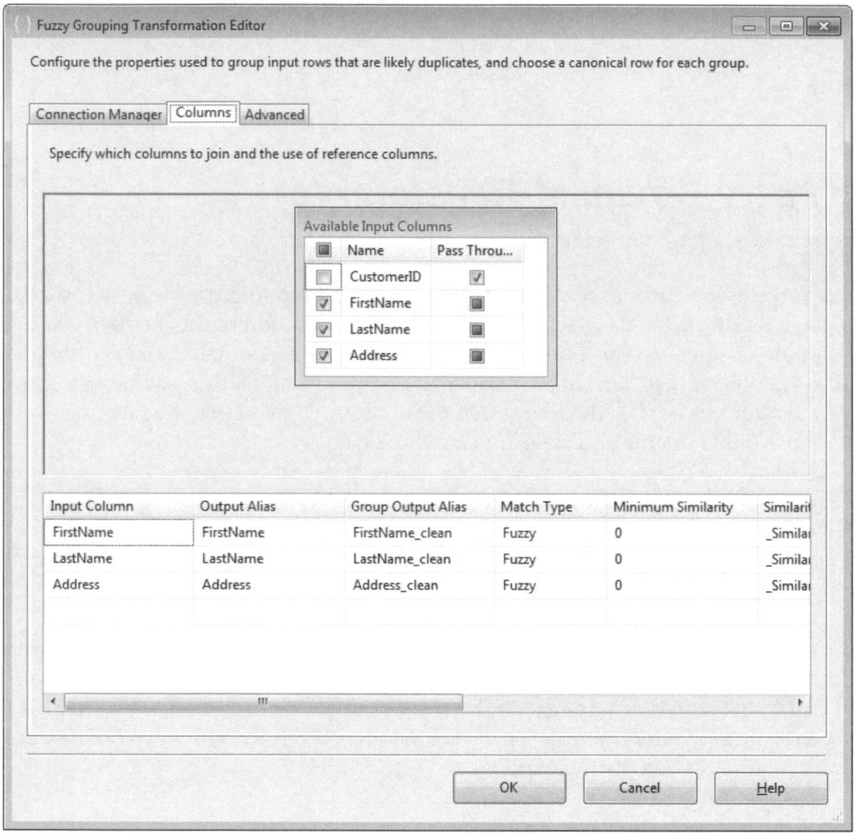

Figure 6-11

Notice that, as you select each of the columns, you can also set the `Minimum Similarity` column. This is a number between `0` and `1`. For example, if you set the `FirstName` column's `Minimum Similarity` to `0.90`, that one column must be at least 90 percent similar to the row with which the transform wants to consolidate the row prior to consolidation.

You can also see in Figure 6-11 that for each column that you select, a new column will be outputted, showing how similar in percentage the row was to the winning row for that given column. For the `FirstName` column, this column is called `_Similarity_FirstName` by default. Additionally, a column shows you the new, clean version of the column after consolidation. For the `FirstName` column, the new column is called `FirstName_clean`.

In the Advanced page (see Figure 6-12), you can set some row-level settings. The _key_in and _key_out columns referenced in the figure show which row was chosen as the winner in a consolidation of rows. The _score shows you how similar the losing row was to the winner. You can type new names for these columns in the Advanced page if you choose to do so.

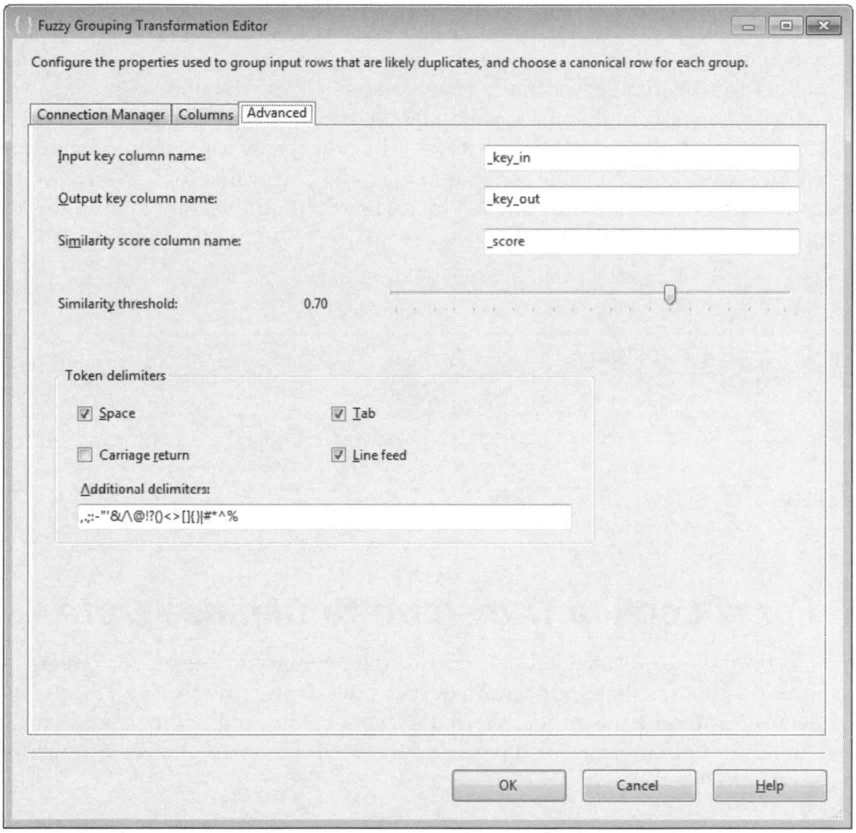

Figure 6-12

The most important setting on this page is the "Similarity threshold." It tells the transform how similar the duplicate row must be to the winning row in order for a consolidation to occur. This percentage is in addition to the column-by-column thresholds in the previous Columns screen. For the purpose of this example, set the "Similarity threshold" to 70 percent, or 0.70.

The last option on this screen is the "Token delimiters." These show which characters represent a new word in a string. For example, does Brian&Knight represent two words or one? Removing as many token delimiters as you can to help with performance of the transform is a good idea.

> It's critical to note that the data for this transform is being written to the transform's connection manager's TempDB database. Be sure to tune this system's TempDB and ensure the database is large enough, or you'll see a slowdown in an already-slow transform.

When you run the package, notice the _key_in column coming out of the Fuzzy Grouping transform is a sequential number from 1 to however many rows you have in the data flow. The _key_out column shows you to which _key_in column the row should be matched. For example, as you can see in Figure 6-13, _key_in 1 through 4 all really match to row 1. The other three rows should be disposed of later in a Conditional Split. If the _key_in value is equal to the _key_out value for a given row, then it is the master record, and similar rows will be matched to it. The "Solution" section later in this chapter provides more details on Fuzzy Grouping.

_key_in	_key_...	_score	CustomerID	FirstName	LastName	Address	FirstName_clean	LastName_clean	Address_clean
1	1	1	1	Brian	Knight	123 Main Street	Brian	Knight	123 Main Street
2	1	0.882605	2	Brian	Night	123 Main Sreet	Brian	Knight	123 Main Street
3	1	0.8832303	3	Bryan	Knight	123 Main Street	Brian	Knight	123 Main Street
4	1	0.7337576	4	Brain	Knight	123 Main Street	Brian	Knight	123 Main Street
5	5	1	5	Denny	Lee	124 Main street	Denny	Lee	124 Main street

Figure 6-13

Using the Fuzzy Lookup Transform to Cleanse Data

After the data has been de-duplicated, other duplicate data may try to enter your system. At that point, you must make a decision whether you want to update the existing row that's already in your system, insert it as a new row, or ignore the duplicate. That's where the Fuzzy Lookup transform comes in to save the day. The Fuzzy Lookup transform performs the same action as a Lookup transform, but through loose, fuzzy means.

In Figure 6-14, you can see a spreadsheet called USCustomers.xls, which you can download from the Wrox Web site (www.wrox.com). You also want to download BIDemo.bak and restore it onto your development database to see the full example. The BIDemo database contains a list of customers that you currently have in your system. The spreadsheet contains a list of customers where you want to look up their CustomerIDs column against the BIDemo database prior to import.

FirstName	LastName	AddressLine1	AddressLine2	City
Lauren	Walker	4785 Scott Street		Bremerton
Ian	Jenkins	7902 Hudson Avenue		Lebanon
Sydney	Bennett	9011 Tank Drive		Redmonds
Chloe	Young	244 Willow Pass Road		Burbank
Wyatt	Hill	9666 Northridge Ct.		Imperial Beach
Destiny	Wylson	8148 W. Lake Dr.		Beaverton
Ethan	Zhang	1769 Nicholas Drive		Bellingham
Seth	Edwards	4499 Valley Crest		Bellflower
Russell	Xie	8734 Oxford Pl.		Concord
Jennifer	Russell	3981 Augustine Drive		National City
Jesse	Murphy	3350 Kingswood Circle		Tacoma
Amanda	Carter	5826 Escobar		Glandale
Megan	Sanchez	1397 Paraiso Ct.		Los Angeles
Nathan	Simmons	1170 Shaw Rd		Glendale
Carol	Rai	6064 Madrid		Chula Vista
Ana	Price	1660 Stonyhill Circle		San Diego
Noah	Powell	9794 Marion Ct		Portland
Angela	Murphy	4927 Virgil Street	# 22	Redmond
Chase	Reed	2721 Alexander Pl.		Downey
Jessica	Henderson	9343 Ironwood Way		La Jolla
Grace	Butler	4739 Garden Ave.		Lebanon

Figure 6-14

To accomplish this job, you do a lookup against the inCustomers table in the BIDemo database with all the columns in the spreadsheet to retrieve the CustomerID. Notice in Figure 6-14 that some of the data is misspelled (rows are highlighted). For example, a "Destiny Wilson" is in the database, but not a "Wylson."

To prepare for this example, follow these steps:

1. Create a new package and a new Data Flow Task.

2. Create an OLE DB Connection Manager to the recently restored BIDemo database and an Excel Connection Manager that points to USCustomers.xls.

3. Finish by creating an Excel Source in the data flow, connecting it to the Excel Connection Manager you just created and to Sheet1$ of the spreadsheet.

The problem with the Fuzzy Grouping and Lookup transform is that they are slower because of having to land the data on the server prior to a comparison. Because of this slowdown with the Fuzzy Lookup transform, you'll want to do a Lookup transform prior to the Fuzzy one to match as many rows as you can through exact matches in order to send fewer rows into the Fuzzy Lookup and help it scale better.

To do the Lookup transform and the Fuzzy Lookup, follow these steps:

1. Drag a Lookup transform over to the data flow design pane.

2. In the Connection page, select the BIDemo Connection Manager and the dbo.InCustomers table from the table drop-down box.

3. In the Columns page, match each of the columns where the columns names are identical, as shown in Figure 6-15. The output that should be checked from the match is the CustomerID.

4. In the General page, select "Redirect rows to no match output" for the bottom redirection option.

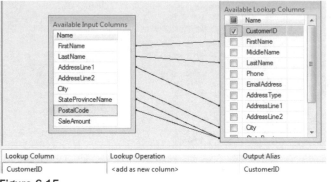

Figure 6-15

5. Drag a Fuzzy Lookup onto the design pane and connect it to the No Match output from the Lookup transform. This sends any rows that don't match the exact match to the Fuzzy Lookup transform.

6. Just as with the Lookup transform, point the connection manager to the BIDemo database in the Reference Table tab, and the "Reference table name" drop-down box to the InCustomers table.

7. In the Columns page, select CustomerID, similar to Figure 6-15.

8. On the Advanced tab (shown in Figure 6-16), set how similar the input row must be to a row in the reference table prior to declaring it a match.

    By default, the "Similarity threshold" is set to 0.00, which means you want the Fuzzy Lookup to pick the best one row. A good threshold to start at is 0.80, and then inch the setting one way or the other. The farther right you move the slider bar, the closer to perfect the match must be prior to returning the CustomerID. If a match is not found within the "Similarity threshold," then the CustomerID will be set to NULL.

Figure 6-16

9. Connect both the outputs from the Lookup and Fuzzy Lookup transform to a Union All transform. When you run the transform, you can see the Fuzzy Lookup transform output produce a number of new columns if you add a Data Viewer between the Fuzzy Lookup and the Union All transform. As shown in Figure 6-17, one of these columns, called _Similarity, shows how similar the entire row is to the row that it was matched against. The _Confidence column shows how confident the Fuzzy Lookup is that it is the same row. For example, you may have a row with the value "Jake" "Smith" for the first and last name columns, respectively. Then, you try to match it against "Smith" and "Jake" for the first and last name. The row won't be similar at all, but the Fuzzy Lookup may be reasonably confident that it is the same row. You can also see a _Similarity_ColumnName for each column, which gives you a column-by-column similarity score.

CustomerID	_Similarity	_Confidence	_Similarity_FirstName	_Similarity_LastName
11013	0.9596...	0.5139394	1	1
11014	0.9840...	0.5292256	1	1
11021	0.9788...	0.5318736	1	0.8316139
11024	0.9374...	0.5025135	1	1
11041	0.9822...	0.5168281	1	1
11067	0.8308...	0.6009938	0.3298856	0.3260759

Figure 6-17

Beyond the Advanced tab in the Fuzzy Lookup transform, you can also customize how similar each individual column must be to the reference table on top of the "Similarity threshold." You can do this customization in the Columns tab by right-clicking on one of the connecting lines, and selecting Edit Mapping. For example, if you set the LastName column to 0.90, and the overall similarity threshold is 0.80, then the LastName column must be at least a 90 percent match to the LastName column on the reference table, and the entire row must be at least an 80 percent match.

A more advanced setting you can turn on is Exhaustive, which performs a more intensive check on your data prior to declaring a match. This setting is in the transform's properties window and is turned off by default. If you turn it on, you may experience a severe slowdown in the transform.

One way to speed up the transform is to materialize the data into a more permanent table. You can do so in the Reference Table tab by selecting Store New Index and then, in subsequent loads, select Use Existing Index. When you use this method, the table that was previously being materialized at run-time will be loaded once, and reused as often as you like. As you can imagine, this index table is only as good as the last time it was refreshed, and will become stale quickly. If you want to keep the index synchronized with the source table, you can select the "Maintain stored index" option, which creates triggers on the source system table. Using this option, as you can imagine, creates latency on your source table. It also requires that Common Language Runtime (CLR) be turned on for your SQL Server instance, because the trigger uses CLR stored procedures to synchronize the table.

Dealing with Multiple Record Types in a Single File

Often, mainframe developers send you a single file that contains information about multiple tables inside the single file, similar to those shown in Figure 6-18. In this extract, you can see in the first column two record types: Record type 1 is the order header and record type 2 is the individual line items for the order. You can download this comma-separated value file (CH6_OrderRecordExtract.csv) from the Wrox Web site (www.wrox.com).

1	43659		0	SO43659	PO522145787		
2	43659	4911-403C-98	1		776	2024.994	2024.994
2	43659	4911-403C-98	3		777	2024.994	6074.982
2	43659	4911-403C-98	1		778	2024.994	2024.994
2	43659	4911-403C-98	1		771	2039.994	2039.994
2	43659	4911-403C-98	1		772	2039.994	2039.994
2	43659	4911-403C-98	2		773	2039.994	4079.988
2	43659	4911-403C-98	1		774	2039.994	2039.994
2	43659	4911-403C-98	3		714	28.8404	86.5212
2	43659	4911-403C-98	1		716	28.8404	28.8404
2	43659	4911-403C-98	6		709	5.7	34.2
2	43659	4911-403C-98	2		712	5.1865	10.373
2	43659	4911-403C-98	4		711	20.1865	80.746
1	43660		1	SO43660	PO18850127500		
2	43660	6431-4D57-83	1		762	419.4589	419.4589
2	43660	6431-4D57-83	1		758	874.794	874.794

Figure 6-18

This section discusses this common example often seen with mainframe extracts, and explains how to parse the file into multiple tables. This example has been simplified dramatically to fit into a chapter, so many of the performance considerations are being ignored in an effort to just show the functionality of how to master this problem.

As you can see in Figure 6-18 (the file being used in this example), there are two orders, which are indicated by the first column being set to 1. Under those two orders are many line items.

You can solve this parsing issue in several ways. In this case, you make a pass at the file to load it into multiple raw files. The second pass of the raw files loads those files into SQL Server tables. Prior to starting this example, run `Chapter6_OrderTables.sql`, which creates the necessary tables in SQL Server. You could, indeed, load the data directly to the target tables in one pass, but certain advantages exist for a two-step process, depending on the business and technical requirements.

One advantage of not making this process two-step is that you only have to load the data into the server's memory buffers a single time. On the contrary, if you were to make two passes at the data, you will ultimately slow down your processing.

The advantage of making the two passes at the data is for both the restartability and availability of the data. If the loading of the data into the production tables were to fail, you would still have the data massaged and in easy-to-access intermediate files. If this first process took three hours and the second pass failed, then all you must do then is execute the second pass, or place checkpoint files on the process to control that execution logic.

Another advantage is availability. In some cases, you may not be able to load the data into the production tables during operational hours. With a two-step process, you could stage the data into raw files, and perform all the transformations during operational hours. Then, during your load window, you would take the final step.

In some cases, you must stage the data in a table or a Raw or text file. Those scenarios usually consist of very complex fixed-width or ragged-right data where the number and length of the columns is variable. The main problem is the length of each column. If that is variable, and multiple record types are in the file, then you must stage each record type into its own file and use a Derived Column transform and the `SUBSTRING()` function to break up the data.

This example assumes that you must break the data into two stages. However, as you can see, this decision depends on your business requirements.

Start stage 1, which loads the raw file by creating a new package called `Chapter6-MultiFileType` `.dtsx` and add a new Data Flow Task onto the control flow.

Next, create a Flat-file Connection Manager that points to `CH6_OrderRecordExtract.csv`. This comma-delimited file contains multiple record types and has no header row. The first column (Column 0) contains the record type. The record type specifies if the row is a header row or detailed data. As you can see in the Columns page (shown in Figure 6-18), Columns 5 and 6 have no data for record type 1.

Although most of the data is not shared between the various record types, a key exists that pairs the records together. In this case, it's the `OrderNumber` column, which is in Column 1. Before exiting the Connection Manager screen, update the common columns to the proper column names and data type.

Change the name of the first column to `RecordType` and the second column to `OrderNumber` in the Advanced page for the Name property, as shown in Figure 6-19. Each column will be a signed integer (`DT_I4`). The last two columns (Columns 5 and 6) are named `UnitPrice` and `LineItemPrice`, respectively, and need to be both be set to Currency (`DT_CY`) as the data type. Leave the other column names and data types alone.

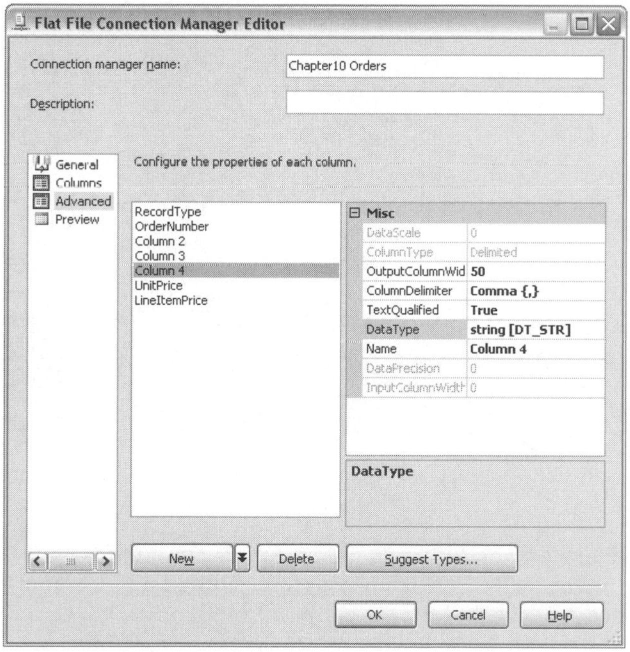

Figure 6-19

Inside the Data Flow Task you created earlier, you're ready to begin using the Flat-file Connection Manager by creating a Flat-file Source in the data flow. Point the source to the Flat-file Connection Manager you just created.

Create a new Conditional Split transform with three conditions, including the default output. The first condition, Orders, will contain all the records that have a RecordType of 1. The expression RecordType == 1 will suffice to only grab the orders. To get the Order Details case, you can use the expression RecordType == 2. The default condition needs to be called Unhandled, and will catch any potential NULL record types or bad data that doesn't meet your requirements. Figure 6-20 shows the final configuration of the transform.

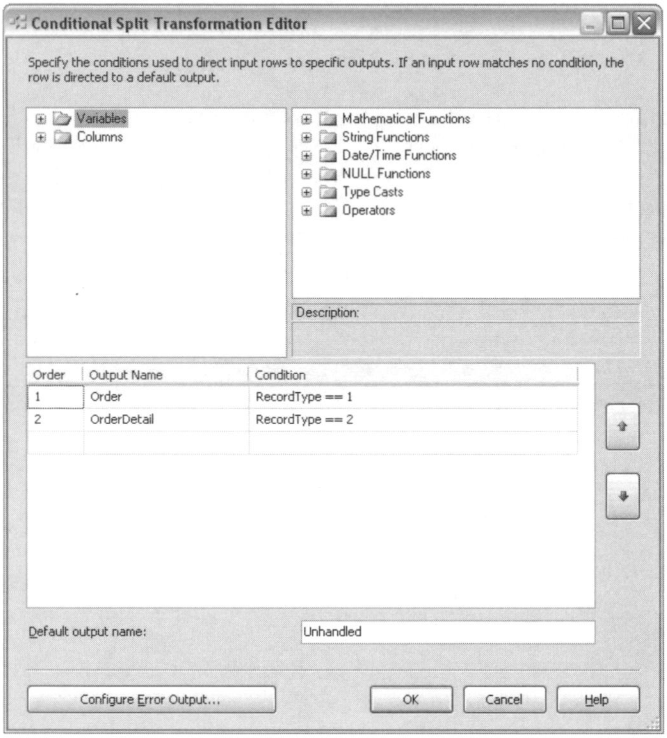

Figure 6-20

Next, create a Data Conversion transform and drag the Order output from the Conditional Split onto the newly created transform. Inside the Data Conversion transform, select Columns 2, 3, and 4 from the Available Input Columns. Change the Output Alias to InternetOrderFG for Column 2, SalesOrderNumber for Column 3, and PurchaseOrderNumber for Column 4. Set the Data Type for InternetOrderFG to Boolean, and the other two columns to a 15-character string, as shown in Figure 6-21.

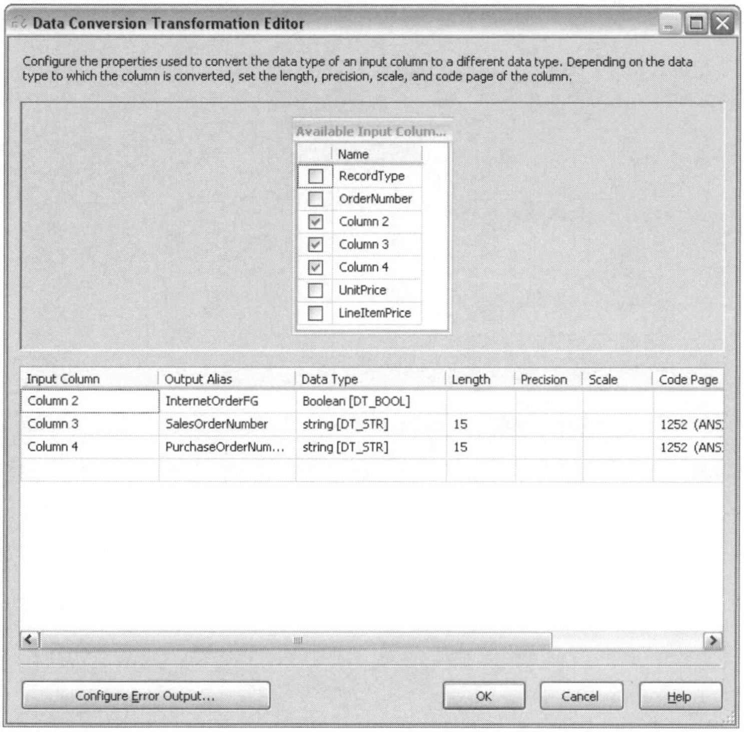

Figure 6-21

Drag over a second Data Conversion transform and connect it to the Order Details output from the Conditional Split transform. Inside the Data Conversion transform, select Columns 2, 3, and 4, as shown in Figure 6-22. Set the Output Alias to CarrierTrackingID for Column 2, OrderQuantity for Column 3, and ProductID for Column 4. For the Data Type use a 20-character string (DT_STR) for CarrierTrackingID and Integer (DT_I4) for the other two columns. Having a Data Conversion transform here, not after the source, is important because the data types will be different for each record type.

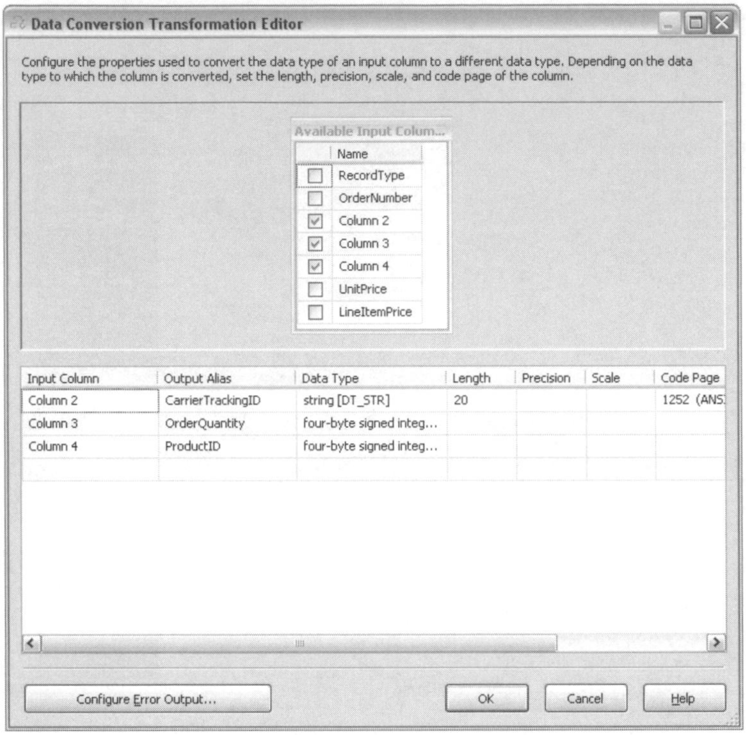

Figure 6-22

With the columns now converted, you're ready to write the data to your raw files. Drag over the first raw file destination and connect it to the Data Conversion that comes out of the Order data. In the Component Properties tab of the raw file destination, ensure that the Access Mode property is set to FileName. Type **C:\Projects\OrderData.raw** (ensure that the C:\Projects folder exists) for the FileName property, and change the WriteOption property to Create Always.

These options will create the .raw file each time the package runs, and you will create a process later to remove the file upon successful completion of the package. This raw file is an encrypted store for your data that contains the data and metadata from a piece of the flat file. In the Input Columns tab, select the OrderNumber, InternetOrderFG, SalesOrderNumber, and PurchaseOrderNumber columns.

Drag over another raw file destination and connect it to the OrderDetails output from the Data Conversion transform. In the destination, configure it just like you did the last raw file destination, except have the destination create the C:\Projects\OrderDetailsData.raw file. This time, in the Input Columns tab, select the OrderNumber, UnitPrice, LineItemPrice, CarrierTrackingID, OrderQuantity, and ProductID columns.

Using the Raw File

Now that you've transformed the data and written two raw files with the first pass, you're ready to consume the raw files. The first process could have been accomplished during a non-maintenance window, and the second process could optionally be untethered from this package and executed independently during the maintenance window.

1. Create another Data Flow Task in the same package and drag a Success (green) precedence constraint from the first Data Flow Task to it.

2. Inside the Data Flow tab for the newly created task, create a new raw file source and name it `Order Extract`. Inside the source, set the `AccessMode` option to `File Name` and type **C:\Projects\OrderData.raw** for the `FileName` property.

3. Drag over an OLE DB Destination. In this destination's Connection Manager page, select the `Order` table in the `AdventureWorks2008` database from the table drop-down box. You must create this table by running `Chapter6_OrderTables.sql` from the Wrox Web site (www.wrox.com) if you haven't already run it. Of course, you will also have to create a connection manager to the `AdventureWorks2008` database. In the Mappings page, the columns will not line up exactly, so you may have to connect them manually. Your final configuration should look similar to Figure 6-23.

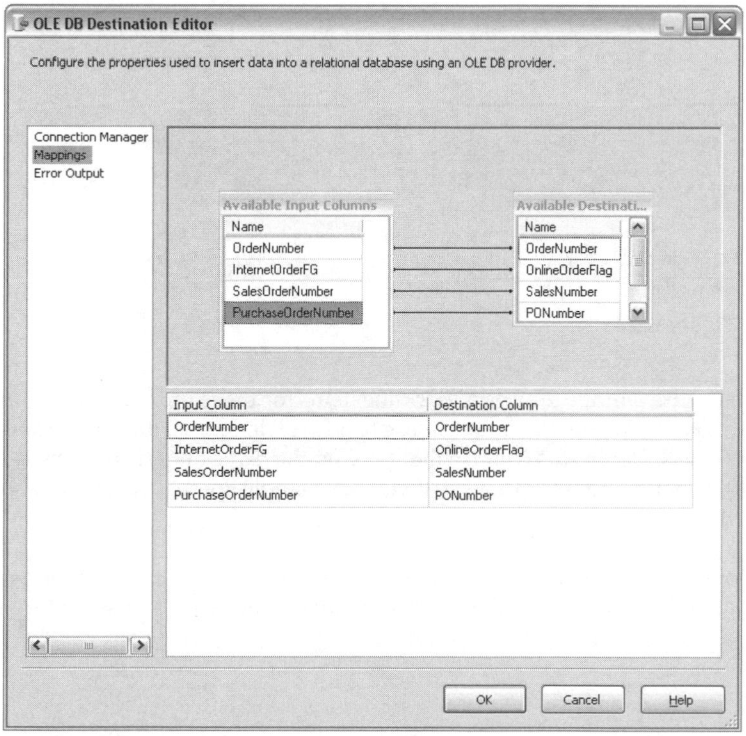

Figure 6-23

For phase 2 of the processing, in the control flow, create a last Data Flow Task and name the task `OrderDetails`. Connect the `Orders` task to the `OrderDetails` task with a Success precedence constraint. In the newly created Data Flow Task, add a raw file source. This time set the raw file source to the `FileName` property to `C:\Projects\OrderDetailsData.raw` in the Component Properties page.

Connect the raw file source to a new OLE DB destination. This time, point the destination to the `OrderDetail` table in the `AdventureWorks2008` connection manager. The Mappings page should align perfectly, and only the `OrderLineNumber` column needs to be set to Ignore.

You're now ready to execute the package. The first Data Flow Task should look similar to Figure 6-24, although your numbers will not match what's in the figure.

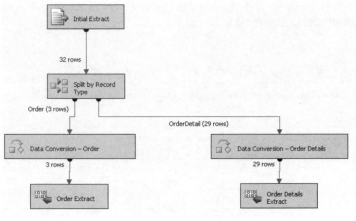

Figure 6-24

As you can see, there are 3 order records and 29 line items for those orders. In the Control Flow tab, you should have three total tasks, but you may choose to add a File System Task to remove the raw files after they've been consumed. Doing this will use the space on the drive only during the execution of the package. This step is not mandatory, though, if you have ample space, because you specified that you wanted the raw file to be always created.

One additional consideration is that, if later on you choose to select data out of the `Order` table, you will need to encapsulate this table in quotation marks or square brackets, because `Order` is a reserved word in T-SQL.

Solution

Now that you've seen many solutions to solve common data-cleansing problems, the time has come to take the next step and build a complete solution. In this solution, the `inCustomers` table in the `BIDemo` database has many duplicate rows caused by years of application neglect. You can download this database from the Wrox Web site (`bidemo.bak` is a SQL Server 2008 backup) at `www.wrox.com`. In this solution, you take the rows in inCustomers, group them together through fuzzy means, and pick which one is the winning row, based on a series of evidence.

Fuzzy Grouping will only be one influencer in your decision of which row is the winning one. After you have the rows grouped with Fuzzy Grouping, you use a voting system to pick the winner. A fuzzy match will give the winning row two points. Then, for each incident in a separate table, you give another point. Whichever row has the most points after those two business rules wins. Normally, you may have a series of rules instead of just these two. You remove the duplicate rows with a Conditional Split prior to insertion into a new table.

To start this example, create a new package with a Data Flow Task. Create an OLE DB Source inside that Data Flow Task and connect the source to the BIDemo database. In the Source, configure the "Data access mode" to be a SQL command and type the following query in the query window:

```
SELECT TOP 1000 * from incustomers
```

Back in the data flow, connect the source to a new Fuzzy Grouping transform. In the transform, use the BIDemo connection manager in the Connection Manager tab. In the Columns tab, select all the columns except the CustomerID, AddressLine2, and AddressType. In the Advanced tab, slide the "Similarity threshold" to 0.70 (70 percent). Keep in mind that the Fuzzy Grouping will not be the only factor to consider when doing the match. Instead, you will also use other evidence of which row is the winning row.

With the Fuzzy Grouping transform now configured, you're now ready to start the scoring system you're going to use throughout this data flow. To do this, drag a Derived Column transform over and connect it to the Fuzzy Grouping transform. Configure the Derived Column transform to create a new column called RowScore. You will use this RowScore column to determine which row is the appropriate winning row.

For the Expression column, type the following code as shown in Figure 6-25:

```
_key_in == _key_out ? 2 : 0
```

Derived Column Name	Derived Column	Expression	Data Type
RowScore	<add as new column>	_key_in == _key_out ? 2 : 0	four-byte signed integer [...

Figure 6-25

This expression code states that if the row is the master row coming from the Fuzzy Grouping, then it will get two points. Otherwise, if the row is pointing to another master row, it will receive zero points.

The next step is to see how many account transactions all the customers have had. For each transaction the customer has had, the customer will receive a point for the RowScore. You determine the number of transactions by using a Lookup transform. In the Lookup transform, configure the General page to "Ignore failures" from the "Specify how to handle rows with no matching entries" drop-down box. In the Connection page, use the following query:

```
SELECT     COUNT(*) TotalTransactions, CustomerID
FROM       CustomerAccountTransactions
group by customerid
```

This query shows you the number of transactions the individual accounts have had by `CustomerID`. In the Columns page shown in Figure 6-26, select the `TotalTransactions` column. You'll use it later to add points to the `RowScore` column. Before exiting, ensure that you're ignoring failures in the General page. Otherwise, you may have issues with those rows where there are no matches.

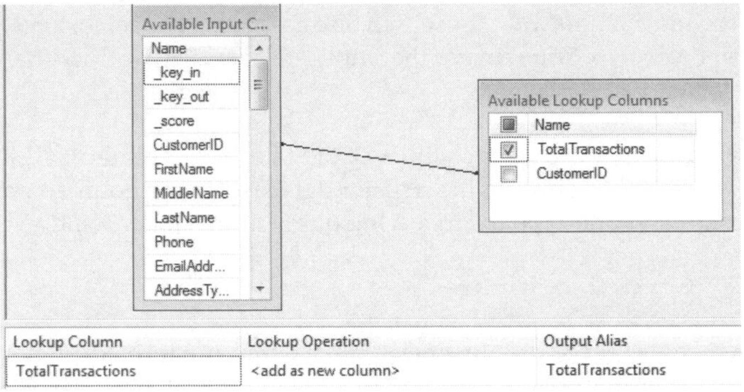

Figure 6-26

Drag a new Derived Column transform over and connect it to the match output off the Lookup transform. In the Derived Column transform, set the Derived Column drop-down box to "Replace RowScore." Then, use the following expression for the Expression, which will add the number of transactions to the overall `RowScore`:

```
RowScore + (ISNULL(TotalTransactions) ? 0 : TotalTransactions).
```

Figure 6-27

As you can see in Figure 6-27, the `ISNULL` conditional statement wrap ensures that nulls are replaced with a `0`.

You could use this same framework in applying additional business rules if you wanted. Perhaps you could query other tables such as comments on the customer's account or sales over the past three months.

To complete the example, you must order all the rows by their `_key_out` column and `RowScore` by using a Sort transform. After you drag the Sort transform over and connect it to the newly created Derived Column transform, select `_key_out` and `RowScore` (in that order). Set the Sort Type to descending for the `RowScore` column, as shown in Figure 6-28.

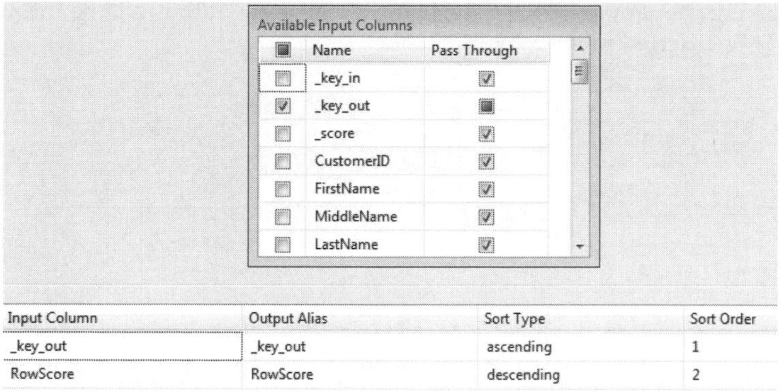

Input Column	Output Alias	Sort Type	Sort Order
_key_out	_key_out	ascending	1
RowScore	RowScore	descending	2

Figure 6-28

You want to have the data sorted prior to the data going into the Script transform. In the Script transform, you select the appropriate row grouped by _key_out based on who has the highest RowScore. Drag a Script transform over and connect it to the Sort transform.

In the Script Transformation Editor, go to the "Input and Outputs" and add a new output column called WinningRow, which is a Boolean column. Next, click Edit Script in the Script page. In the script, you first need to initialize a variable called MyKey to -1. This must be right above the ProcessInputRow subroutine.

```
Dim MyKey As Integer = -1
```

Next, add the following code in the ProcessInputRow subroutine. Because the rows are already ordered, the MyKey variable holds the previous row's _key_out data. If the _key_out does not match the variable, then it must be the master record, and the WinningRow column will be set to True.

```
Public Overrides Sub Input0_ProcessInputRow(ByVal Row As Input0Buffer)


    If MyKey = -1 Then ' Handles the first row in overall system
        Row.WinningRow = True
    Else

        If MyKey <> Row.keyout Then ' Row must be the first row in grouping
            Row.WinningRow = True
        End If ' End row must be the first row in grouping

    End If ' End Handles the first row

    MyKey = Row.keyout

End Sub
```

Now that you know which row is the winning row, you must remove the duplicate rows. You can do so with a Conditional Split transformation. After you connect it to the Script transform, configure the Conditional Split transform as shown in Figure 6-29. Create two conditions: one called Winning Rows and one called `Duplicate Rows`. Rows in the `Duplicate Rows` output will be thrown away, but they could just as easily be inserted into a reference table.

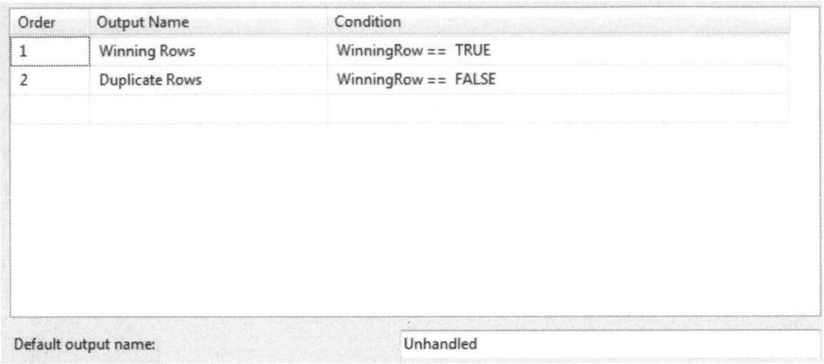

Order	Output Name	Condition
1	Winning Rows	WinningRow == TRUE
2	Duplicate Rows	WinningRow == FALSE

Default output name:	Unhandled

Figure 6-29

The last step is to connect the `Winning Rows` output from the Conditional Split transform to the OLE DB Destination. Configure the OLE DB Destination to insert into the `inCustomersClean` table. Run the package, and the results should look like Figure 6-30. As you can see, three rows are removed prior to insertion into the `inCustomersClean` table.

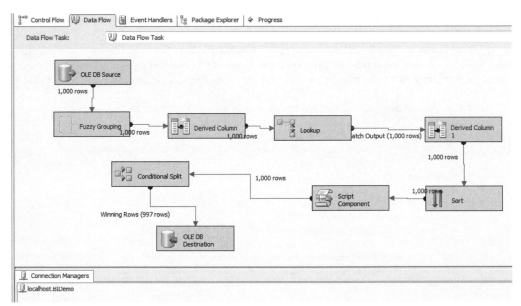

Figure 6-30

Summary

In this chapter, you saw how to handle many common scenarios for bad data. You cleansed data as it came in by using the Script transform and regular expressions. You also used tools such as Fuzzy Grouping and Fuzzy Lookup components to help you de-duplicate your data quickly, or retrieve data through less-than-exact means. Those two transform (which are only available in Enterprise Edition) provide a powerful tool in the battle to cleanse your data better than ever before.

In Chapter 7, you'll see how to solve data warehouse dimension ETL requirements in an SSIS solution.

7

Dimension Table ETL

The next three chapters focus on the problems and solutions of data warehouse *extraction, transformation, and loading (ETL)* and business intelligence (BI) processing. This chapter examines how to process dimension tables using SSIS. Dimension tables are a data warehouse concept, which this chapter describes. The chapter then discusses how to move data from your data sources to your data warehouse dimension tables. Similar to this, Chapter 8 reviews the same things, but only applied for fact tables. Chapter 9 also covers BI, but looks at the integration of SSIS with SQL Server Analysis Services (SSAS). Integration between SSIS and SSAS involves cube and dimension processing, as well as SSAS data mining querying and training.

This chapter is divided into two Problem-Design-Solution sections. The first lays out the fundamental dimension ETL problem and then walks you through the basic design and solution with SSIS. The second problem deals with advanced dimension ETL that you may experience when dealing with high volumes or more complex dimension types.

Problem — Fundamental Dimension ETL

Arguably, when looking at the development time investment required for a data warehouse ETL solution, dimension table ETL takes the longest and is the most complex component. You may have experienced this time investment, especially when the requirements call for tracking the history of changes that a dimension goes through.

Does this user requirement sound familiar: "I want to be able to look at the history of list price changes for a product so I can understand the supply and demand curve"? In other words, what the business user is really asking is how the change in list price affects sales historically. To handle this type of request, a single product must have a new version created in the dimension table any time the list price changes. Furthermore, the sales activity (tracked in the appropriate fact table) must be associated with the right dimension record for the sales (the one with the list price at that point in time). Sound complicated? Add to that a second or third dimension attribute change (like department) that must be tracked historically, and soon you will be pulling your hair out!

The good news is that SSIS comes with out-of-the-box functionality to handle dimension scenarios just like this one. Specifically, it comes with a data flow transformation called the Slowly Changing Dimension (SCD) Wizard. As you will see, using the wizard has advantages, as well as some limitations you must consider, and ways to work through those limitations to create a scalable dimension process in your ETL. This Problem-Design-Solution section deals with using the SCD Wizard to handle your fundamental dimension ETL.

But, before going any further with the SSIS designs and solutions for dimension table ETL, let's first step back and review the basics of dimension tables, and some of the challenges with ETL design and the tracking of history.

Dimensions: The Basics

This chapter focuses on dimension ETL. But, in order to understand the full picture of dimension ETL, some dimension theory is required. For a complete picture of a dimension design, the following are the best resources to read:

❑   *The Data Warehouse Toolkit: The Complete Guide to Dimension Modeling, Second Edition*, by Ralph Kimball and Margy Ross (Indianapolis: Wiley, 2002)

❑   *Data Warehouse Design Solutions,* by Christopher Adamson and Michael Venerable (Indianapolis: Wiley, 1998)

For the purposes of this discussion on dimension ETL, the following is a high-level summary.

The *dimension* itself is an organized grouping of categories and properties about a particular entity. These categories and properties are called *attributes*, and they form hierarchies with levels and members used to slice and query a cube or *fact table*.

For example, Table 7-1 shows data focusing on geography. The attributes are the Country, State/Province, and City, which combine together because of their relationship to one another.

Table 7-1

Country	State/Province	City
Germany	Bavaria	Augsburg
Germany	Bavaria	Munich
Germany	Niedersachsen	Hannover
United States	California	Palo Alto
United States	California	Woodland Hills
United States	New York	Cheektowaga
United States	New York	Lake George

Naturally, this data can be used together to create a hierarchy, which provides drill paths to data and the capability to slice and dice data based on certain records. Figure 7-1 shows one of the hierarchies within this geography dimension. The members are the names of the countries, state/provinces, and cities. The hierarchy is made up of levels that usually correspond to the column names used in the hierarchy.

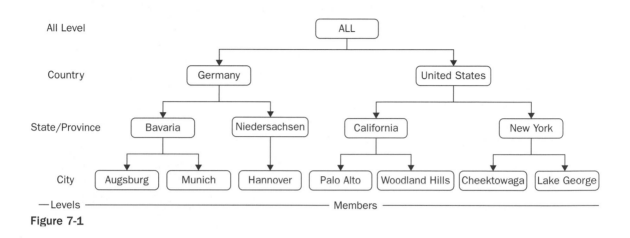

Figure 7-1

In this example, the hierarchy is made up of the levels Country, State/Province, and City, in that order. When querying the dimension, the lower levels roll up to higher levels, so analysis can be done drilling up or down the hierarchy.

Understanding how dimensions relate to fact tables is also important. Chapter 8 examines the topic of fact table ETL, but some background in dimension-to-fact relationships can help you grasp the ETL requirements for dimension processing. Because the AdventureWorksDW2008 sample databases are used to illustrate this chapter, Figure 7-2 shows one of the fact tables with its related dimension. It is an example of a single fact table, FactResellerSales, one of the six fact tables in the AdventureWorksDW2008 database.

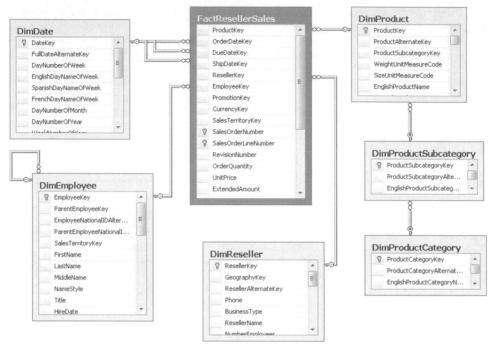

Figure 7-2

Related to this fact table is a product dimension, a reseller dimension, an employee dimension, and a date dimension (plus others not shown). In all, they are typical dimensions. You might notice that the product dimension has multiple tables associated with it in what's called a *snowflake design*. The employee dimension is also a different type of dimension, called a *parent-child*, given its self-referencing nature.

Each dimension contains a *surrogate key*, as shown in Figure 7-2. The surrogate keys are identifiable by the `Key` suffix in the column name (such as `ProductKey`). This defines the primary key for the table itself, and relates to the fact table foreign key field. Typically, these data types are numeric, most likely integer and auto-incrementing (called an `IDENTITY` column in SQL Server). Some designers prefer to use a unique identifier (GUID), but these column types are wider (16 bytes) and more difficult to read. The best-practice recommendation is to use integer data types — either a 1-, 2-, 4-, or 8-byte integer based on the number of projected members within the dimension table.

The business keys are still tracked in the dimension table, but are not marked as the primary key to identify uniqueness, nor are they used for referential integrity in the database. Instead, they help identify source system data associations for the ETL. In the `AdventureWorksDW2008` database, each dimension's business key is called the `[DimensionName]AlternateKey` for standardization, but simply contains the source system's primary key value. This business key column is sometimes called the *candidate key*. Most dimension tables name the business key with the same name as the source system name.

A surrogate key, more precisely, is a single column with a value that is unrelated to the dimension table's members. These keys provide the central foundation to dimensional modeling, critical to tracking history and designing a BI system that performs well. Here are a few advantages to using a surrogate key:

❑ *Surrogate keys consolidate multivalue business keys* — A source table or file with multicolumn business keys can be difficult to manage, and takes up extra unnecessary space if used as the primary key. Some dimensions are sourced by multiple source systems, which also creates the situation of multiple business keys that a single surrogate key can handle.

❑ *Surrogate keys allow tracking of dimension history* — Tracking of a dimension attribute's history (such as the list price example discussed in the opening section of this chapter) is not possible without surrogate keys. The surrogate key allows multiple versions of a single source record to be tracked and associated with the fact table history.

❑ *Surrogate keys standardize dimension tables* — Having an identical relationship mechanism to every dimension creates simplicity in reporting and standardization or consistency in the design.

❑ *Surrogate keys improve query performance* — From an optimization standpoint, surrogate keys limit a fact table width. In other words, the combined total data type size for the fact table is small, allowing more fact table rows to fit in memory and, therefore, improving query performance.

> **Make the surrogate key as narrow as possible. If you have a dimension table that only has 100 potential rows (considering future additions), a 1-byte integer (`tinyint`) would be the best choice. Based on the number of members in the dimension, make your data type as small as possible, but be sure you account for future rows! The performance gains will be fairly significant. Simply by going from a 7-byte `int` to a 2-byte `int` (just 2 bytes), you may improve performance by as much as 4–5 percent. And, optimizing all the dimension surrogate keys can translate into big performance gains on queries, which, in turn, reduces a server's resource load. In other words, don't make every dimension key a 7-byte integer. If you can take the fact table width and cut it in half, that's twice as many rows you can put in a SQL page that goes into memory. Inserts, updates, and queries will run much faster.**

Later in this chapter, you learn about the Problem-Design-Solution ETL for a few advanced dimension forms:

❑ Snowflake dimension tables

❑ Parent-child dimension

❑ Junk and profile dimension

These types have their own challenges and unique solutions with SSIS.

Dimension ETL: The Challenge

As already mentioned, dimension ETL often consumes the largest portion of a data warehouse ETL effort. But even beyond the challenges presented by handling history, managing surrogate keys, and accounting for different dimension designs, dimension ETL must manage the source system complexities, and must consolidate them down from the source to the dimension structure in the data warehouse. Figure 7-3 compares the table structures of the product dimension destination in the `AdventureWorksDW2008` database with the multiple related product tables from the `AdventureWorks2008` database source.

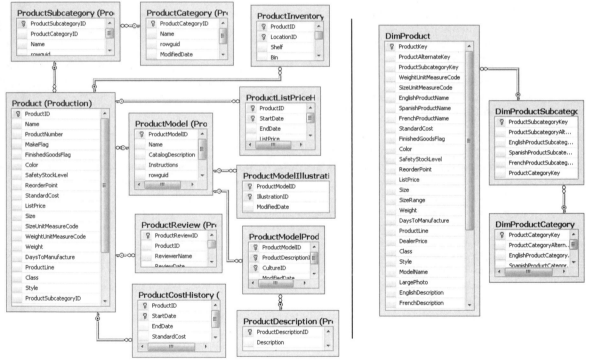

Figure 7-3

The left side of the table layout represents the `AdventureWorks2008` transactional system, with 11 related tables that focus on the product dimension. These tables involve many-to-many relationships and one-to-many primary-to-foreign key relationships, organized into a transactional third normal form. The challenge for the ETL process is taking the source data and transforming it to a structure that can be compared with the dimension in order to handle dimension history and changes. The challenge is also ensuring that the ETL is scalable and manageable, simple for people to follow when administering it, and flexible to handle changes.

The three tables on the right side of the table layout represent the product dimension organized into a snowflake structure. These tables are considered dimensionally normalized, which is a very different organization than the transactionally normalized tables from the source.

So far, this discussion has looked at the theory of dimension tables and the problems with ETL. As the discussion progresses to the design of the ETL process for ETL, you will see how the dimension data changes are solved in ETL. After the design section, the solution section walks you through how to process standard dimension within SSIS.

Design — Fundamental Dimension ETL

Fundamentally, dimension table ETL design is about handling changes from your source data through to your dimension tables in your data warehouse. This often includes new records, changes of data because of updates, and sometimes handling missing records.

This section reviews the fundamental steps involved in dimension ETL design:

❑ Data preparation

❑ Dimension data changes

❑ Missing records (called inferred members)

Data Preparation

Before you even get to the point of handling dimension changes, the first step is preparing your data for dimension loading.

Source data is often messy. And, added to that, you may need to pull from multiple tables or files that must be joined together. The most common data preparation steps involve handling NULLs, blanks, and formatting. Chapter 6 reviews source data profiling with the SSIS Data Profiling Task. In this chapter, you apply transformation logic to the data quality issues for the purpose of dimension ETL.

Figure 7-4 shows an example of some pre-processed source data from the Product tables.

	Name	Color	Size	Class	ProductModelID
1	Front Derailleur Cage	Silver	NULL	NULL	NULL
2	HL Mountain Frame - Silver, 46	Silver	46	H	5
3	HL Road Frame - Red, 44	Red	44	H	6
4	HL Road Frame - Red, 48	Red	48	H	6
5	LL Crankarm	Black	NULL	L	NULL
6	LL Grip Tape	NULL	NULL	L	NULL
7	Long-Sleeve Logo Jersey, S	Multi	S	NULL	11
8	ML Grip Tape	NULL	NULL	M	NULL
9	ML Road Rear Wheel	Black	NULL	M	77
10	Road-650 Black, 44	Black	44	L	30

Figure 7-4

In the data shown in Figure 7-4, a few data-cleansing and preparation steps must be taken. To begin, most of the attribute source columns contain NULLs. Usually, in BI systems, NULLs are replaced with a default value such as Unknown or Not Applicable (NA). Also, the Size column contains discrete values that must be turned into a range for easier analysis. Notice also that the Product Model is an ID column that must be replaced with Model Name.

Figure 7-5 shows these same attributes, but transformations have been applied to standardize cleansing and consolidate the data.

	Name	Color	SizeRange	Class	ModelName
1	Front Derailleur Cage	Silver	NA	NA	NA
2	HL Mountain Frame - Silver, 46	Silver	42-46 CM	H	HL Mountain Frame
3	HL Road Frame - Red, 44	Red	42-46 CM	H	HL Road Frame
4	HL Road Frame - Red, 48	Red	48-52 CM	H	HL Road Frame
5	LL Crankarm	Black	NA	L	NA
6	LL Grip Tape	NA	NA	L	NA
7	Long-Sleeve Logo Jersey, S	Multi	S	NA	Long-Sleeve Logo Jersey
8	ML Grip Tape	NA	NA	M	NA
9	ML Road Rear Wheel	Black	NA	M	ML Road Rear Wheel
10	Road-650 Black, 44	Black	42-46 CM	L	Road-650

Figure 7-5

In order for the source dimension data to be loaded into the dimension table, the first step is to prepare the data by performing data cleansing and transformation to get it into the form shown in Figure 7-5. The "Solution" section for fundamental dimension ETL later in this chapter walks you through the SSIS steps that perform these operations.

Dimension Change Types

The phrase *slowly changing dimension* refers to the tracking of dimension changes over time, and, although the phrase is specific to one of the types of tracking, the name has been used to identify the built-in transformation for SSIS.

> *Much of dimension change tracking theory (including the slowly changing dimension) was driven by Ralph Kimball of the Kimball Group, Inc. Kimball and the Kimball Group have written extensively on the theory and practicalities of creating dimension models, handling ETL, and planning a data warehouse project. These theories have proven themselves critical to answering the challenge of BI and data warehousing. In addition to theory, the Kimball Group has produced the* Microsoft Data Warehouse Toolkit *(Indianapolis: Wiley, 2006), which looks at applying data warehousing theory to the SQL Server BI technologies.*

The question is, as information changes in your dimensions, how do you track those changes? In some situations, data may need to be updated, while other data must be tracked historically. Each different tracking requirement is classified as a certain *dimension change type*. Although several different change types exist, the following are the three most common ones that relate to dimension ETL with SSIS:

❑ *Change Type 0 (fixed)* — Also called a *fixed attribute*, this change type specifies an attribute that should not change over time. An example of this would be gender.

❑ *Change Type 1 (changing)* — Often, tracking the history of changes for a dimension attribute may not provide value. A Type 1 change (also called a *changing attribute*) is useful when you're not interested in the previous value of the attribute. For example, if the Color attribute of the product doesn't provide significant value, then, when the color changes, its old value could be overwritten. This technique is also known as *restating history*, because, for example, changing the product color from yellow to red would reflect the new color in all previous sales, too.

❑ *Change Type 2 (historical)* — A Type 2 change is the slowly changing type in dimension tracking. Also called a *historical attribute*, this change type is handled by adding a new row. If a customer location changes from New York to Atlanta, rather than overwriting the new location, a second record is created for the customer. Otherwise, if the location is overwritten, the sales history for New York will not include that customer, but rather all the sales will appear to have come from Atlanta. This technique is also known as *tracking history*, because all changes to dimension attributes can be accurately tracked through time without loss of fidelity.

Two other scenarios are also an important part of an SSIS-based ETL design:

❑ Creating new members when the data source presents a new record

❑ Handling missing dimension member processing, called an *inferred member*

The SCD Wizard within SSIS supports both of these other dimension processes.

Type 1 (Changing) Attribute: A Closer Look

As previously described, a Type 1 (or changing) attribute requires an in-place update. With this type, you are restating history, and when that update happens, no possibility exists of querying the older value. Overall, a Type 1 change proves fairly simple to understand and execute. Figure 7-6 shows one record from a source data set that matches a record in a dimension table.

Reseller Source

ResellerID	AW00000047
Phone Number	141-555-0172
Business Type	Specialty Bike Shop
Reseller Name	Greater Bike Store

Reseller Dimension

ResellerKey	10
ResellerAlternateKey	AW00000047
Phone Number	141-555-0172
Business Type	Classic Bikes
Reseller Name	Greater Bike Store

Figure 7-6

In the Reseller Source record, the ResellerID matches the ResellerAlternateKey in the Reseller dimension. The BusinessType attribute in the Reseller dimension is identified as a changing attribute (change Type 1), and the current value is Classic Bikes. The Reseller Source record, however, indicates that this particular reseller store now is classified as a Specialty Bike Shop. Because the attribute is marked as changing, the value is simply updated. Figure 7-7 shows the updated dimension table record with the new value.

Reseller Dimension

ResellerKey	10
ResellerAlternateKey	AW00000047
Phone Number	141-555-0172
Business Type	Specialty Bike Shop
Reseller Name	Greater Bike Store

Figure 7-7

Type 2 (Historical) Attribute: A Closer Look

A column that is identified as a Type 2 (or historical) attribute is a little more difficult to handle than a Type 1 changing attribute because it involves adding a row and tracking details of the change. Figure 7-8 shows a record for the Product Source and the matching record in the Product Dimension table.

Product Source

ProductID	BK-T79U-60
Class	Mid Tier
ModelName	Touring-1000

Product Dimension

ProductKey	576
ProductAlternateKey	BK-T79U-60
Class (Type 2)	High Perf
ModelName (Type 2)	Touring-1000
StartDate	7/3/2007
EndDate	NULL

Figure 7-8

Notice that two of the attributes, ModelName and Class, are marked as Type 2 historical attributes. In other words, if a change occurs, you are interested in keeping the history of the change. In this example, the Class of the product changed from Mid Tier to High Perf. Because a change happened in a Type 2 historical attribute, a new record must be added, with a new surrogate key. Figure 7-9 shows the dimension table with the changes applied.

Product Dimension

ProductKey	576	763
ProductAlternateKey	BK-T79U-60	BK-T79U-60
Class (Type 2)	High Perf	Mid Tier
ModelName (Type 2)	Touring-1000	Touring-1000
StartDate	7/3/2007	6/30/2009
EndDate	6/30/2009	NULL

Figure 7-9

The High Perf Class value remains in the original record, but is updated in the new record. Surrogate keys are the lynchpin to handling Type 2 changes, because they allow a new record to be created with the same business key, and all the history in the fact table references the first key, and any new fact records would reference the new surrogate key. This allows someone to run a query to say "show me the sales of the Mid Tier bicycles." If the change were not tracked historically, the Mid Tier sales would not be available for that bicycle. It would appear as if all the sales for that bicycle were High Perf if querying on Class.

Notice that there are metadata columns to help track the Type 2 historical change — a StartDate and an EndDate. The StartDate for the new record is set to 6/30/2009 and the EndDate is NULL, which indicates the dimension member is the current row. When this new record was added, the EndDate of the original record was updated to the date of that change. The StartDate and EndDate columns provide the capability to know when a dimension member was active, and the capability to identify the current record (that is, when the EndDate is NULL). In this example, two records now exist for this product. However, having many different versions of this record is possible.

Another common technique is to use a Boolean column that identifies the current record (which would be marked as True), and the outdated records (which would be marked as False).

Inferred Members

At times, the ETL system may need to handle missing dimension records. When the fact data is being loaded, if the dimension member is not available, the fact row should not just be ignored, but inserted into the fact table with a temporary dimension assignment. An *inferred member* is a dimension record that has been added during the fact load when the business key from the fact source doesn't have a match in the dimension table. You might have an inferred member for many reasons:

❑ If the data in the dimension source or fact source is dirty and the match is not available, then the dimension member may not be available or found in the dimension table.

❑ Depending on source system requirements, if the dimension source cannot be extracted as often or before the fact table source is extracted and processed, a missing dimension record may occur.

❑ A dimension source that is not updated as often as the fact source may result in missing dimension records during the fact load.

Having missing dimension members is a problem known as an inferred member, but is also commonly called a *late-arriving dimension* scenario.

For example, at some retailers, products may go on the shelf at a store to be sold before the master product table is updated at a corporate office. Store managers are often given autonomy to sell extra products in their stores outside of the corporate product list. Therefore, data may not enter into the centralized item inventory until later, but the sale is still recorded, causing a late-arriving dimension scenario.

When dealing with inferred members, there are really two aspects of the ETL:

❑ *Inserting* the inferred member during the *fact load*

❑ *Updating* the inferred member during the *dimension load*

Adding Inferred Members During the Fact Load

The SSIS mechanisms for this aspect of inferred members is discussed in Chapter 8, but here are some of the basics of what must happen during the ETL. During the fact load, if a dimension record is not available, a placeholder record is added to the dimension table. If you get a business key for a product, but the product doesn't exist in the dimension table, instead of using a generic *unknown* that is not associated with any business key, you can add an *unknown* specific to the business key for the missing record. Later, if or when the dimension record comes in from the source, you can update it with all the attributes. Inferred members are the most complicated part of dimension processing.

Figure 7-10 shows a transactional source for a sales type fact table on the left, and a couple of rows from a related dimension table on the right. The source contains a `ProductID`. However, there's no match in the dimension table itself. The `ProductID` (business key) `BK-8006F` sold for $439.99, but a matching dimension record is not in the dimension table.

Product Dimension

No Match				ProductKey	436	763
				ProductAlternateKey	BK-R64Y-40	BK-T79U-60
				Class	High Perf	Mid Tier
				ModelName	ROAD-550-W	Touring-1000
ProductID	Customer	Sales Amount		StartDate	7/1/2007	6/30/2009
BK-8006F	R Torres	$439.99		EndDate	NULL	NULL

Figure 7-10

Handling this kind of change as an inferred member, you must add a record to the dimension table during this fact load. What you don't have are values for all the other attributes of the dimension, which must be set to an unknown value. Figure 7-11 shows the resulting dimension table after the load.

Product Dimension

ProductKey	436	763	975
ProductAlternateKey	BK-R64Y-40	BK-T79U-60	BK-8006F
Class	High Perf	Mid Tier	Unknown
ModelName	Road-550-W	Touring-1000	Unknown
StartDate	7/1/2007	6/30/2009	6/30/2009
EndDate	NULL	NULL	NULL
Inferred Member Flag	No	No	Yes

Figure 7-11

Notice that the inferred member has been added with a new surrogate key, but the attributes in the dimension are set to `Unknown`. Furthermore, there's another column in the dimension table called the `Inferred Member Flag` column. It should be set to `Yes` (or `True`), because the dimension process needs to know the record is an inferred member created during the fact load. That will impact how dimension processing handles that ETL.

Updating the Inferred Member During the Dimension Load

As just discussed, when you're loading the fact table, if there's a missing record, you add the record to the dimension table as an inferred member. When you process the dimension table later, if the dimension source becomes available for an inferred member, it can be updated with the missing dimension attributes.

The ETL process works by essentially updating all the columns for that table. Every attribute becomes like a Type 1 changing attribute, even the Type 2 historical attributes. In other words, instead of creating a new record with the changes, the original record is updated. Figure 7-12 shows one row in the data source for a dimension (on the left), and a few rows from the dimension table. The source contains details for a record that currently exists in the dimension table as an inferred member.

Product Source

ProductID	BK-8006F
Class	Mid Tier
ModelName	All Terrain-800

Product Dimension

ProductKey	576	763	975
ProductAlternateKey	BK-T79U-60	BK-T79U-60	BK-8006F
Class	High Perf	Mid Tier	Unknown
ModelName	Touring-1000	Touring-1000	Unknown
StartDate	7/3/2007	6/30/2009	6/30/2009
EndDate	11/30/2006	NULL	NULL
Inferred Member Flag	No	No	Yes

Figure 7-12

If the matching record table in the dimension was added during a normal dimension load, the change in the `Class` or `ModelName` column (because they are Type 2 historical) would cause a new record to be generated. However, because the dimension member is marked as an inferred member, instead, every attribute is updated to the new values. Figure 7-13 shows the now updated dimension table.

Product Dimension

ProductKey	576	763	975
ProductAlternateKey	BK-T79U-60	BK-T79U-60	BK-8006F
Class	High Perf	Mid Tier	Mid Tier
ModelName	Touring-1000	Touring-1000	All Terrain-800
StartDate	7/3/2007	6/30/2009	6/30/2009
EndDate	6/30/2009	NULL	NULL
Inferred Member Flag	No	No	No

Figure 7-13

Not only are all the attributes updated with the new value, but also the `Inferred Member Flag` column is marked as `No` (or `False`), because you now have the full details of that dimension member. An inferred member turns all the attributes into Type 1 changing until the dimension member details come in from the source.

> You may have a scenario where you want the dimension table to act like an inferred member, even though the dimension is added from the dimension source. If you have a dimension source record that goes through lots of column value changes until at some point the record is stable, consider treating that dimension record as an inferred member until it stabilizes. The drawback in handling the dimension record like a normal dimension with Type 1 changing and Type 2 historical attributes is that every change to a Type 2 historical attribute causes a new record. Waiting until the stabilization will reduce the number of dimension records and, therefore, avoid too much confusion with so many records for a single member.

Solution — Fundamental Dimension ETL

Now that you've seen the challenges and objectives of dimension table ETL, it's time to dive into how SSIS solves these problems. This section looks at how to apply the SSIS SCD Wizard to fundamental dimension ETL. After this Solution, you find out how to handle more complex dimensions and high-volume dimension processes in the Problem-Design-Solution titled "Advanced Dimension ETL."

Preparing Your Source Data for Dimension ETL

Before diving into the details of applying SSIS to handle dimension changes, let's begin with data preparation.

With SSIS, several out-of-the-box transformations will become key to your transformation and data-cleansing steps, before even getting to the core of dimension processing. Here are some selective transformations that are very useful for this purpose:

❑ The Data Conversion transformation is valuable to handle data type conversions, such as conversions between Unicode and non-Unicode data types, numeric and float, or text and numeric.

❑ The Lookup transformation provides the capability to associate sources without requiring relational joins.

❑ The Derived Column transformation is especially useful in handling NULL values, performing calculations, or applying date functions.

Figure 7-14 shows several data preparation steps useful in the processing of the Product source data which you must perform before you can use the SCD Wizard. The first objective is to take the third normal form of the transactional system and transform it into a structurally equivalent copy of the dimension table in the data flow pipeline.

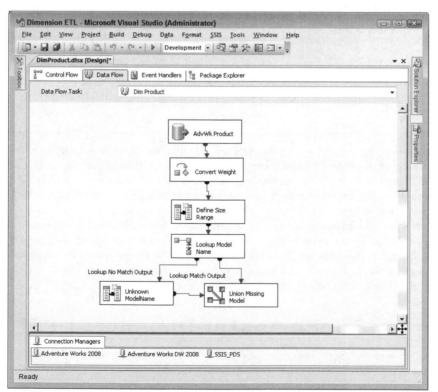

Figure 7-14

The first component is the source adapter, which extracts the source table (`Production.Product`, in this example). The very next component is a Data Conversion transformation, which changes the data type of the `ProductWeight` from a `Numeric` to a `Float`. This is because the destination table stores this attribute as a float, as opposed to a numeric. Figure 7-15 shows the Data Conversion Transformation Editor. The output column is aliased as `Weight` to match the column names of the product dimension table.

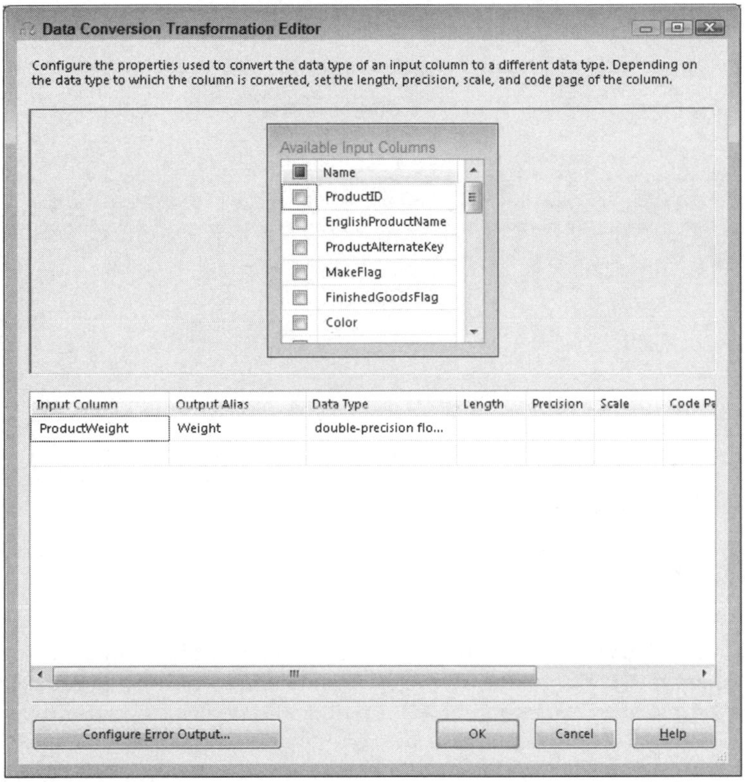

Figure 7-15

Next, in the product dimension table (which contains the products related to the sale of bicycles and bicycle parts that `AdventureWorks2008` sells), a column exists called `SizeRange`. This dimension attribute is an example of a dimensional-modeling technique called *data banding*, where ranges are built from usually numeric sources that have several discrete values, but must be consolidated for grouping. Instead of reporting off of the bicycle sizes one size at a time (38, 40, 42, 43, 45, and so on), there are groupings of the discrete size values, such as 38–40, 42–46, and so on. To handle this requirement, a Derived Column transformation is employed, which considers the size and, based on certain values, how the output is grouped. Figure 7-16 shows the Derived Column transformation used.

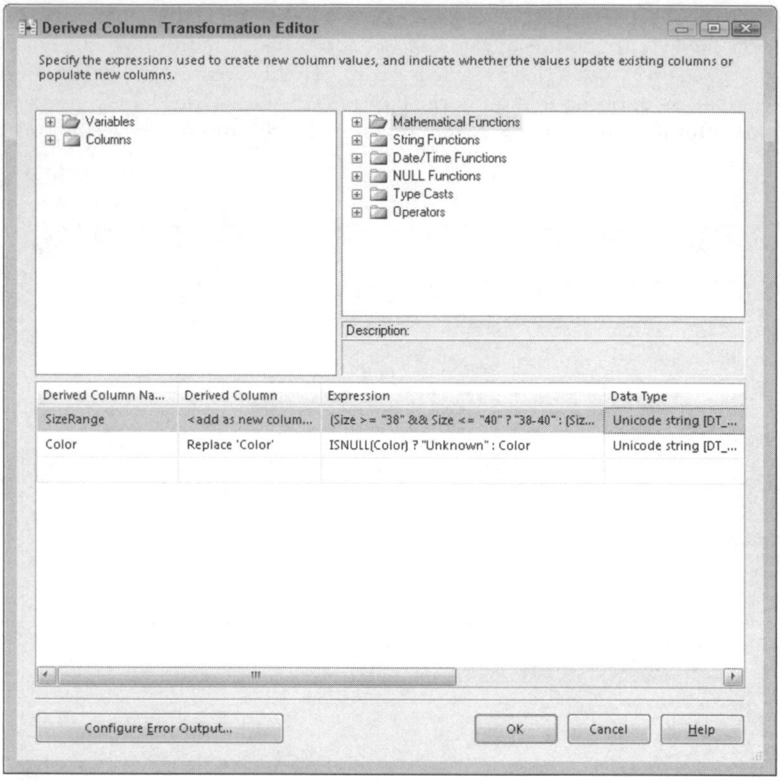

Figure 7-16

The first column in the Derived Column transformation handles the banding by using an SSIS expression to compare the size to groups of ranges, as shown in the following code. Critical to this expression is the use of an expression-based conditional statement, «boolean_expression» ? «when_true» : «when_false». In this case, the conditional evaluator is recursively embedded to perform multiple comparisons in one statement.

```
(Size >= "38" && Size <= "40" ? "38-40" :
    (Size >= "42" && Size <= "46" ? "42-46" :
        (Size >= "48" && Size <= "52" ? "48-52" :
            (Size >= "54" && Size <= "58" ? "54-58" :
                (Size >= "60" && Size < "62" ? "60-62" :
                    ISNULL(Size) ? "NA" : Size
                )
            )
        )
    )
) + (ISNULL(SizeUnitMeasureCode) ? "" : " " + SizeUnitMeasureCode)
```

In the first condition, if the size for the row being evaluated is 38, then the output range is returned as 38-40. Otherwise, the next condition is checked, and so on, recursively.

The second column used in the example shown in Figure 7-16 deals with unknown values. If there's a `NULL` in the `Color` column, it is trapped and replaced by an `Unknown`. If the column is not `NULL`, the actual `Color` value is used.

The next transformation in the data flow is an example of data preparation. A Lookup transformation is used to query a second source table that contains an additional attribute needed for the product dimension. Because the Lookup transformation is referencing a source table, the `AdventureWorks2008` Connection Manager is selected. In this case, the attribute `ModelName` comes from a different table in the source. Figure 7-17 shows the Columns tab of the Lookup Transformation Editor.

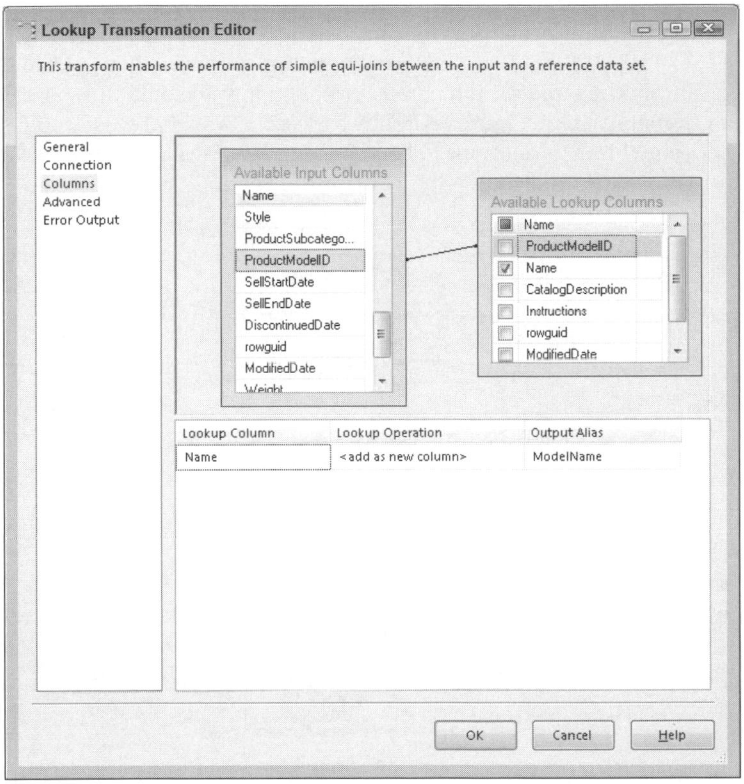

Figure 7-17

The available input columns shown on the left come from the `Production.Product` table that was defined in the source adapter. The available lookup columns on the right come from the `Production.ProductModel` table, also in the source, which was defined in the Reference Table tab in the same editor.

The lookup is done across the `ProductModelID` and the `Name` column is checked, which returns the column into the pipeline column list. The `Name` column is also aliased as `ModelName` to match the product dimension table column. In effect, what you have achieved is to take the incoming `ProductModelID` values and augment them with the corresponding `Product Names` from a separate table in the source.

The data flow highlighted earlier in Figure 7-14 also shows that the Lookup transformation sends rows for both matches (Lookup Match Output) and no matches (Lookup No Match Output) as outputs. When a product model is not found, the row is sent to a derived column transformation and replaced with an unknown product model. A final Union All transformation brings the data back together.

The output of all these transformations is a *pipeline*, or a set of columns that align with the dimension table itself. When that preparation process is achieved, then the source data is ready to be matched with the existing dimension data for the handling of dimension changes.

SSIS Slowly Changing Dimension Wizard

Now it's time to look at the built-in support for dimension ETL, called the Slowly Changing Dimension (SCD) Wizard. The SCD Wizard is a data-flow transformation and initially works like all the other transformations — simply drag and drop the transformation into the data flow, and connect it to the upstream source or transformation. Figure 7-18 shows the data flow that was used earlier in the chapter with a couple of additional transformations to handle the name translation columns and the subcategory key. These transformations are followed by the SCD transformation.

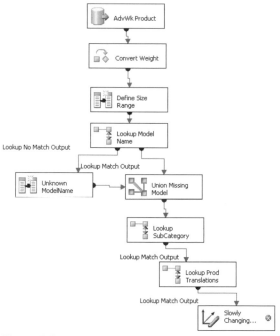

Figure 7-18

Double-clicking the transformation invokes the wizard. Like other user-interface wizards, several windows prompt you for configurations, in order to build the dimension ETL process. One of the nice advantages of the SCD Wizard is that it allows for very rapid ETL development.

The SCD Wizard supports Type 1 changing attributes, Type 2 historical attributes, inferred members, and Type 0 fixed attributes, all out of the box.

When the source is connected to the SCD component, and the wizard invoked, the first screen prompts you to identify the target dimension table, then the mapping of source columns from the data flow pipeline to the dimension columns in the dimension table, and, finally, the business keys in the source and dimension table. Figure 7-19 shows the mapping between the source rows generated for the product dimension and the dimension columns themselves.

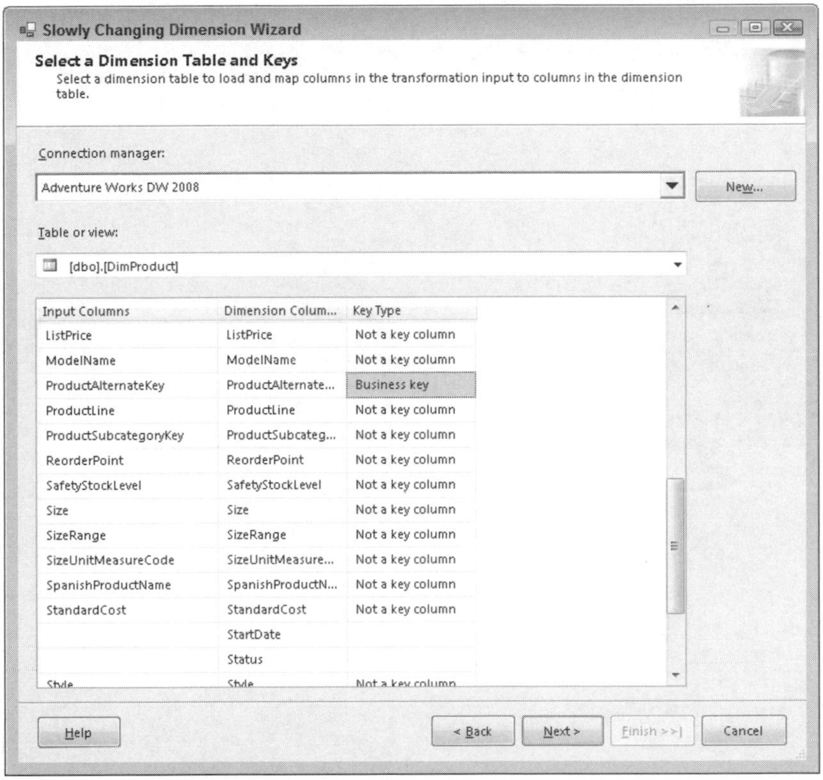

Figure 7-19

Note that the data types must match in order for the source columns to be compared with the dimension table columns, which may require the use of the Data Conversion transformation in the upstream data-cleansing logic. For the wizard to handle the matching automatically, the column names must be the same. Matching names is not a requirement, because the matching can be done manually. Furthermore, if you have any columns in the dimension table that are not attributes, but rather management or metadata columns (such as `StartDate` and `EndDate` columns that identify when the row is active), they will not be matched. Later options in the wizard give you the opportunity to specify the use of these columns.

The final step in the first screen is to identify the business key or keys. In Figure 7-19, the `ProductAlternateKey` is the business key manually matched to the source column `Product ID` (which has been aliased as `ProductAlternateKey`). The business keys help identify dimension records that must be added as new members. The business keys also provide part of the equation for identifying matching records that must be evaluated for changes.

The next screen of the wizard is about associating the dimension columns that have just been matched with the dimension change type. The wizard does not use the common dimension changing type numbers (Type 0, Type 1, or Type 2). Rather, it uses the descriptive terms to identify the type of change (fixed, changing, or historical).

Figure 7-20 shows the matching of the dimension changes. The column on the left contains any non-business key matches identified in the prior screen, and the column on the right is a drop-down of the three different change types.

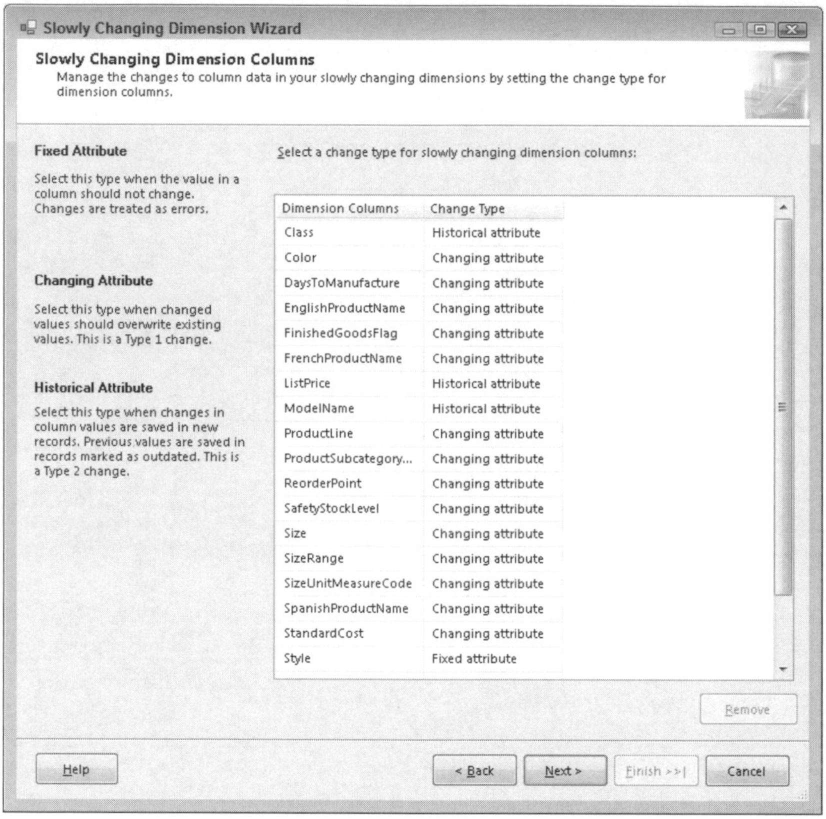

Figure 7-20

In this example, the following groupings were made:

- ❏ *Fixed attributes* — Style (changes in size will generate a new product, therefore, this is fixed)

- ❏ *Historical attributes* — Class, ListPrice, ModelName

- ❏ *Changing attributes* — Color, DaysToManufacture, EnglishProductName, FinishedGoodsFlag, FrenchProductName, ProductLine, ProductSubcategoryKey, ReorderPoint, SafetyStockLevel, Size, SizeRange, SizeUnitMeasureCode, SpanishProductName, StandardCost, Style, Weight, WeightUnitMeasureCode

The matching shown in Figure 7-20 can be a tiresome process if you have dozens of dimension columns and you are using your mouse to select the column in the drop-down. A quicker way to fill in these values is to use the Tab key and the up- and down-arrow keys. After finishing a row, the Tab key sends the cursor to the next row and automatically selects the next column in the list.

Now that you have defined the column matches and identified the change types, the next few screens help you to manage the advanced requirements for the dimension ETL process.

In the Fixed and Changing Attribute Options screen, shown in Figure 7-21, some specific requirements are asked about "Fixed attributes" and "Changing attributes" members.

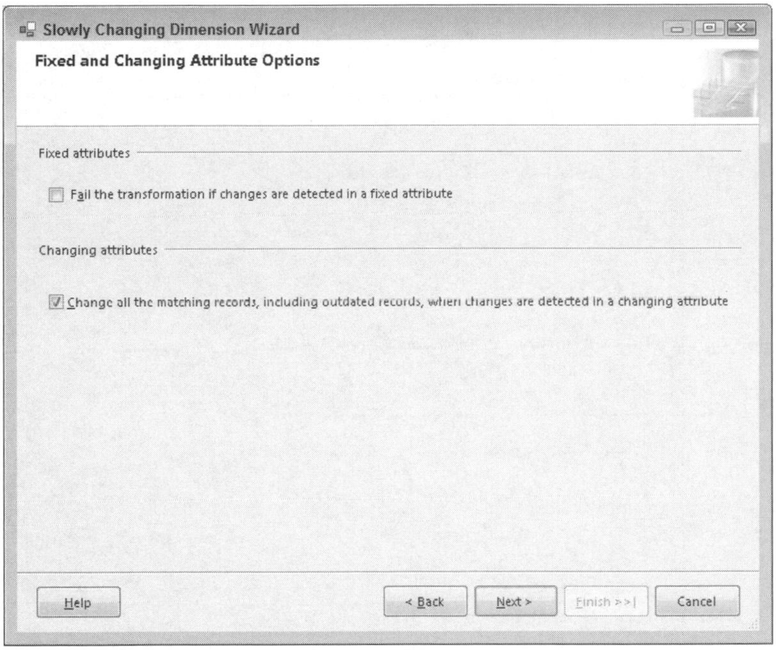

Figure 7-21

If you do not identify any "Fixed attributes" or "Changing attributes" columns, then the respective detail questions shown in the screen shot is grayed out.

The option for fixed attributes asks, "If there is a change in a fixed attribute, what should happen?"

❑ By leaving the box unchecked, the change will be ignored and the value in the dimension table will stay the same as it was originally.

❑ By selecting the box, if a change is detected in a Fixed attribute column, then the transformation will intentionally generate an error, so the data can be reviewed. This may be useful if, when a change is identified, it indicates a bigger problem.

The option for "Changing attributes" (Type 1) identifies which records to update when a change happens. In other words, if the dimension record has any Type 2 historical attributes, there may be multiple records for the same business key.

217

❑   When the box is selected, all the related records (the current dimension member and the outdated members) are updated.

❑   When the option is cleared, only the current record gets updated with the new value of the column. For example, if there's a change in `Color` from `blue` to `aqua`, and the particular business key had five historical changes, then only the last record would be updated with aqua. When the "Changing attributes" box is cleared, and color is marked as a Type 1, only the current record gets updated from `blue` to `aqua`. The rest of the historical records remain as `blue`.

If any historical attributes have been selected, then the next screen prompts you to identify how the current row is identified. Figure 7-22 shows the Historical Attribute Options screen.

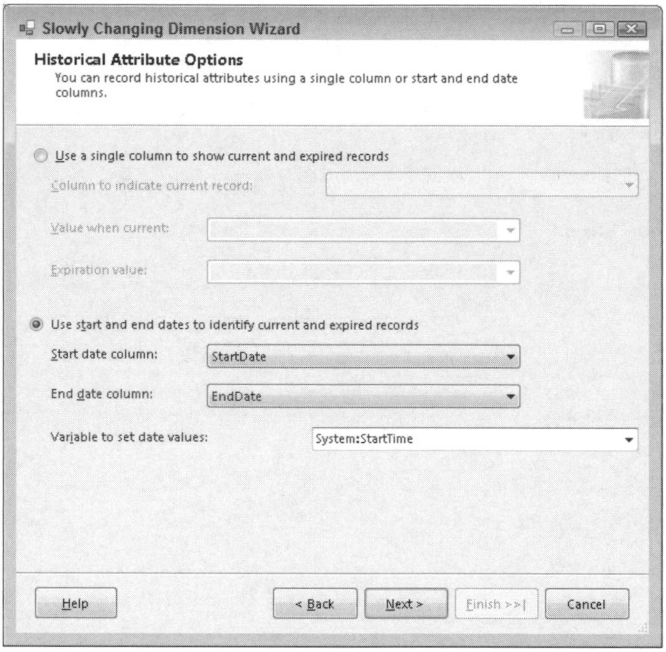

Figure 7-22

Following are the two choices to identify a current row:

❑   *Use a flag column (usually Boolean) to identify whether a row is current or not* — Besides just selecting the column that should be used, the SCD Wizard also supports defining what values identify a current record and expired record. Note also that the columns in the drop-down list are any dimension columns that have not been matched from the source. That is because these are considered metadata columns that are used for management purposes like this.

❑   *Use a* `StartDate` *and* `EndDate` *combination to manage when a dimension record is active* — The `StartDate` and `EndDate` column selections must be dimension table columns defined with a `datetime` data type. Furthermore, one other option exists if taking the approach of start time and end time columns — that is, choosing which package variable should be used as the value to update the record with. In other words, when a new dimension member needs to be added, because there is a change in a Type 2 historical attribute, the prior record must be first updated with a new `EndDate` and the new record must be initiated with a new `StartDate`. Any system or user variable can be used. One good choice is to use the `System::StartTime` variable, which is automatically updated when the package is executed. And, in this example, the `StartDate` and `EndDate` columns are used in conjunction with the `System::StartTime` variable.

Using `StartDate` and `EndDate` columns gives you the advantage of knowing exactly when a particular dimension member was active, either for reporting purposes or even to handle the scenario when a fact record arrives late and a historical dimension record must be selected instead of the current member.

The SSIS inferred member support is found in the next screen, Inferred Dimension Members. As a reminder, inferred members are added during the fact ETL and updated during the dimension ETL. The built-in support for inferred members revolves around the dimension update. Figure 7-23 shows the options available for inferred members.

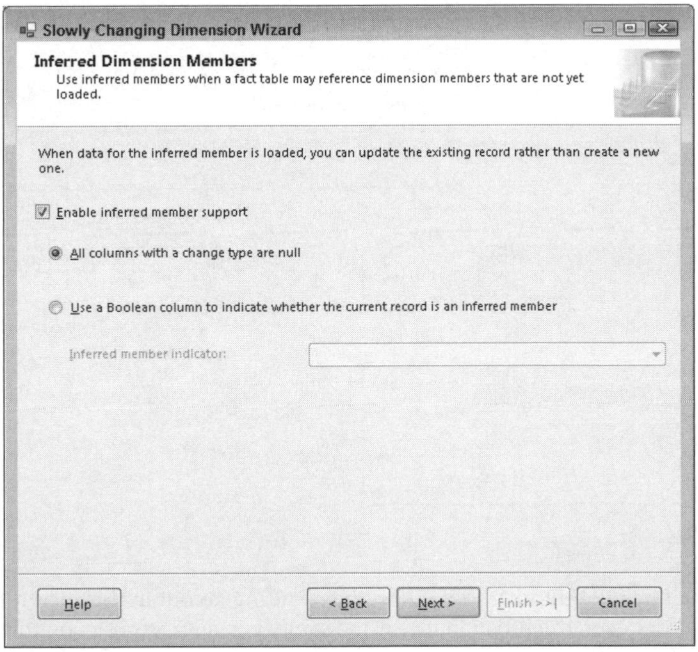

Figure 7-23

First of all, inferred member support is either enabled or disabled. If enabled, the SCD Wizard must know how to identify whether a record is an inferred member. The two choices are to leave all the dimension columns in the dimension table as `NULL`, or to use an `Inferred Member` Boolean column in the table that identifies which rows are inferred members.

Because the product dimension table in the `AdventureWorksDW2008` database does not have an inferred member column, the first choice is selected.

> Using the first choice for inferred members (all attributes contain **NULL** values) is not often practical, because it assumes that the columns in the dimension table allow **NULL** values, and it makes for difficult querying. Using an unknown value, for example, is often a better way to see data for a reporting system. But, in addition, if Analysis Services is used for analytics, **NULL** values are also not a good choice. The best practice is to define an inferred member column and handle the identification by setting the Boolean value to **True** or **False**.

The final screen (not shown here) presents a summary of the outputs that will be created. When you select Finish on this screen, the SCD Wizard takes all the configuration options and creates several downstream transformations and destinations. Figure 7-24 shows the end result of the SCD Wizard — the SCD transformation remains, but it contains several outputs to handle the different attribute types.

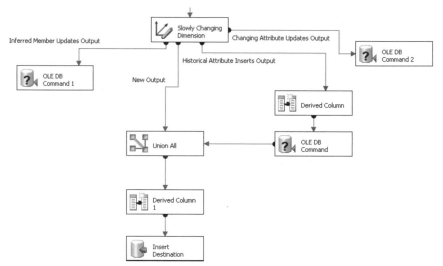

Figure 7-24

Because SSIS dynamically builds the data flow, the resulting layout in this example may not look exactly like your testing. However, the functionality is the same. For this example, on the right are changing attributes. Down the center are new members and historical attributes. On the left are inferred members.

Starting with the SCD transformation, when a dimension row is processed, the SCD will determine which (if any) attribute changes occur, and whether there are new members to be added or inferred members to update. Consider the SCD transformation to be like a Conditional Split — it evaluates every row, one at a time, and sends each record to zero, one, or more outputs, depending on the change.

The simplest output to understand is the Changing Attribute Updates Output, which is linked to the OLE DB Command 2 transformation, connected to the `AdventureWorksDW2008` database. The following code shows the `SQLCommand` property, which defines the `UPDATE` statement:

```
UPDATE [dbo].[DimProduct]
SET [Color] = ?
,[DaysToManufacture] = ?
,[EnglishProductName] = ?
,[FinishedGoodsFlag] = ?
,[FrenchProductName] = ?
,[ProductLine] = ?
,[ProductSubcategoryKey] = ?
,[ReorderPoint] = ?
,[SafetyStockLevel] = ?
,[SizeRange] = ?
,[SizeUnitMeasureCode] = ?
,[SpanishProductName] = ?
,[StandardCost] = ?
,[Style] = ?
,[Weight] = ?
,[WeightUnitMeasureCode] = ?
WHERE [ProductAlternateKey] = ?
```

What you should note in the UPDATE statement is that only the columns that were defined as changing attributes (Type 1) are included in the UPDATE statement, simply because this output is only for the Type 1 changing attributes. Also notice that the SQL statement is an OLE DB parameterized statement with question marks, which is the way that the OLE DB provider handles the parameterization. Figure 7-25 shows the Column Mappings tab, which maps (in order) the pipeline input columns to the parameterized query.

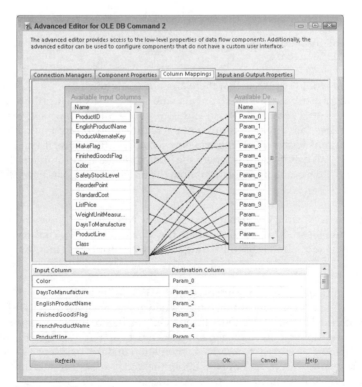

Figure 7-25

The order of the question marks defines the order of the mappings.

The second output is the Inferred Member Updates Output. This output is very similar to the Changing Attribute Updates Output because it also performs an UPDATE statement. Just like the first output, the inferred member output uses an OLE DB Command transformation to handle the updates (in this case, the OLE DB Command 1 transformation). The UPDATE statement defined in the SQLCommand property is as follows:

```
UPDATE [dbo].[DimProduct]
SET [Class] = ?
,[Color] = ?
,[DaysToManufacture] = ?
,[EnglishProductName] = ?
,[FinishedGoodsFlag] = ?
,[FrenchProductName] = ?
,[ListPrice] = ?
,[ModelName] = ?
,[ProductLine] = ?
,[ProductSubcategoryKey] = ?
,[ReorderPoint] = ?
,[SafetyStockLevel] = ?
,[Size] = ?
,[SizeRange] = ?
,[SizeUnitMeasureCode] = ?
,[SpanishProductName] = ?
,[StandardCost] = ?
,[Style] = ?
,[Weight] = ?
,[WeightUnitMeasureCode] = ?
WHERE [ProductAlternateKey] = ?
```

The difference, as you would expect, is that there are more columns in the UPDATE statement. Not only are the Type 1 changing attributes updated, but also the Type 2 historical attributes. Included in the UPDATE statement are the Class, ModelName, and ListPrice columns, which were defined as a Type 2 historical attributes. These are updated because of the nature of an inferred member, which requires updates to all the columns without generating a new record. Furthermore, if you had defined an Inferred Member Flag column, this is where the inferred member column would also be updated. Just like the first OLE DB Command transformation, the order of question marks defines the order of the mapping.

The next two outputs to consider are also related. Both the New Output (new members to be added) and the Historical Attribute Inserts Output add rows to the dimension table. What you can see in Figure 7-24 is that a Union All transformation is used to bring these two outputs together for a single destination insert.

If the business key from the source does not exist in the dimension table, it's identified as a new member that must be inserted. The New Output that handles new members goes directly to the Union All transformation. With the Historical Attribute Inserts Output, before the records are brought together in the Union All, a couple of metadata management tasks must happen. Whether the new historical attribute record is marked as current through a combination of dates or a separate column, the old record must be updated before the insert can happen. Either the End Date column is updated, or a current flag column is updated, which is handled in a two-step process:

1. The Derived Column transformation that is attached to the Historical Attribute Inserts Output adds either an `EndDate` column to the data flow (as in this example), or it adds the expired flag value. Figure 7-26 shows the Derived Column editor that defines an EndDate column and then also uses the System::StartTime variable as specified in the SCD Wizard.

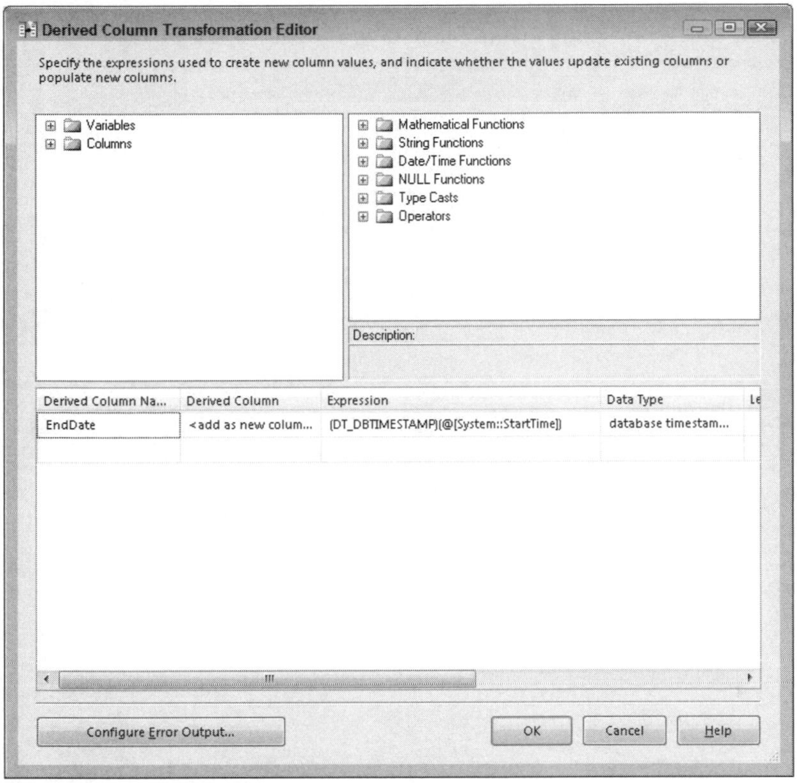

Figure 7-26

2. Another OLE DB Command transformation is used to update the `End Date` for the expired record, based on the business key and the current indicator (in this case, the record to be expired will currently have an `End Date` of `NULL`). The `SQLCommand` property of this OLE DB Command transformation is as follows:

```
UPDATE [dbo].[DimProduct]
SET [EndDate] = ?
WHERE [ProductAlternateKey] = ? AND [EndDate] IS NULL
```

One nice feature of the OLE DB Command transformation, as this example shows, is that the records from the pipeline can perform the UPDATE statement, and then still be available downstream for other purposes. After the expired record has been updated, then the record is ready to be "union-ed" with the new member output.

Before the final insert for the new members and Type 2 historical attributes, one final step is necessary — you must add the `Start Date` (or current record flag). The SCD Wizard uses a Derived Column transformation, which adds a column to the pipeline called `StartDate` (in this example). Figure 7-27 shows the details of the Derived Column transformation that falls just below the Union All transformation and before the OLE DB Destination (from the data flow shown earlier in Figure 7-24).

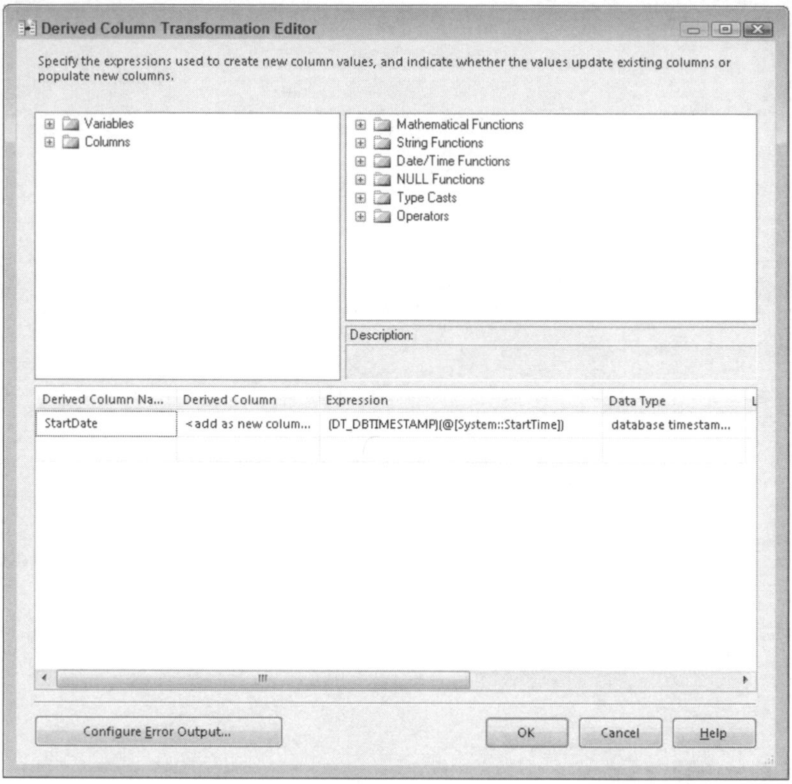

Figure 7-27

Just like the `EndDate`, the `StartDate` uses the `System::StartTime` variable, which is used for the new record. New records that are new members or Historical Attribute Inserts require the `EndDate` to be `NULL`. (If you have specified a current indicator, you put the indicator's current value in this Derived Column transformation.)

When executed, the SCD transformation routes the rows from the source to the different outputs. Notice in Figure 7-28 that the 504 input rows are sent out to the various outputs. In fact, a single row can be routed to multiple outputs if the row meets more than one SCD criteria. Furthermore, some of the records do not go through any changes, so they are effectively ignored. If you are executing the example provided in the files on this book's companion Web site (www.wrox.com), and want to run the package more than one time, you will need to restore the `AdventureWorksDW2008` database to see the rows sent out to the multiple destinations. After the first run, the dimension table has been updated.

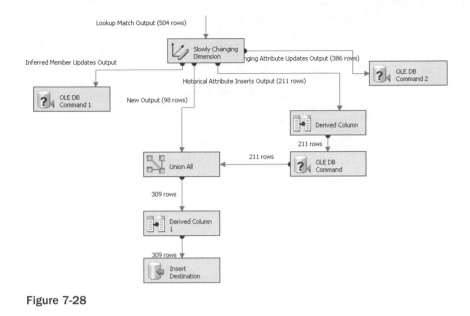

Figure 7-28

Advanced Properties and Additional Outputs of the SCD

Two advanced properties of the SCD can be used to customize how the SCD transformation handles the processing:

❏ The CurrentRowWhere property identifies how the current dimension row for a source record is identified. If you have configured the SCD to use a Current Flag column, then, by default, this property would filter on the Current Flag where the value you defined in the wizard is current. Alternatively, if you specified Start Date and End Date, then, by default, the property would assume that the End Date column IS NULL. This property can be changed if you need to redefine how the SCD transformation searches for the current record. For example, if your organizational standards do not allow NULL values, then you would have to modify this property to check the End Date for the default value set for the column (often, a date far out in the future is used to accommodate this, such as 1/1/2050).

❏ The SQLCommand property contains the SQL syntax used for the lookup against the dimension table to either determine whether a new member must be created, or whether there have been any changes in a Type 0 fixed attribute, Type 1 changing attribute, or Type 2 historical attribute.

You can find both of the properties referenced here by reviewing the Properties window when the SCD transformation is selected on the SCD transformation, as shown in Figure 7-29, or by looking at the advanced editor of the SCD transformation.

Properties ▾ ‑⊞ ✕
Slowly Changing Dimension Data Flow Component

⊟ **Common Properties**	
ComponentClassID	{70909A92-ECE9-486D-B17E-30EDE908849E}
ContactInfo	Slowly Changing Dimension;Microsoft Corporation; N
Description	Updates a slowly changing dimension.
ID	2445
IdentificationString	component "Slowly Changing Dimension" (2445)
IsDefaultLocale	True
LocaleID	English (United States)
Name	**Slowly Changing Dimension**
PipelineVersion	0
UsesDispositions	False
ValidateExternalMetadata	True
Version	3
⊟ **Custom Properties**	
CurrentRowWhere	[StartDate] IS NOT NULL AND [EndDate] IS NULL
DefaultCodePage	1252
EnableInferredMember	True
FailOnFixedAttributeChang	False
FailOnLookupFailure	False
IncomingRowChangeType	Detect
InferredMemberIndicator	
SqlCommand	SELECT [Class], [Color], [DaysToManufacture], [EnglishF
UpdateChangingAttributeⱵ	True

Figure 7-29

Furthermore, the SCD transformation contains two additional outputs that are not used by default, but are useful for auditing and data validation.

The first output enables you to capture the rows that have not gone through any change. Very likely, if you are pulling the entire dimension source (as opposed to just targeting new and changed records), you will have many dimension records from the source that are unchanged, or are completely in synch with the dimension table. Although a change has not happened, you may have a need to count the number of rows that are unchanged, or capture the unchanged rows in a table or file for review. The Unchanged Output is accessible by selecting the green path output from the SCD transformation, and connecting it to another transformation or destination. When you make this connection, you will be prompted to choose one of the remaining output of the SCD. In Figure 7-30, a Row Count transformation is used to capture the number of rows that are unchanged into a variable that is later captured for auditing purposes.

Figure 7-30

The second additional output is the Fixed Attribute Output, which sends out any rows where a fixed attribute column has changed when it should not have. Rather than a Row Count, a better use of this output is to capture the records to a staging table for review, because a change was not supposed to happen.

Only when the "Ignore fixed attribute changes" option is selected will the Fixed Attribute Output be used. Otherwise, if a fixed attribute change occurred, the SCD would intentionally fail.

As you can see, the Slowly Changing Dimension transformation can handle a variety of requirements, and putting together a dimension ETL package is relatively straightforward. However, some drawbacks exist that the next section addresses, and not all situations can leverage the SCD transformation.

The remainder of this chapter focuses on the Problem-Design-Solution for advanced dimension ETL.

Problem — Advanced Dimension ETL

If the first half of this chapter addressed most dimension ETL challenges, then processing dimensions would be relatively straightforward. However, you are likely run into more complex challenges. This Problem-Design-Solution section covers advanced dimension ETL, including the following:

❑   Optimizing the SCD transformation

❑   Handling parent-child and snowflake dimensions

❑   Dealing with profile dimensions

❑   Building your own dimension ETL process

SCD Wizard Advantages and Disadvantages

The SCD Wizard is a very powerful tool, and will be appreciated by ETL developers who commonly deal with managing complicated ETL processes for dimensions. Several benefits can be achieved by using the built-in SCD support. However, a few limitations also surround the SCD that we should mention.

Before considering the problems with the SCD transformation, be aware of some good benefits:

❑   *Simplicity* — The SCD Wizard can handle most dimension scenarios. It makes the often complicated dimension processing straightforward, and helps standardize ETL development for dimensions.

❑   *Rapid development* — The SCD Wizard can save time in the development life cycle by reducing the design and development time, and also easing the management and testing. This leaves more availability for other areas of an ETL process.

❑   *Wizard allows changes* — If the inputs entered into the SCD Wizard require changing, the wizard can be re-invoked, and these changes will propagate down to the downstream-generated components automatically. A caveat to this benefit is presented in the limitations discussion that follows.

❑   *Customized output transformations* — Because the SCD Wizard generates transformations rather than a black-box approach, the output can be customized. For example, you can remove and replace the OLE DB Command transformation used for Type 1 changing attributes with a staging table in order to achieve set-based updates, which often perform faster than row-by-row updates.

❏ *Beyond dimension processing* — You can use the SCD transformation beyond just dimension processing, such as with table synchronization. Even though the name suggests that the SCD Wizard focuses exclusively on dimension processing, one alternative use is to just leverage the Type 1 changing attribute support (and the included new member support).

The limitations of the SCD support focus mostly on scalability for large-dimension scenarios:

❏ *Dimension table lookup scalability* — The dimension table is not cached in memory. Therefore, for every row coming in from the source, a separate lookup statement is sent to the dimension table in the underlying relational engine.

❏ *All updates are row-based* — Relational updates are required for the Type 1 changing attribute output, the Inferred Member output, and the Type 2 historical attribute output (to expire the previous record). Because the OLE DB Command transformation is employed, every row coming through these transformations sends a separate UPDATE statement to the dimension table, in a cursor-like fashion. When dealing with several thousand updates, this feature can be limiting.

❏ *Customized outputs are overwritten by changes* — Although the wizard can be rerun (with the prior run's values remaining), if you have customized the output and then run through the wizard again, when the wizard finishes, it overwrites any changes you made (the transformations will be orphaned by a new set of transformations). Be careful with that if you're making customizations. The wizard will overwrite them.

❏ *Locking issues and inserts* — At the same time that data may be queried from the dimension table for comparison, it may be updated in the dimension table to handle a Type 1 change, and it may also be inserted for new members and Type 2 historical records. All this activity on the dimension table happens at one time and can slow down the dimension ETL process. Furthermore, the inserts cannot take advantage of the Fast Load option because of the locking contentions, thus resulting in row-by-row inserts.

Dimension Volume and Complexity

Some of the dimension tables you will deal with will either have complexities that require advanced ETL, or they will contain hundreds of thousands or millions of dimension members and require special handling to optimize the ETL. And, in some cases, you must deal with both volume and complexity.

The most common complexities in dimension ETL involve parent-child, snowflake, profile, or junk dimensions. Each of these is not supported directly by the SCD transformation in SSIS. However, in some cases, you can use the SCD transformation with some additional logic, but, in other cases, you can't use the SCD at all.

The advanced dimension ETL design and solution sections of this chapter address each of these problems.

Design — Advanced Dimension ETL

To solve advanced dimension ETL problems with SSIS, the first step is to understand the design principles and aspects involved in the ETL. This section begins with the background to optimizing the SCD transformation, and then addresses the ETL aspects involved in snowflake, parent-child, date, profile, and junk dimensions. The section concludes with a look at building a custom dimension ETL process.

Optimizing the Built-in SCD

One of the benefits of the SCD transformation is that it is not an "all-or-nothing" proposition. In other words, optimization techniques are available to help tune the SCD. Later in this chapter, you learn about writing an SSIS package for dimension ETL without using the built-in SCD Wizard support. However, if you are dealing with a large dimension table, you can use a few techniques to achieve better performance with the out-of-the-box SCD transformation.

Index Optimizations

Because the dimension lookups and updates both are row-by-row operations, be sure to check the indexes on your dimension table to speed up the identification of the current record. If you are seeing very poor performance with the SCD (anything less than approximately 2,000 rows per minute), then chances are the SCD lookups are requiring relational table scans or bookmark lookups after identifying the record key. For best ETL optimization, create your dimension table's clustered index on the business key, rather than the dimension surrogate key. Including the current indicator flag or end date as the second column in the index improves the performance even more.

> You must balance index optimization between the ETL and the query usage. Optimization for query patterns should take priority over optimizations for ETL. However, some situations may require ETL-focused optimization as a priority to achieve the service-level agreements (SLAs) identified for processing times. Also, be cautious that too many indexes can slow down operations.

Update Optimizations

Dimension table updates to handle Type 1 changing attributes are a common occurrence in any dimension table ETL process. Although the inferred member output also requires updates, the number of rows are typically a fraction of the number of Type 1 changing attributes, because inferred members are considered an exception to the rule. Because the updates are row by row (this is the way the OLE DB Command transformation works), then dealing with thousands of updates will create a processing bottleneck.

One way to improve performance is to replace the OLE DB Command update with a set-based update approach. In Figure 7-31, the OLE DB Command that handles the Type 1 changing output has been replaced with an OLE DB Destination to a staging table.

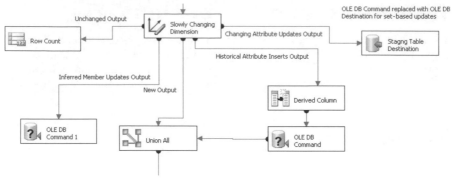

Figure 7-31

Using a staging table for this scenario improves performance, because it allows a single set-based UPDATE statement to be run. The UPDATE statement is handled with an Execute SQL Task in the control flow.

The set-based statement comprises an inner join between the staging table and the dimension table across the business key, where any matching rows (already identified as requiring a Type 1 changing update) will require the attributes to be updated. The following highlights the Transaction SQL (TSQL) code that performs this operation:

```
UPDATE [dbo].[DimProduct]
SET
 [Color] = STG.[Color]
,[DaysToManufacture] = STG.[DaysToManufacture]
,[EnglishProductName] = STG.[EnglishProductName]
,[FinishedGoodsFlag] = STG.[FinishedGoodsFlag]
,[FrenchProductName] = STG.[FrenchProductName]
,[ProductLine] = STG.[ProductLine]
,[ProductSubcategoryKey] = STG.[ProductSubcategoryKey]
,[ReorderPoint] = STG.[ReorderPoint]
,[SafetyStockLevel] = STG.[SafetyStockLevel]
,[SizeRange] = STG.[SizeRange]
,[SizeUnitMeasureCode] = STG.[SizeUnitMeasureCode]
,[SpanishProductName] = STG.[SpanishProductName]
,[StandardCost] = STG.[StandardCost]
,[Style] = STG.[Style]
,[Weight] = STG.[Weight]
,[WeightUnitMeasureCode] = STG.[WeightUnitMeasureCode]
FROM [dbo].[DimProduct]
INNER JOIN [SSIS_PDS].[dbo].[stgDimProductUpdates] STG
ON [DimProduct].[ProductAlternateKey]
 = STG.[ProductID]
```

Be sure to truncate your staging table for every ETL run (by adding an Execute SQL Task at the start of the control flow); otherwise, you will be updating data from old rows from a prior execution.

Snowflake Dimension Tables

A *snowflake dimension table*, as briefly described in the beginning of this chapter with the product dimension (refer to Figure 7-2), requires some unique ETL handling aspects. In a snowflake dimension, the higher-level tables (subcategory and category in this example) also have surrogate keys. With the product snowflake dimension, the `ProductCategoryKey` cascades down as a foreign key in the `DimProductSubCategory` table, and the `ProductSubCategoryKey` cascades down to a foreign key relationship in the `DimProduct` table. The `ProductKey` itself relates directly to the fact table, whereas the surrogate keys in the category and subcategory tables do not relate directly to the reseller fact table.

The design is called a snowflake because when viewed in relationship to the fact table, the table layout looks like a snowflake as opposed to a star. (A *star schema* has dimension tables one level out from the fact table. A single-table dimension is often called a *star dimension*.) Generally, most dimensions are designed as a star dimension. However, two very valuable reasons exist for breaking out a dimension table into a snowflake design:

❑ When a dimension table has several attributes that relate directly to a higher level within a dimension hierarchy, managing those dimension changes can be a lot easier with a snowflake design. For example, suppose that the product subcategory table contains the English, Spanish, and French names of the subcategory. If these columns were included in the base product table, and the subcategory changed for the dimension, ensuring that the Spanish and French names were in synch with the subcategory would be much more difficult. Otherwise, if they were not included, reporting of these attributes would be misleading with the incorrect association.

❑ A second and more compelling reason to use a snowflake is when you have multiple fact tables related to the same dimension table at different levels. For example, if the `Reseller Sales` fact table tracked sales at the Product Level, but the `Sales Quota` facts were assigned to a Product Category, if the Product dimension only had one table, the Category could not be effectively joined. Using a snowflake design, the fact tables can be related to one another because they share a common table at different levels of the product dimension hierarchy. Sharing dimension tables between fact tables is a driving emphasis of dimensional modeling called *conforming dimensions*.

A snowflake dimension table can still leverage the SCD transformation. The section on the Solution reviews how to solve the snowflake ETL challenge in SSIS.

> *Analysis Services supports having a standard dimension relate to different measure groups, at different levels. (A measure group in Analysis Services is equivalent to a fact table in the database.) It understands how to do the right aggregations. The Analysis Services engine naturally understands how to associate this data and perform aggregations.*

Parent-Child Dimension ETL

The next dimension design to consider is the *parent-child dimension*. A parent-child is a self-referencing dimension table and also has special ETL requirements. Simply put, a parent-child dimension has a surrogate key and a parent surrogate key, which gives the dimension a self reference. In addition, parent-child dimensions usually have a business key and a parent business key. The self-referencing business key nicely illustrates the parent relationship in the table.

An organizational structure is a great example. An organization typically has common attributes for all the individuals in the organization, such as location, office, salary, and so on. All of these attributes relate to higher levels in the hierarchy. A parent-child enables you to build a hierarchy where members at different levels have common attributes. A parent-child dimension also allows the hierarchy to be unbalanced, where not every drill path in the hierarchy goes down to the same level.

The `Employee` dimension table, as shown earlier in this chapter in Figure 7-2, is an example of an organizational structure. Figure 7-32 shows a subset of data and columns within the `Employee` dimension table.

Employee Key	Parent Key	Name	Title
112	NULL	Ken Sanchez	Chief Executive Officer
23	112	Peter Krebs	Production Control Manager
7	112	David Bradley	Marketing Manager
44	112	Jean Trenary	Information Services Manager
143	112	Laura Norman	Chief Financial Officer
275	7	John Wood	Marketing Specialist
276	7	Mary Dempsey	Marketing Assistant
214	23	Brenda Diaz	Production Supervisor - WC40
204	23	Hazem Abolrous	Quality Assurance Manager
188	23	Jack Richins	Production Supervisor - WC30
189	23	Andrew Hill	Production Supervisor - WC10
105	44	Dan Bacon	Application Specialist
120	44	Francois Ajenstat	Database Administrator
154	44	Stephanie Conroy	Network Manager

Figure 7-32

As you can see, some dimension members relate to other dimension members. For example, Dan Bacon reports to Jean Trenary. (Dan's parent employee key is 44, which is the employee key of Jean.) At the top of the table, the Chief Executive Officer, Ken Sanchez, has no parent key and, therefore, no manager. Every member in the table is a member at a different level in the hierarchy. Taking this subset of data and building the hierarchy for the parent-child relationship turns into the hierarchy shown in Figure 7-33.

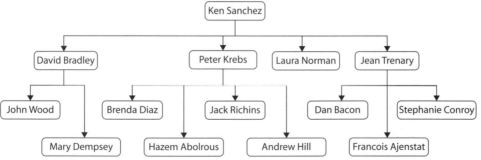

Figure 7-33

Note a few points about this parent-child dimension:

❏　This is an *unbalanced hierarchy*. The levels within this dimension don't all extend to the lowest level. (Laura Norman, for example, has no direct reports.) Within an unbalanced hierarchy, there are levels that don't cascade all the way down.

❏　A parent-child dimension can also be a *ragged hierarchy*. A ragged hierarchy has holes in the hierarchy. You could be at the top level, skip the next level, and go directly to the level below. You must be aware of these variations when processing ETL.

❏　Parent-child dimensions have shared attributes. Most of the records (except at the top level) share common attributes, such as `Employee Address`.

Date Dimension ETL

The *date dimension* is probably the most common and conformed dimension in any data warehouse or data mart structure. In other words, most fact tables have relationships to a `Date` table. A date dimension can have many different attributes. Besides the year, month, and date, it might include the following:

❏　Day of week

❏　Week of year

❏　Holiday

❏　Fiscal hierarchy

The attributes combine to create different hierarchies. An example of a natural calendar hierarchy would be Year-Quarter-Month-Date or Year-Week-Date. In the natural calendar, weeks do not line up with months (a week can span two months). Therefore, there are two natural calendar hierarchies. Because of this challenge, organizations have come up with different (and often unique) fiscal hierarchies. Your organization may have its own fiscal hierarchy.

A common approach to a custom fiscal hierarchy is to break a quarter into three periods: four weeks in period 1, four weeks in period 2, and five weeks in period 3 (commonly called a 4-4-5 fiscal date hierarchy). A period essentially replaces a month to accommodate the week-month challenge. One organization we worked with had at least ten different fiscal hierarchies — every branch of the organization wanted to see the sales data from a different perspective.

When it comes to handling the date dimension ETL, the dimension is relatively easy to process because when a new date record is added, it is usually never updated. The date dimension is commonly not snowflaked into multiple tables. A couple of approaches are examined later in the Solution discussion on how to handle date dimension ETL.

> **The date dimension is not typically snowflaked, even if you have higher-level fact tables and a multigrained scenario. For example, account balances might be tracked at a week level, whereas sales come in at a day level, and inventory at a month level. The date dimension almost always uses the day for granularity. You would use the first period of that grain as the key. For example, if inventory is at the month level, use the first day of the month as the key for the month.**

Profile Dimension and Junk Dimension ETL

Two other dimensions are found in dimensional models, but not as often as the other dimension types already discussed. The first is a *profile dimension*, which contains a summarized subset of attributes that relate to a source entity. The difference is that a profile dimension does not go down to the lowest grain of the source data. Instead, the dimension uses attributes that have fewer discrete values. This makes the dimension table much smaller from a row-count perspective.

For example, if the number of customers you have in your sales system is in the multimillions, you may not need to report on the detailed customer, but you still want to be able to analyze by customer attributes. This is a great example of when to use a profile dimension.

Figure 7-34 shows data from a customer profile dimension.

Age	Maried	Gender	Children	Education	Occupation	House Owner	Cars Owned
29	M	F	0	Bachelors	Clerical	0	0
30	S	F	0	Bachelors	Management	0	1
61	S	M	4	High School	Professional	0	2
62	M	F	2	Bachelors	Management	1	0
53	S	M	3	Partial College	Professional	1	2
44	S	F	2	Partial College	Clerical	1	2
44	S	F	3	Bachelors	Management	0	4
35	M	M	3	Partial College	Clerical	0	2
91	S	M	2	High School	Skilled Manual	1	2

Figure 7-34

This `Customer` profile dimension table has significantly less rows than a customer dimension table that contains the detailed customers.

Junk dimension tables are similar to profile dimensions in that they contain attributes that do not have discrete values (less unique values). The ETL challenge with these dimensions is that neither a profile dimension nor a junk dimension contains a business key. Therefore, the ETL must handle new records by identifying the unique combination of all the attributes in the table. In the Solution section later in this chapter, a proposed SSIS approach is provided that can ease the complexity of the ETL and still perform well.

Creating a Custom Slowly Changing Package

The built-in SCD transformation handles many (but not all) dimension processing situations. Its limitations were pointed out earlier in this chapter.

The natural question is: "How can I build a dimension ETL package that mimics the functionality of the built-in SCD support, but scales to handle high volumes?"

If you are now comfortable with the SSIS data flow features and the SCD concepts covered thus far, then the answer will be surprisingly easily. Before laying out a couple of variations, consider the different aspects of the dimension process:

❑ Data correlation between the source records and the dimension table

❑ Comparisons between the column values from the source and the dimension tables

❑ Updates to handle Type 1 changing records and inferred members

❑ Inserts to handle Type 2 historical changes and new dimension members

When considering the built-in SCD support, the SCD transformation (not including the downstream transformations) handles the first two aspects listed here. So, the objective is to first re-create this process by using out-of-the-box features.

Joining Source Data to Dimension Data

The first step you want to do is correlate the data, comparing the source to the dimension. Within SSIS, two primary transformations can help you correlate data: the Lookup transformation and the Merge Join transformation.

In both cases, you must use the business key in the source and associate it with the current record in the dimension. When you join those records together, you can then compare the different attributes to see whether there are changes:

❑ Using a *Lookup* transformation, the dimension table can be fully cached, which will limit the relational database management system (RDBMS) impact, as opposed to the row-by-row lookup approach of the SCD transformation. However, on a 32-bit server with 4GB of memory, the Lookup cache will max out in the neighborhood of 2 to 6 million dimension members in the cache, depending on the availability of system memory, the data type of the surrogate key and business key, and the number of columns needed to be returned by the lookup for comparison.

❑ A *Merge Join* transformation allows the dimension members to be joined with source records. When the source or dimension can be pre-sorted, this approach will allow greater memory scalability. Instead of keeping everything in cache, when a key match occurs, the row is sent downstream and no longer held up by the Merge Join. This approach requires a Left outer join, taking rows from the source on the left side, and the dimension on the right side, and merging across the business key.

Determining Data Correlation Approach

Before continuing with the review of this custom SCD package, here are a few considerations when determining what SSIS approach you should use to correlate data in the data flow. These approaches employ different uses of the Merge Join and Lookup transformations for bringing source and dimension data together:

❑ *Merge Join with Sort* — The Merge Join requires the sources be sorted on the joining keys. You could use a Sort transformation in each source before the Merge Join. However, this approach requires a lot of memory because the Sort must encapsulate all the records, and then sort them before sending the rows downstream.

❑ *Merge Join with Presorted Input* — Relational engines do a great job of sorting data because, in many cases, the join keys in the source are already indexed. If this is the case, use a simple ORDER BY statement in the source, and then tell the source adapter that the input is sorted (the approach identified earlier in this chapter).

❑ *Fully Cached Lookup* — The Lookup transformation allows full cache, partial cache, and no cache. Partial and no cache don't scale well, because database calls are expensive. However, if your dimension table size is manageable (less than a few hundred thousand members), then caching the dimension table in memory can provide great performance without the data sources having to be sorted.

❑ *Filtered Cache Lookup* — If you have millions of rows in your dimension table and are able to target only new and changed records during the dimension source extract, one option is to land the business keys from those dimension tables in a staging table, then use that staging table to filter the lookup itself. This method allows all the needed records to be loaded into the Lookup cache, but not the entire dimension table.

On a 64-bit server, the fully cached Lookup scales very well. The benefits of 64-bit are in both the size of the cache (millions of records) and the capability to load the records into cache much faster than a 32-bit environment.

Handling Dimension Inserts and Updates

The next step after you correlate the data involves comparing the columns from the source to the dimension. To do this, the best component is the Conditional Split transformation, because it can evaluate whether values have changed and direct the rows accordingly. The section, "Solution — Advanced Dimension ETL," later in this chapter shows an example of the Conditional Split used this way (see Figure 7-49).

If a change exists or a new record must be created, the final step in the dimension table ETL is to handle inserts and updates.

The SCD Wizard approach also handles inserts and updates by using a series of OLE DB Command transformations and OLE DB Destinations. When considering how to deal with changes in a custom dimension process, the same options are available:

❑ *Dimension Updates* — Updates for Type 1 changing attributes and inferred members can be handled by the OLE DB Command transformation, or a set-based update approach, which would leverage a staging table and an Execute SQL Task, as described earlier in this chapter.

❑ *Dimension Inserts* — Inserts should use an OLE DB Destination adapter or other destination that optimizes the inserts. If updates are handled through a staging table approach, the OLE DB Destination can be configured with fast load support. Otherwise, database table-locking contentions can happen if the updates are happening at the same time as the inserts.

An example of a custom dimension ETL process is provided in the Solution discussion next.

Solution — Advanced Dimension ETL

The final section of this chapter looks at how to solve the advanced dimension ETL problems reviewed earlier with SSIS.

Snowflake Dimensions

A straightforward method to processing snowflake dimensions in SSIS is to use multiple SCDs embedded in different data flows, linked by precedence constraints in the control flow starting at the top level of the snowflake tables and working down to the lowest level. Figure 7-35 shows the control flow of the product dimension package. Note the very first task is an Execute SQL Task that truncates the staging table used for the set-based update, followed by the three Data Flow Tasks.

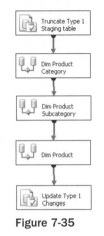

Figure 7-35

The first data flow shown is the product category dimension table, followed by the subcategory dimension table, and concluding with the product data flow. The final Execute SQL Task handles the set-based updates for Type 1 changing attributes as discussed earlier.

The product category data flow is the most straightforward because it only requires one Lookup transformation to get the category translation attributes, and, furthermore, it only contains Type 1 changing attributes. Figure 7-36 shows the product category data flow.

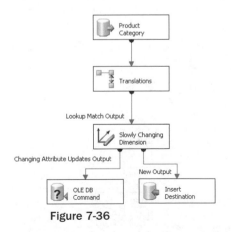

Figure 7-36

Next, you process the product subcategory. When processing data within intermediate snowflake tables in the hierarchy, a Lookup transformation is also required to reference the parent table surrogate key. For example, as you process the product subcategory table, include a Lookup transformation to pull the surrogate key of the category, as shown in Figure 7-37.

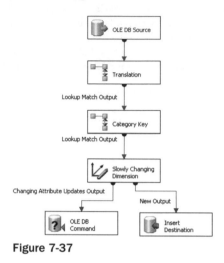

Figure 7-37

The ETL processing in the lowest-level product table has already been discussed.

Parent-Child Dimensions

When processing parent-child dimensions in SSIS, the unique ETL requirement is to acquire the parent dimension key. You can do so either with an UPDATE statement after the data flow that contains the dimension ETL, or you can use both an UPDATE statement and a Lookup transformation inside the dimension ETL. The Lookup must also be followed by an UPDATE statement when the child dimension member and the parent are added as new dimension members at the same time.

As an example, the DimEmployee dimension in the AdventureWorksDW2008 database contains several employee attributes plus a ParentEmployeeKey in the table. Figure 7-38 shows the Data Flow Task that handles the ETL.

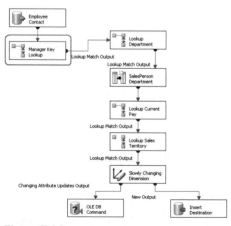

Figure 7-38

This data flow has similarities to the product dimension data flow, because several transformations are used to prepare the data for the SCD transformation (to handle the `DepartmentName`, `Salary`, and `SalesTerritory` columns). Also note that the first Lookup transformation is used to acquire the parent surrogate key. In this case, the Lookup transformation joins the parent employee business key of the source to the matching employee business key from the employee table. Figure 7-39 shows the Columns tab of the Lookup Transformation Editor.

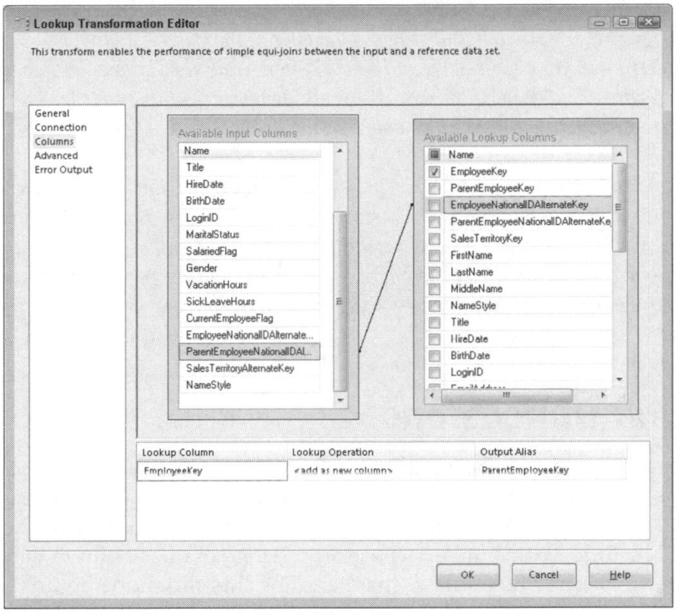

Figure 7-39

In addition to the join being across the parent business key to the business key in the reference table, the surrogate key that is returned is aliased to match the `ParentEmployeeKey`.

You must also add an Execute SQL Task to the control flow after the Data Flow Task to handle any `NULL` parent keys. This happens if the manager is added during the same ETL run as the employee. In fact, you do not even need the manager key lookup in the data flow. However, it helps optimize the ETL, because it reduces the number of rows that must be updated.

The Execute SQL Task that should run after the data flow must update the `ParentEmployeeKey` of the dimension records. The following SQL code is used to perform the operation:

```
UPDATE dbo.DimEmployee
   SET ParentEmployeeKey =
      (SELECT EmployeeKey
       FROM dbo.DimEmployee Parent
       WHERE EmployeeNationalIDAlternateKey =
             DimEmployee.ParentEmployeeNationalIDAlternateKey
         AND EndDate IS NULL)
FROM dbo.DimEmployee
WHERE ParentEmployeeKey IS NULL
```

The query could be handled by a self join or a correlated subquery. In this case, a join is used between the `Employee` table and the `Employee` table (aliased as `Parent`) matching across the child employee with the parent manager record. The `ParentEmployeeKey` is updated with the `EmployeeKey` of the `Employee` table joined as the parent table. Also important to note is that the only records affected are those with the `ParentEmployeeKey` set to `NULL`, which targets and, therefore, optimizes the updates.

As a final note about parent child dimension ETL, the example here assumes that all the columns are Type 1 changing attributes. Because the SCD transformation supports Type 2 historical attributes, you can certainly configure the SCD to handle them. However, if the parent member is also identified as a Type 2 historical attribute, then your ETL will be a lot more complex. This is because a change anywhere in the hierarchy requires new dimension records for all members underneath the changed hierarchy member. If the hierarchy changes often, that could result in thousands of changes daily!

The best approach is to leave the parent key as a Type 1 changing attribute with the current hierarchy, but then create a new table that contains the historical hierarchy keys. This table would have the dimension key, the parent key, and also a hierarchy version date. The hierarchy version date is simply the day that the hierarchy was captured. The ETL should just capture the hierarchy on a weekly or monthly basis, and you can use this table to go back in time to see what the hierarchy was for analysis purposes.

Profile and Junk Dimensions

As mentioned in the advanced ETL Design discussion earlier in this chapter, the challenge with profile and junk dimensions is that they do not have a business key. In fact, the candidate key is simply the combination of all the attributes. When all the attributes are part of a composite key, the attributes in effect become Type 2 historical attributes, because any change in one attribute value will cause a new record to be generated. You may be thinking that handling this situation should be pretty straightforward. And, in fact, if you only had to deal with loading the dimension table, then loading a profile or junk dimension would be pretty easy to handle. You could just use a Lookup transformation to determine whether the combination of attributes exists in the dimension table already. If it doesn't, then a new record must be added.

However, the challenge is actually in the fact table load, because if you go through a set of transformations to cleanse the data for the profile and junk dimensions, then you would have to perform the same set of steps in the fact table load so that you could identify the right key. This characteristic makes the fact table load very cumbersome, and introduces redundancy in the code. It's not a great solution. One way to approach this problem is to create a staging table that contains the cleansed attributes, along with the lowest-level business key — yes, the key that is not actually used in the dimension table. What this technique will allow is a fact load that can use the staging table to find the right surrogate key without having to duplicate all the transformation logic!

Figure 7-40 shows an ETL example of a dimension called `DimCustomerProfile`.

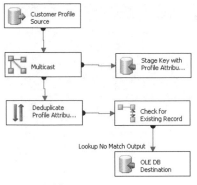

Figure 7-40

This data flow is a simple example. Depending on the complexity of the attributes, you may need several data flow components to handle the data cleansing and transformations required for your profile dimension. This data flow contains five primary steps:

1. A source adapter that runs a query returning the business key of the customer and the attributes of the customer profile dimension.

2. A Multicast and OLE DB Destination that lands the rows to a staging table for later use during the fact ETL process.

3. A Sort transformation that selects only the attributes used in the customer profile dimension (the business key is not included). The Sort has the "Remove rows with duplicate sort values" option checked, as shown in Figure 7-41. The purpose of this component is to remove duplicates so that only unique combinations of attributes are returned.

4. The Lookup transformation joins the attributes to the DimCustomerProfile dimension, and the configuration for errors sends the missing matches out the Lookup No Match Output.

5. The Destination loads rows into the DimCustomerProfile dimension that were not found in the Lookup transformation immediately above.

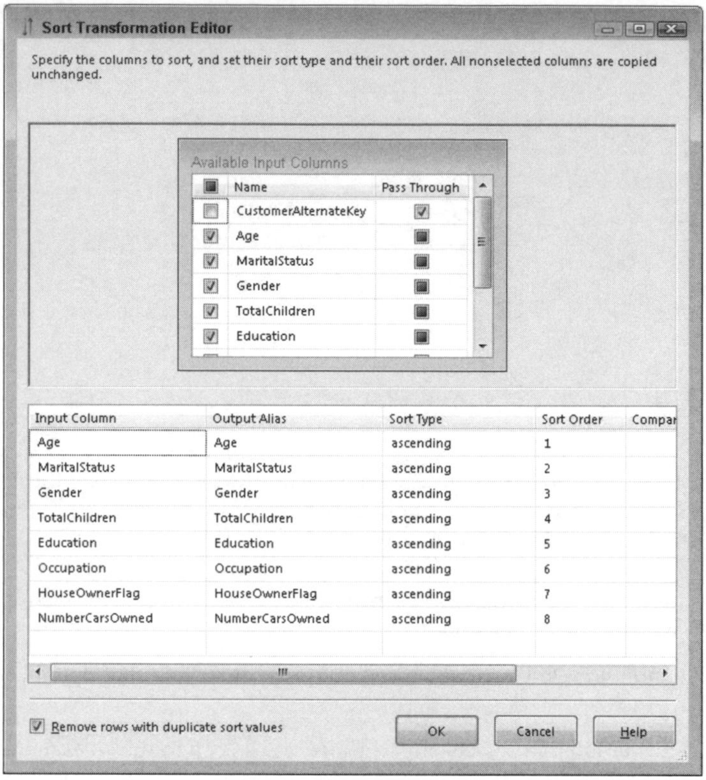

Figure 7-41

This dimension ETL package will load the records into the dimension where the combination of dimension values had not existed before. During the load, a new surrogate key is automatically generated because of the identity specifications in the table.

Chapter 8 deals with the fact table load, but because this dimension ETL solution requires special handling of the fact table load, here is a glimpse of how the fact ETL will acquire the customer profile surrogate key. The solution uses the staging table joined to the profile dimension across the profile dimension attributes as the following query shows:

```
SELECT DIM.CustomerProfileKey, STG.CustomerAlternateKey
  FROM dbo.DimCustomerProfile DIM
 INNER JOIN SSIS_PDS.dbo.stg_DimCustomerProfile STG
    ON DIM.Age = STG.Age
   AND DIM.MaritalStatus = STG.MaritalStatus
   AND DIM.Gender = STG.Gender
   AND DIM.TotalChildren = STG.TotalChildren
   AND DIM.Education = STG.Education
   AND DIM.Occupation = STG.Occupation
   AND DIM.HouseOwnerFlag = STG.HouseOwnerFlag
   AND DIM.NumberCarsOwned = STG.NumberCarsOwned
```

Because the staging table contains the `CustomerAlternateKey`, this key is returned in the `SELECT`, along with the `CustomerProfileKey` surrogate key of the profile dimension.

This query can then be used in the fact table load, and the only thing that is needed is the customer business key from the source. Figure 7-42 shows the Columns tab of the Lookup transformation in a fact table load to get the `CustomerProfileKey`. The Lookup uses the previous query.

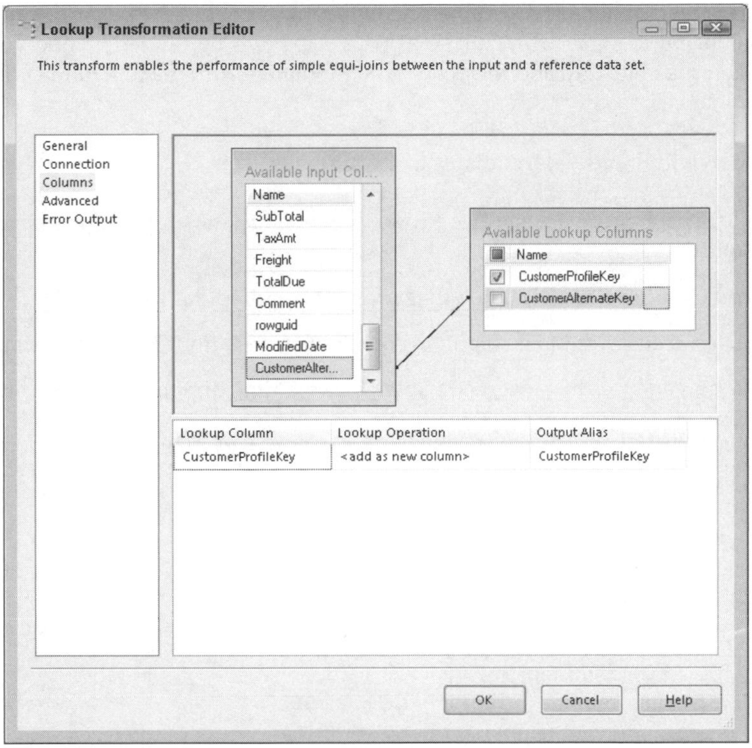

Figure 7-42

Date Dimension ETL

There are a few different ways to process date dimension ETL. Because the date dimension table is fairly static with usually only inserts of new rows, the most common approach is to run a procedure that performs all the date attribute logic and inserts new date dimension rows.

Another solution is to use a data flow that leverages the SSIS expression language to handle the date dimension ETL. This approach involves identifying the first new date and the last date to add, followed by a data flow to handle the inserts. Figure 7-43 shows the control flow of a package with an Execute SQL Task followed by a data flow.

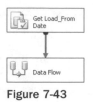

Figure 7-43

Defined in the package are two user variables, FromDate and ToDate, which are populated by the Execute SQL Task using a single-row result set. The FromDate is populated by querying the MAX date in the time dimension plus one day, and the ToDate is populated from the MAX date in the sales header table source.

The data flow, shown in Figure 7-44, contains five components:

❑ A Script Component that generates a row for every day starting with the Start Date and ending with the End Date

❑ A Derived Column transformation that adds the required date attributes

❑ Two Lookup transformations to pull in some date translations from a translation table

❑ A destination adapter that inserts the rows into the time dimension table

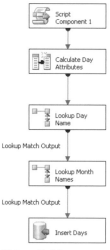

Figure 7-44

Because the Script Component can be used as a source (as described later in Chapter 11), it is a great candidate to generate rows from the FromDate to the ToDate values. The following code takes the SSIS variables and, using a Do While loop, iterates over the dates from the FromDate to the ToDate, adding a date for every loop:

```
Public Overrides Sub CreateNewOutputRows()
'
' Add rows by calling AddRow method on member variable called "<Output Name>Buffer"
' E.g., MyOutputBuffer.AddRow() if your output was named "My Output"

        Dim vFromDate As Date = Me.Variables.FromDate

        Do While vFromDate <= Me.Variables.ToDate
            With NewDatesOutputBuffer
                .AddRow()
                .FullDateAlternateKey = vFromDate
            End With
            vFromDate = DateAdd(DateInterval.Day, 1, vFromDate)
        Loop

End Sub
```

The second component to highlight is the Derived Column transformation. Figure 7-45 shows the Derived Column Transformation Editor, which contains several additional columns using the DATEPART SSIS expression function to pull out common attributes.

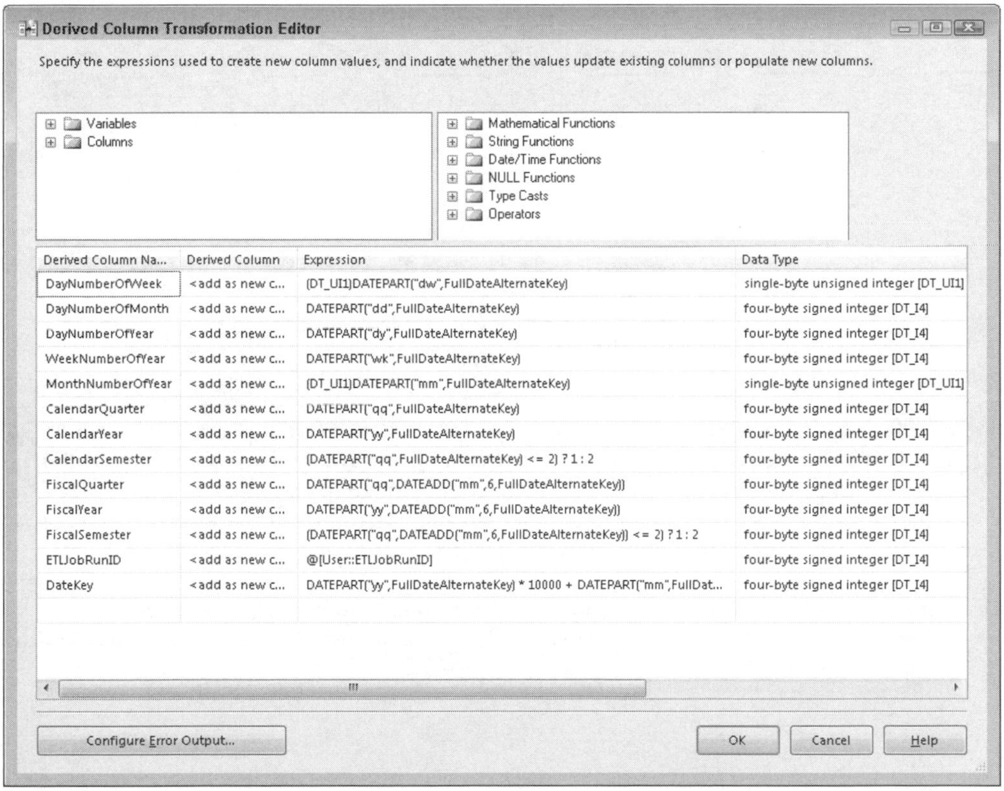

Figure 7-45

Before the OLE DB Destination (which is just an insert into the DimDate table), two Lookups handle the translation, because the time dimension table supports multiple languages for the month- and day-related attributes.

Overall, the package is straightforward, performs well, and leverages SSIS capabilities.

Custom Dimension ETL

The final solution described here demonstrates how to build a custom dimension ETL package without the SCD transformation. The reasons, benefits, and design choices were discussed in the advanced ETL Design section earlier in this chapter

Figure 7-46 shows the sample data flow for the customer dimension.

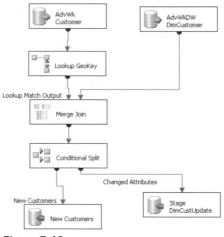

Figure 7-46

On the left, the customer source records are extracted (along with a Lookup to acquire the geography surrogate key), and on the right, the customer dimension records are pulled. Both of these sources are joined together with a Merge Join. As you recall, the Merge Join requires that the data sources are sorted. However, neither input is sorted using the Sort transformation. Rather, these sources use a SQL ORDER BY statement in the source adapter, sorting by the business key.

To accomplish this task, the Advanced Editor allows the sources to be flagged as pre-sorted. Figure 7-47 shows that the IsSorted property is set to True on the OLE DB Source Output of the dimension table source.

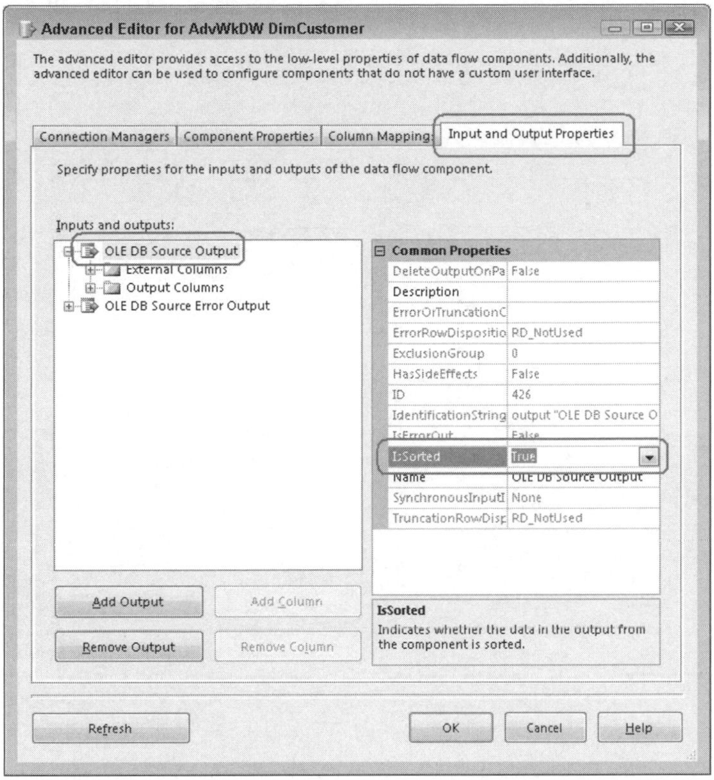

Figure 7-47

To be sure, the `IsSorted` property is only a flag. It does not perform any actual sorting itself. It is merely a contract by the developer to the component to state that it should "trust this source is already sorted."

The second required step to mark a source to be pre-sorted is to drill into the Output Columns folder in the same window, and change the `SortKeyPosition` (not shown) of the appropriate sorted column to an integer that delineates which columns are sorted in which order (negative indicates descending).

As a reminder, both inputs into a Merge Join must be sorted on the join column in order for the Merge Join to validate. Because both sources have been marked as pre-sorted, the Merge Join will recognize the sort columns. Figure 7-48 shows the Editor window of the Merge Join transformation.

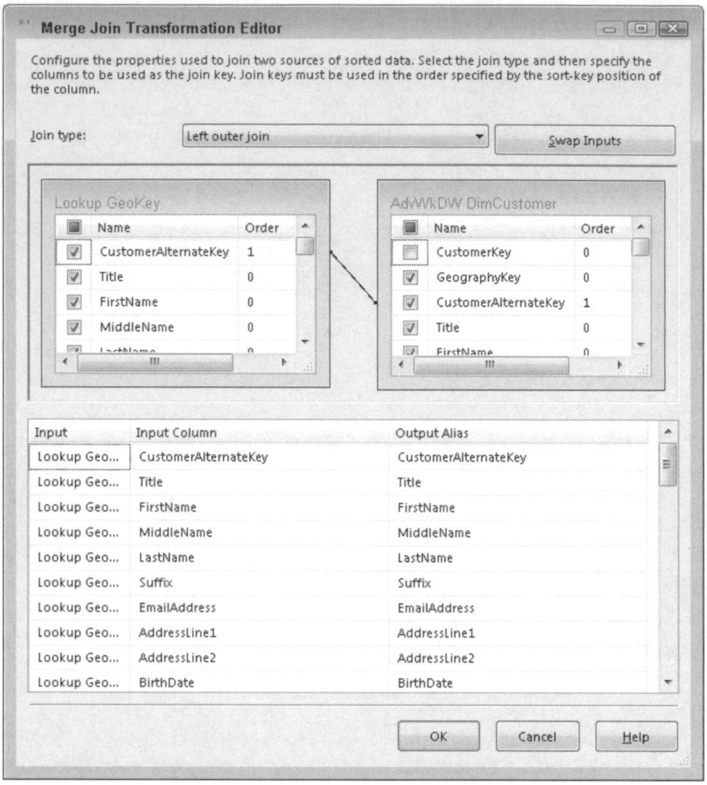

Figure 7-48

The Left outer join Join type allows the new source records to be identified. Notice also that the attribute columns are selected on both inputs. This is to allow the comparison of the columns in the next step. Because many of the column names are repeated, the columns from the right input (the Dimension table) are prefixed with a DW_.

Determining Dimension Changes

Now that the dimension source has been joined with the dimension table, the records must be routed to the appropriate output for the dimension change handling. As Figure 7-46 showed previously, the next step after the Merge Join is a Conditional Split, which helps determine where the records should go.

The Customer dimension in AdventureWorksDW2008 contains only Type 1 changing attributes, which simplifies this example. Therefore, only new members and changes must be accommodated. The comparison is handled through the Conditional Split transformation, the editor shown in Figure 7-49.

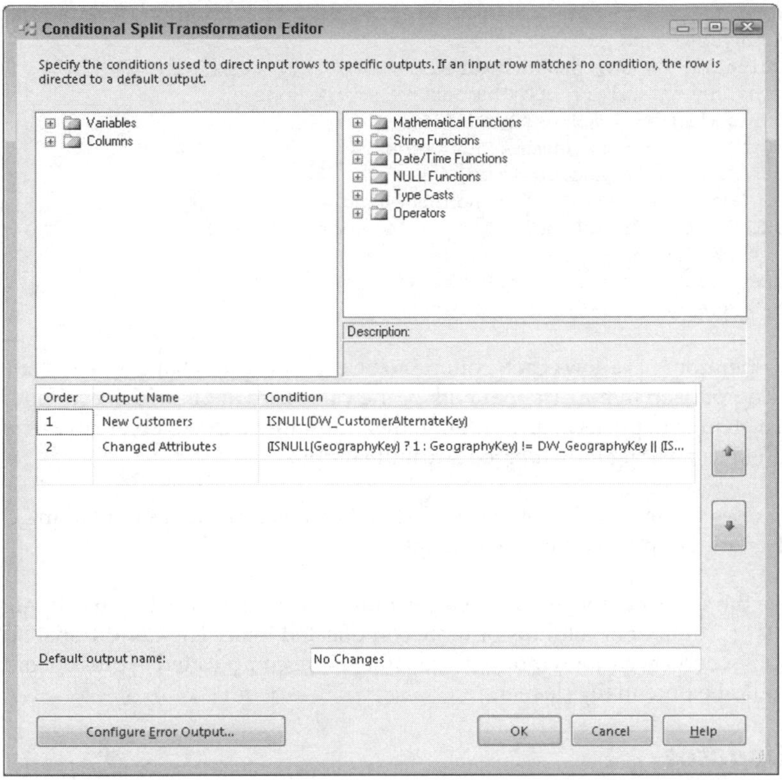

Figure 7-49

As you can see, the first criterion evaluated is whether the business key is NULL in the dimension table, ISNULL(DW_CustomerAlternateKey). If it is NULL, then this indicates the dimension record does not exist, and, therefore, the source record is New Customers, as the output name indicates.

The second criterion is to determine whether a change has happened in any of the attribute columns, using an SSIS expression, as shown in the following code:

```
   (ISNULL(GeographyKey) ? 1 : GeographyKey) != DW_GeographyKey
|| (ISNULL(Title) ? "" : Title) != (ISNULL(DW_Title) ? "" : DW_Title)
|| FirstName != DW_FirstName
|| (ISNULL(MiddleName) ? "" : MiddleName)
   != (ISNULL(DW_MiddleName) ? "" : DW_MiddleName)
|| LastName != DW_LastName
|| BirthDate != DW_BirthDate
|| MaritalStatus != DW_MaritalStatus
|| (ISNULL(Suffix) ? "" : Suffix) != (ISNULL(DW_Suffix) ? "" : DW_Suffix)
```

```
|| Gender != DW_Gender
|| EmailAddress != DW_EmailAddress
|| TotalChildren != DW_TotalChildren
|| NumberChildrenAtHome != DW_NumberChildrenAtHome
|| HouseOwnerFlag != DW_HouseOwnerFlag
|| NumberCarsOwned != DW_NumberCarsOwned
|| AddressLine1 != DW_AddressLine1
|| (ISNULL(AddressLine2) ? "" : AddressLine2)
   != (ISNULL(DW_AddressLine2) ? "" : DW_AddressLine2)
|| Phone != DW_Phone
|| DateFirstPurchase != DW_DateFirstPurchase
|| CommuteDistance != DW_CommuteDistance
```

The Logical OR operator (||) allows each column to be evaluated for changes. The ISNULL function helps to perform the comparison in the case that both of the values are NULL, which evaluates as not equal. In other words, if a change happens in any column, then the entire expression evaluates as TRUE, and the record is identified as meeting the Changed Attribute output.

Finally, if a row does not meet either of these criteria, then it is consider as not having changed, and, therefore, the Default Output is called No Changes.

You can also use the script component to do the conditional comparison, because it might be easier when dealing with a large number of columns or more complicated logic. The Conditional Split expression box does not allow a secondary editor window to generate more complicated expressions. Therefore, a Script Component would be potentially cleaner.

Inserts and Updates

Continuing with the previous example, a set-based approach is taken to handle the updates. Therefore, the output of the Conditional Split requires two OLE DB Destination adapters, as Figure 7-46 demonstrated earlier: one for the dimension inserts and a second for the staging table inserts.

Because the ETL process controls the data in the dimension table and the updates will not be happening at the same time, a Fast Load with a Table Lock is used to handle the inserts. Figure 7-50 shows the OLE DB Destination adapter editor for the dimension inserts.

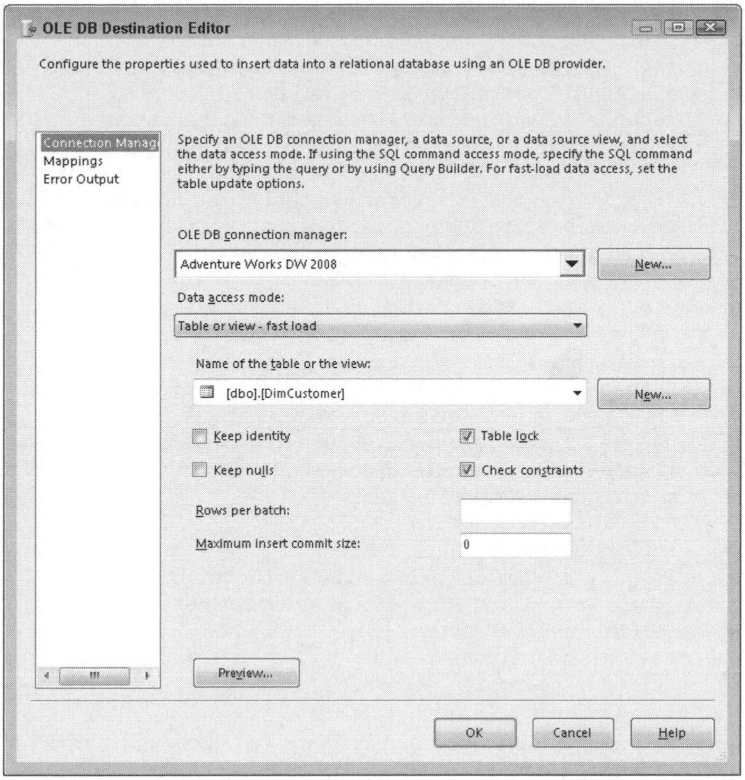

Figure 7-50

When it comes to the dimension updates, after the rows requiring an update are loaded to the staging table, the set-based update can be performed. Figure 7-51 shows the control flow of the Customer package, which ends in an Execute SQL Task to perform the update, called Batch Updates. This control flow also begins with a truncation statement to clear out the same staging table used for the updates.

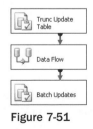

Figure 7-51

The update itself is formed by joining the dimension table with the staging table, and replacing the values in the staging table with the current values in the dimension table.

```
UPDATE AdventureWorksDW2008.dbo.DimCustomer
   SET AddressLine1 = stgDimCustomerUpdates.AddressLine1
     , AddressLine2 = stgDimCustomerUpdates.AddressLine2
     , BirthDate = stgDimCustomerUpdates.BirthDate
     , CommuteDistance = stgDimCustomerUpdates.CommuteDistance
     , DateFirstPurchase = stgDimCustomerUpdates.DateFirstPurchase
     , EmailAddress = stgDimCustomerUpdates.EmailAddress
     , EnglishEducation = stgDimCustomerUpdates.EnglishEducation
     , EnglishOccupation = stgDimCustomerUpdates.EnglishOccupation
     , FirstName = stgDimCustomerUpdates.FirstName
     , Gender = stgDimCustomerUpdates.Gender
     , GeographyKey = stgDimCustomerUpdates.GeographyKey
     , HouseOwnerFlag = stgDimCustomerUpdates.HouseOwnerFlag
     , LastName = stgDimCustomerUpdates.LastName
     , MaritalStatus = stgDimCustomerUpdates.MaritalStatus
     , MiddleName = stgDimCustomerUpdates.MiddleName
     , NumberCarsOwned = stgDimCustomerUpdates.NumberCarsOwned
     , NumberChildrenAtHome = stgDimCustomerUpdates.NumberChildrenAtHome
     , Phone = stgDimCustomerUpdates.Phone
     , Suffix = stgDimCustomerUpdates.Suffix
     , Title = stgDimCustomerUpdates.Title
     , TotalChildren = stgDimCustomerUpdates.TotalChildren
  FROM AdventureWorksDW2008.dbo.DimCustomer DimCustomer
 INNER JOIN dbo.stgDimCustomerUpdates
    ON DimCustomer.CustomerAlternateKey
       = stgDimCustomerUpdates.CustomerAlternateKey
```

In this case, because the Customer dimension only contains Type 1 changing attributes, every non-key attribute is updated. In the case where Type 2 historical attributes are involved, the UPDATE statement would only target the Type 1 changing attributes, and leave any changes in the Type 2 historical attributes to an insert.

When this package is run with a large volume, the differences will be stark compared to the built-in SCD Wizard. A customer dimension with hundreds of thousands or millions of records will process in a fraction of the time that the SCD would take, given how the SCD works.

Summary

As demonstrated, when working through your list of dimension change and processing requirements, SSIS provides great out-of-the-box support to handle a majority of the cases and data volumes in your organization. The SCD Wizard can deal with Type 0 fixed, Type 1 changing, and Type 2 historical attributes, and even handle the unique update requirements that inferred members require. But even in situations where the complexity or volume go beyond what the SCD Wizard can handle out-of-the-box, you can tweak the SCD outputs or even use other data flow features and components to build a custom solution that does scale and can deal with your unique situations.

As a natural extension to dimension ETL, Chapter 8 focuses on the requirements around fact table ETL practices using SSIS. Then, Chapter 9 shifts to processing your dimension and fact data into the supporting Analysis Services objects that your BI solution leverages for analytics.

8

Fact Table ETL

When it comes to loading data into data warehouses, dimension table ETL is only half the story. The next major aspect of ETL involves fact tables. But the good news is that dimension ETL usually represents the majority of the complexity in the overall warehouse ETL. To be sure, a data warehouse involves more than just dimension and fact ETL (such as data lineage, auditing, and execution precedence). But in terms of business data, dimensions and facts contain the core information.

This chapter focuses on using SSIS to solve the ETL challenges involved with fact table ETL, and addresses the following:

❑ The "Problem" section outlines what fact tables are, and the challenge with loading data into them.

❑ The "Design" section considers the theory behind fact table ETL, including data mapping, workflow, and precedence. Included in the "Design" section is a discussion of how to identify dimension surrogate keys, measure calculations, fact table updates, and inserts.

❑ The "Solution" section applies the SSIS features and demonstrates two complete packages to handle fact table ETL.

Problem

The core of data warehousing is measuring data. In Chapter 7, you learned about the descriptive data (mostly text columns) and entities called *dimension tables* that allowed easy browsing for attributes and hierarchies. This chapter focuses on the measuring of data (mostly numeric data) by working with entities called *fact tables* that contain numeric measures used to track the core business processes, such as sales, orders, procurement, inventory, account balances, and events.

This section provides an overview of fact tables, including a description of the different types of fact tables used in data warehousing. In addition, you will become familiar with the primary aspects of fact table ETL, including capturing the measures, acquiring the dimension surrogate keys, and handling grain changes for different types of fact tables. The section begins by presenting fact table design principles.

Fact Tables: The Basics

Instead of containing attributes about an entity as dimension tables do, a fact table contains the metrics or numbers that a report presents, or a cube aggregates, as well as trends. Examples of these *measures* include sales amount, account balance, discount amount, and shipping quantity. Figure 8-1 shows the Internet sales fact table, which contains several measures related to the direct sales to consumers, such as OrderQuantity, UnitPrice, ExtendedAmount, and so on.

Dimension Surrogate Keys

Degenerate Dimensions and Lineage

Measures

Degenerate Dimensions

FactInternetSales		
Column Name	Data Type	Allow Nulls
ProductKey	int	☐
OrderDateKey	int	☐
DueDateKey	int	☐
ShipDateKey	int	☐
CustomerKey	int	☐
PromotionKey	int	☐
CurrencyKey	int	☐
SalesTerritoryKey	int	☐
SalesOrderNumber	nvarchar(20)	☐
SalesOrderLineNumber	tinyint	☐
RevisionNumber	tinyint	☐
OrderQuantity	smallint	☐
UnitPrice	money	☐
ExtendedAmount	money	☐
UnitPriceDiscountPct	float	☐
DiscountAmount	float	☐
ProductStandardCost	money	☐
TotalProductCost	money	☐
SalesAmount	money	☐
TaxAmt	money	☐
Freight	money	☐
CarrierTrackingNumber	nvarchar(25)	☑
CustomerPONumber	nvarchar(25)	☑
		☐

Figure 8-1

In addition to the measures, a fact table also contains the relationships between the measures and the dimensions. As Figure 8-1 shows, the fact table contains the foreign key relationship from the dimension tables. Essentially, the primary key in the dimension table is the dimension's surrogate key. The surrogate keys from the related dimension tables are included in the fact table. This fact table also contains degenerate dimension values and lineage columns (which often overlap) to provide the transaction IDs to allow tracing back to the source data, and filtering by transaction numbers.

The three types of columns in the fact table are dimension keys, measures, and metadata. These columns map directly to the ETL processing requirements for fact table ETL, mapping dimension keys, calculating measures, and adding metadata.

There are different types of fact tables, just like dimension tables had variations. Dimensions ETL involves dealing with different change types and managing change history. Fact table ETL has similar concepts, which involve different types of fact tables, managing history and change, and data grain changes from the source to the fact table.

Figure 8-2 shows the primary sales fact tables within the `AdventureWorksDW2008` database: reseller sales and Internet sales. Notice that the fact tables are identical, except for the `ResellerKey` in the `FactResellerSales` table and the `CustomerKey` in the `FactInternetSales` table.

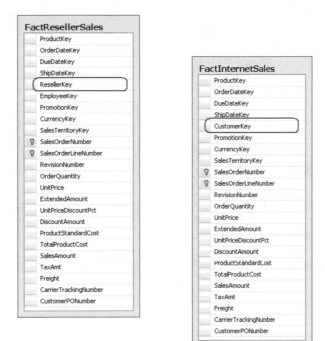

Figure 8-2

These fact tables are *transaction fact tables*. This means that the fact tables contain transactional activity. In this case, the transactions are sales activity. Instead of having one fact table for sales, two transactional fact tables are appropriate because they contain different grain (level of detail). One table represents sales activity when selling directly to an end consumer. The other fact table contains the sales when selling to a reseller store.

Other transactional fact tables may have a different type of transaction, such as system alerts, shipping activity, and so on. Furthermore, in this case, both the reseller sales and Internet sales fact tables come from the same source tables. This is an example of a *data grain change*.

Another fact table type is called a *snapshot fact table*. Figure 8-3 shows the schemas of the finance fact table, currency rate fact table, and call center fact table, which are examples of snapshot fact tables.

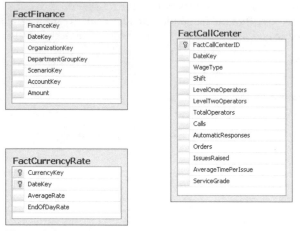

Figure 8-3

A snapshot fact table is a point-in-time picture of the levels or balances of the source. The finance fact table, for example, contains account balance snapshots of the amounts on a monthly level. The advantage to this design is that it allows quick querying of the balances historically without having to compile the transactions in order to answer the query. But it also allows trending over time of the balances at different grains of the dimensionality. As an example, Figure 8-4 shows the monthly account balances of administrative salaries, reported off the finance fact table.

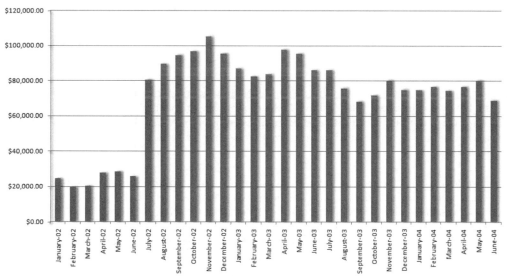

Figure 8-4

If the finance fact table were treated as a transactional table of all the financial account debits and credits, then creating a chart like the one shown in Figure 8-4 would be much more difficult. You would need to know the beginning balance and then apply the transactions against the balance monthly, bringing forward the prior month balance and being sure to take into account any journal entry adjustments. A snapshot fact table for a financial accounts table makes reporting and analytics much easier to handle.

The call center fact table is also a snapshot fact table because it combines the details of call center activity and summarizes the activity at the day level, tracking counts of the number of calls, escalations, operators, and orders.

Although not shown, another common type of snapshot fact table targets inventory levels. Instead of tracking account balances over time, an inventory-level fact table tracks in-stock levels at different locations at various times.

Fact Table ETL: The Challenge

Fact table ETL is similar to dimension ETL in that the source system may come in a different structure than the destination dimensional fact structures. Figure 8-5 shows (on the left) the transactional tables that participate in the sales activity for `AdventureWorks2008`. On the right, it shows the table structures that are involved in the dimensional model.

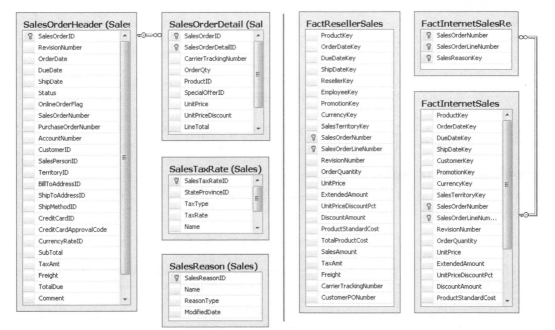

Figure 8-5

If you look carefully, you can see that the tables are structured differently and do not even correspond one-to-one from the transactional system to the data warehouse. Two sales transaction tables are in the source (a header and a detail), plus a couple supporting tables. The dimensional model has three fact tables, with the two primary fact tables being the Internet sales fact and the reseller sales fact table. Essentially, to perform the ETL, the header and detail transactional tables are combined, and then broken out based on whether the sale was direct-to-consumer (through the Internet), or sold to a reseller. The ETL performs both consolidation and a breakout (or partitioning) of the data.

This is the challenge of fact table ETL — to perform the data changes, consolidation, calculations — and to do it in a way that is scalable, manageable, and flexible. But before diving into ETL design, take a close look at the following list of the various aspects of fact table ETL:

- ❏ Data preparation
- ❏ Dimension surrogate keys
- ❏ Measures
- ❏ Metadata
- ❏ Fact table updates
- ❏ Fact table inserts

Preparing the Data

In many ways, the data preparation for fact table ETL is similar to dimension ETL, because most of the time, the data is coming from the same place. The source tables are typically transactional systems or operational data stores, and, therefore, require associating data and handling missing or dirty data.

Transforming and loading fact tables does have some unique data preparation steps. For example, at times, you may need to summarize data, which is typically not done during dimension table ETL. You may also need to combine multiple streams of data into a single feed if, for example, you have multiple field offices that send in data files nightly that then populate the same fact table. Both of these examples are shown later in this chapter in the "Solution" section.

Mapping Dimension Keys

Data warehouse project plans should include some mechanism to map source tables or files to both the dimension and fact tables.

The fact table mapping must include not just where and how the measures are calculated, but also *how the dimension relationships are mapped to acquire the related dimension's surrogate key.* In other words, when you are loading a fact table, you must have the business keys of the dimension available that are used to join to the dimension table to identify the surrogate keys that are inserted into the fact table. The business keys are sometimes called *candidate keys.* There may even be situations when one fact table uses one set of business keys to look up against a dimension, and a second fact table uses a second key (or keys) to identify the dimension record for the same dimension table.

Calculating Measures

Measures in fact tables may be generated from multiple source columns and tables, or files. At times, a measure may be derived in the ETL process without a direct mapping from a source value. A common example of this is when Analysis Services (or other cubing engine) is involved, and a counting or occurrence measure is needed. Such measures usually assume the values of 0 or 1, based on a source occurrence. These measures are additive in nature, and fit nicely with Analysis Services aggregations.

Adding Metadata

Fact tables (and dimension tables) often include metadata columns that provide information about the rows in the table. These metadata columns include `datetime` columns, batch identifiers, and lineage columns. `datetime` and batch identifiers help to identify when a row was added, and with what ETL processing group the row was executed. Lineage, on the other hand, identifies where a record came from in the source system down to the source row or records.

Fact Table Updates

Several situations may require data updates to the fact table. This can include when you must make data corrections, or when you are updating. Here are the most common circumstances that require fact table updates:

❑ *Updates to inventory balances or account balances* — If you have a snapshot fact table such as an inventory table that is captured at a week level, you may need to make daily updates to the current week until the new week begins.

❑ *Updates to accumulating fact tables* — If you are consolidating activity records such as alerts into a single fact table that is tracking multiple dates (such as occurrence date, escalation date, or resolution date), you may need to update the fact records as changes occur in the source system.

❑ *Data corrections or adjustments* — Data changes happen in any transactional system because of errors or simply because of required changes. You may need to update your fact table records when these changes occur.

In contrast to fact table volumes, dimension tables typically don't have many records — most often less than a million records. However, fact tables can scale into millions of records, and even billions, depending on how much data is coming across from the transactional sources. Column optimization of the fact table is, therefore, critical to performance. Because of this, fact tables may not always have metadata in order to reduce the overall row width for performance reasons. By keeping the fact table narrow, you trade off the benefits of the metadata for better overall performance, both when querying and loading data.

Fact Table Inserts

Of course, every fact table involves inserts. This is the most critical piece of a fact table to design optimally for performance. Inserts can be as simple as just inserting new transactions into the fact table, or they can involve working with complex indexes within your table partitioning strategy to optimize how the new rows are added.

If you need your fact table inserts to run as fast as possible, then just using an SSIS destination adapter by itself will not do the trick without the support of other table management tasks. Both the "Design" and "Solution" sections of this chapter describe how to leverage SSIS for fact table insert optimization. If you are working with partitioned tables and need direction on how to optimize the inserts, then see Chapter 12, which shows an example of managing partitions in a partitioned table for faster inserts.

Design

Handling fact table ETL often involves many unique scenarios. In fact, you have many ways you can approach each data processing requirement, even in SSIS. Some approaches are better than others.

This section shows you a few ways in SSIS to handle the most common situations, and considers some of the rationale behind each design area. You can combine these SSIS design approaches based on the overall challenges you face. Following the "Design" section, the "Solution" section of this chapter demonstrates two SSIS fact table ETL examples, plus some advanced ETL.

Data Preparation

Data preparation for fact tables has many flavors. Commonly, data preparation involves correlating sources, summarizing data, filtering, or splitting data. Here are some data preparation requirements you may come across:

❑ *Consolidating sources* — This can include combining multiple tables or files together, or joining sources to produce a complete set of business keys needed for the fact table. A common situation is when multiple locations within an organization use different copies of the same system. To report off of a combined fact table, these sources must be consolidated.

❑ *Splitting out sources* — This may be required if you have a single table that populates multiple fact tables. For example, an enterprise resource planning (ERP) system may export a file that contains the transactions for two different fact tables, based on transaction category. In this case, the rows would need to be divided.

❑ *Roll-up summarizations* — These are a common grain change, where the source feed is at a lower level of detail than the required fact table based on reporting needs. Many situations do not require the detail grain of the source for reporting, which has a side benefit of performance gains and reduced storage requirements.

❑ *Pivot or un-pivot dimensionality* — This converts source data and columns to rows, or rows to columns. The most common pivoting needed for fact table data is when the source is coming from a fourth-normal form design, or key-value pair. This data may need to be un-pivoted to de-normalize the data for the fact table match.

Of course, other types of data preparation scenarios exist, and may even involve more than one of these requirements for a single fact table.

Data Preparation with SSIS Transformations

How is this data preparation handled with SSIS? SSIS includes several built-in transformations to help manage fact table grain changes from the Aggregate transformation to the Pivot. Table 8-1 describes several transformations and potential uses to handle different grain changes.

Table 8-1

Transformation	Data Usage
Pivot	Converts columns to rows. Useful in a flattened record set to normalize the grain of a source that will be used for a fact load.
Un-pivot	Converts rows to columns. Useful for key-value pairs that are common in auditing tables to collapse rows to columns, and to de-normalize the grain.
Conditional Split	Allows data routing and filtering. Useful when a source feed must be filtered for a fact load, or a single source must be split to different fact loads.
Aggregate	Summarizes source data. Useful for sources that must be rolled up to a higher-level grain for the fact table load. Can also be used to aggregate across multiple key sets for multiple fact table outputs.
Sort	De-duplicates data (and sorts). Provides the capability to remove duplicates across the sort key columns. Useful for sources that must be pared down based on duplicate records.
Union All	Stacks rows of data from multiple sources. Useful when more than one source table or feed match in structure and must be combined for a fact table load. Rows are not joined, but rather passed through. Provides similar semantics to a relational UNION ALL operation.
Merge Join	Joins two sources on a set of keys. Useful when several sources' entities must be consolidated for a single fact load. Joins across rows, rather than stacking rows, which allows for columns from both inputs to be included in the output. Also allows the capability to allocate rows to a lower grain by providing multiple output rows across matches. Provides similar semantics to relational JOIN operations (INNER JOIN, LEFT OUTER JOIN, FULL OUTER JOIN).
Lookup	Allows you to include columns from a reference table to the output. Useful to also correlate sources, by providing the capability to augment columns from a relational table to the pipeline based on matching source key columns. Can also be used as a filter mechanism to identify matches and non-matches.
Derived Column	Allows calculations for allocation with a row. Useful when combined with other transformations.
Script Component	Provides advanced grain-changing capabilities. Useful for many complex scenarios not included in the out-of-the-box capabilities, such as advanced pivoting, filtering, combining, and so on.

Even beyond what you see in Table 8-1, you can also achieve data changes by combining these different out-of-the-box transformations, thus allowing for a fairly comprehensive toolset to handle unique scenarios.

Data Preparation Examples

As an example of data preparation, one common scenario is handling data correlation. Essentially, when you must join multiple tables or files in a source together, you can do so in SSIS with the Merge Join transformation.

You can do joins, of course, in a database query, but you don't often have the luxury of having all the source data in the same database to perform them, or maybe your data is coming from files, or you may need to minimize the impact to the source system.

Therefore, in the case when the source feed does not come from a database system, or the database cannot optimize the join effectively enough without either straining the source system or slowing down the extraction, you should use the Merge Join transformation in SSIS. Figure 8-6 shows a data flow that contains two source adapters extracting data from a sales header table and sales detail table. The ultimate goal of this data flow is to prepare this data for the fact tables.

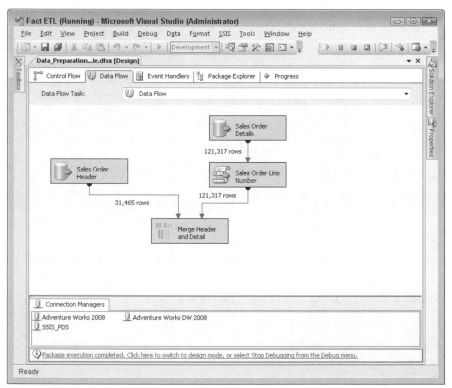

Figure 8-6

To perform the correlation from both source files, a Merge Join transformation is used. Figure 8-7 shows the Merge Join Transformation Editor.

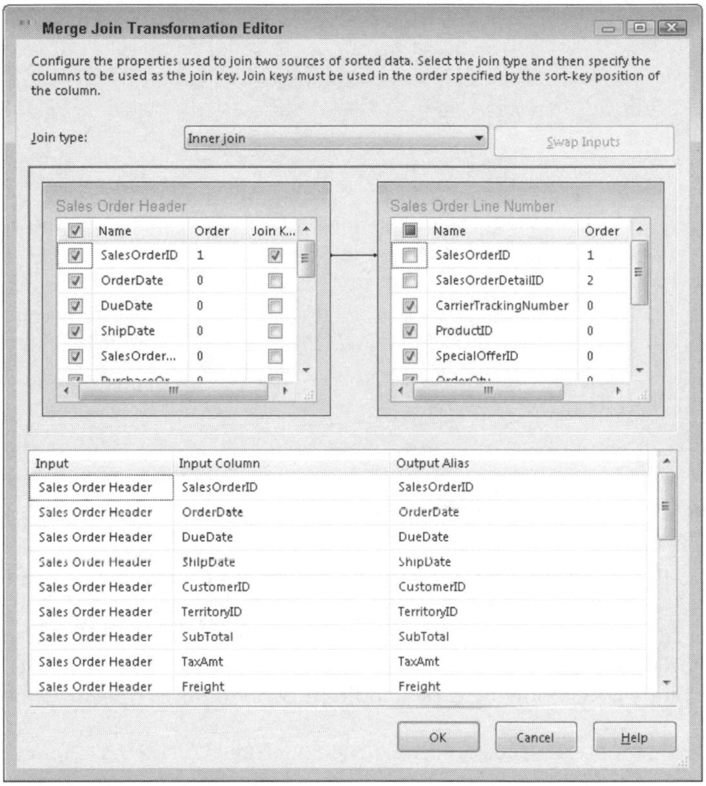

Figure 8-7

In this data flow, both source adapters contain SQL statements with explicit ORDER BY *operations on the* SalesOrderID *key. Because the Merge Join requires the sources to be sorted, you can either use a Sort transformation or you can pre-sort the data. In this case, the tables have indexes that help the sort operation. The source adapters are marked as pre-sorted, as described in Chapter 7, which is a requirement if you will use an* ORDER BY *operation.*

An INNER JOIN is used in the Merge Join transformation, because the source system that created the files uses referential integrity. Therefore, no records will be lost in the join. A Lookup transformation could have been used in this example with the sales header in the Lookup transformation reference table, because the lookup would be across the SalesOrderID and the SalesOrderID, which has a unique constraint as the primary key. However, if your sales header and sales detail tables were coming from files, a Merge Join approach would be required, because the Lookup component is unable to directly read in flat-file data.

Another useful example of data preparation within this data flow is the Script component, which is placed just below the Sales Order Details source in Figure 8-6. In the sales fact table, sales transactions are grouped by the `SalesOrderID` (named `SalesOrderNumber` in the fact tables). Within each `SalesOrderNumber` group, the detail line records have a line number called `SalesOrderLineNumber` that is auto-incrementing. Figure 8-8 shows an example of the sales line numbers.

	SalesOrderNumber	SalesOrderLineNumber
1	SO43664	1
2	SO43664	2
3	SO43664	3
4	SO43664	4
5	SO43664	5
6	SO43664	6
7	SO43664	7
8	SO43664	8
9	SO43665	1
10	SO43665	2
11	SO43665	3
12	SO43665	4
13	SO43665	5
14	SO43665	6
15	SO43665	7
16	SO43665	8
17	SO43665	9
18	SO43665	10

Figure 8-8

Notice that there are two sales order numbers, and each group has incrementing numbers starting at 1 for the detail lines. Because the sales detail table in the source does not contain the numbers, they must be generated in the ETL process. The Script component handles this task. The rows coming into the script are already sorted by `SalesOrderID`. Therefore, the script evaluates the sales orders and updates the numbers accordingly. The following code handles this job in the Script component:

```
Public Overrides Sub Input_ProcessInputRow(ByVal Row As InputBuffer)
    '
    If (Row.SalesOrderID = Me.PreviousSalesOrderID) Then
        Me.SalesOrderLineNumber = Me.SalesOrderLineNumber + 1
    Else
        Me.SalesOrderLineNumber = 1
    End If
    Me.PreviousSalesOrderID = Row.SalesOrderID 'set up for next row
    Row.SalesOrderLineNumber = _
        CSByte(System.Convert.ToSByte(Me.SalesOrderLineNumber))

End Sub
```

The script has an output column called `SalesOrderLineNumber`. For each row, the script captures the `SalesOrderID` and saves it in a variable called `PreviousSalesOrderID`. When the next record is evaluated, if the current `SalesOrderID` is different from the `PreviousSalesOrderID`, then the `SalesOrderLineNumber` is reset to 1. Otherwise, the `SalesOrderLineNumber` is incremented by 1. The end result is a new column that has incrementing integer values, starting at one for each sales order group.

Scripts are a powerful way to handle more complex data preparation in a single step. Chapter 11 dives into how to best leverage scripts both in the data flow and the control flow.

Acquiring the Dimension Surrogate Key in SSIS

As you process fact source records (such as transactions or inventory), you must also pull the surrogate key from the dimension tables. To accomplish this task, you must have the business key from the transactional source that maps to the business key in the dimension table. This process of loading a dimension table involves looking up the surrogate key from the matching business key.

Identifying the Dimension Surrogate Keys with SSIS

The best SSIS approach for acquiring surrogate keys is to take advantage of the data flow and use one of the following transformations:

❑ *Derived Column transformation* — This method can be used for smart keys such as a date surrogate key.

❑ *Lookup transformation* — This method is the primary one to use because it performs well when the dimension table can fit into the transformation cache.

❑ *Merge Join transformation* — This method works well if the dimensions are large and do not fit easily into memory for cache.

❑ *Fuzzy Lookup transformation* — This method is useful with dirty data. If no match exists when you're performing a lookup on the dimension, the Fuzzy Lookup can find the "best guess" match. It indexes and caches the data. It also requires some startup time and overhead, so the best approach is to leverage the Fuzzy Lookup in tandem with the Lookup transformation, by handling the missing records from the Lookup transformation with the Fuzzy Lookup.

Another approach is to use a control flow Execute SQL Task to handle the dimension association to the fact table with an Execute SQL Task. This requires staging the fact data and using a SQL JOIN to get the surrogate key. However, this approach is synchronous — it requires one step at a time:

1. Landing the fact source data to a staging table

2. Performing the joins across all the related dimension tables (and either performing an UPDATE to the staging, or taking the join results and loading the fact table)

3. Loading the fact table

A data flow approach will scale better than this control flow approach because it reduces the impact on the database (eliminating expensive joins) and reduces the steps involved in the dimension association.

Surrogate Key Examples in SSIS

This discussion shows a few examples of how to use the SSIS data flow to acquire the dimension key during your fact table loads.

Basic Dimension Key Examples Using the Derived Column and Lookup Transformations

The currency rate fact table process provides some nice examples of how to get the dimension surrogate keys in SSIS. Figure 8-9 shows a data flow that loads data into the `FactCurrencyRate` table. Two transformations have been highlighted, a Derived Column transformation and a Lookup transformation, that add the `DateKey` and `CurrencyKey` columns to the data flow.

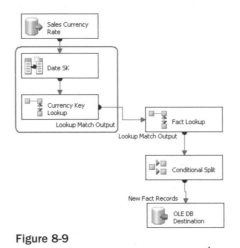

Figure 8-9

The `DateKey` used in the `AdventureWorksDW2008` warehouse is in the form YYYYMMDD. This design is common for date keys, because it allows for easy fact table filtering and partitioning. To handle these tasks, a Derived Column transformation can take the `datetime` column from the source and convert it into the YYYYMMDD format with a few SSIS date functions. The following function is used in the Derived Column to handle this task:

```
  YEAR(CurrencyRateDate) * 10000
+ MONTH(CurrencyRateDate) * 100
+ DAY(CurrencyRateDate)
```

The `YEAR`, `MONTH`, and `DAY` functions return those date parts in integer form, which can then be multiplied by a factor and added together to generate the YYYYMMDD output.

The second example, right below the Derived Column transformation, uses the Lookup transformation to get the `CurrencyKey` dimension surrogate key. Figure 8-10 shows the Columns tab of the Lookup Transformation Editor.

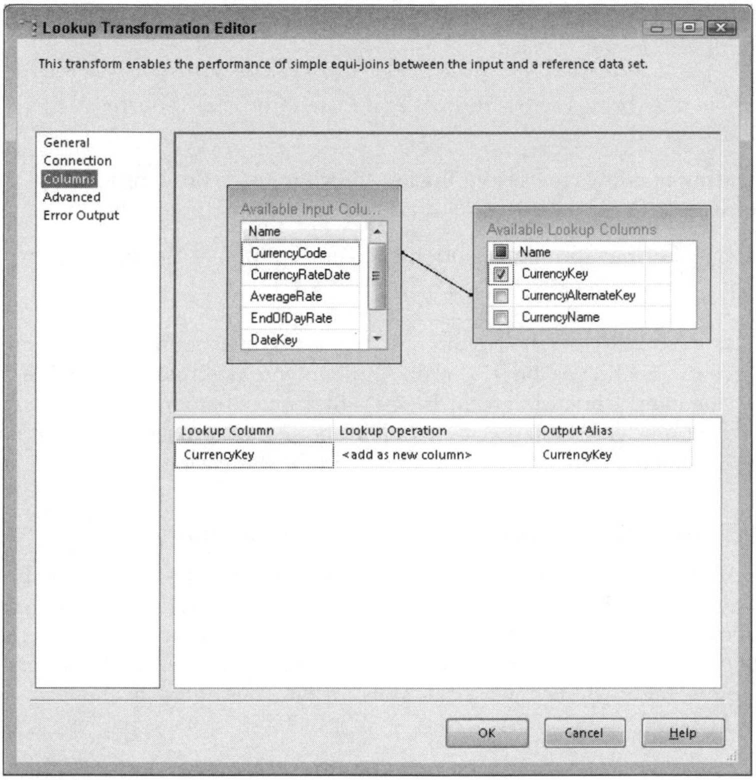

Figure 8-10

In this example, the CurrencyCode from the source is joined to the CurrencyAlternateKey (the business key) in the dimension table. The CurrencyKey is returned. The Lookup transformation is configured to be fully cached, so all the rows in the dimension table are stored in memory, and the transformation performs very well.

This approach is the most common, but because the dimension rows are stored in memory, be sure that you have enough memory on the server to handle the volume. For dimensions with more than 1 million or 2 million members, unless you have a 64-bit server with 16GB or more of RAM, you should consider a different approach, such as the one discussed next.

Using the Merge Join Transformation to Identify the Dimension Key

The Merge Join transformation presents another alternative to getting the dimension's surrogate key for the fact table load. With the Merge Join transformation, the source records can be merged with the dimension table across the business key, which makes the surrogate key available. The Merge Join transformation allows three join types:

❑ An *inner join* only brings across records that match from both sources. Any record without a match is discarded.

❑ The *left outer join* allows rows from the left source input to flow through the transformation, either with a matching record, or without a match on the right input.

❑ A *full outer join* brings rows from both the left and right, whether or not there is a match between sources.

If the source has the possibility of missing dimension records, then a left outer join should be used in the join with the source rows acting as the left input. A full outer join would not provide the right solution, because there may be many dimension records (the right input) that have no current match in the source, and, therefore, are not needed. Similarly, an inner join should not be used because it would filter out new dimension members that are in the source, but not yet in the dimension.

Using Fuzzy Lookup to Pull Dimension Keys Based on Similarity

Using a Fuzzy Lookup transformation for dimension lookups provides greater flexibility when the source data does not match absolutely with the source. In some cases, the match to acquire the surrogate key will not be across a single business key, but rather a column or several columns that may not have exact matches. Because the Fuzzy Lookup matches on column value similarity, its use allows non-equal matches. For example, Figure 8-11 shows a data flow for the sales quota fact table.

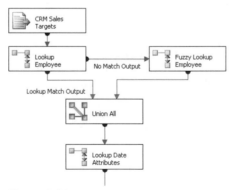

Figure 8-11

In this case, the source is coming from a flat file generated from the customer relationship management (CRM) system, which does not have a single matching key for the employee lookup. The Lookup transformation joins across FirstName, LastName, LoginID, and Department to try to find the right match.

The challenge is that when this package is executed, several Employee dimension records do not return a match, even though the Employee record actually exists in the table. The reason no records were found is because of misspelling and minor differences between the source and the dimension table itself.

Therefore, to handle this problem, the No Match Output from the lookup is sent to a Fuzzy Lookup transformation, as Figure 8-11 shows.

The Fuzzy Lookup columns mapping is identical to the Lookup configuration. Figure 8-12 shows the Columns tab of the Fuzzy Lookup transformation.

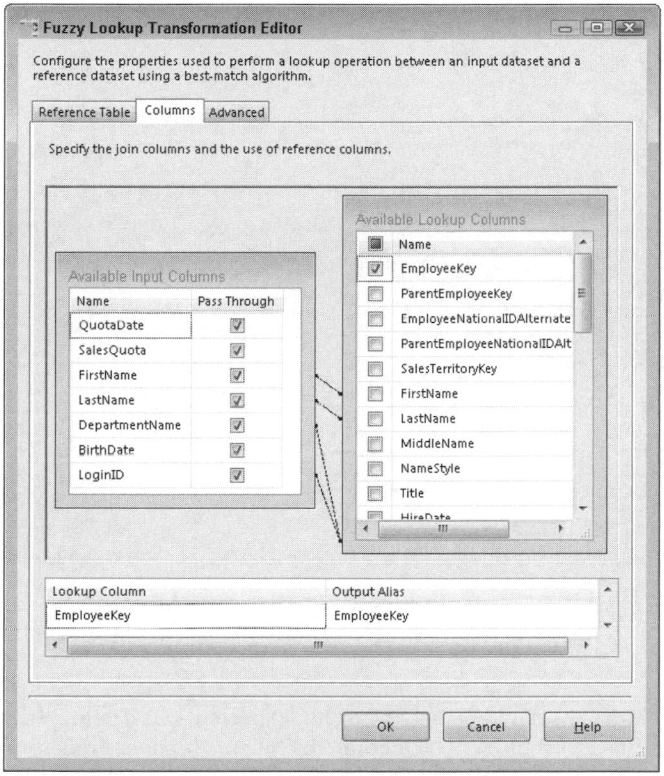

Figure 8-12

The Fuzzy Lookup will evaluate the joins, calculate a similarity, and, therefore, look for the closest match. This transformation has advanced options for configuring the thresholds for the comparison. Figure 8-13 shows the options available on the Advanced tab of the Fuzzy Lookup Transformation Editor.

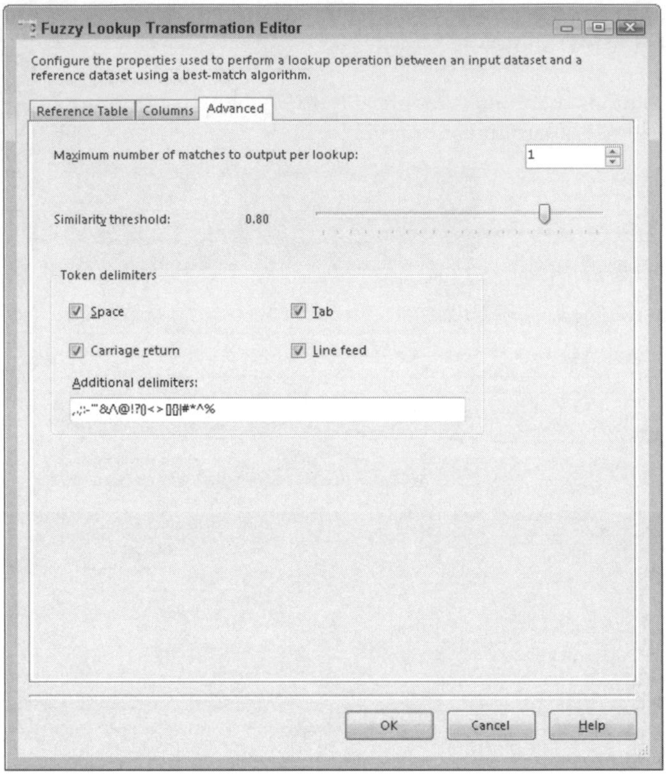

Figure 8-13

In this case, the "Similarity threshold" is set to 0.80 (or 80 percent), indicating that only employee matches that are over this threshold will be identified. Only the highest similar match is pulled, as indicated by the "Maximum number of matches to output per lookup" property set to 1. Although not shown, the Fuzzy Lookup outputs a confidence value, which identifies the overall possibility that the highest match selected is the right one. In other words, if multiple good matches are possible between the source and reference tables, the confidence value would be lower, because there would be some lack of confidence on which match is the right one.

After all is said and done, the sales quota fact table package uses both the Lookup and the Fuzzy Lookup transformations to accomplish acquiring the dimension surrogate keys. A Union All transformation brings the records back together in the data flow from both the Lookup and the Fuzzy Lookup outputs. As shown earlier in Figure 8-11, after the Union All, a Lookup transformation is used to pull the DateKey, CalendarYear, and CalendarQuarter, and the completed data flow for the dimension lookups and the execution results are shown.

An alternative approach would be to use the Fuzzy Lookup in place of the Lookup transformation. However, for optimization purposes, the No Match Output was used. This is because the majority of records do match directly (which the lookup handles efficiently), and only the missing rows are sent through the Fuzzy Lookup (which, behind the scenes, requires staging, indexing, and tempdb overhead to perform the matches). The general rule of practice is to separate the exception to the rule to handle the one-off situations, and then bring the data back into the main stream of processing.

Measure Calculations

Another major component of a fact table load involves calculating measures, which, in most cases, is relatively straightforward.

Measure Calculation Types

Calculating measures involves a few different types of transformations from the source:

❑ *No change from a source column* — In the case where the source column matches one-to-one with the destination fact table column, the measure can be passed through from the source to the fact table without change.

❑ *Standard calculation* — Often, a measure involves standard arithmetic calculations, such as dividing one column by another, or determining the difference between two values. For example, the number of items in the sale record multiplied by the price of the item returns the transaction subtotal, or the subtotal sales divided by quantity provides the average price.

❑ *Derived calculation* — In some cases, the measure must be derived in the ETL process. As mentioned earlier in this chapter, a measure often may simply be the value 0 or 1, based on certain conditions in the source feed. An example of this is an *occurrence* measure, where the measure indicates the happening of an event (1), or the non-happening of the event (0). Such measures are usable in additive scenarios when aggregating to determine the number of occurrences of the event.

❑ *Advanced calculations* — In rare cases, a calculation is required that goes beyond simple math or derivation, such as aggregating a subtotal of a group of records, divided by a part, or using advanced algebraic expressions, or parsing out values in a string.

Handling Measure Calculations in SSIS

The good news is that measure calculations are relatively straightforward in SSIS. Here are a few methods for handling the calculations:

❑ *Using a Derived Column transformation to perform the calculation with SSIS expressions* — SSIS provides many standard mathematical functions to perform calculations from associated columns in the same row of data.

❑ *Including the calculation in the source query* — If the source pull is a relational database, as opposed to a flat-file extraction, the calculation expression can be handled in-line in the SQL statement. This typically has low impact on the source system, as long as the query is straightforward.

❑ *Using an aggregate to handle the calculation* — In the case where the measure is a SUM, MAX, MIN, or COUNT of a grouping of source rows, the Aggregate can perform this functionality. Combining the Aggregate transformation with an ensuing Derived Column transformation will enable both aggregates and calculations based on the aggregates.

Leverage the data flow Script component as a transformation to handle advanced calculations. The Script component unlocks a full-featured Visual Basic and Visual C# environment, which can take advantage of many more functions, and the capability to compare values across rows of data. When dealing with more advanced situations, consider the Script component to provide that extended capability beyond what the SSIS expression language can provide. Chapter 11 dives into several examples.

To exemplify measure calculations, the sales fact table load package referenced earlier requires some common calculations. Figure 8-14 shows the Derived Column Transformation Editor with the data flow that calculates several measures used in the fact table. The full example of the sales fact table package is described later in the "Solution" section.

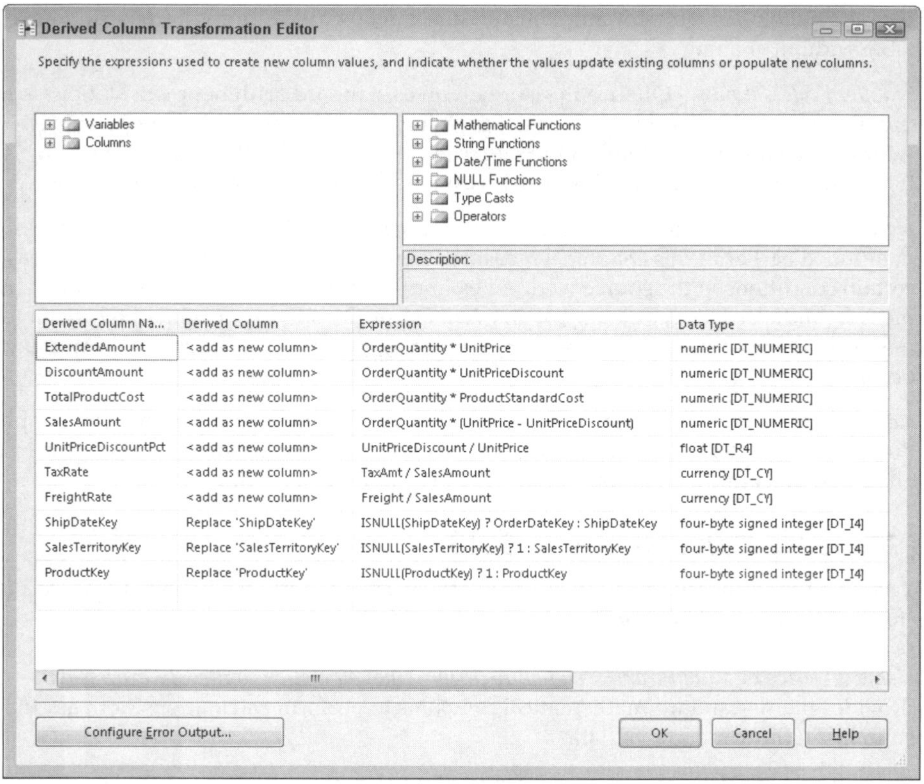

Figure 8-14

As you can see, these calculations use common mathematical equations that generate the needed output for the destination measure. For example, the ExtendedAmount involves multiplying the OrderQuantity by the UnitPrice. The UnitPriceDiscountPct involves dividing the UnitPriceDiscount by the UnitPrice.

In summary, measure calculations are often easy to handle in SSIS. But when the situation requires more advanced computations, SSIS also provides the Aggregate transformation and the Script component.

Later, in the "Solution" section, the FactCallCenter example demonstrates the use of an Aggregate transformation to handle the measure calculations.

Managing Fact Table Changes

At times, a matching fact table record in the source may change, which, therefore, must propagate through to the fact table. Changes are often required to handle corrections in the source, or to update keys for accumulating fact tables (like updating the ShipDateKey in the sales fact table when the product is shipped).

To handle the change, a few different data warehousing approaches are common:

❑ A simple UPDATE to the fact table to modify the existing record with the change

❑ A newly generated record in the fact table with the new values, and a flag in the table to indicate the status of the record (current or expired)

❑ An offset change record that calculates the difference between what was in the fact record and the new value

Each approach comes with its advantages and disadvantages.

To enable you to deal with the design in SSIS, this section presents some common approaches of identifying changes as well as how to best perform fact table updates when required in the ETL. One of the approaches uses the SQL Server MERGE command, which can handle inserts and updates at the same time.

Approaches to Identifying Changed Fact Records

Some sources include a way to identify whether the record requires a change or a new fact row. For example, a source column may provide the Data Manipulation Language (DML) type. DML is the cause for the row being sent to the ETL, commonly a value of I (insert), U (update), or D (delete). Alternatively, the source feed may include both a create date and a modified date. Comparing these dates together in conjunction with the last incremental change identifier (as discussed in Chapter 5) allows the identification of the row as a new row or a modified row.

A new row is when the creation date is greater than the last incremental change identifier date. A modified row is when the create date is less than the incremental extraction date, and the modified date is greater than the last incremental extraction date.

In both of these cases, the source records do not need to match the source rows to existing records in the fact table.

Unfortunately, when a source for a fact table goes through changes, most cases will not provide this capability, and the source row will need to be matched with the fact row to identify the DML type of the record. Even if you are using the SQL MERGE, you may want to identify records that have either changed or are new.

Just like the other aspects of dimension and fact ETL, two general categories exist in SSIS to associate source rows with fact rows:

❑   *Database joins between the source data and the fact table* — These enable the comparison of the source to the fact table. This approach comes with a couple drawbacks. For starters, it requires the source data to be in a table in the same database engine and on the same server as the fact table in order to perform the join efficiently. If the source data is on a different system or is in a flat-file form, then the data must be staged, which generates more disk IO and creates a multistep process. On the other hand, fact tables often contain millions of rows and would consume tremendous memory if brought completely into the SSIS pipeline buffers. When you're dealing with large volumes, an RDBMS can provide invaluable help in scaling an ETL solution.

❑   *Data correlation with the data flow* — As mentioned previously, two primary data transformations exist that assist in associating sources together: the Lookup transformation and the Merge Join transformation. Using these, the source feed can be correlated with the fact table, which is the first step in processing changes. The general benefit of these transformations is that the source feed can come from any source system or files, and still be joined to the fact table. The lookup will have more memory overhead when the fact table is fully cached. However, the Merge Join requires the inputs to be sorted, which would use just as much memory as the lookup if the Sort transformation is used (because of the Sort's data blocking nature). However, sources can be marked as pre-sorted, which gives the Merge Join an advantage when the source can be sorted efficiently.

Fact Update Examples in SSIS

To demonstrate how to handle updates for fact tables, two examples are provided. The first uses a Lookup transformation to identify fact records; the second uses a SQL Server MERGE statement.

A third example is provided in the "Solution" section for the fact sales package, which uses a Merge Join transformation to identify fact records.

Using a Lookup Transformation to Identify Fact Updates

The sales quota fact table, demonstrated earlier in the section, "Surrogate Key in SSIS," is the perfect example of when a lookup can be used to help identify existing fact records. Because the fact table itself is rather small in volume, the entire table can fit into memory, which is a requirement of the lookup if you want scalability.

Figure 8-15 shows the full data flow for the steps involved in the fact table inserts and updates. Earlier, Figure 8-11 showed the other steps upstream in the data flow.

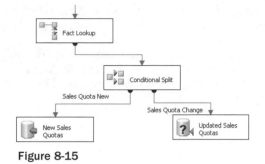

Figure 8-15

In this example, the Lookup transformation joins the source records to the fact table. Because the EmployeeKey and the DateKey have already been acquired, the lookup will join across these columns. Figure 8-16 shows the Columns tab of the Lookup Transformation Editor.

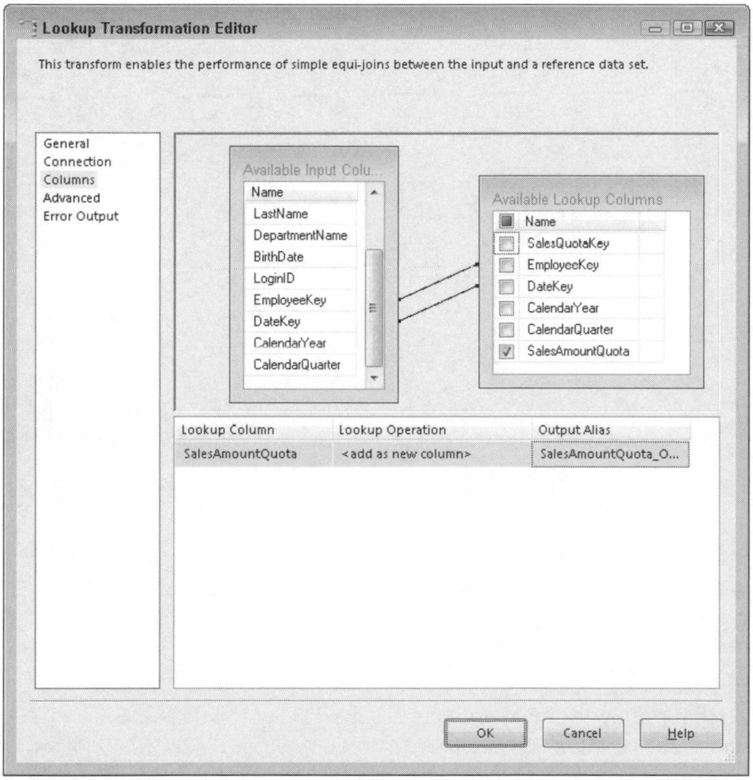

Figure 8-16

The `SalesAmountQuota` column from the fact table is also returned in the lookup because it will be used to see whether a change has happened. It is aliased as `SalesAmountQuota_Original`.

The other critical setting is found on the General tab. You must set the drop-down named "Specify how to handle rows with no matching entries" to Ignore Failure. If a match is not found (meaning that the record is new), the row still gets sent to the next transformation. The only difference when a match is not found is that the `SalesAmountQuota` will be `NULL`.

In the next transformation, the Conditional Split, the records are checked to determine whether the record is new or must be updated (or there is no change!). Figure 8-17 shows the Conditional Split Transformation Editor.

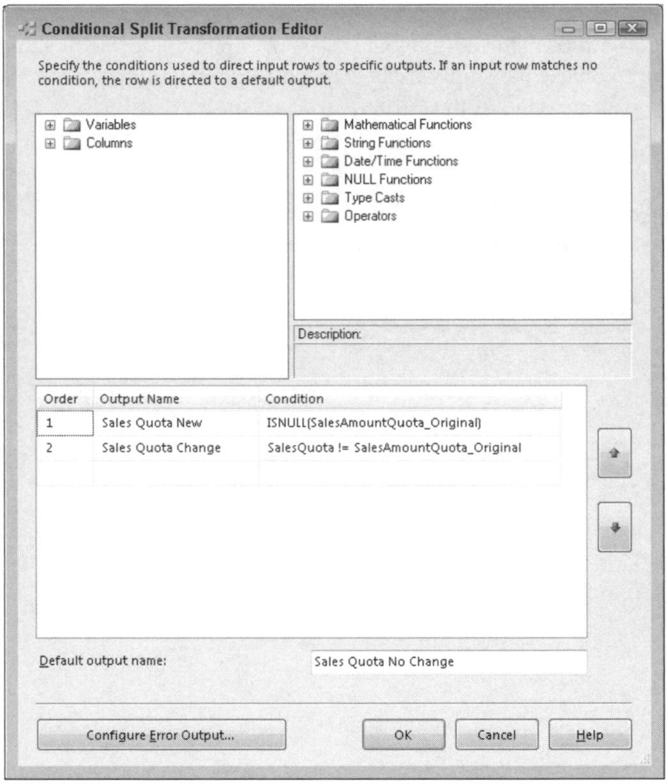

Figure 8-17

The first condition that the Conditional Split checks is whether the `SalesAmountQuota_Original` is `NULL` using the statement `ISNULL(SalesAmountQuota_Original)`. If this Boolean expression evaluates to `true`, then the record is a new fact record and gets assigned to the Sales Quote New output.

The second condition checks the current sales quota from the source with the sales quota amount from the fact table using the expression `SalesQuota != SalesAmountQuota_Original`. If the values do not match, then the record must be updated.

Finally, if the row is neither a new or changed record, then nothing must be done, and it is assigned to the default output named Sales Quota No Change.

The Conditional Split outputs as shown earlier in Figure 8-15 are either sent to an OLE DB Destination (for the inserts) or an OLE DB Command (for the updates). Because this fact table has relatively few updates, the OLE DB Command is a good choice. For high-volume updates, you should stage the data to a staging table and perform a set-based update. Chapter 7 demonstrated this, plus, the next immediate section shows you how to use the `MERGE` to handle this with a staging table.

Using SQL Merge to Simultaneously Handle Updates and Inserts

One way to simultaneously handle inserts and updates is to use the `MERGE` statement of SQL Server 2008. The statement compares a table to another table, performing either an insert or update, depending on whether the record already exists.

As an example, you can design the same `FactSalesQuota` process to handle this requirement.

The first step is to create a staging table that is identical to the fact table DDL. A create table script is provided in the chapter sample files available on the Wrox Web site (`www.wrox.com`). In the control flow, you must add an Execute SQL Task that uses a `TRUNCATE TABLE` statement to clear out the staging table. Next, in the data flow, after you have acquired all the dimension keys and calculated all the measures, you must stage all the records to a staging table, as shown in Figure 8-18.

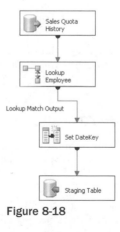

Figure 8-18

After the staging table is loaded with the records, you can then perform the following TSQL operation. Add this code to the control flow right after the data flow that stages the data.

```
MERGE dbo.FactSalesQuota AS T
USING SSIS_PDS.dbo.stgFactSalesQuota AS S
ON T.EmployeeKey = S.EmployeeKey
AND T.DateKey = S.DateKey
WHEN NOT MATCHED BY target
   THEN INSERT(EmployeeKey, DateKey, CalendarYear
            , CalendarQuarter, SalesAmountQuota)
         VALUES(S.EmployeeKey, S.DateKey, S.CalendarYear
            , S.CalendarQuarter, S.SalesAmountQuota)
WHEN MATCHED AND T.SalesAmountQuota != S.SalesAmountQuota
   THEN UPDATE SET T.SalesAmountQuota = S.SalesAmountQuota
```

Figure 8-19 shows the final control flow layout.

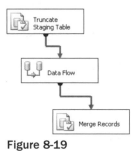

Figure 8-19

This approach is very straightforward and can be designed quickly. The benefits are that you can rely on the SQL Server engine to determine when a match exists or not. Especially when your fact table is very large (millions or billions of rows) and you cannot easily identify updates versus inserts, then consider the MERGE statement. However, its drawbacks are performance if you have a large number of source rows (in the millions or billions). If inserts and updates are identifiable without checking the destination fact table, then a faster approach is to fast-load the inserts and perform a set-based update for the updates.

Optimizing Fact Table Inserts

Every fact table package requires inserts. Furthermore, optimizing inserts is critical to any fact table process for performance gains. This section examines how to optimize inserts by tuning the destination adapter and dealing with indexes effectively.

This brief section presents the fundamental designs for fact table inserts, fast loads, and index management. Chapter 12 deals with optimizing and scaling SSIS packages, and provides more insights and examples on tuning your packages, including SSIS practices on dealing with partitioned tables.

When inserting data into fact tables, you should take the following first two steps:

1. Making sure the inserts are handled in bulk
2. Dropping indexes before the data load and re-creating them after the data inserts

Optimizing Inserts with Fast Load

The OLE DB Destination adapter is the most common destination adapter used. When you are working with an insert operation, be sure to set the adapter to use the fast load setting. Figure 8-20 shows the OLE DB Destination Editor. The "Data access mode" is set to "Table or View — Fast Load." This is the staging table insert from the previous merge example, but the settings should be set identically for fact table loads.

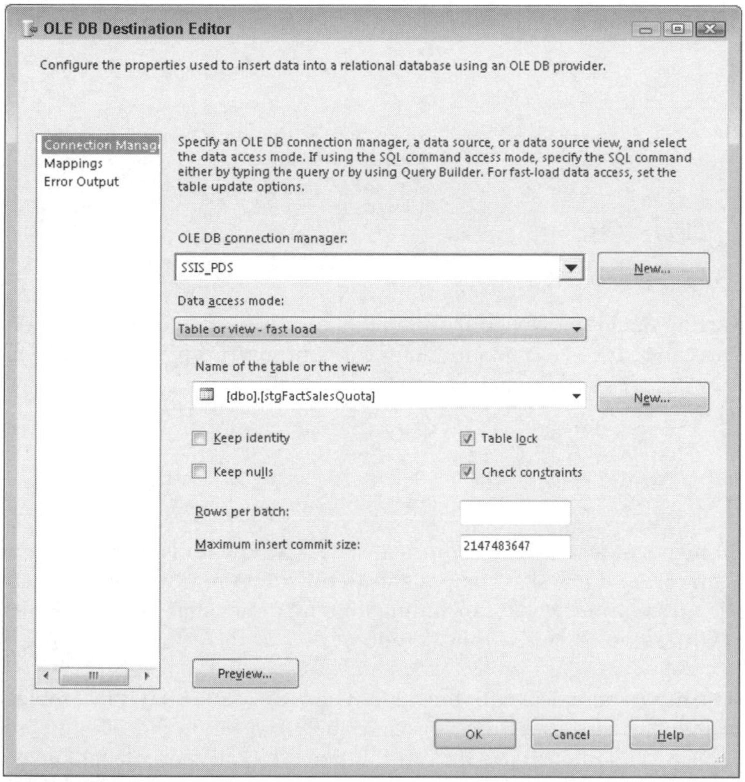

Figure 8-20

You should also consider using the SQL Server Destination adapter if your package runs on the same server as the destination, and your data flow is not too complicated. The SQL Server Destination works best if you are pumping records in from a source with minimal transformations, and it will run 2 percent to 4 percent faster than the OLE DB Destination adapter.

Optimizing Inserts with Index Management

The second most important thing to consider for fact table inserts is dropping your fact table indexes and then rebuilding them after the load. This is often the most overlooked optimization technique. You may think that it is counterintuitive, but the difference in performance can be significant in probably 75 percent of the cases. The reason is that building an index from scratch is a lot easier than shuffling the index pages around when data is being inserted into a table. Figure 8-21 shows a package control flow that drops the indexes on the sales fact, runs the data flow, and then creates the indexes.

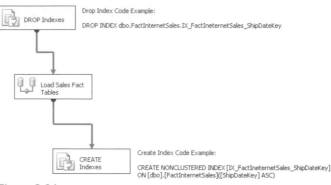

Figure 8-21

In conclusion, inserting data is a given, but optimizing inserts is often overlooked. With a couple of simple steps, you can reduce your execution time if your inserts are slowing down your fact table data flow.

Solution

With all the requirements of fact table ETL processes in SSIS, how do you put all the pieces together? This section takes you from the design components to the solution. In addition, you may experience some unique challenges with fact tables, including missing dimension keys and late-arriving facts. This section concludes with some advanced considerations.

The primary two examples here deal with the AdventureWorks2008 sales fact tables and the call center fact table. Some of the sales fact table processes were shown earlier in the "Design" section, but this section closes the loop and demonstrates the full solution. The call center fact table is a unique snapshot type fact table. That example shows how to convert transactional audit records into a single fact table.

Internet and Reseller Sales Fact Table ETL

So far, the sales fact table package reviewed in this chapter demonstrated consolidating sources and handling measure calculations (see Figure 8-6, Figure 8-7, and Figure 8-14). However, these design examples are only a portion of the overall solution for the sales fact table process.

The overall fact ETL process requires the following steps:

1. Consolidating the sales header and sales detail tables

2. Adding the SalesOrderLineNumber to the detail records

3. Identifying new fact table records

4. Data cleansing of missing values

5. Associating sales order transaction records with columns from other tables

6. Acquiring the dimension surrogate keys

7. Calculating the measures

8. Splitting the records into Internet sales and reseller sales

9. Inserting the rows into fact tables

As you can see, the process involves several steps. To best handle these steps, the ETL process has been broken into two distinct packages, leveraging a staging table at the completion of the first package, and extracting rows from the staging table at the start of the second package.

Fact Internet and Reseller Sales Extraction and Transform Process

The first two steps listed previously (associating the sales order header and detail tables, and creating the sales order line number) were demonstrated earlier in Figure 8-6 and Figure 8-7.

The next step in this package involves identifying which records have already been inserted into the fact table, so that only new records will be added to the fact table. For demonstration purposes, record changes are not required for this ETL. Figure 8-22 shows a Merge Join and Conditional Split transformation being used to identify new records.

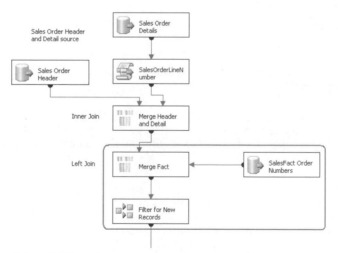

Figure 8-22

The new source adapter on the right is extracting the sales order numbers that have already been added to the fact table. These records are then merged together with data flow that contains the source data. To identify new source records, this data flow must determine which rows already exist in the fact table. This can be done by using a left outer join, and then filtering the data to only the rows that do not have a match in the fact table.

Figure 8-23 shows the Merge Join Transformation Editor configured to use a left outer join.

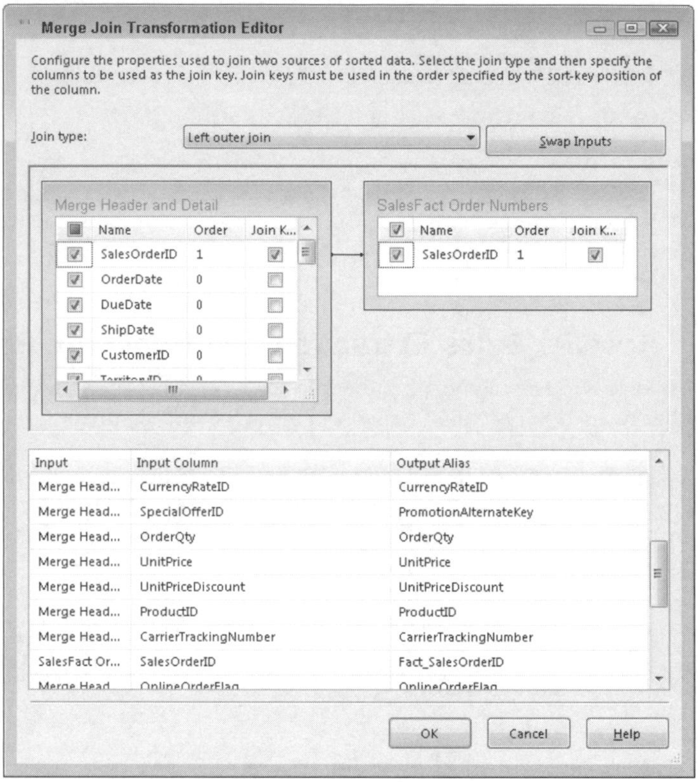

Figure 8-23

Because the left outer join will find matches and non-matches, you want to filter out the matches. (The matching records already exist in the fact table.) To filter out the records, you use a Conditional Split transformation.

Notice that, in the Merge Join, the `SalesOrderID` is included from the fact table in the output and aliased as `Fact_SalesOrderID`. This is used in the Conditional Split to determine which records do not match and, therefore, must be added. The following code is the Conditional Split's Boolean expression used to identify source rows that are not matched in the fact table:

```
ISNULL(Fact_SalesOrderID)
```

The one output of the Conditional Split is named New Sales Facts.

Now that the records have been identified, the next few transformations perform a series of data-cleansing and correlation operations. Figure 8-24 shows the rest of the data flow for the first data flow used to process the fact records. The data flow shown begins with the New Sales Facts output of the Conditional Split.

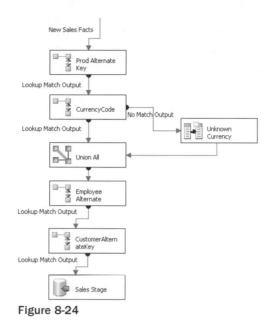

Figure 8-24

The rest of the data flow in this first sales fact package handles a few data-cleansing operations:

❑ Gets the Product number from the `Production.Product` source table. This is needed to get the dimension surrogate key, and is handled by a simple Lookup transformation.

❑ Uses the `CurrencyRateID` in the sales table to find the `CurrencyCode` of the source transactions. A lookup is also used. The one caveat to the lookup is that when the currency rate is `NULL`, the currency code must be defaulted to USD, which is handled by redirecting the No Match Output rows to a Derived column, and replacing the `NULL CurrencyCode` column with the following expression:

```
(DT_WSTR,3)"USD"
```

❑ If you branch the data in the data flow and must bring the rows back together, you can use a Union All transformation, which is used in this data flow.

❑ Immediately below the Union All, a Lookup transformation is used to get the `NationalIDNumber` of the employee sales person. Only reseller records have sales employee associations. Therefore, a large majority of the rows will not have matches, and the non-matches should be ignored. Figure 8-25 shows the Lookup Transformation Editor configured to "Ignore failures" when no matches are found, which will return a `NULL` in the `NationalIDNumber` column.

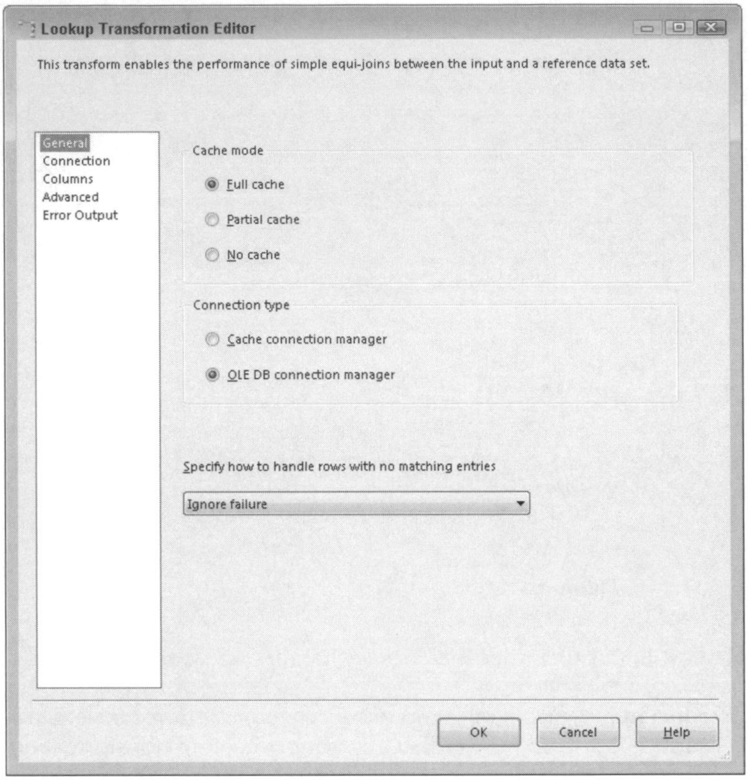

Figure 8-25

❑   The final transformation step is identical to the employee lookup, except that it is pulling the reseller customer number for the reseller fact table.

❑   The last component is an OLE DB Destination that lands the records to a staging table before the next data flow.

Because a staging table is used, you must truncate the table before running the package. This is done in the control flow immediately before the data flow just shown is executed. Truncating the staging table before a new run of the package is always a best practice because, most of the time, you want to keep the records in the staging table in case you need to research an error.

The package just examined is available in this chapter's example code found on the Wrox Web site (www.wrox.com) and is called FactInternetAndResellerSales_Stage.dtsx.

Fact Internet and Reseller Sales Load Process

In the sales fact table ETL example, the data load package is the second package involved. The first package just demonstrated is a staging package that consolidates source rows, cleanses data, and filters the records required for the load. Because of the complexity of the data cleansing and correlation, an intermediate staging table was chosen to simplify the ETL and provide a data restartability point.

The data load package handles Steps 6 through 9 described earlier in this example, which includes getting the dimension keys, calculating the measures, splitting the records, and loading the fact tables.

Figure 8-26 shows the sales fact table load data flow containing several surrogate key lookups for the dimension key.

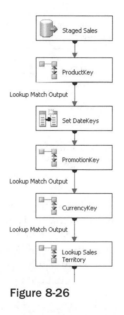

Figure 8-26

This example highlights how to design an SSIS package for a fact table with several dimension keys. What you may be wondering is how efficient this will be, because it looks like the lookups happen one after the other. In fact, this package runs very efficiently with the lookup designed sequentially in this manner. Although it may appear that the data flow might require the first dimension lookup to be completed before the second, what is actually happening is that the lookup transformations are being handled in parallel. Figure 8-27 shows a midstream picture of the data flow execution, before the records are completely landed into the fact table.

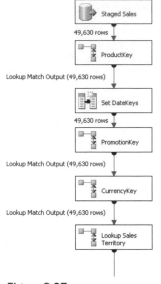

Figure 8-27

Based on the record count shown, note that the lookups are all happening at the same time, because the record count (49,630) is identical for all the lookups. The reason this is an important point is that it underscores the architecture of SSIS.

In this case, the Lookup transformation output is synchronous, meaning that the output of the lookup is synchronously connected to the input of the next lookup. This means that as soon as the rows in a pipeline data buffer (typically about 10,000 rows) completes in one lookup, it is immediately available to the next lookup to perform its work. So, rather than the multiple lookups having to be performed in serial, the data is actually being performed in parallel, which gives a tremendous advantage to how SSIS can scale, and makes for a compelling case to use the Lookup transformation for dimension key lookups.

Although not shown, it will become apparent later that, while rows are still coming in from the source, transformed data is already landing to the destination. Chapter 12 reviews in more detail the architecture of the SSIS pipeline and how to take advantage of it for scalability.

The lookups in the data flow all connect to the dimension tables that contain the keys. As an example of one of the lookups, the `ProductKey` comes from the `DimProduct` table. In this case, the Lookup transformation is configured to use the results of a SQL query as follows:

```
SELECT ProductKey, ProductAlternateKey
FROM DimProduct
WHERE EndDate IS NULL.
```

Because the product dimension contains Type 2 historical changes, there is an `EndDate` column. A `NULL` in the `EndDate` indicates that the dimension record is current, and the Lookup cache will, therefore, only be populated with the current records in the Product dimension, so the join across the business key will still yield the right current match. Figure 8-28 highlights the Columns tab of the Lookup Transformation Editor.

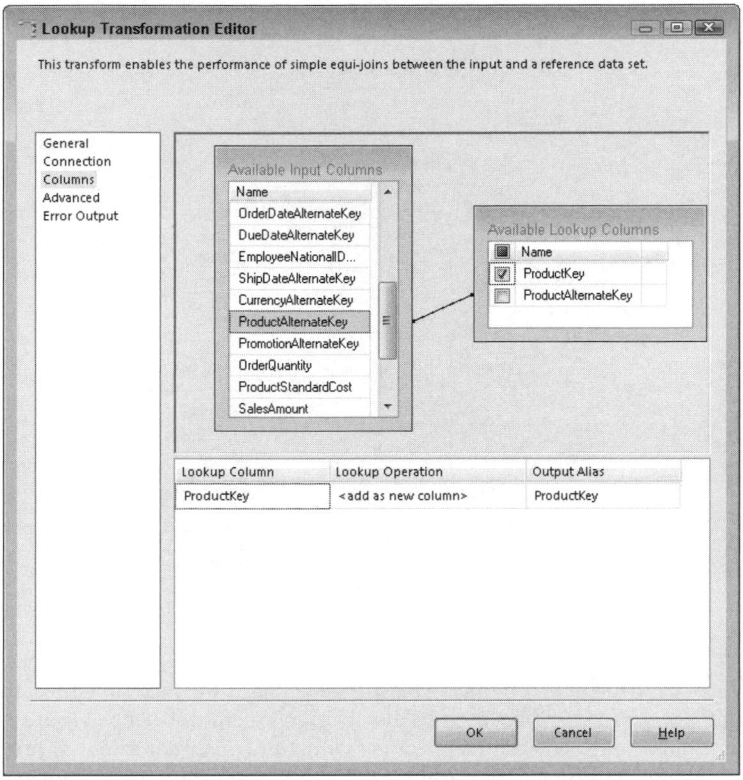

Figure 8-28

Essentially, this configuration will assign the current Product surrogate key to the fact record.

After the dimension keys are acquired, the remaining tasks outlined in the beginning of this example include calculating the measures, splitting the fact records into reseller sales and Internet sales, and inserting the rows into the fact tables. Figure 8-29 shows the rest of the data flow after the sales territory lookup.

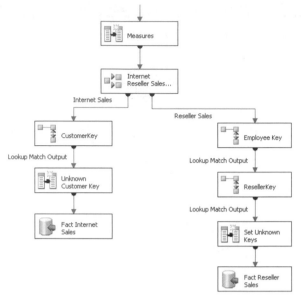

Figure 8-29

The Derived Column transformation named Measures calculates the fact table measures based on columns in the data flow, and was discussed in the "Design" section (refer to Figure 8-14). With the sales fact tables, any record marked as an online order is a direct-to-consumer sale that originated through the Internet. Therefore, these rows must be inserted into the Internet sales fact table. Alternatively, any record that is not an online order originates from a reseller transaction and, therefore, should be loaded into the Reseller fact table.

The Conditional Split handles the routing of the fact records to the appropriate fact table. The Conditional Split below the Derived Column uses the condition `OnlineOrderFlag == TRUE` to identify Internet sales (the output is named Internet Sales). Any record not meeting this criterion is sent out the default output, which is named Reseller Sales.

You will notice that the output of the Conditional Split contains a couple of Lookup transformations on the Internet Reseller Sales output, and one Lookup transformation on the Internet Sales output. This is because the two sales fact tables contain a couple of different dimension keys. A Customer dimension relationship exists in the Internet Sales fact table, and a reseller and employee dimension relationship exists in the Reseller Sales fact table. Finally, the data flow destinations perform fast loads into the two fact tables, respectively.

Both OLE DB Destination adapters are configured to use the fast load option so that the rows are batch-inserted for performance.

This concludes the sales fact table examples. This last package is available in the chapter code examples on the Wrox Web site (`www.wrox.com`) and is named `FactInternetAndResellerSales_Load.dtsx`.

Snapshot Fact Table Example — Call Center Fact Table

The second example focuses on the `FactCallCenter` table contained in the `AdventureWorksDW2008` database. It contains data related to a network technology call center handling network alarms, customer service calls, and outages.

The fact table is a snapshot fact table that captures statistics related to the call center shifts in each day. There is one record per shift per day. Figure 8-30 shows a sampling of data from the fact table.

DateKey	Shift	LevelOneOperators	LevelTwoOperators	Calls	AutoResponses	Orders	Issues	AverageTimePerIssue	ServiceGrade
20061130	AM	2	8	380	218	280	2	79	0.05
20061130	PM1	3	10	461	391	375	0	79	0.08
20061130	PM2	3	12	403	221	243	2	87	0.17
20061130	midnight	1	4	193	115	125	0	89	0.18

Figure 8-30

The measures are mostly count measures, such as the number of issues, orders, calls, and responses, with a few other measures like average response time and service grade (which evaluates how the shift performed).

This data is not sourced from the `AdventureWorks2008` database. Rather, it comes from a trouble ticket system in a legacy engine. A nightly export process creates a flat file that is made available to the ETL operation.

Unfortunately, the data is not in an aggregated format. Rather, it comes from an audit table that tracks the changes to each call center issue and, therefore, generates multiple records per issue. Figure 8-31 shows a sample of the audit data in the flat file.

IssueID	AuditDatetime	DDLType	OperatorID	OperatorLevel	AlertType	ResolvedFlag	OrderRequiredFlag	OutageIssueFlag	AlertLevel
43888	2006-12-02 05:15:12.000	Insert	josé1	2	Alarm	0	0	0	1
43888	2006-12-02 05:17:08.000	Update	josé1	2	Alarm	0	0	0	3
43890	2006-12-02 05:18:54.000	Insert	garrett1	2	Phone Call	0	0	0	1
43888	2006-12-02 05:19:33.000	Update	josé1	2	Alarm	0	0	0	2
43878	2006-12-02 05:19:45.000	Insert	AUTO	0	Alarm	0	0	0	1
43888	2006-12-02 05:20:31.000	Update	josé1	2	Alarm	0	0	0	1
43888	2006-12-02 05:20:31.000	Update	josé1	2	Alarm	1	0	0	3
43878	2006-12-02 05:24:42.000	Update	AUTO	0	Alarm	1	0	0	1
43890	2006-12-02 05:25:06.000	Update	garrett1	2	Phone Call	0	1	0	1
43890	2006-12-02 05:25:30.000	Update	garrett1	2	Phone Call	0	1	1	5
43890	2006-12-02 05:28:48.000	Update	garrett1	2	Phone Call	0	1	1	5
43890	2006-12-02 05:35:58.000	Update	garrett1	2	Phone Call	1	1	1	5

Figure 8-31

So, the ETL objective is to take the thousands of audit records and summarize the data for each shift. This task is difficult, because the measures in the fact table are based on either a per-issue basis, or they apply to the whole shift.

The solution using SSIS will rely on the Aggregate transformation as the main driver for the calculations of the measures. In fact, the Aggregate transformation will need to be used in a few places. The ETL workflow involves the following general aggregation steps:

1. An aggregation across the day and shift data that performs a distinct count of the LevelOneOperators and LevelTwoOperators.

2. An aggregation that groups by the IssueID and consolidates all the issues for each IssueID audit record into one record.

3. An aggregation of the consolidated issues by the date and shift. This must be done after the issue grouping.

If this is making your head spin, let's take a look at the completed data flow first, then break out into the details. Figure 8-32 shows the complete data flow from the flat file to the destination.

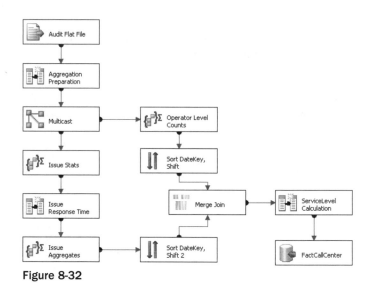

Figure 8-32

Notice that the data flow branches at the Multicast. One branch aggregates at the entire day and shift (to the right of the Multicast). The other branch aggregates first at the issue level (below the Multicast) and then the day and shift in a second aggregate. The branches are eventually merged together again after the calculations are performed for each data flow branch.

One key to the aggregation approach is the addition of a few columns that are used in the aggregations. Figure 8-33 shows the Derived Column Transformation Editor for the first transformation component.

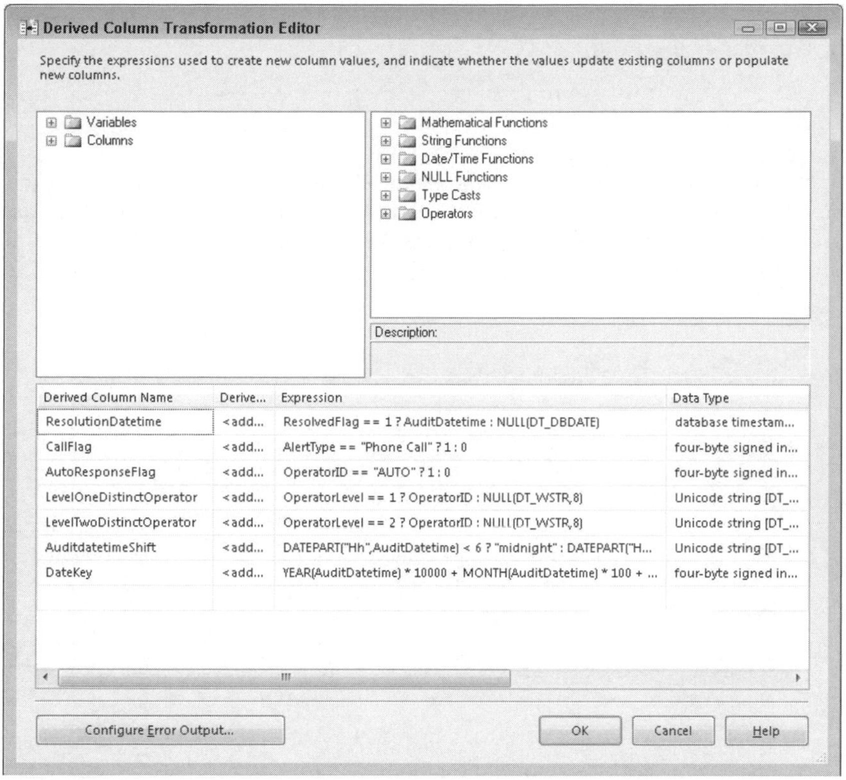

Figure 8-33

The derived columns are used for the aggregate. For example, the `CallFlag` determines whether the `AlertType` was a "Phone Call." If it was, a 1 is returned to the column; otherwise a 0 is returned. The `AuditShift` column uses the following SSIS expression to determine in which hour that the audit record was generated:

```
DATEPART("Hh",AuditDatetime) < 6 ? "midnight" :
        DATEPART("Hh",AuditDatetime) < 12 ? "AM" :
                DATEPART("Hh",AuditDatetime) < 18 ? "PM1" : "PM2"
```

As another example, counting the operators is a distinct count operation, but before that can be done, the `OperatorID` must be broken out into two columns: one column that has the `OperatorID` if the operator is level 1, and a second column if the operator is level 2. `NULLs` are used if an `OperatorID` does not apply, so that the distinct count will not include a level 1 operator in the level 2 count, for example.

Next, the Aggregate transformation that is on the right side of the Multicast then performs the distinct counts for the operator level counts with the following configuration:

❑   `DateKey` — Group by operation

❑   `Audit Shift` — Group by operation

❑ LevelOneOperators — Count distinct operation on the LevelOneDistinctOperator column created earlier

❑ LevelTwoOperators — Count distinct operation on the LevelTwoDistinctOperator column created earlier

The most important step in correctly generating the measures is the Aggregate transformation just below the Multicast. Its collapses each IssueID into one record through a group by, and then uses Maximum and Minimum operations to generate count columns that will be used in the final count for the fact table. Figure 8-34 shows the Aggregate Transformation Editor for the "Issue Stats" transformation.

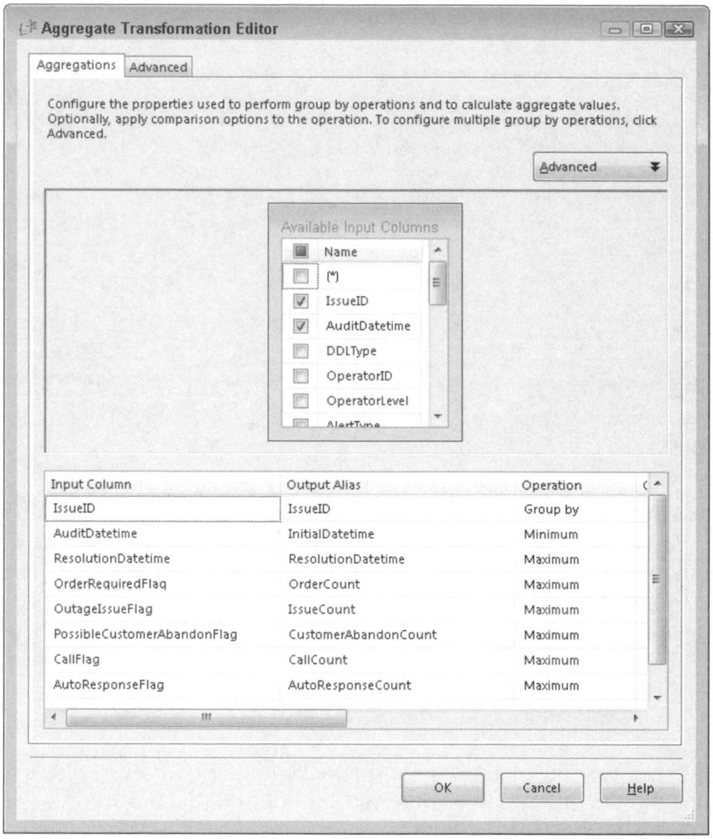

Figure 8-34

The Output Alias names help define what each column is. For example, the InitialDatetime column is generated by a Minimum operation on the AuditDatetime, and the ResolutionDatetime is a Maximum operation on the ResolutionDatetime column (generated in the Derived Column transformation). These columns are needed to get the time it took to resolve the issue.

All the "Flag" input columns are also Maximum operations. This is because the source value is a 0 or a 1 in all the cases. A Maximum will return a 1 if any of the IssueID records had that flag value and the result can be used to count all the issues, or calls, or auto responses, and so on.

The Derived Column after the "Issue Stats" aggregate computes the response time (using a DATEPART SSIS function) of the Issue from the initial alarm or call to the resolution.

Two aggregates are needed because, after the issues are collapsed by IssueID, the records must be aggregated again at the day and shift level. Figure 8-35 shows the final Aggregation transformation named "Issue Aggregates."

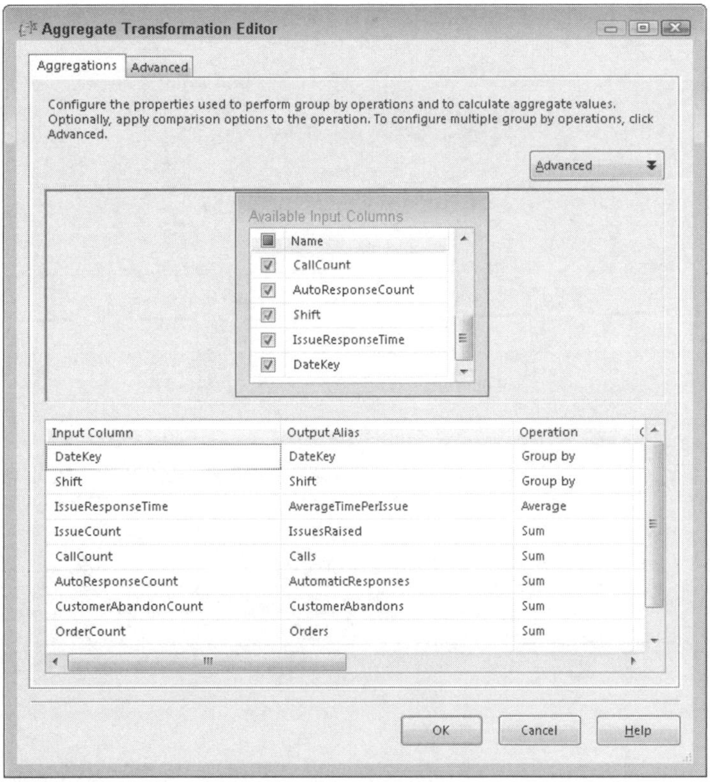

Figure 8-35

Many of the measures are finalized in this transformation, which uses a Sum operation for all the count columns and an Average operation for issue response time.

Before the fact records can be inserted, the two branches of the data flow must be brought back together. The data flow uses a Merge Join for this purpose, which requires a Sort operation before each input. Both branches are sorted by DateKey and Shift, and joined across those columns. The final Derived Column transformation computes a ServiceGrade, which is the number of potential customer abandons divided by the number of calls, and is used to rate the overall satisfaction of the customers during the shift.

When the ETL is run, you can see the end result and how the thousands of input records are collapsed down to four records for the single day that this is processed. Figure 8-36 shows the package execution, the row counts, and a data viewer showing the values.

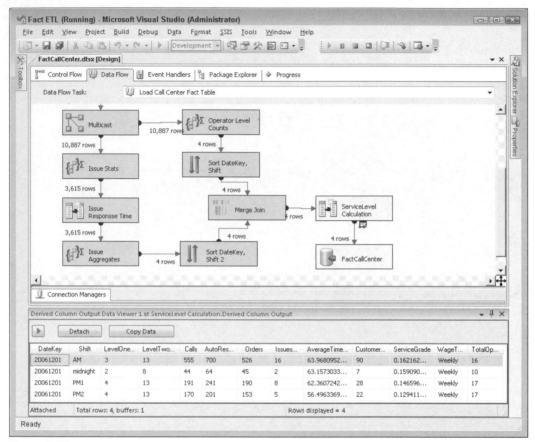

Figure 8-36

This example is available in the chapter example files available on the Wrox Web site (www.wrox.com) and is named FactCallCenter.dtsx. Chapter 11 takes this example and uses a Script component to simplify the process down to only a couple components in the entire data flow.

Advanced Fact Table ETL Concepts

Before this chapter concludes, a couple advanced concepts should be discussed:

- ❑ Dealing with missing dimension members, called *inferred members*, when data is dirty or the dimension member arrives late in the dimension table

- ❑ Handling late-arriving fact records when a dimension table is tracking Type 2 changes

Handling Missing Dimension Lookups

Sometimes, you may work with a dimension table that does not have current data, or some of the data is not immediately available. This can cause missing dimension keys during the fact table load, which may require you to add placeholder records in the dimension table.

When the fact table is being loaded and a dimension key is not available, then the fact ETL must assign a placeholder surrogate key for the row to be successfully inserted. Dimension foreign keys in the fact table usually do not allow NULL values. To handle this issue, you can use one of two common approaches:

- ❑ Option 1 involves using a generic unknown surrogate key for the missing key. Commonly, a surrogate key value of 0, 1, or –1 is reserved for the missing key.

- ❑ Option 2 involves adding a placeholder record in the dimension table with the business key that previously did not exist in the dimension.

Option 1 can be handled through a Derived Column transformation, replacing any NULL values in the surrogate keys with the generic unknown surrogate key. However, this choice will not allow the fact row to ever be updated with the right dimension key, should the dimension source record be available at a later date.

The second option, called an *inferred member*, offers greater flexibility and is the focus of this section. In Chapter 7, consideration was given to updating the inferred member dimension record when the missing dimension source is available. This section looks at creating the inferred member during the fact load.

You have at least three ways to handle inferred member creation during the fact-loading process:

- ❑ *Create a pre-data flow check of the source rows* — This allows you to see whether any missing dimension members exist, and subsequently create them first, before you load the primary data flow for the fact table.

- ❑ *Use a post-data flow process* — During the primary fact load data flow, only fact source records that have every dimension match immediately available are loaded into the fact table. Any row with at least one missing dimension member is staged to a temporary table. After the primary fact load data flow, the inferred members are added to the dimension table, and then the staged fact source rows are re-processed with complete matches.

- ❑ *Use an in-line data flow approach* — During the fact row processing, if a missing dimension record exists, add the dimension record midstream in the data flow, and bring the new surrogate key back so that all the fact source records can be added to the fact table.

Unfortunately, none of these approaches comes with an Easy button. Each has its complexities, benefits, and drawbacks.

The pre-data flow choice works well when only one or two dimensions require inferred members, and it is okay to scan the source file or table two times (the first to check for inferred members, and the second to load the fact rows). It involves an initial data flow with dimension lookups, where any missing lookup records are sent to a dimension destination.

The post-data flow requires a few steps: staging records with missing dimensions, adding the inferred members, and then running the fact load process a second time to associate the newly created inferred member keys, and loading the rows into the fact table.

The in-line data flow choice comes with some advantages, but requires more complex data flow component configuration. One thing to keep in mind is that, if a dimension record is missing for one fact source row, the possibility exists that the same dimension record may come across a second time (or more) during the same load. In this common case, the inferred member should be added only once; otherwise, duplicates will be generated in the dimension table.

Using out-of-the-box transformations, one data flow approach involves redirecting the missing record, handling the inferred member, and joining back the new record into the data flow. Figure 8-37 shows the sales fact data flow, with inferred member handling of the product dimension.

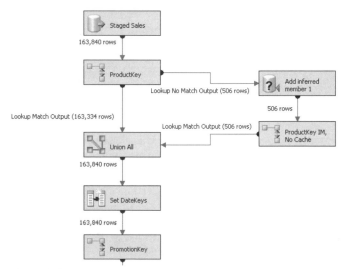

Figure 8-37

The product dimension lookup is configured as a full-cached lookup, and the No Match output is used in the event of a missing record. All missing lookups are sent out the Lookup No Match into an OLE DB Command transformation. This component calls a SQL stored procedure, passing in the ProductAlternateKey (or ProductID from the source). The following code shows the details of the TSQL procedure:

```
CREATE PROCEDURE csp_CreateInferredMember
@ProductAlternateKey nvarchar(25)
AS

IF NOT EXISTS
  (SELECT ProductAlternateKey FROM [dbo].[DimProduct]
   WHERE ProductAlternateKey = @ProductAlternateKey)
BEGIN

    INSERT INTO [dbo].[DimProduct]
    ( [ProductAlternateKey]
    ,[EnglishProductName],[SpanishProductName]
    ,[FrenchProductName],[FinishedGoodsFlag]
    ,[Color],[StartDate],[EndDate],[Status])

    VALUES
    (@ProductAlternateKey,'NA','NA','NA',1,'NA'
    ,GETDATE(),NULL,'Inf')
END
```

Within the stored procedure, the IF NOT EXISTS line checks to see whether the business key already exists, in which case the procedure does not need to re-add it. If the business key does not exist, then the procedure adds the inferred member with the business keys and unknowns for attributes.

Because the OLE DB Command transformation cannot receive any returned value, the surrogate key must be acquired in a second step. The output of the OLE DB Command transformation is passed to a second Lookup transformation. This lookup is configured with a disabled cache, as shown in Figure 8-38. Disabling the cache has the effect of forcing the Lookup component to query the database directly for the required values, instead of utilizing an in-memory cache. A partial-cache could also be used in this context, where the cache is built as new matches are received from the lookup reference table.

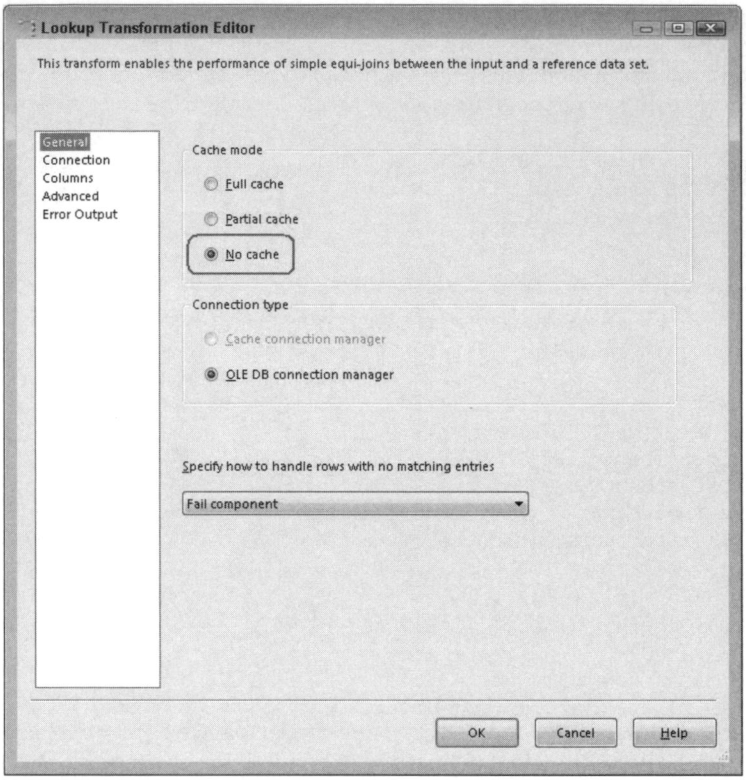

Figure 8-38

Every row passed through the OLE DB Command transformation needs the product surrogate key. The lookup queries the product dimension and returns the right surrogate key. Figure 8-39 shows the lookup Transformation Editor Columns tab with the returned surrogate key added as ProductKey_inferred to the data flow.

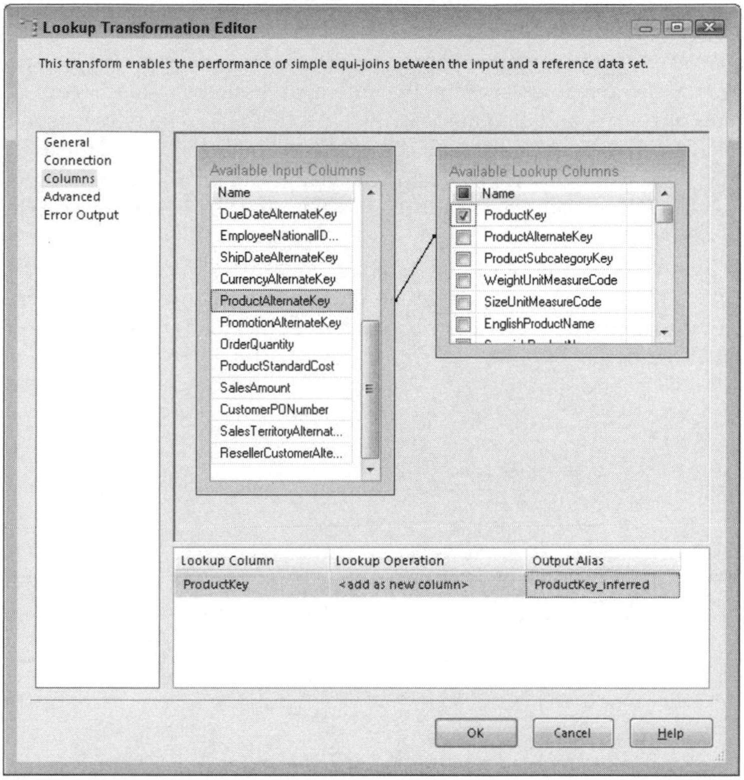

Figure 8-39

The final step is to bring the fact row back into the main pipeline of records that initially matched the dimension records. This is handled with a Union All transformation.

Of note, the `ProductKey` column from the product lookup is matched with the `ProductKey_inferred` from the inferred member lookup, thus giving a complete set of product surrogate keys from the source fact rows that can then be inserted into the fact table destination.

If you have been counting, this model requires three queries against the product dimension table for a new inferred member. The first checks for the record, the second adds the record, and the third gets the surrogate key. Furthermore, every time the same `ProductAlternateKey` comes through the inferred member process, the product dimension is queried again to check for the record, and again to return the key. When considering that the inferred members should make up a very small minority of source records, this solution may work well and not pose scalability issues.

You can use a Script component to perform a similar process, but at the same time, increasing the performance by reducing the queries against the dimension table. Chapter 11 examines how to use the Script component. You could create the Script component to call the procedure listed earlier and return the surrogate key in the same step (rather than two steps), as well as also maintain an internal cache of `ProductAlternateKey` with matching surrogate keys in the event the same business key resurfaces.

The bottom line is that choices are available to handle inferred members, and although the processes and code may add complexity to the ETL, the overall benefits are significant for missing dimension handling.

Handling Late-Arriving Facts

Like it sounds, a *late-arriving fact* is when a fact source row comes through the ETL process at some amount of time after the source row was actually generated. Perhaps a sales record is delayed for a day or so for verification purposes, and then made available to the ETL. The only reason this may require special handling is when a dimension contains Type 2 historical attributes. If the associated record in the dimension table has gone through a Type 2 historical change, then the late-arriving fact row may need to look back to an outdated dimension record for the most accurate dimension association.

One approach for this scenario is to check the current dimension StartDate with the fact transaction date and, if the dimension StartDate is later than the fact transaction date, then send the row out for special handling. Figure 8-40 shows an example of the sales fact load data flow, again focused on the product dimension lookup.

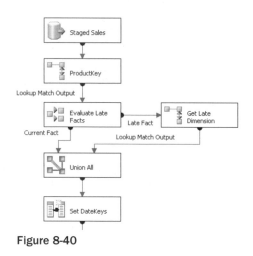

Figure 8-40

The lookup for the product dimension returns both the product surrogate key and the StartDate (aliased as ProductStartDate) of the dimension, because the product dimension contains Type 2 historical attributes. The very next transformation, a Conditional Split, compares the dates. Figure 8-41 shows the Conditional Split Transformation Editor.

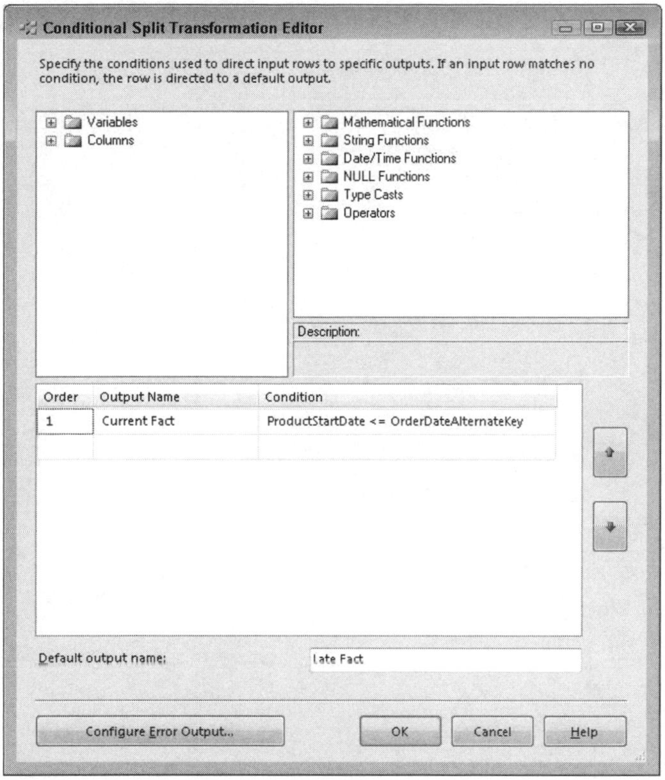

Figure 8-41

If the order date of the sale (OrderDateAlternateKey) is less than or equal to the dimension's start date, then the surrogate key must be replaced with the correct outdated surrogate key. The rows redirected to the default output called Late Fact are sent into another Lookup transformation, with special configuration to handle the date range. Figure 8-42 shows the Advanced tab of the second Lookup Transformation Editor.

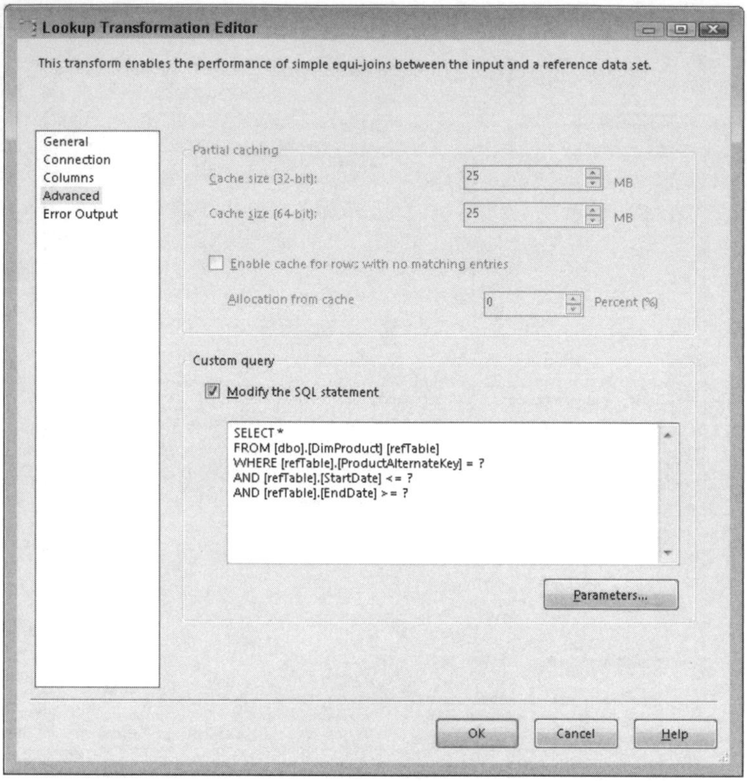

Figure 8-42

Notice that the "Modify the SQL statement" checkbox is selected, which allows a custom query to be entered. The query is redefined with parameters to handle the date range. These parameters are mapped to the ProductAlternateKey, the OrderDateAlternateKey, and the same OrderDateAlternateKey again, as Figure 8-43 shows (by clicking the Parameters button shown in Figure 8-42).

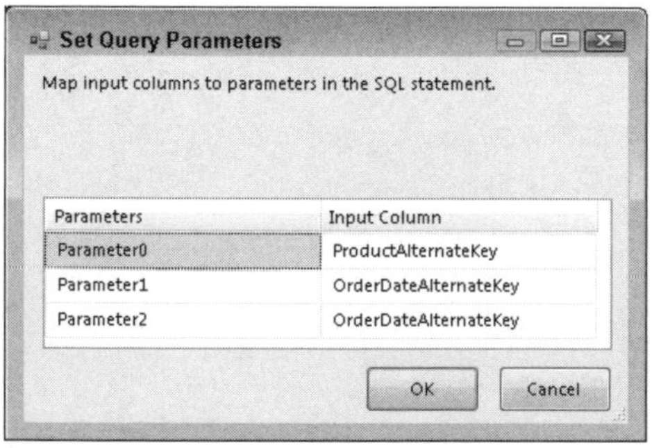

Figure 8-43

Using this approach does not allow caching. However, the number of records requiring this handling is usually significantly small. One trick is required to get the modified SQL statement to work. The Column Mappings tab must include the `OrderDateAlternateKey` mapped to a column in the reference table (mapped to `StartDate` because it made the most sense) so that the lookup can see the `OrderDateAlternateKey` for parameterization. Without this, the transformation will fail with the error referencing the `OrderDateAlternateKey` as not existing. Also note that, because the SQL statement is being modified, the configured column mapping will not apply, so it is, therefore, okay to map the `OrderDateAlternateKey`.

Summary

Fact table ETL involves several central (but simple) aspects, such as dimension key lookups and measure calculations. Beyond these two common components, many fact table processes require preparing the data, which adds a layer of difficulty. And, in more rare instances, unique dimension processing requirements (such as inferred members and late-arriving facts) are more complex and require more planning, development, and testing. But, in all, SSIS provides the tools to meet your fact table ETL requirements successfully.

As an extension to this chapter and Chapter 7, Chapter 9 focuses on SSAS integration, mainly processing SSAS dimensions and cube partitions.

SSAS Processing Architecture

This final chapter of the Business Intelligence chapter trio targets the integration points between SSIS and SQL Server 2008 Analysis Services (SSAS). Business Intelligence (BI) solutions that involve SSAS cubes typically include a method for processing the objects from the data warehouse or data mart database sources into the Online Analytical Processing (OLAP) cube structures. With the focus of Chapters 7 and 8 on handling dimension and fact table ETL, the final step in the process is to load the related SSAS objects, which, in most cases, is the responsibility of the ETL process. This chapter contains one Problem-Design-Solution to discuss SSAS processing and partition management techniques and best practices. The "Problem" section discusses the integration points between SSIS and SSAS, and some of the considerations to look at during that integration. The "Design" section looks at the out-of-the-box basics, and how to handle more complicated situations. Lastly, the "Solution" section shows how to create a set of packages to utilize the tasks and components, and manage the entire SSAS solution.

Problem

After you've designed your data warehouse and loaded it with data, you must provide the users with a way to access the data. By creating an Analysis Services database with cubes and dimensions, you give the users accessibility, and you can encapsulate business terms and business logic within the cube. Analysis Services will also contain aggregations to speed up querying and hierarchies for drill-down capabilities. Even though SSAS can provide a great number of benefits, you must work through a number of considerations before just throwing a cube at your solution. The following processing design questions should be considered in more detail:

❑ Which method should you use to populate SSAS objects?

❑ When should you run the population?

❑ What happens with late-arriving or new data?

❑ How do you incorporate everything together?

SSAS Object Population

An SSAS database will not do you much good if no data is inside of it. As is discussed later in more detail, SSAS objects can be populated in two different ways: processing and direct loading. You typically pull your data from the data warehouse that was already loaded during the ETL process. This ensures that you can reload that data at any time by reprocessing that object. For dimensions and partitions, you can alternatively load the data directly into the object.

Choosing one option over the other depends on the data with which you are working. So, how do you decide which to use? The "Design" section of this chapter discusses how both options work, how you can perform them in SSIS, and the benefits of both.

Schedule

Enterprise BI systems often have recurring ETL schedules that are predicated on the availability of source data. Often, these schedules are set to run nightly when either a source system is idle or has downtime, or when some prior batch process or precedence is complete. However, sometimes scheduling is required more or less frequently, such as when an inventory system sends data updates weekly or monthly, or on the flip side, when data is made available several times a day. You may even have a situation that contains a diversity of processing schedule requirements, from monthly to near real time.

The common thread in most of the enterprise ETL processes is that the load times are known. The ETL schedules kick off at either predefined times, or via scheduling tools that work in conjunction with other environment precedences. This can be for ETL jobs that run every five minutes to once a month. And, when a job finishes, the scheduling tool or package that coordinates execution can spawn off another process.

ETL scheduling is important in a discussion on SSAS processing because, in the majority of cases, when an Enterprise BI system involves SSAS, the processing of the SSAS objects is the responsibility of the ETL subsystem. Therefore, you must take into consideration the aspects and methods involved in it.

To be sure, a handful of BI solutions are real time or very near real time, meaning the transactions that are happening from the source systems are trickled through to the BI solution throughout the day as they happen. This scenario requires leveraging some of the real-time and near real-time features of SSAS, including Relational Online Analytical Process (ROLAP) storage for objects and proactive caching. These are both out of the scope of this chapter, but important in describing the overall picture of SSAS processing. You can refer to SQL Server's online documentation on "proactive caching" for more information on near real-time processing.

Partition Management

When discussing SSIS integration with SSAS, just reviewing partition processing is not the complete story. Any enterprise BI solution involving SSAS almost always requires more than one partition per measure group for data management, processing, and performance reasons.

In other words, in your ETL, you often have to create new partitions before processing them. The easy way out may be to create several partitions a couple years out into the future. Just don't give them your phone number if you leave the project or organization, because you might get a call in two years asking why the processing is breaking!

Although you can hope that your data will always come from the source system in the correct order on the correct day that you request it, this is most often not the case. As previously discussed in Chapter 8, late-arriving facts are very common. If a fact record comes in after that partition has already been processed, how do you handle it?

Understanding how your data comes from the source system into your data warehouse is an essential part of working with Analysis Services. That information can help you determine what new structures must be created and modified.

The Complete Package

The end goal is to create a set of SSIS packages that incorporate everything that has been discussed up to this point. The packages must utilize the correct population method for all SSAS objects. The correct SSIS task or component should be selected for the requirements. The packages should run on the correct schedule, either in tandem with the ETL packages, or on a different schedule. If data arrives after a partition has already been processed, or when new data comes into the system, partitions must be created and/or reprocessed. Each of these factors is examined in the "Solution" section later in this chapter.

Design

To recap the problem, you must create a set of SSIS packages that can manage the SSAS portion of your data warehouse. The packages should create new partitions if needed, and process or reprocess partitions with new data. The packages should also contain a way to process the dimensions associated with the cube. SSIS provides a number of tasks and components that can be used for these purposes.

Let's start by reviewing SSAS and processing options. Then, let's look at each SSIS item in depth and determine which ones can be used in this particular scenario. Finally, this discussion wraps up with ways to create and manage measure group partitions. After all the options have been explored, you can learn about the best items to use in the "Solution" section.

SSAS Objects and Processing Basics

Before jumping into the details of SSAS processing, here's a quick refresher on the concepts and components involved in SSAS processing.

The main types of objects in SSAS that must be processed are dimensions and partitions. If you are using the data-mining features of SSAS, you will also be processing data-mining objects. You may ask, "What about processing the SSAS database, cubes, and measure groups?" True, these objects can be processed, but they are just containers for subordinate objects, and when you choose to process them, you are really identifying the set of dimensions, partitions, and mining objects to process.

Note that even though a cube doesn't contain data itself (only its related dimensions and measure group partitions), when a cube is processed, that cube does have a script cache that is refreshed. In other words, you should process the cube object itself if you made any changes to calculations or to the Multidimensional Expressions (MDX) script.

Dimensions

An SSAS dimension, as you would guess, maps very closely to a dimension table in the database. In fact, when you have a dimensionally structured modeled data warehouse or data mart (with an ETL process, as described in Chapters 7 and 8), then the SSAS dimensions are loaded directly from their underlying dimension tables. However, it's not always the case that the mapping is exactly one to one, because at times you may need to combine multiple tables or use a single-source dimension table for more than one SSAS dimension. Furthermore, an SSAS solution can be built on top of a transactional system where several source tables are involved. However, a transactionally sourced SSAS solution is limited in size and the tracking of history, and this is mostly reserved for proof-of-concept, specialized, or smaller-scale solutions.

Figure 9-1 shows the Employee dimension in the `AdventureWorks` example SSAS solution.

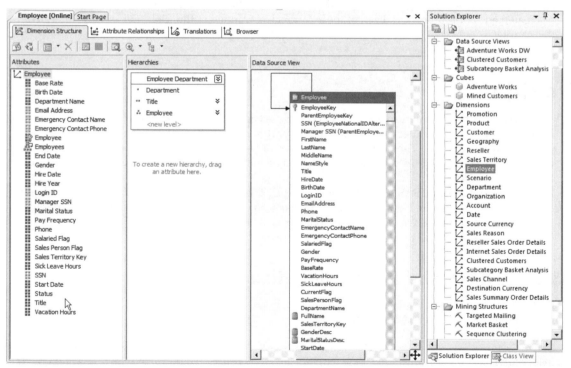

Figure 9-1

The main Business Intelligence Development Studio (BIDS) designer window shows the dimension editor. The Solution Explorer (on the right) shows the list of dimensions created in the SSAS solution. Dimensions contain attributes and defined hierarchies, which come into play when loading the underlying table data into the SSAS objects.

Several processing types exist for SSAS dimensions, including the following:

❑ *Full process* — A full process involves a rebuild of the data structure underlying the SSAS dimension, which requires full rescans of the dimension table to populate the attribute's structures, hierarchies, and indexes created for optimization. A full process is required when you make any structural change to the dimension (such as adding attributes and hierarchies, and moving or adding attribute relationships).

When you perform a full process, the data is dropped in any associated measure group partitions because the structures are rebuilt.

❑ *Process update* — A process update is similar to a full process in that the underlying dimension table is rescanned. However, the attribute, hierarchy, and index structures in the SSAS dimension are merely updated with changes and additions. This choice is the best when processing an SSAS database because it preserves the related structures.

Some dimension changes, including deletes, may not be allowed based on the design, which has implications in dimension ETL change types. This topic is discussed later in this chapter when reviewing the implications of rigid and flexible attribute relationships.

❑ *Unprocess* — Occasionally, you may want to *unprocess* your dimension to perhaps free space, or perhaps to force a full rebuild of a partition with the full processing.

❑ *Process data* — Process data is similar to the process update, but only involves processing the data structures for the attributes and the hierarchies, excluding the attribute bitmap indexes.

❑ *Process index* — The complement to process data is process index, which only processes the indexes. The requirement for this type is that the SSAS dimension must first be processed, because process index does not require rescanning the dimension table.

❑ *Process add* — Process add enables you to add dimension members to the SSAS dimension without requiring the entire dimension table to be rescanned. This option is not available in the UI processing features found in SQL Server Management Studio (SSMS) or SSIS, but is a method that can be used programmatically or through XML for Analysis (XMLA), which is the industry specification message for interacting with OLAP structures.

Partitions

The second SSIS object involved in processing is the measure group partition. A *measure group partition* is most often sourced from a fact table when you are loading data from a data warehouse or data mart. If you are loading data from an active transactional database system, your partitions would map to your primary transaction tables. But again, enterprise-scale solutions are best designed with a dimensionally normalized underlying database. When you are associating SSAS objects with fact tables to SSAS objects, the mapping is at the measure group level. The partitions are a subordinate object to the measure group, and provide the data storage for the measure group. Therefore, when a measure group contains more than one partition, the partition only contains a subset of the measure group's entire data set.

As already mentioned, SSAS has the capability to drive the scheduling and processing times of the partitions. This feature is called *proactive caching*. Furthermore, you may have some partitions that act like database views where the structure allows queries, but the queries are passed through to the database that contains the cube data. This is called *Relational OLAP* (ROLAP), which is useful for a rapidly changing subset of data. For most of your partitions (if not all), you will be using *Multidimensional Online Analytical Process* (MOLAP) storage, where the underlying data is completely pulled into the partition structure and aggregates can be added.

Figure 9-2 shows the cube designer in BIDS, with the Partitions tab selected, which highlights the partition management UI for SSAS.

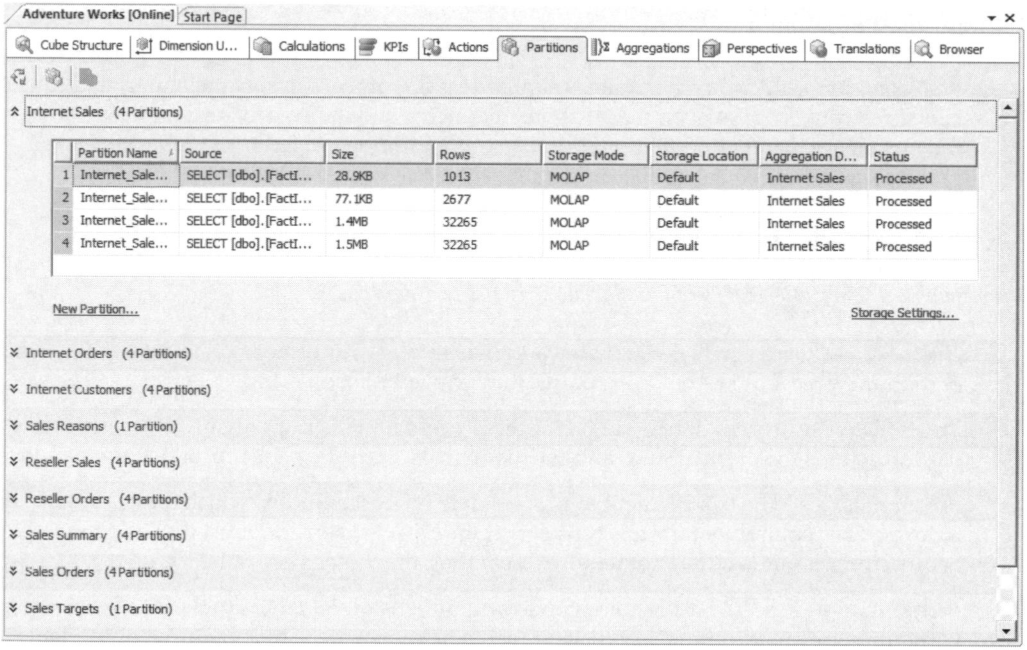

Figure 9-2

As you can see, the partitions are associated with measure groups, and, furthermore, each partition has a different name and, although not shown, also a different underlying query to keep the partition data separate from one another.

When you are processing partitions, the following options are available:

❑ *Process full* — A process full for partitions is equivalent to both the process update and process full for dimensions. The underlying partition's data is rescanned and the partition is rebuilt with any changes and updates. When process full is complete (or the transaction that it is contained in), the new data will be made available, and during processing, the old data is still online.

❏ *Incremental process* — An incremental process is the equivalent of *process add*, where data can be added to the partition without the need to rebuild it. However, process add does not update any data currently in the partitions; it only brings in new underlying fact rows. In other words, if you have a fact record that is updated, you must perform a process full. Alternatively, you could use a change-record approach to offset the original value in the partition.

❏ *Unprocess* — Unprocess drops the data, aggregates, and indexes from the partition.

❏ *Process data* — Process data, just like the equivalent on the dimension side, only loads the detailed data into the partition's MOLAP structure without processing the indexes or aggregates. Because ROLAP and *Hybrid Online Analytical Processing* (HOLAP) keep data in the underlying database, this option only applies to MOLAP structures.

❏ *Process index* — Process index processes both the bitmap indexes and the aggregation, provided that at least the partition's core data is already loaded. In other words, the process index does not need to access the underlying table data.

Mining Structures

When processing data-mining objects in SSAS, you are really dealing with processing mining structures and mining models, which are very different in regard to what the processing is doing.

The *mining structure* is the base organization of data that the mining models are built upon. Mining structures define the organization of data to be mined (hence, *structure*), as well as the training data that give the mining models the capability to perform predictions and associations. Figure 9-3 highlights the Targeted Mailing mining structure in SSAS, which contains a series of columns that will be used in the mining.

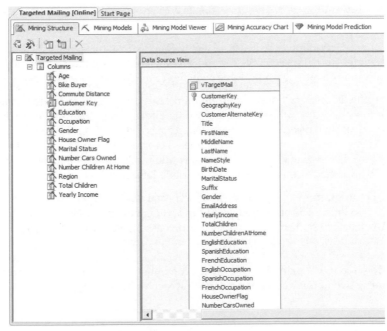

Figure 9-3

When processing the mining structures in SSAS, what you are doing is loading the training data into the structure so that the mining models can perform their analysis. When you process the mining models, you are applying the chosen mining model algorithms to the content of the mining structures.

Both mining structures and mining models have only two general processing types: *process full* (called *process structure* for mining structures) and *unprocess* (called *process clear* for mining structures). As you would expect, a process full rebuilds the structures or models. However, be aware that a process full on a mining structure does not automatically perform a process full on the associated mining models. Therefore, if you process a mining structure, you must then process the mining models created on top of that structure.

SSIS Tasks and Components

Now, the solution starts to come together. When you have an SSAS solution involved in your BI solution, just what are the different methods that you can use to process these related objects in your SSIS-based ETL process?

There are several, which involve leveraging different aspects of SSIS in the data flow and control flow:

❑ Using the control flow object Analysis Services Processing Task is the most straightforward approach, and is discussed in the next section. This allows any SSAS objects (that involve processing) and their processing method to be selected. A few drawbacks are listed in the next section.

❑ Although the Analysis Services Execute DDL Task may sound as if it only allows objects to be modified, created, or deleted, its functionality goes way beyond Data Definition Language (DDL). This task runs an SSAS XMLA script. XMLA includes the capability not just to run DDL, but also query and process. Therefore, this task is very useful for SSAS processing, because the XMLA can be modified in an SSIS package before it is executed.

❑ Another approach involves using the Execute Process Task to call the ASCMD executable that comes with SSAS. This executable can run MDX, Data Mining Expressions (DMX), and XMLA, and also contains some command-line switches to make your processing more dynamic.

❑ The data flow in SSIS includes two destinations: the *Dimension Processing destination* and the *Partition Processing destination*. These allow data directly from the pipeline to be pushed into either an SSAS dimension or SSAS partition, respectively. Unlike all the other SSIS approaches discussed here, this approach is the only one where data is pushed directly to SSAS. The other approaches essentially tell SSAS to start pulling the data from a data source. Like the other SSIS approaches, this approach is described later in this chapter.

❑ Finally, the programming API for SSAS, called Analysis Management Objects (AMO), allows the interface into the SSAS object model and can leverage the processing methods to process any of the SSAS objects described. To use AMO for processing, you must leverage either the Script Task in the control flow, or the Script Component in the data flow.

When it comes down to it, your situation may use a combination of approaches as the needs arrive, or even a one-off derivative of these choices. Let's review each of these methods in more detail.

Analysis Services Processing Task

The Analysis Services Processing Task is a control flow task designed to process objects selected in a list with the capability to set processing types, handle errors, order and relate objects, and manage transactions. Figure 9-4 shows the Analysis Services Processing Task Editor.

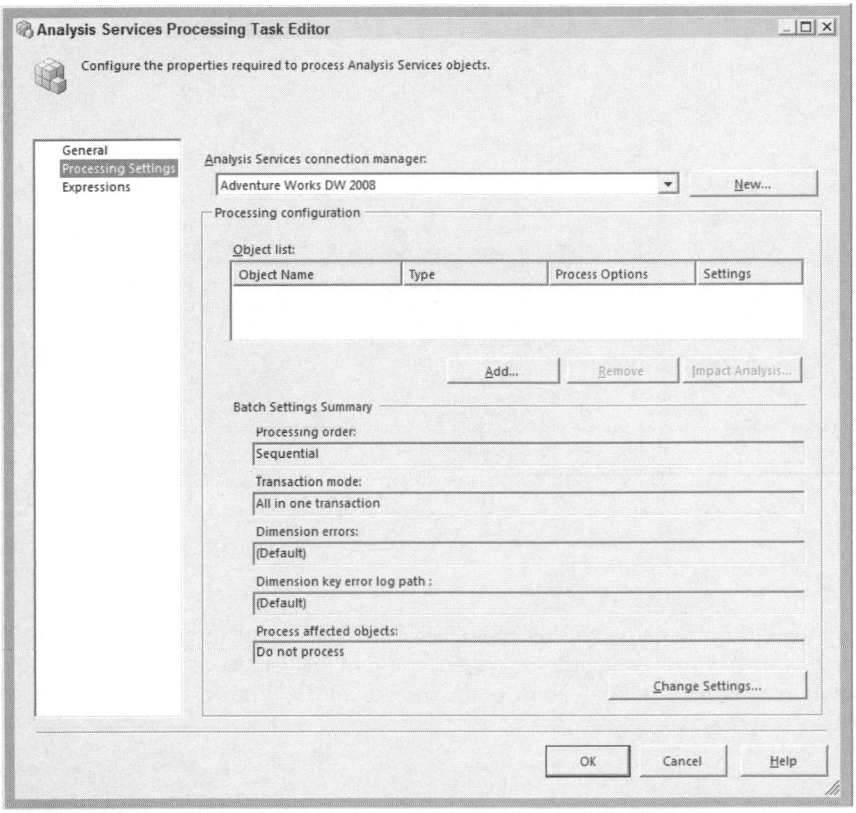

Figure 9-4

Adding objects to the Object list is very straightforward. You select Add below the Object list to enable an entire SSAS database to be selected, or specific cubes, dimensions, or mining models. When selecting a cube or mining model, you are merely instructing the task to process the underlying measure groups and partitions or mining structures. You can also select these individually, as Figure 9-5 shows.

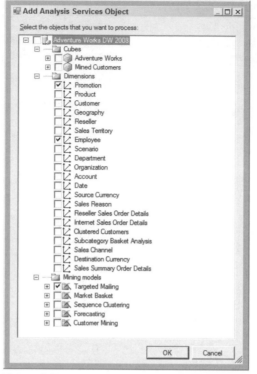

Figure 9-5

After clicking the OK button, you will see the selected items in the Object list on the main screen. Here is where you can select the processing types. For each item in the list, choose the processing option from the drop-down list. Figure 9-6 shows some of the choices for the Product dimension.

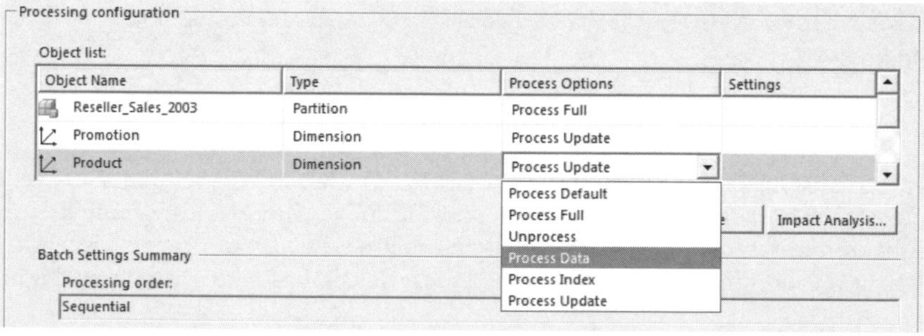

Figure 9-6

If you have selected a parent container with the intention of processing the underlying objects, the list will only show the processing options that are in common with all the objects. So, you may need to select the different objects individually. Also, if you have selected the Process Incremental option for a partition, you will be prompted to configure some advanced settings. This is because when adding data to a partition incrementally, you must define which data should be added. The configuration screen (not shown) allows for a table, view, or query to be specified as the source for the rows being added to the partition.

The second aspect of this task involves setting how to handle the processing batch. The lower half of the Analysis Services Processing Task Editor window shown earlier in Figure 9-4 has settings related to the batch. Selecting Change Settings opens a window to modify the advanced properties, with a "Processing options" tab and a "Dimension key errors" tab. The first tab allows some general settings to be updated, such as whether to run the processing sequentially or in parallel, and how to handle SSAS transactions initiated by the task. Also, a writeback table selection exists, along with the option to process affected objects.

Figure 9-7 shows the "Dimension key errors" tab, which controls the action taken when a partition is being processed, and a dimension key is referenced in the underlying fact, but the associated key doesn't exist in the SSAS dimension itself.

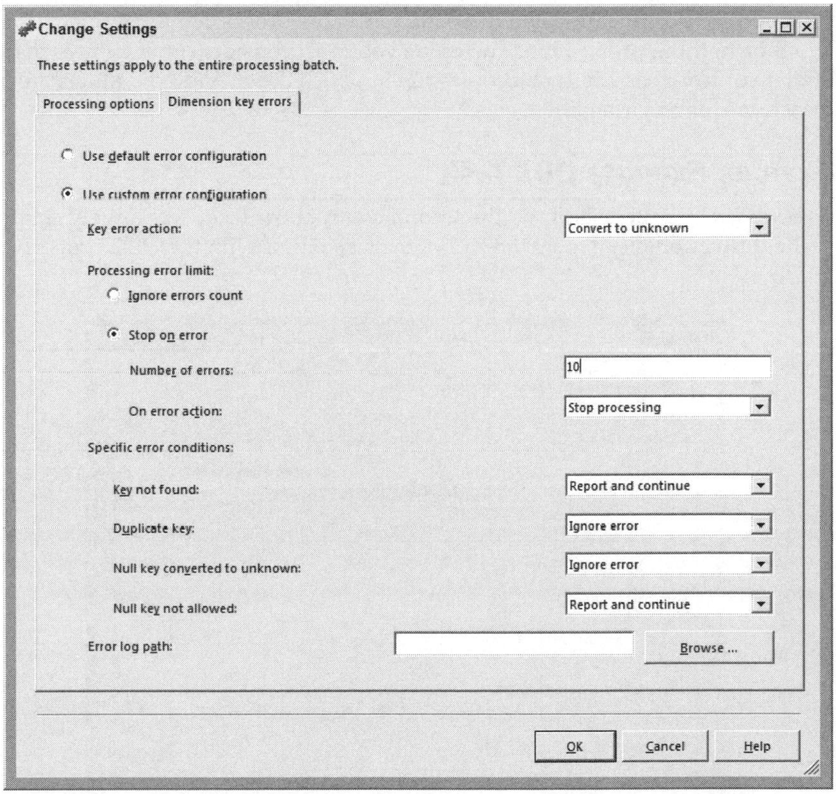

Figure 9-7

You can define similar settings within a given measure group, and the "Use default error configuration" option will then default to those settings. The "Use custom error configuration" option enables you to override these settings. For example, you are able to set a threshold number (property "Number of errors") so that if processing errors reach the threshold, either the task can fail, or it can stop reporting the errors.

Several key errors also cause issues in processing, including missing keys, duplicates, and NULL values. These settings can ignore, report, and continue processing, or report and stop the processing. In this case, you are able to define which types of errors you allow to happen, and which indicate a bigger issue that may need to be addressed (and, therefore, stop the processing).

The following are some drawbacks to the Analysis Services Processing Task:

❏ Although some of the general properties are configurable through property expressions or SSIS Configurations, what is not changeable is anything related to the list of objects and the batch setting. In essence, when you use this task, you are hard-coding the list of objects and how the objects should be processed. In many cases, this will not meet your requirements, especially if partitions are involved. The good news is that even if you have multiple partitions, typically your dimension list doesn't change, nor the processing type. This makes the processing task a good choice for defining dimension processes.

❏ A second drawback is that the SSAS Processing Task either requires every object to be processed one at a time (in separate transactions), or the entire process set to run in parallel in the same transaction. The drawback when choosing to run the processing in parallel is that the processing is an all-or-nothing proposition. Therefore, you must consider other choices that allow for better granular control over which objects get run in which order, and how things are batched for transactions for restartability.

Analysis Services Execute DDL Task

The Analysis Services Execute DDL Task, the second control flow task, is relatively simple in form, but provides excellent functionality. Figure 9-8 shows the task editor with the DDL property page selected.

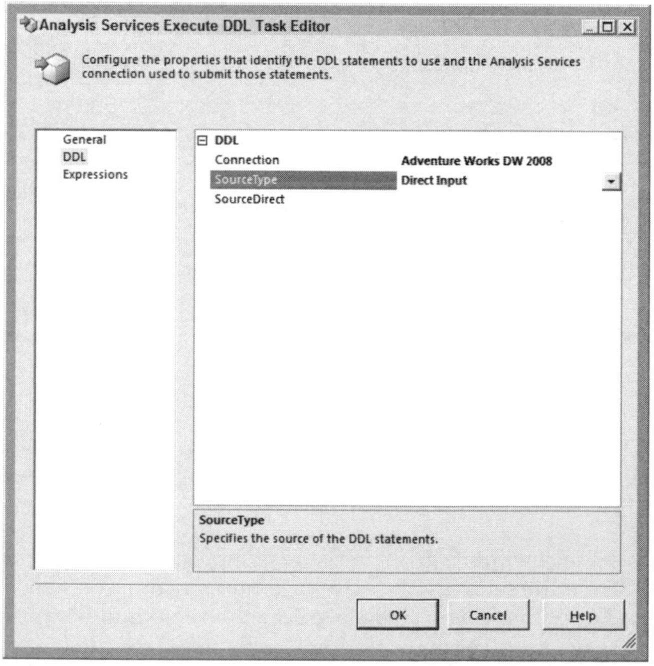

Figure 9-8

There are only three properties. The `Connection` property, as you would guess, defines which SSAS package connection should be used. The `SourceType` property allows three different methods to input the XMLA statement:

❑ Choosing Direct Input changes the third property to `SourceDirect`, where the XMLA can be hard-coded into the task.

❑ Selecting File Connection changes the third property to `Source`, so that a file connection manager can be selected, which identifies the file system file that contains the XMLA to run.

❑ Choosing Variable in the `SourceType` means that the XMLA will be embedded in a variable of type string. The `Source` property becomes the package variable that the task will use.

Because these properties are exposed, you are able to modify them through expressions and configurations. You can use the Analysis Services Execute DDL Task for processing dimensions or facts.

Dimensions

Because dimension processing is generally straightforward (except for some potential unique precedence handling or transaction management), the keep-it-simple corollary dictates that some of the approaches would be overkill.

Leveraging the Analysis Services Processing Task is often sufficient, and has already been described. Another straightforward approach involves creating an XMLA script for processing the dimensions. Rarely do dimension structures change, and, in most scenarios, a process update is performed on the dimensions. In most cases, the XMLA script doesn't need to be dynamic. Therefore, the XMLA can be generated, and then just executed using the Analysis Services Execute DDL Task.

Facts

The next choice works well for cases where the partition count is dynamic. Using the Analysis Services Execute DDL Task, you can modify XMLA before the DDL task is run. Earlier, Figure 9-8 showed how the Execute DDL Task works, by reading the XMLA (or MDX or DMX) either through the direct input, a package variable, or from a file.

Because the SSIS expression language does not support iterative functions, using a property expression with the direct input option will not allow the partition count to be dynamic. Instead, the Script Task is a good alternative to dynamically generate the XMLA, and either outputting the script to a file, or the contents into a variable. If you are proficient with TSQL, the XMLA could be generated within a stored procedure and returned with the Execute SQL Task. But be mindful of output parameter length limitations.

Execute Process Task with ASCMD

Similar to the Analysis Services Execute DDL Task, the approach to create and modify XMLA script can be used in conjunction with the Execute Process Task. This approach executes an XMLA script by leveraging the `ASCMD.exe` executable that you can find as part of the "Microsoft SQL Server Product Samples: Analysis Services" download at `http://msftasprodsamples.codeplex.com`.

As mentioned earlier, the `ASCMD.exe` contains the capability to run XMLA scripts, MDX queries, and DMX queries. Refer to `http://msdn2.microsoft.com/en-us/library/ms365187.aspx` for an article that describes the full feature set of `ASCMD.exe`. in SSIS through an Execute Process Task. For example, you can save the prior XMLA script to a local directory file, and you can use the Execute Process Task in the control flow to run ASCMD.exe, identifying the file containing the XMLA script.

When looking at the properties of the Execute Process Task, you can see that the task is configured to run the ASCMD.exe executable and pass in three primary arguments. Figure 9-9 shows the Execute Process Task Editor.

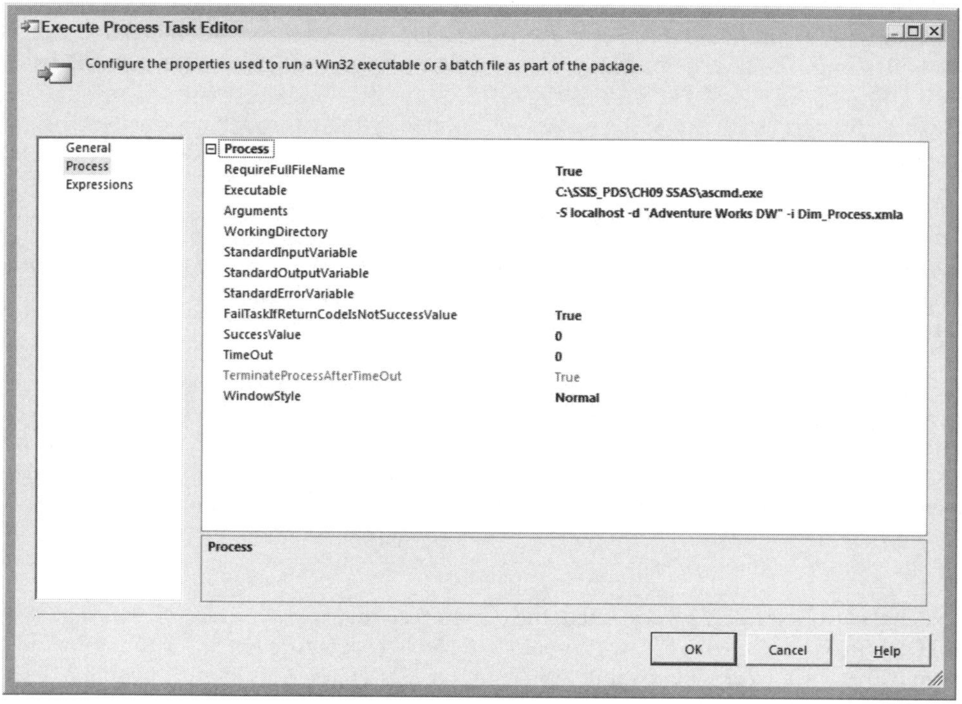

Figure 9-9

The first argument, -S localhost, specifies the server to run the script. The second argument, -d "Adventure Works DW", identifies which SSAS database the script should be run against. The third argument, -i Dim_Process.xmla, specifies the name of the file containing the XMLA script to run.

ASCMD.exe also supports the capability to dynamically update the contents of the XMLA, MDX, or DMX code with variables passed into the command line through the arguments.

Among other benefits (such as more comprehensive logging), the ASCMD.exe utility also contains the capability to accept parameters as arguments, and then apply those parameters to the XMLA code being executed.

In conclusion, this approach works well in the case where a fixed number of partitions must execute, and the XMLA can be parameterized to handle the fixed number, which would map to pre-defined package variables. The drawback is that the parameterization requires a fixed number of partitions. To circumvent this problem, you could update the file with the correct number of partitions before the execution, if needed, or use the Analysis Services Execute DDL Task, as described next.

Data Flow Destinations for SSAS Objects

The final consideration for the built-in features involves the data flow destinations: *Dimension Processing* and *Partition Processing*.

As briefly mentioned earlier, these two data flow destinations are the only SSIS methods where the ETL process is actually pushing the data into SSAS. The other choices listed earlier instruct SSAS to begin its processing, which causes the SSAS engine to pull data in from defined sources for the various objects being processed. These destinations are a very powerful mechanism to load data into SSAS from non-standard sources and for near real-time processing.

Dimension Processing Data Flow Destination

The Dimension Processing destination is connected directly to the data flow pipeline, which allows any type of transformation to influence the data before it is pushed into the SSAS dimension structures. The property pages include pages for specifying the dimension (and processing option), column mappings from the source data into the dimension attributes, and dimension key error handling. Figure 9-10 shows the Connection Manager property page in the Dimension Processing Destination Editor, which identifies the SSAS connection manager, the dimension (in this case, Geography), and the type of processing.

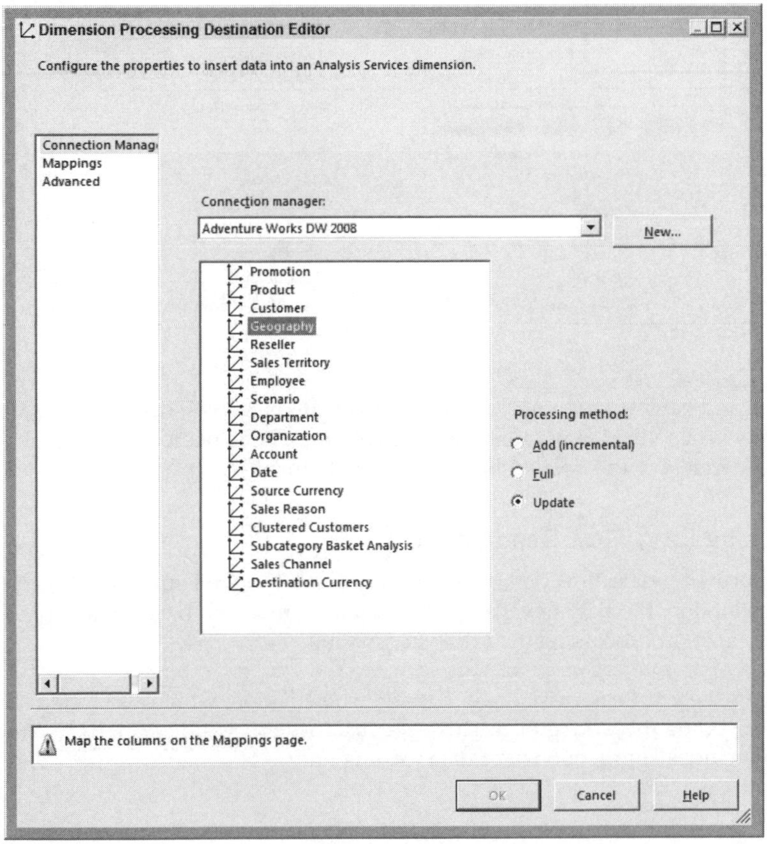

Figure 9-10

Mapping the source columns from the pipeline to the dimension attributes is handled in much the same way as any other source-to-destination mapping within the pipeline. Figure 9-11 shows the Mappings page of the Geography Dimension Processing destination.

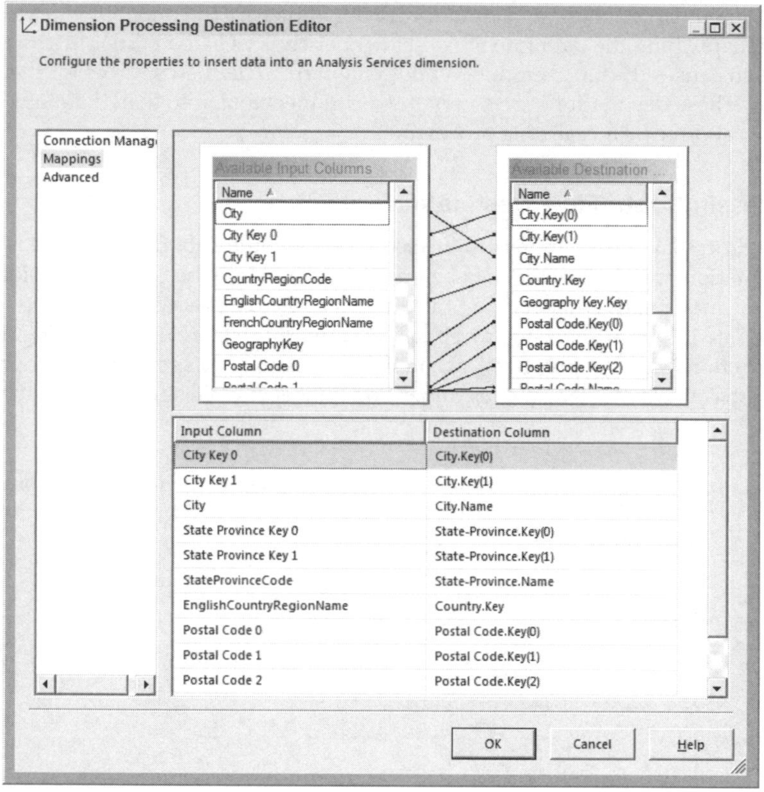

Figure 9-11

Attribute names and keys are required for the processing to be successful. The keys are defined within SSAS, which may be a collection of more than one column. The Advanced tab (not shown) allows key error handling, identical to the details shown earlier in Figure 9-7.

Partition Processing Data Flow Destination

The Partition Processing data flow destination is very similar to the Dimension Processing destination. As with any destination, the data flow can pull from any source and perform a variety of transformation logic before the Partition Processing data flow destination.

Figure 9-12 shows the Connection Manager tab of the destination, which is selected on the sole partition of the Currency_Rates measure group. This page includes processing options to handle additions, full process (which includes aggregations), or data loading only.

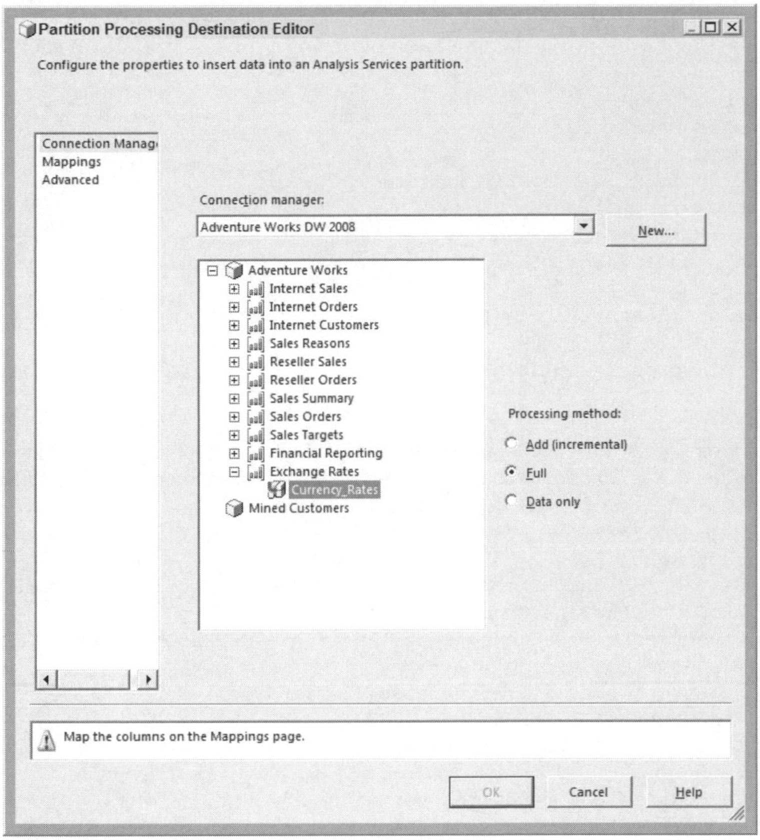

Figure 9-12

The Mappings tab and the Advanced tab are identical to the Dimension Processing destination, where the columns are mapped and key error handling can be defined.

Script Task with AMO

You can also handle the processing of SSAS objects programmatically by using the Analysis Services object model API, called AMO (see the complete object model reference at `http://msdn2.microsoft.com/en-us/library/ms345088.aspx`). AMO contains all the methods, properties, and objects needed to perform many tasks such as creating SSAS partitions or other objects, modifying settings at all levels, performing administrative operations (such as backups and restores), and processing objects.

As a preview to using AMO, the following code in the Script Task loops through all the SSAS dimensions in the Adventure Works DW 2008 database and performs a process update on each one:

```
Imports System
Imports System.Data
Imports System.Math
Imports Microsoft.SqlServer.Dts.Runtime
Imports Microsoft.AnalysisServices

<System.AddIn.AddIn("ScriptMain", Version:="1.0", Publisher:="",
    Description:="")> _
<System.CLSCompliantAttribute(False)> _
Partial Public Class ScriptMain
    Inherits Microsoft.SqlServer.Dts.Tasks.ScriptTask.VSTARTScriptObjectModelBase

    Enum ScriptResults
        Success = Microsoft.SqlServer.Dts.Runtime.DTSExecResult.Success
        Failure = Microsoft.SqlServer.Dts.Runtime.DTSExecResult.Failure
    End Enum

    Public Sub Main()
        ' Get Server and Database name from SSIS connection managers
        Dim oConnection As ConnectionManager
        oConnection = Dts.Connections("Adventure Works DW 2008")
        Dim sServer As String = _
            CStr(oConnection.Properties("ServerName").GetValue(oConnection))
        Dim sDatabase As String = _
          CStr(oConnection.Properties("InitialCatalog").GetValue(oConnection))

        ' Connect to the requested server
        Dim oServer As New Microsoft.AnalysisServices.Server
        oServer.Connect(sServer)

        ' Connect to the database
        Dim oDB As Database = oServer.Databases.FindByName(sDatabase)
        Dim oDimension As New Microsoft.AnalysisServices.Dimension

        'Process update each dimension
        For Each oDimension In oDB.Dimensions
            oDimension.Process(ProcessType.ProcessUpdate)
        Next

        Dts.TaskResult = ScriptResults.Success
    End Sub
End Class
```

Note that the Microsoft.AnalysisServices namespace reference has been added to the script to allow interaction with AMO references. The script also references the SSAS connection (named Adventure Works DW 2008 as the script references) within the SSIS package, which prevents the need to hard-code the server or database. You can find the full AMO reference in Books Online, or online at MSDN.

This design only requires a single Script Task, but you can also use the code in a Script component in the data flow, with the connection information included in the `PreExecute` subroutine.

Creating and Managing Partitions

Before you even begin processing your partitions, you must ensure that they exist. If you have an SSAS solution that does not contain more than one partition per measure group, or your design has a static set of partitions and you do not have the need to dynamically add or process them, then you can use one of the prior solutions.

When it comes to managing SSAS partitions (creating, modifying, and deleting), here are your choices in SSIS: Use an Analysis Services Execute DDL Task to run a dynamically built XMLA script, which uses the `Alter` and `ObjectDefinition` commands of XMLA, and dynamically modifies the partition list that must be created.

❑ Leverage the `ASCMD.exe` executable to run the same XMLA DDL statement, and parameterize the XMLA file with the partition and measure group names.

❑ Use AMO in a Script Task or Script component to create or modify the partition.

With the first two choices, you would use an XMLA script similar to the one used in the earlier section, "Execute Process Task with ASCMD." As with the other examples provided earlier in this chapter, you can generate the XMLA in a Script Task, or use it in a file with ASCMD parameters to update the properties.

The third choice for creating or modifying partitions is to use AMO. One advantage of AMO is the capability to clone an existing partition to a new partition. In other words, you can have a template partition in each of your measure groups that is used as the basis for any new partition that must be created; then the AMO code is a simple template-copy operation. This option is explored further as part of the "Solution" section.

Overall Design

Now that you are familiar with the different methods that you could use in your packages, let's put everything together. You will create a set of packages that use the processing methods discussed. For the partition management portion, you will create a metadata table that can be populated during the execution of the fact package. Let's look at each of these in more detail in the "Solution" section.

Solution

To complete the full BI solution, you will create SSIS packages that utilize the built-in SSAS components discussed in the "Design" section. You'll create two packages that will accomplish the following tasks:

❑ Process Dimensions

❑ Process Partitions

Because different dimensions can have different loading methods, the Process Dimensions package will show how to load several different dimensions. The Process Partitions package will contain the logic to manage partitions and process only partitions where the underlying data has recently changed. Let's start by setting up the package, and then dig into the fun details!

Preparation for SSAS Integration

The two built-in control flow components already mentioned that interact with SSAS are the Analysis Services Processing Task and the Analysis Services Execute DDL Task. The two data flow components that interact with SSAS are the Dimension Processing destination and the Partition Processing destination. All of these components leverage an Analysis Services connection that you must define in the Connection Managers window pane. A Script Task with AMO can also pull the server and database information from an Analysis Services connection.

To use any of these methods, create a new connection in a blank package. To create the connection, right-click in the Connection Manager window pane and select New Analysis Services Connection, which opens the Add Analysis Services Connection Manager window with a connection string. When you select Edit next to the connection string, the standard Connection Manager editor opens, as shown in Figure 9-13.

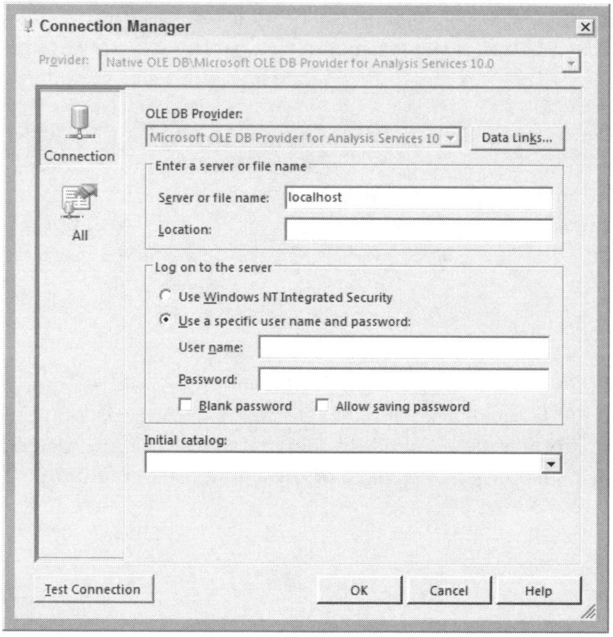

Figure 9-13

The "Server or file name" entry is the name of the SSAS server, and the "Log on to the server" selection defines how the connection should pass its authentication to the SSAS server. SSAS only supports Windows authentication (local machine or Active Directory security), so the two choices for security both relate to Windows security.

❑   *Use Windows NT Integrated Security* — This option uses the existing security account for the user who is logged in during either design or execution. When you execute a package through the command line, it is the account that runs DTExec, which may be a service account or a proxy account when you're using SQL Agent or Windows scheduler, or a third-party scheduling tool.

❑   *Use a specific user name and password* — This option allows a Windows account and password to be entered, so that you can define a different Windows account for the connection to use. Because a password must be entered, even if you select the "Allow saving password" check box, you must still handle the password storage or un-encryption (through an SSIS configuration entry, command-line switch, or property expression).

For this solution, use the Adventure Works DW 2008 catalog, so select it in the "Initial catalog" drop-down. Now you are ready to add the other tasks and components to the package.

Process Dimensions Package

When working with SSAS dimensions, you have learned that you have many options to process a dimension to pull the information from the underlying dimension table. Let's create a package that handles just a few dimensions. This discussion separates this package into two sections: "Process Task" and "Parallel XMLA."

Process Task

For the sales territory dimension, you want to load data from the underlying table. You know that you want to perform a process update, so use the Analysis Services Processing Task. The final package should look like Figure 9-14.

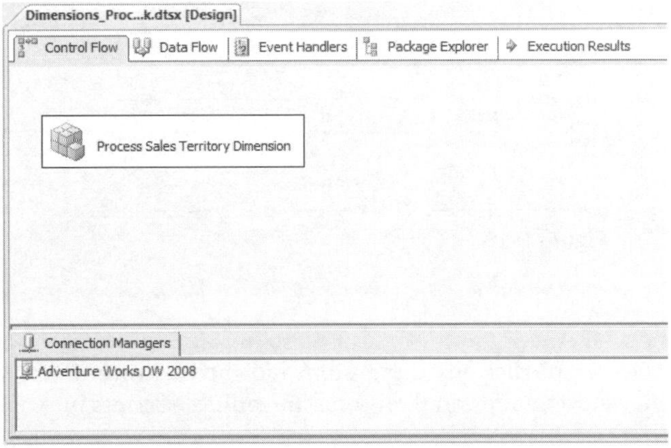

Figure 9-14

This task is one of the most straightforward SSAS tasks to configure. Use the preparation steps already described to create an Analysis Services connection. Then, using the screens shown in the "Design" section as a guide, set the task to perform a process update against the Sales Territory dimension.

You can also add additional dimensions from within this task, or change the processing order from sequential to parallel if you want them to run at the same time.

> All dimensions must have previously been processed at least once using the process full option before you can process using the process update option. If you expect to redeploy your SSAS dimensions often, you may want to add logic that will check the processed status of the dimension before executing either a process full or process update.

Parallel XMLA

To start, set up a load of the Product, Employee, and Date dimensions. The data for each of these dimensions will be available at the same time, so you can run them in parallel. The new data will be pulled from the relational data warehouse, so you can perform a process update. To handle all of these, you'll use an XMLA script that can be executed in an Analysis Services Execute DDL Task. The final package will look like Figure 9-15.

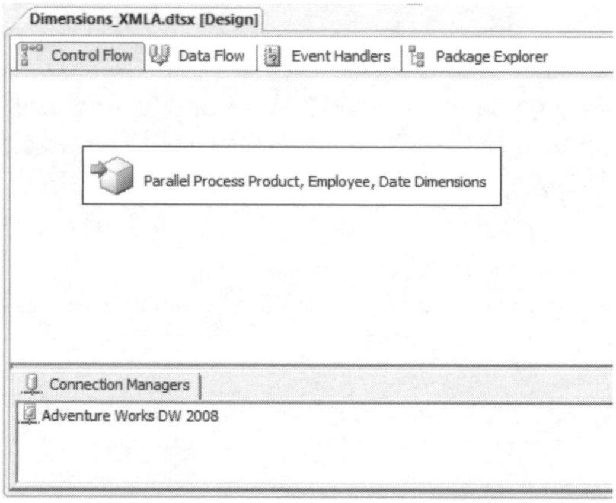

Figure 9-15

Go ahead and build the XMLA script first. You can do so in SSMS by connecting to the SSAS instance. The Processing dialog box (right-click any dimension, and choose Process) contains the capability to script out the processing settings. You can then combine multiple scripts into one, which will look like the following:

```
<Batch xmlns="http://schemas.microsoft.com/analysisservices/2003/engine">
  <Parallel>
    <Process xmlns:ddl100_100="http://schemas.microsoft.com/analysisservices/2008/
    engine/100/100">
      <Object>
        <DatabaseID>Adventure Works DW 2008</DatabaseID>
        <DimensionID>Dim Product</DimensionID>
      </Object>
```

```
      <Type>ProcessUpdate</Type>
      <WriteBackTableCreation>UseExisting</WriteBackTableCreation>
    </Process>
    <Process xmlns:ddl100_100="http://schemas.microsoft.com/analysisservices/2008/
      engine/100/100">
      <Object>
        <DatabaseID>Adventure Works DW 2008</DatabaseID>
        <DimensionID>Dim Employee</DimensionID>
      </Object>
      <Type>ProcessUpdate</Type>
      <WriteBackTableCreation>UseExisting</WriteBackTableCreation>
    </Process>
    <Process xmlns:ddl100_100="http://schemas.microsoft.com/analysisservices/2008/
      engine/100/100">
      <Object>
        <DatabaseID>Adventure Works DW 2008</DatabaseID>
        <DimensionID>Dim Time</DimensionID>
      </Object>
      <Type>ProcessUpdate</Type>
      <WriteBackTableCreation>UseExisting</WriteBackTableCreation>
    </Process>
  </Parallel>
</Batch>
```

Note that the XMLA process script uses the dimension's ID rather than the dimension's name. You can see a prime example with the Date dimension, which, in comparison to its name of Date, *has an ID of* Dim Time. *Keep this in mind when building or reviewing your XMLA scripts.*

After you have your script, set up the package as described earlier in the section, "Preparation for SSAS Integration." Then, create a variable named XMLA with a data type of String. The value of the variable should be the XMLA script that you just created. Drag over an Analysis Services Execute DDL Task to the control flow and configure it to use the connection manager you just created. After you change the SourceType to use Variable, you can select the User::XMLA variable.

You can now execute this package to process all three dimensions in parallel. If, at any time, you must change which dimensions are processed, or remove one of the dimensions from being processed, you can easily do so by adding a configuration to modify the variable named XMLA.

Process Partitions Package

Now that the dimensions are ready, you must load the data for the measure groups. As previously mentioned, it is rare to only have one partition per measure group. More commonly, a measure group has multiple partitions based on a date range. This means that you will need to create new partitions as time passes. The package should automatically create the partition when needed before completing its processing.

> The Process Dimensions package must complete before the Process Facts package begins execution. If all dimension keys are not available, the fact processing will either fail, or produce inaccurate results, depending on your error settings.

327

To ensure full integration with the fact ETL packages, you must create some metadata objects and modify the existing fact table. After you have those in place, you can create a separate package to handle the SSAS partition management and processing.

Storing and Loading Metadata

To begin the solution, you must create a table to hold a list of the partitions that must be processed. The lowest time grain of any of the measure groups within the Adventure Works cube is a year, indicating that each partition is comprised of one year's worth of data. You can create your process management table with three columns: measureGroup, year, and an isProcessed flag.

If your data is partitioned into smaller pieces, you can modify this schema. For example, if you partition by month, your table would include a fourth column named month. You can create the original version of this table by running the following script:

```
USE [SSIS_PDS]
GO

CREATE TABLE [dbo].[PartitionProcessStatus](
    [measureGroup] [varchar](100) NOT NULL,
    [year] [smallint] NOT NULL,
    [isProcessed] [bit] NOT NULL
)
```

As part of your fact load, you insert or update records in this table. Because this designation occurs during the load of the underlying data warehouse tables, you ensure that any late-arriving data gets processed into your SSAS cube. Before you even get to the Process Partitions package, you already know exactly which partitions must be loaded. Start by creating the following stored procedure in the SSIS_PDS database:

```
USE [SSIS_PDS]
GO

CREATE PROC LoadPartitionProcessStatusTable
  @measureGroup varchar(100)
  ,@year int
  ,@isProcessed bit
AS
BEGIN
  MERGE dbo.PartitionProcessStatus AS oldprocstat
  USING (SELECT @measureGroup, @year, @isProcessed)
      AS newprocstat (measureGroup, year, isProcessed)
    ON oldprocstat.measureGroup = newprocstat.measureGroup
      AND oldprocstat.year = newprocstat.year
  WHEN MATCHED THEN
    UPDATE SET
      isProcessed = newprocstat.isProcessed
  WHEN NOT MATCHED THEN
    INSERT (measureGroup, year, isProcessed)
    VALUES (newprocstat.measureGroup, newprocstat.year, newprocstat.isProcessed);
END
```

The `LoadPartitionProcessStatusTable` stored procedure will accept the name of the measure group, the year that the partition designates, and whether the partition has already been processed (1) or needs to be processed (0). Based on the measure group name and the year, the stored procedure will either insert a new record if the row does not exist, or update the `isProcessed` status if the row does exist.

Within your fact table load, you can add an Aggregate transformation to get a distinct list of years from the record date. For each year, you will execute an OLE DB Command that contains a statement similar to the following:

```
EXEC LoadPartitionProcessStatusTable 'ResellerSales',?,0
```

You've hard-coded the measure group name of `ResellerSales` because you know exactly from which fact this data came. Likewise, this command will only be executed if you must pull new data into the partition, so you set the `isProcessed` flag to 0 to say that it must be processed.

SSAS Processing

Now you can start creating the package. After you put everything together, you should end up with the package shown in Figure 9-16. Start with the steps to set up your Analysis Services connection. Although you won't use this connection directly, you will reference the server and database name to use in your logic. You'll also need a connection to the `SSIS_PDS` database to retrieve the metadata.

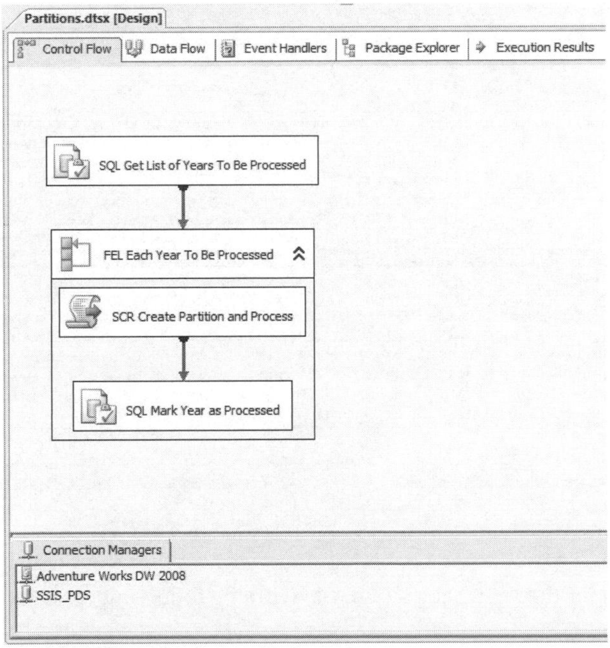

Figure 9-16

The next step is to use the table that you just created and populated to consume the metadata stored. Use an Execute SQL Task against the SSIS_PDS database to pull all records where the measure group name is the desired name of ResellerSales and the isProcessed flag is set to 0. The query to use is as follows:

```
SELECT year
  FROM [dbo].[PartitionProcessStatus]
WHERE measureGroup = 'ResellerSales'
  AND isProcessed = 0
```

Store this information into a variable of Object data type named oNeededPartitions. You then use a Foreach loop to enumerate over an ADO rowset, using oNeededPartitions. Store the data into a variable of data type Int16 named nYear.

Drag a Script Task to the inside of the Foreach loop. This is where the bulk of the work will take place because you are checking for the existence of, possibly creating, and doing the processing of the partition. Add the nYear variable to the Script Task's ReadOnlyVariables property, and set the Script Task to use the ScriptLanguage: Microsoft Visual Basic 2008.

When you begin editing the script, you must add the AMO (Analysis Management Objects) assembly to the project. Under the My Project page's References menu, click the Add button. You want to select the version as shown in Figure 9-17.

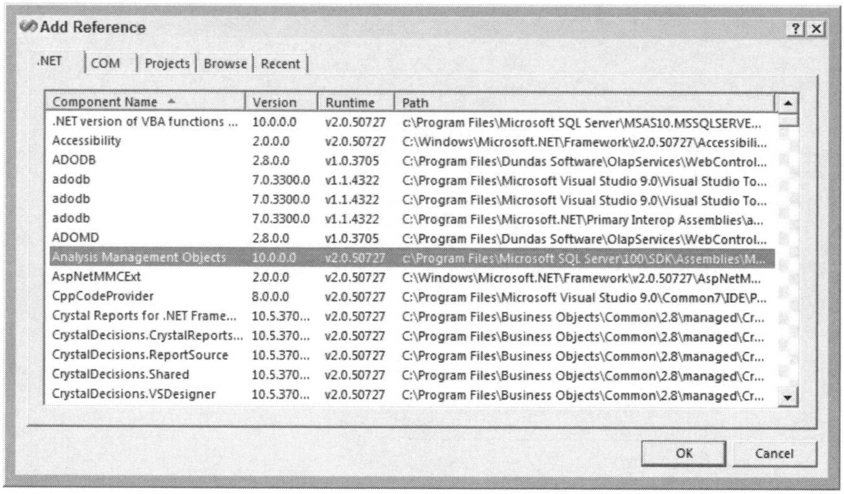

Figure 9-17

Replace everything under the ScriptMain.vb file with the following code:

```
Imports System
Imports System.Data
Imports System.Math
Imports Microsoft.SqlServer.Dts.Runtime
Imports Microsoft.AnalysisServices
```

```vb
<System.AddIn.AddIn("ScriptMain", Version:="1.0", Publisher:="",
    Description:="")> _
<System.CLSCompliantAttribute(False)> _
Partial Public Class ScriptMain
    Inherits Microsoft.SqlServer.Dts.Tasks.ScriptTask.VSTARTScriptObjectModelBase

    Enum ScriptResults
        Success = Microsoft.SqlServer.Dts.Runtime.DTSExecResult.Success
        Failure = Microsoft.SqlServer.Dts.Runtime.DTSExecResult.Failure
    End Enum

Public Sub Main()

    ' Set Partition name we are interested in
    Dim sYear = Dts.Variables("nYear").Value.ToString
    Dim sPartitionName = "Reseller_Sales_" & sYear
    Dim sYearTemplate = "2004"
    Dim sPartitionTemplate = "Reseller_Sales_" & sYearTemplate

    ' Get Server and Database name from the connection manager
    Dim oConnection As ConnectionManager
    oConnection = Dts.Connections("Adventure Works DW 2008")
    Dim sServer As String = _
      CStr(oConnection.Properties("ServerName").GetValue(oConnection))
    Dim sDatabase As String = _
      CStr(oConnection.Properties("InitialCatalog").GetValue(oConnection))

    ' Connect to the requested server
    Dim oServer As New Microsoft.AnalysisServices.Server
    oServer.Connect(sServer)

    ' Connect to the database, cube, and measure group
    Dim oDB As Database = oServer.Databases.FindByName(sDatabase)
    Dim oCube As Cube = oDB.Cubes("Adventure Works")
    Dim oMeasureGroup As MeasureGroup = oCube.MeasureGroups
        ("Fact Reseller Sales")

    ' Check for the partition existence, clone as needed
    If Not oMeasureGroup.Partitions.Contains(sPartitionName) Then

        Dim oPartitionTemplate As Partition = _
          oMeasureGroup.Partitions.FindByName(sPartitionTemplate)
        Dim oNewPartition As Partition

        oNewPartition = oPartitionTemplate.Clone()
        oNewPartition.Name = sPartitionName
        oNewPartition.ID = sPartitionName

        If Not IsNothing(oNewPartition.Slice) Then
            oNewPartition.Slice = _
                oPartitionTemplate.Slice.Replace(sYearTemplate, sYear)
        End If
```

```
            Dim oSource As QueryBinding = CType(oPartitionTemplate.Source,
                QueryBinding)
            Dim sQuery As String = oSource.QueryDefinition.Replace
                (sYearTemplate, sYear)
            Dim sDS As String = oSource.DataSourceID

            oNewPartition.Source = New QueryBinding(sDS, sQuery)
            oMeasureGroup.Partitions.Add(oNewPartition)
            oNewPartition.Update()
            oNewPartition = Nothing

        End If

        ' Process the partition
        oMeasureGroup.Partitions(sPartitionName).Process(ProcessType.ProcessFull)

        Dts.TaskResult = ScriptResults.Success
    End Sub

End Class
```

This script connects to the Analysis Services database from the connection manager named `Adventure Works DW 2008`. It uses the cube named Adventure Works and the measure group with an ID of `Fact Reseller Sales`. These values are hard-coded, because it is assumed that this script will only be for one partition at a time. If you want to make that information dynamic, you can add more columns to your metadata table, or you can extract that information out to a variable that is configurable.

When you have the values set, check whether the partition name based on the `nYear` variable passed in exists. If it does not, create a new partition, using the 2004 partition as the template, but modifying the slice and source values to use the correct year. Finally, process the cube using the `Process Full` type, whether or not it existed before.

After configuring the Script Task, you want to attach an Execute SQL Task to it using a success precedence constraint. This task sets the record's `isProcessed` flag to `1` for that year when the Script Task has succeeded. The SQL command to use in the Execute SQL Task is as follows:

```
UPDATE [dbo].[PartitionProcessStatus]
SET isProcessed = 1
WHERE year = ?
```

Now that everything is set up, this package will loop through every year that needs to be processed, create a new partition if needed, process the partition, and reset the metadata table for that combination. If, at any time, you must reprocess a partition without having run the fact ETL package, you can directly modify the process table to set the `isProcessed` flag to `0`. The package will then include that partition in its list of years to be processed the next time the package runs.

Overall Solution

At this time, you've created two separate packages: one to process your dimensions, and one to manage and process your fact partitions. Although these packages provide a full solution for managing your

SSAS objects, you will need to extend them to fit your data warehouse. You will also need to decide on when the packages must run to ensure the data is available for reporting.

The dimension package should include all of your dimensions, and you may need to use different methods for each one. Depending on the availability of your source data, you may create multiple packages for your dimension set to allow them to be run at different times during your load window. You must modify the fact partition package to include all measure groups, with the appropriate template partition and IDs used.

One way to execute your packages is to execute them using a master package, as shown in Figure 9-18. Use Execute Package Tasks to execute each processing package, and group all of your dimension processing packages in a sequence container. By connecting the sequence container to the partition processing package, you ensure that the dimensions are processed before the partitions. You do not need any precedence constraints between dimensions, because they can run in parallel.

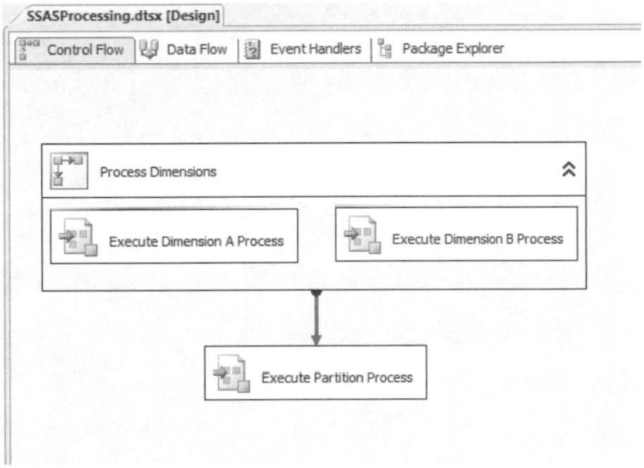

Figure 9-18

An alternative method to running your package is to call them from a SQL Server Agent job. This method gives you control over sequential ordering of your packages. This may be a good idea if you are already running your ETL loads from within a job, and you can include the SSAS packages as well.

Summary

The built-in support for Analysis Services object processing handles some situations, but, overall, doesn't provide the flexibility needed to handle many enterprise BI processing requirements (such as transaction grouping or dynamic partition processing and creation). As you have seen in this chapter, SSIS includes the tools to create much more robust solutions to process your SSAS objects.

Now that you have learned about SSIS principles in loading data warehouse structures and processing cubes, the rest of the book focuses on high availability and reliability. Chapter 10 discusses ways to have SSIS handle failovers, transactions, and restartability.

10

Implementing Scale-Out ETL Process

Now that you've worked through several aspects of building an SSIS solution, let's turn now to some advanced concepts. In this chapter, you learn how to scale out SSIS, where SSIS packages are working in tandem on multiple machines. This effective way to handle large volumes of data has the added benefit of fault tolerance if one of the servers goes down.

Chapter 11 transitions to review advanced scripting in those situations when you just can't accomplish what you need to with out-of-the-box components and you need to compose code to help accomplish your goals (both control flow and data flow). The final chapter, Chapter 12, is about troubleshooting performance issues and optimizing packages for efficient use of the data flow, and other advanced topics (such as how to handle partitioned tables). Overall, these last chapters give you the direction you need to deal with both complexity and high volumes of data.

One of the biggest benefits of SSIS is its capability to process and transform data in memory, effectively reducing disk I/O, and taking advantage of better memory availability and 64-bit architecture as well. With BI solutions now becoming more commonplace than just a few years ago, companies are realizing the need to process larger and larger amounts of data, and to try to do so as quickly and efficiently as possible. As a result, ETL architects and SSIS developers must start thinking about ways to scale out ETL processes so that they have the capability to deal with varying workloads, and take advantage of cheap commodity hardware.

This chapter directs you toward the architecture planning and implementation of an SSIS-based ETL solution that scales out. It accomplishes this primarily through an example based on a real-life solution:

❑ The "Problem" section briefly defines the need for a scale-out solution, and walks you through some of the requirements of the real-world example.

❑ The "Design" section walks you through the possible components of a scale-out solution in the context of an example that requires handling thousands of XML files daily.

❑ The "Solution" section provides the full case study-like solution that is designed with SSIS for a scale-out ETL solution.

Building a scale-out solution has a lot of benefits beyond just increasing the amount of data that a single server can handle. You can also use it to balance resource utilization across various servers.

You can use a number of scale-out scenarios to achieve better parallelization of data processing, including running different ETL processes on different servers. SSIS provides some easy ways to achieve this type of scale-out, where you can execute different packages remotely by calling the SQL Agent jobs on the remote servers. Other scale-out scenarios require that the same package be executed on multiple servers, using resources on those servers and processing different data sets for the same destination. Throughout this chapter, you will see a simple variation of this type of process where you need aggregated data sets in the central data store.

Problem

The main question you should ask to determine the need for a scale-out solution is, "When is a scale-out solution required?"

Scale-out is ideal when you must process large amounts of data files on a frequent interval, and you require the capability to scale to large current and future loads.

The business and technical problem you are trying to handle is to build a comprehensive and scalable solution that allows reliable file management, as well as data processing, in a timely fashion. Common examples of such a need are processing log files coming from a large number of Web servers on a regular interval, or processing very chunky XML data that requires more processing power to parse the files and data. Often, this granular data also needs significant aggregation before it reaches the final destination tables.

To help you conceptualize an SSIS scale-out solution, this chapter walks you through an example of handling thousands of log files on a near real-time basis. This example is based on a real-world example with the following problem aspects:

❑ The scale-out example requires handling XML log files generated by ever-increasing numbers of servers powering a cloud computing platform. These XML log files are generated every five minutes. The solution must keep up with current demand and frequency, and scale out to accommodate additional log files, as well as increase in the log file size caused by additional attributes being captured.

❑ The granular transaction log data must be aggregated into hourly and daily aggregates for analytics, reporting and usage history, and trend tracking. This example does not require storing the granular transaction data.

❑ Because the data is also being exposed for analytics by the end users, you must expect a maximum latency being no greater than two to four hours before the user can query against the aggregate data.

In addition to these requirements, some of the technical challenges include the following:

❑ Managing high parallelism of raw log data processing, concurrency in table operations, and the size of stage tables that may arise because of resource constraints on the stage databases

❑ Ensuring data consistency and integrity

❑ Keeping up with incoming volumes

The scale-out challenges include having the capability to do the following:

❑ Dynamically increase data-processing capacity

❑ Automatically manage consequences of existing data-processing servers going offline

With all these challenges and requirements in mind, the "Design" section walks you through the design aspects needed to build a scale-out SSIS environment. The "Solution" section later in this chapter brings together these design principles to present an SSIS architecture meeting these needs and requirements.

Design

This section reviews the overall solution components and the detailed design aspects of how these components integrate.

A scale-out solution consists of two major components:

❑ The scale-out SSIS ETL servers that handle the file processing, including the data import, transformations, and aggregations.

❑ The central database that retains the consolidated data after the file data is processed and aggregated. Each scale-out server consolidates data into the single central database.

Figure 10-1 shows the scale-out servers in the middle. Also shown is the central database server that retains the post-processed data, and also contains the shared services.

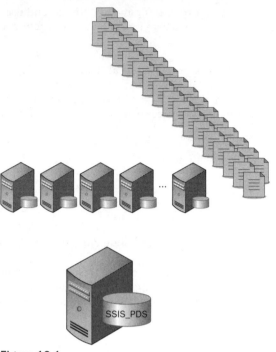

Figure 10-1

Design Components Overview

This section reviews the design components, the services, and other roles that each component must play in the scale-out solution, including the central common services server and the scale-out servers.

Central Common Services Server

The central common services server is a single place where you put all control mechanisms in place for managing the workload and the scale-out processes, and for ensuring data reliability. This central server is the heart and soul of the scale-out process described later, and you implement all the major services here. Separating your operational or control database from your data marts or data stores may also be prudent in order to enhance manageability of the data.

File Processor and Pre-Aggregation Scale-Out Processes Servers

File processor and pre-aggregation scale-out processes servers represent a set of databases and services that work independently, and depend on work assigned by the central server when appropriate requests are made. Each file processor and pre-aggregation server is self-contained with the resources required to process the raw log files and data, and to make them available in a standardized and consistent fashion to the central services server when requested.

When the listener process detects new source data files, it adds information about these files in a table in the central server. On a frequent basis, jobs on the file-processing servers kick off and make a request to the central server for some work assignments, as shown in Figure 10-2.

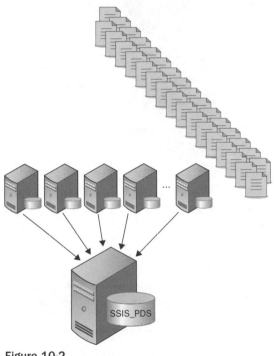

Figure 10-2

Based on queue depth and other configurations, the services on the central server assign different sets of files to the different file-processing servers. After these servers get work, they begin to process the data, store it in their individual stage databases, and provide appropriate status information back to the central server, as shown in Figure 10-3.

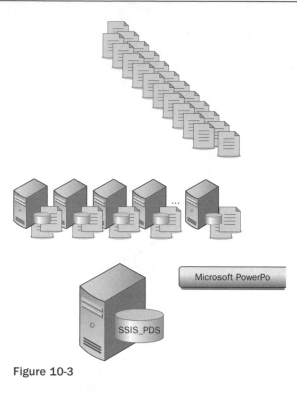

Figure 10-3

At some frequent interval, the central server consolidates the processed data, potentially aggregates the data, and then stores the data in the central data store for business use, as shown in Figure 10-4.

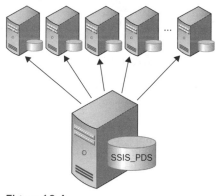

Figure 10-4

Design Details

Each of these main components requires a set of detailed work tasks to handle the processing. Some of these tasks are duplicated on each scale-out server so that, if a server fails or you add a new server, the processes can scale out. This duplication accounts for the robust automated scale-out solution. In other words, with this architecture, you can bring new data-processing servers online that compensate for existing servers going offline.

The following elements make up the details of the solution:

- ❏ File management and processing tasks
  - ❏ Data file management
  - ❏ Work allocation process
  - ❏ Scale-out source file process
  - ❏ Work re-assignment process
- ❏ Data aggregation tasks
  - ❏ Hourly data pre-aggregation process
  - ❏ Hourly data aggregation process
  - ❏ Daily data aggregation process
- ❏ Archival and clean-up process tasks
  - ❏ Data file archival process
  - ❏ Stage table clean-up process

The remainder of this section outlines each of the design components in this list so that you can understand the roles they play in the overall solution.

File Management Tasks

The coordination of the scale-out processes requires the tracking of the files that must be processed, plus the central administration and assignment of files and processes to the scale-out servers. Sometimes files must be re-assigned if one of the server processing the files goes offline. When a file is scheduled to be processed, but no response is received from the processing server, then the file is re-assigned.

Data File Management

In the file management process, you must manage a comprehensive list of source data files that the source system generates. You can collect these files in one or more locations.

In the solution described throughout this chapter, you expect that the path and filename combination is unique for each file. Typically, such files may have unique names that include the name of the server (or source) generating the log files, as well as the date and time stamp when the file was generated. Also, in this solution, you assume that you can assign all the content of the log file to a single hour interval that is derived from the date and time stamp of the filename. The aggregation processes, where you aggregate the data into the hourly data tables, uses this derived date and time interval.

In this example, you also assume that any scale-out in terms of file storage and disk-I/O balance is taken care of outside this solution. For these processes, you must simply have the knowledge of all files coming in, their locations, and the filenames. Also, this example assumes that the archival mechanism follows some archival strategy. The discussion in this chapter does not go into details of the same, except to pass on information about files that are ready for archival to the archival process, and then marking those files as having been archived in the audit tracking tables.

The file management process starts with having a "listener" process poll for the files being added to the file server(s). When it detects new files, this process retrieves the filename and location details, parses the date and hour that the file belongs to, and makes an entry in an audit table that you will call `FileLog`. The `FileLog` table manages the complete list of all files and their process status. So, when the files are initially entered into the `FileLog` table, their status is set to `UNPROCESSED`.

As the file goes through the various process stages all the way to archival, the file management process manages all the details in this table.

Work Allocation Process

The work allocation process is one of the key components of the scale-out process. This process determines which data files get processed by which server. Various data-processing servers make a request on a regular basis to this work allocation process, and then request work. This process then allocates a set of files to the requesting process based on certain configurable constraints (such as the number of files that should be allocated for a single request).

The process looks for files that meet the following criteria:

❑ Unprocessed files.

❑ Files already allocated for processing to this particular data-processing server. The assumption here is that if the file is in an `UNPROCESSED` state by this server, it means that a previous process failed to process this file.

❑ Files assigned to this data-processing server where processing had started.

This process then marks the list of files as `ASSIGNED FOR PROCESS`, and also includes the name of the processing server in the `FileLog` records. This process also assigns the `BatchLogID` and the `PackageLogID`, enabling you to tie in the package management framework to this process.

To achieve scale-out on a single server, the SSIS packages that do file processing are designed with parallel processes so that each process can manage the processing for a set of files. When allocating the files, this procedure also takes into account parallelization within the package, and accordingly allocates files for each parallel process on the server.

Because the work allocation process may be called in parallel from multiple servers, you must also take precautions to manage any deadlock situations when assigning files. Later in this discussion, you find out the details of the implementation.

The current work allocation process and implementation assume that each data-processing server has only a single process that runs serially, and that, on a given data-processing server, no parallel processes exist that can request files.

Scale-Out Source File Process

The scale-out source file process takes place on multiple scale-out processing servers. Each server executes a file processor package that processes a unique set of files that are assigned by the work allocation process when the package makes a request for work. As part of the request, the file processor package passes back information about the server on which it is executing.

After the server receives a list of files that it must process, it then spawns off some parallel threads, each of which processes individual files assigned to it. Before the work threads are spawned, the server also takes into account configuration variables that might regulate the amount of parallelism for processing files. Each thread also writes raw data to its own stage table in order to increase parallelism for processing the raw log files. A pre-process step takes care of creating the new tables for this process on the individual staging database on that server.

After the individual threads parse and process the raw log file data from all the files assigned to them, a single process combines this data from the individual stage tables, and puts it into a stage table that is created to hold all raw data (slightly aggregated) for that date-hour. Future date and hour data would get individual stage tables that are dynamically created based on incoming data.

Through this process, as files start getting processed, the status is updated accordingly in the `FileLog` table, and, when all the file data is finally processed into the aggregated tables, then the `FileLog` records are marked as PROCESSED.

Next, a process checks for queue depth of unprocessed files, and, if the queue depth at this point is zero, the process finishes until the next time that the job schedule kicks off the file processor. Otherwise, it repeats the entire process again until such time that the queue depth is zero.

In the "Solution" section later in this chapter, you find out how many servers are required to process the files such that the unprocessed file queue is exhausted within a five-minute interval, at which point, more files would start showing up in the queue. You also record processing data for each file so that you can measure the performance, as well as any performance trends, over time.

An ever-increasing queue depth signals a file processor bottleneck, which indicates that additional scale-out servers are required. Each file processor stage server has its own local database where it writes all the temporary raw data, and creates and manages the required tables and objects. These servers are unaware of the existence of any other file processor servers, and rely solely on the work allocation process that resides on a central server to assign them work.

This process also adds a single record in an `HourlyServerProcessLog` table if a record does not already exist for that date-hour-server name combination. This table is also updated regularly with incremental counts of the number of files and records processed for audit information. A flag also denotes whether the data for that date-hour on that server has been pre-aggregated. When a new record is created in this table, the process also creates a new record for the date-hour (no server name this time) in the `HourlyProcessLog` table if a record does not already exist for that date-hour.

Work Reassignment Process

The work reassignment process is the heart and soul of reliability for this scale-out process, because existing file processor servers can easily go offline (or be taken offline).

The process is designed to run at frequent intervals (usually hourly). It first reads a configurable setting for the number of minutes for timeout. Based on that setting, it polls the `FileLog` table for last reported activity from each file-processing server. If the process detects a lag between the maximum process date time and the last process date time from any particular server that exceeds the timeout threshold, then it assumes that the server is offline.

At this point, for all servers that it deems to be offline, it performs the following actions:

❑ Gets a list of all unique date-hour details where data has not been aggregated by the hourly aggregation process from this server.

❑ Flags all the files belonging to those date-hours and assigned to that server as `UNPROCESSED`.

❑ Deletes the record from the `HourlyServerProcessLog` table for that server for those date-hour records.

Data Aggregation Tasks

After the file processors extract the raw log data, several data process tasks handle the aggregation of data, as well as the consolidation of the aggregated data to the common process server. This happens in three distinct steps:

1. An hourly pre-aggregation process prepares the data in a managed staging table.

2. An hourly aggregation process takes the pre-aggregated data and groups it together in preparation for the daily rollup.

3. A daily aggregation process takes all the data from an hourly grain and combines it into a daily grain table.

Hourly Data Pre-Aggregation Process

Once an hour, when the file processor package starts encountering data for the next date-hour interval, it triggers the hourly data pre-aggregation process. This process first reads the `HourlyServerProcessLog` table for all the date-hour combination records that have not yet been pre-aggregated for that particular server. For each date-hour that is not pre-aggregated, it then creates a table (drops and re-creates the table if one already exists for that date-hour) to store the pre-aggregated data for that date-hour on that particular staging server.

Next it reads all the slightly aggregated data from the combined data table for that date-hour, and aggregates it to the hourly interval down to the required grain of the fact table for the other dimensions. It then flags the record in the `HourlyServerProcessLog` as `Pre-Aggregated`, and pre-aggregates the next non-pre-aggregated date-hour until all the non-pre-aggregated date-hour records are pre-aggregated (except for the latest date-hour, which is assumed to still be the active hour).

As a fail-safe measure to manage the scenario in which a previously pre-aggregated date-hour data was being reprocessed by the pre-aggregator (which invalidates any further aggregation by the hourly and daily aggregation process), you would update the records in the `HourlyProcessingLog` and `DailyProcessingLog` tables to invalidate the process if it had already taken place. This way, the data would get re-aggregated.

Hourly Data Aggregation Process

The hourly data aggregation process is a single process that runs on the central server every hour. When scheduling this process, be sure to give enough time for the various pre-aggregation processes that are taking place on the scale-out servers to complete for the previous hour. In your observations for this example, you find that, typically, within 10 minutes of the hour having completed, all the raw log files for the previous hour are processed, and the data was pre-aggregated on the individual stage servers. So, providing some buffer, you run this process at around 20 minutes past the hour.

This process first reads the `HourlyProcessLog` table to find all records where the date-hour (except the latest record) has not yet been processed by the hourly data aggregation process. Then, for each record, it reads information from the `HourlyServerProcessLog` table, where it gets details of all the servers where pre-aggregated data for that date-hour is waiting to get aggregated. If it encounters records for that date-hour where the stage server has not yet completed pre-aggregation, the process does not aggregate that data.

After it finds details for the date-hour that is ready for aggregation, it connects to each individual server, collects the data from the pre-aggregate tables on the server for that date-hour, and aggregates the data to the hourly grain. It then stores the data in appropriate tables in the central database.

After the data has been successfully aggregated for the hour, the process flags the appropriate records to indicate that the date-hour data has now been processed and aggregated.

If additional date-hour records are ready for processing, then the process aggregates them as well, using the same process.

Daily Data Aggregation Process

The daily data aggregation process takes data from the hourly grain table and aggregates it to the day grain. The process further marks the appropriate log records to indicate that the day has been processed. The process is again scheduled after taking into account latency of the hourly aggregator for processing the records for the previous day. It is also able to identify all days where data is not aggregated at the daily grain, and aggregates the data.

Both the hourly and daily aggregation processes also ensure that any existing data in the destination tables for the time period is first deleted if it exists. This allows you the flexibility of reprocessing some old files (or older days) without any significant manual intervention into the processes.

Archival and Clean-up Processes

The files and table data also must be cleaned up, including cleaning up the staging tables.

Data File Archival Process

When dealing with large volumes of files, having a good archival process in place is important. The data file archival process works on certain configuration settings that define how many days files should be kept in the main storage location. The archival process gets a list of all processed files that are ready for archival from the `FileLog` table, and then provides the list to the archival process. The process archives the files, and then updates the appropriate `FileLog` records to signal that the files have been archived.

You may optionally extend this process to also update the `UNCPath` to the new location if you so choose.

Stage Table Clean-up Process

A standalone package that checks the duration required to keep the stage data, and then drops all tables that have data older than the required latency, can initiate a stage table clean-up process. This is provided that the downstream processes that must read the data has already processed the data from those tables. This step is important to prevent your stage databases from getting very large, because they contain a lot of unaggregated and partially aggregated raw data.

Design Conclusions

As you can see, designing a scale-out process requires several tasks and coordination steps. However, the benefits are significant! Here are two notable advantages when you implement a scale-out server:

❑ Better high-volume data-handling and the capability to add additional processing servers as scale requirements increase.

❑ Reliability advantages when servers become unavailable (that is, other servers in the scale-out architecture can take on the workload of the offline servers).

The "Solution" section takes into consideration the outlined business and technical challenges presented thus far, as well as the scale-out design just examined, and demonstrates the solution.

Solution

Although the solution demonstrated here has some complexities surrounding the scale-out administration, the overall complexity of the data processing is minimal. This section walks you through the technical solution, and outlines the overall structures, code, and packages that participate in the SSIS-based solution.

This section highlights the following aspects of the implementation:

❑ The service infrastructure

❑ The supporting metadata and log tables that maintain the configuration, file processing, and logging

❑ The stored procedures (both on the central server and the staging servers) that are used to interact with the configuration and staging tables

❑ The SSIS packages that perform the actual data processing and aggregations

The solution code is available for download on the Wrox Web site (www.wrox.com) .

Central Server Services

This solution entails the following set of operations that run and execute on the shared central server:

❏ Manage the list of all files requiring processing

❏ Manage the distribution of files to various file-processing servers on request (that is, the workload is controlled by configuration)

❏ Manage assignment of failed files for processing

❏ Manage file reassignments in case of a lack of request from a file-processing server

❏ Provide a list of each file-processing server that is processing data for a particular hour

❏ Control the hourly processing/aggregation process

Multiple File Processor and Pre-Aggregator Processes

The file process servers each handle the following set of redundant tasks:

❏ Manage a personal stage database

❏ Request an unprocessed file list from a central server

❏ Create hourly stage tables to hold raw data

❏ Process raw XML log files and load data into a stage table

❏ Retrieve dimension keys from the data mart

❏ Pre-aggregate information at the end of the hour into an hourly pre-aggregate table

❏ Provide regular status reports back to central server

❏ Scale-up to process multiple files in parallel

Database Tables Required on the Central Server

Most (if not all) ETL operations require a set of administrative tables for ETL tasks such as logging, configurations, and administration. When you build a scale-out solution, you need several administrative tables to assist in the tracking and coordination of the processes. You use the following key database tables to manage the scale-out process. Figure 10-5 highlights the table entity-relationship diagram (ERD) for the supporting ETL entities.

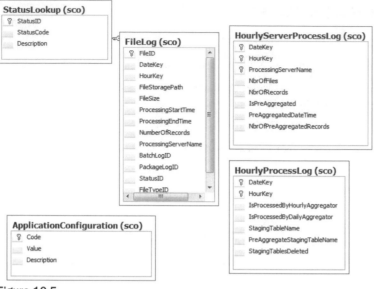

Figure 10-5

Table 10-1 describes the function of each table in the process.

Table 10-1

Table Name	Description
FileLog	Has a record for each unique file that must be processed. It also stores processing information and status for each file.
FileLogArchive	Is optional (but recommended); keeps the data in the FileLog table to a minimum. It also requires an archival process to move the FileLog records to a different table.
HourlyServerProcessLog	Contains a single record for each date-hour of data being processed by a single FileProcessor. It also contains other processing information and appropriate flags used for downstream processes.
HourlyProcessLog	Contains a single record for each date-hour of data being processed.
ApplicationConfiguration	Holds many configuration values that drive the process. This is kept separate from the SSISConfiguration tables mentioned in Chapter 2 because the role of this table is to support the application logic, and not SSIS operations. Aside from that, there can be other supporting tables to hold different lookup or reference information.

Stored Procedures

You use stored procedures on the central server and the staging server to interact with the configuration and stage tables.

Procedures on the Central Server

You implement many of the business processes in stored procedures that are called from different SSIS packages. Table 10-2 lists the key procedures used for this implementation. These procedures are located on the central processing server.

Table 10-2

Procedure Name	Description
RecordFile	Typically called by the "listener" process that finds new file lists, and records the information in the FileLog table. This procedure is only included for reference, because the sample implementation does not include an implementation of the listener process.
GetFileList	Called by a file-processing server, and retrieves a list of available files for processing.
UpdateMultipleFileStatusStaged	Updates the status of multiple FileLog records to STAGED for the files being processed by a given file-processing server.
CheckServerHourlyPreAggregateReadiness	Checks for the number of records in HourlyServerProcessLog table, and determines whether any date-hour combination data that was processed by that server is ready for pre-aggregation. If this server has already started processing data for the next hour, then the procedure returns back an indication that the data for the previous hour can be pre-aggregated.
ExecutePreAggregatorPackageJob	The only procedure that is deployed on the stage server. It kicks off the PreAggregator SQL Agent job, and then waits for the job to complete execution before returning the control to the FileProcessor package.
GetHourlyPreAggregateDateAndHour	Retrieves the minimum date and hour for the pre-aggregate process from the HourlyServerProcessLog table for that file-processing server.

(continued)

Table 10-2 (*continued*)

Procedure Name	Description
GetHourlyAggregatorWorkLoad	Returns a record set of all unprocessed date-hour keys that are ready for aggregation at the hourly level. It pulls the initial list from the HourlyProcessLog table, where the hourly aggregation is not yet done, and then eliminates all date-hour keys where there are either unprocessed files in the FileLog table for those date-hour keys, or any of the file-processing servers have not yet pre-aggregated their data.
GetPreAggServerListForHour	Returns the list of servers and table names of the server where pre-aggregated data is stored for the hour in the HourlyServerProcessLog table.
UpdateHourlyAggregatedFileStatus	Updates the file status in the FileLog table to FINISHED for the date-hour.
UnassignFileProcessorWorkLoad	Unassigns any server workload if a certain time threshold has been reached without reported activity. The timeout threshold is retrieved from the ApplicationConfiguration table.
GetDailyAggregatorWorkLoad	Returns all unprocessed date keys, except the latest one from the HourlyProcessLog table, where the hourly aggregation process for the day is complete, but the daily aggregation process is still pending.
GetRawTablesToBeDropped	Returns a list of server, database, and table names to be dropped, based on the configuration value of number of days of history to be stored.
GetFilesToBeDropped	Returns a list of server and filenames to be dropped, based on the configuration value of number of days of history to be stored.
DropHourlyData	Deletes any old hourly data, based on the amount of history required. You can also appropriately modify it to archive the old data before deleting it from the main hourly table.
DropDailyData	Deletes any old daily data, based on the amount of history required. You can also appropriately modify it to archive the old data before deleting it from the main daily grain table.

Procedures on the Staging Servers

The staging server has only a single stored procedure (listed in Table 10-3) that is required to kick off a job and wait for a response. This stored procedure is called from within the `SCOStage 01 - File Processor.dtsx` package when the workflow process identifies the need for the pre-aggregator to execute. The following section describes SSIS packages.

Table 10-3

Procedure Name	Description
ExecutePreAggregatorPackageJob	Kicks off the `PreAggregator` SQL Agent job, and then waits for the job to complete execution before returning the control to the `FileProcessor` package.

SSIS Packages

The entire workflow is controlled by a number of SSIS packages that execute at varying intervals. The packages related to the scale-out file processor are deployed to various scale-out servers. These packages are designed to be self-contained, with the exception of requiring an accompanying staging database on the same server where the package will write data for the files that it processes.

The packages are also designed to assume that the `ServerName` is the same name as the machine name. As a result, the current solution, as implemented, does not work with named instances. However, if named instances were required, modifying the logic to work with named instances would not be too difficult.

Further, the credentials that run this package have permissions to create and drop tables on that stage database. The packages also adhere to the common framework design described in Chapter 2, and use `BatchLogID` and `PackageLogID` to help extend the framework reporting to the scale-out process. In order to scale out the file processing to another server, you must simply deploy the packages, the database creation script, the job creation script, and any server framework components (such as the environmental variable and the XML Config file) to make your new server operational.

File-Processing Server Packages

Following are the packages that are deployed to the file-processing servers:

- ❑   SCOStage 01 - File Processor.dtsx
- ❑   SCOStage 02 - Hourly PreAggregator.dtsx

SCOStage 01 - File Processor.dtsx

This package does most of the heavy lifting around processing raw log files. The package is set to execute frequently (in this case, every five minutes). The package has an internal loop counter and a configurable `MaxLoopCount` value. This loop helps to manage workload, while ensuring that the package does not keep running all the time in the event of an increase in workload beyond the capacity of the current scale-out servers.

An unprocessed queue depth that keeps increasing over a period of time probably indicates that you should increase the number of scale-out file processors, or find potential ways to optimize the file processing. You implement the loop using a Foreach Loop container and user variables, as shown in Figure 10-6.

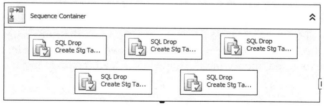

⊟ For Loop Properties	
InitExpression	@UnProcessedFileCount = 1
EvalExpression	@UnProcessedFileCount > 0 && @CurrentLoopCount <= @MaxLoopCount
AssignExpression	@CurrentLoopCount = @CurrentLoopCount + 1
⊟ General	
Name	FLP While UnProcessedFileCount > 0
Description	For Loop Container

Figure 10-6

Within that loop, you first drop and create a set of temporary tables that will be used for processing raw data. Because the package allows five files to be processed in parallel, you create five sets of tables — one for each raw log file parse process. This process is implemented using Execute SQL Tasks inside a Sequence container, which is inside the Foreach Loop container, as shown in Figure 10-7.

Figure 10-7

After you create these temporary tables, an Execute SQL Task calls the GetFileList procedure, which then gets back a list of files that are assigned to this server for processing. The file lists are also broken down by threads by the stored procedure so that each thread is assigned its own set of files.

After the file list is received, a Foreach Loop container enumerates through the record set, and then calls the required processes to parse the files and load the data into the respective temporary tables. Figure 10-8 shows this process. Behind the scenes, each thread has its own set of variables that it uses to process files assigned to the thread.

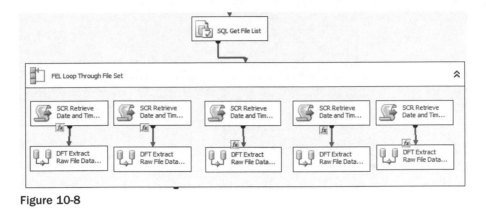

Figure 10-8

After all the raw data for all files assigned to this package loop is parsed into the respective tables, then the downstream processes are responsible for collating the data and putting it in the respective hourly raw data stage tables, as shown in Figure 10-9.

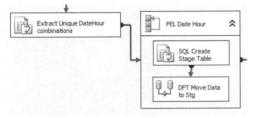

Figure 10-9

You first extract unique date-hour combinations from the raw file data. Then, for each set of date-hours, you create the raw hourly table if one does not already exist in the staging database, and then combine and load the data from the raw log files into the hourly raw data table. You can choose to do some aggregations at this point if doing so makes sense. This way, for this example, data will get aggregated to a five-minute interval.

After the data from the assigned files has been processed, you call a `Status Update` method to flag the `FileLog` records as processed. You then do a quick check to see whether the data on that stage server is ready for pre-aggregation. You determine this status if the stage server has already started processing data for a new date-hour.

If you find that data is indeed ready for pre-aggregation, you call the pre-aggregation job by executing a stored procedure. If the data is not ready for pre-aggregation, then you simply call a process to get the queue depth for unprocessed and unassigned files. If the queue depth is more than zero, then the loop logic considers doing another iteration of the loop within the boundaries of the `MaxLoopCount`. Figure 10-10 shows this flow.

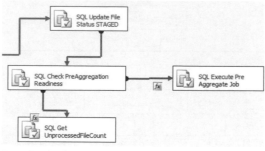

Figure 10-10

SCOStage 02 - Hourly PreAggregator.dtsx

This simple package first gets the necessary information on the earliest date-hour that is still to be pre-aggregated. It then drops and re-creates a pre-aggregate storage table for that time period, and pulls the data from the hourly raw data table. After the desired aggregation to the hour level, it then loads the data into the `Hourly` table. Finally, it flags the appropriate `HourlyServerProcessLog` record to indicate that this date-hour is now aggregated on this file server.

Figure 10-11 shows this simple flow. This package is set up as a non-scheduled job that is called via a stored procedure when initiated by the `File Processor` package.

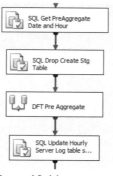

Figure 10-11

Central Server Packages

In addition to the two packages that are on the file process server, some packages also reside on the central server to aggregate data as described below. These packages are scheduled at appropriate intervals to achieve the desired latency.

Two main packages collect and aggregate the data to an hourly or daily grain. In addition, a third sample package performs clean up.

Following are the packages on this central server:

❑   SCOMain 01 - Hourly Aggregator.dtsx

❑   SCOMain 02 - Daily Aggregator.dtsx

❑   SCOMain 03 - Cleanup.dtsx

SCOMain 01 - Hourly Aggregator.dtsx

This package is scheduled to kick off on the central server every hour, taking into account some latency, as described previously. The package first gets the workload of all the date-hour combinations that are now ready to be aggregated and brought into the central data store.

Then, for each hour, it drops and re-creates stage tables for holding some temporary process data. It gets a list of all the staging servers and the tables names where the pre-aggregated data is stored for that particular hour. Using an enumeration loop, it connects to each individual file-processing server and brings down the data into the temporary tables it created previously. After this step is complete, the package further aggregates the data to the appropriate hourly grain, and puts the data in the hourly table in the central data store. It updates the HourlyProcessLog table to flag this hour as being aggregated, and updates all the FileLog records belonging to that hour with a status of FINISHED.

At the very end, after all available date-hours data have been aggregated based on the workload, the package kicks off the work reassignment process. Figure 10-12 shows the flow.

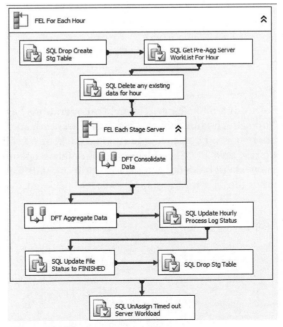

Figure 10-12

SCOMain 02 - Daily Aggregator.dtsx

This simple package is scheduled to kick off once a day. (Or, you can schedule it a bit more often to ensure that delays in other processes do not postpone the processing of daily data for the previous day by 24 or more hours.) It first finds out the workload of all unprocessed days. Then, for each day, it deletes any existing data in the daily table in the central data store for that date key. Then it reads and aggregates the data from the hourly table for that day, and inserts it into this table. Finally, it updates the `HourlyProcessLog` table records to flag the daily aggregation process as being completed for the date.

Figure 10-13 shows this implementation.

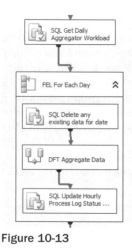

Figure 10-13

SCOMain 03 - Cleanup.dtsx

The clean-up package performs different clean-up or archival operations based on historic needs and configurable parameters. You can schedule this package based on need, and have it occur daily, weekly, or even at more frequent intervals. You don't want to run this package too infrequently, because a large number of tables containing raw data sit on the file processor databases that should be regularly cleaned up. You should however, leave enough latency to perform audit or quality assurance activities for your data loads. Figure 10-14 shows the flow for the sample clean-up package.

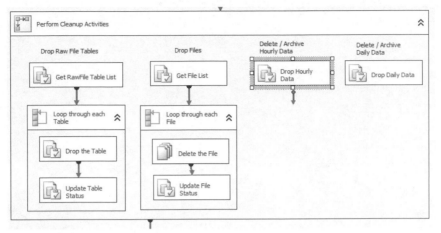

Figure 10-14

Summary

Although this chapter deals predominantly with a solution that requires significantly aggregated data in the central data store, you can also apply many of the scale-out principles to scenarios where you simply need more resources (including memory, CPU and disk I/O for processing, and doing complex transformations to your data your main server can afford). Other aspects (such as sizing) and additional parallelization of the scale-out services (such as dynamic thread management and the capability to increase parallel processes) have not been examined here, but with a little tweaking of the base processes, you can certainly accomplish similar scale-out tasks.

Scale-out ETL may fit only a small percentage of ETL solution needs. But if your data volumes are high, or the requirements are for near real-time data processing, then you should consider implementing a scale-out SSIS solution.

Chapter 11 deals with advanced scripting for those times when you just can't efficiently use the built-in processes in SSIS, and you need the power of a script to handle complex control flow and data flow situations.

11

Scripting Design Patterns

Whether applying SSIS toward data integration or DBA tasks, extending SSIS through scripting to handle logic not handled by the out-of-the-box components can be a useful and powerful tool. By using the Script Task or the Script component, you can write code to accomplish things that are better suited to a full-blown programming language than the items provided. Writing scripts enables you to create workflow tasks in the control flow, or data-centric operations in the data flow.

This chapter is split into two separate "Problem-Design-Solution" sections. The first "Problem-Design-Solution" section delves into the Script Task inside of the control flow. The discussion walks through an example of needing to check the attributes of files for archiving files. The second "Problem-Design-Solution" section continues the scripting adventure with the Script component inside of the data flow. This scenario re-creates the call center fact ETL that was introduced in Chapter 8.

Problem — Advanced File Management

Throughout the previous chapters of this book, you've learned how to configure several control flow tasks, including the Execute SQL Task and Execute Package Task. The control flow is the SSIS workflow designer, where you can decide which and in what order processes should execute. The next section offers a look at another control flow task, the Script Task.

Script Task

The Script Task is the first foray into adding a programming language to an SSIS package. Following are a few of the reasons you would want to use a Script Task:

❑ *No available standard task* — The SSIS tasks included out of the box will not always suffice to reach your package's end goal. If you come across one of these scenarios, your best bet is to utilize the Script Task.

❑ *Use business logic from an alternative assembly* — If you have business logic that is used across your company, and is already provided in a set of assemblies, there is no reason to re-create that logic. Instead, you can use a Script Task to reference that assembly and perform the task inside of your SSIS package.

This chapter is specifically addressing the Script Task, not the ActiveX Script Task. The ActiveX Script Task is available for backward compatibility with DTS, but is deprecated for future versions of SSIS. Do not use the ActiveX Script Task for any new development.

Scenario

Older backup systems used a method to determine the necessity of backing up a file that included checking the attributes of a file. If the archive attribute was set, the file had been recently modified, and the program knew that it should be backed up. Newer systems tend to use the date that the file was last modified. However, if your data extract system still uses the archive attribute, you will want to match that logic in your backup solution to only archive the files that were just loaded.

Let's create a system to archive files from one directory to another. This system should be extendable to multiple packages and multiple archive directories. The following sections take a look at the design for creating this system.

Design — Advanced File Management

As described in the "Problem" section, you need to create an archiving system for files that fall under the "needs to be archived" category, designated by the archive attribute being set on the file. Unfortunately, for people who like using the canned SSIS components (but, fortunately for this example), SSIS does not provide any way to directly check what attributes a file has. The only way that you will be able to answer this question is by using a Script Task.

You must also provide this file capability to multiple packages, so you will extract that data out to its own assembly. This assembly can then be referenced from multiple packages in their Script Tasks. Before examining the full solution, you must make a number of design decisions, including the following:

❑ Which script language should you use?

❑ How do you access SSIS objects from your script?

❏ Do you really need a custom assembly?

❏ What logic do you need to script?

Script Language

The very first choice you must make is what scripting language to use in your Script Task. Starting with SQL Server 2008, you have the option of using either Microsoft Visual Basic 2008 or Microsoft Visual C# 2008 in the Visual Studio Tools for Applications 2.0 environment (versus the 2005 "option" of only Visual Basic .NET under Visual Studio for Applications). Figure 11-1 shows this choice.

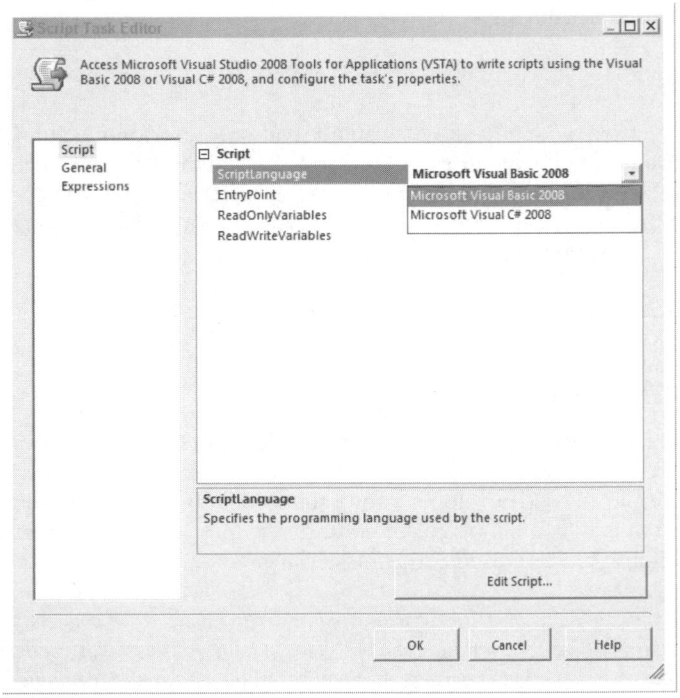

Figure 11-1

Although many debates exist about which language is better, neither Visual Basic nor C# is specifically recommended here, except to suggest that you pick one language to use exclusively in your packages. Doing so enables you to become more proficient in your scripting skills without needing to learn two different syntaxes, as well as makes maintaining your packages and scripts in the future easier for someone. For example purposes in this chapter, use Visual Basic.

Accessing Objects

If the Script Task were completely isolated from the rest of the package, it wouldn't be of much help to your package workflow! By using the `Dts` object inside of the Script Task, the Script Task can interact with the package through access to variables, connection managers, and events.

In this example, you must access the values of variables within your script. You have two specific ways to access variables: the easiest way is the `Variables` object, and the other is the `VariableDispenser` object. The `Variables` object requires less code, but is slightly less efficient and requires more interaction in the GUI. The `VariableDispenser` locks variables for a slightly shorter period of time.

To access a variable with the `Variables` object, you can use the following code. This code gets the value of the variable to be used in your logic.

```
Dts.Variables("sourceDirectory").Value.ToString
```

The other option for letting a Script Task know about read-only, user-defined variables is to use the `Dts.VariableDispenser.LockOneForRead` method. This method could be considered a late-binding approach because the task is only aware of the variable at runtime, and nothing in the task itself must be configured to make the code aware of the variable. Previously, the variable was set up through the Script Task Editor, which is an early-binding approach.

For this example, use the early-binding approach and specify the variables through the user interface.

Custom Assemblies

Script Tasks are valuable tasks for handling custom functionality because you can write code within the task. However, when you want to use the same code over and over again, why rewrite or cut and paste code for each Script Task? A good developer knows that code reuse makes developing code efficient and easier to maintain. That is why building custom libraries so that you can use them as functional components and building blocks within Script Tasks is a good practice.

Another great case for code reusability is writing custom components. Your code may not be suitable for a custom component because of its unique variability, or perhaps your company policies prevent registering such components on your servers. In these cases, the Script Task combined with custom libraries is the right solution, so you can still consolidate redundant code.

Because the requirement is to provide a way to access the code over many packages, you will be using a custom assembly for this example. Although in this example you start by creating your own assembly, your situation may vary in that the assembly may have already been created for your use.

Scripting

When you set up your script, there is a property called EntryPoint, which has been set to Main by default. The value of EntryPoint tells the Script Task which method in the script to execute when the task executes. If you do not modify this value, all code that you write should start in the Main subroutine. You can create other functions as well. However, they must be called from within the Main function.

There can be a tendency (especially by those who feel comfortable with programming languages) to resort to scripting more often than not. Resist the urge to use a Script Task or Script component if another item can perform the same function. Doing so results in a cleaner, more manageable, and often, better performing package.

Finally, the Main function must return a success or failure value for the package to recognize. An enumeration value has been created for you, as you can see in the following code, so be sure to set the Dts.TaskResult to one of the following options:

```
Enum ScriptResults
      Success = Microsoft.SqlServer.Dts.Runtime.DTSExecResult.Success
      Failure = Microsoft.SqlServer.Dts.Runtime.DTSExecResult.Failure
End Enum
```

Solution — Advanced File Management

As previously discussed in the "Problem" and "Design" sections, you are putting together a package that will archive files. This logic must reside in one location so that multiple packages can use the same logic. The following sections break up this solution into the following manageable chunks:

❑   Create an external assembly

❑   Access the external assembly

❑   Archive the files

Create an External Assembly

For this example, start by creating a custom assembly. In other scenarios, this assembly may already have been created. If that is the case, you can skip down to the section, "Access the External Assembly," where you learn about installing the assembly on the appropriate server, and including it in your Script Task.

To create a new assembly, open Visual Studio 2008 and create a new Visual Basic class library, as shown in Figure 11-2. You can also add this project to your existing SSIS solution to keep every dependency organized in the same container. A class library project is the type of the project to use when you need to create assemblies.

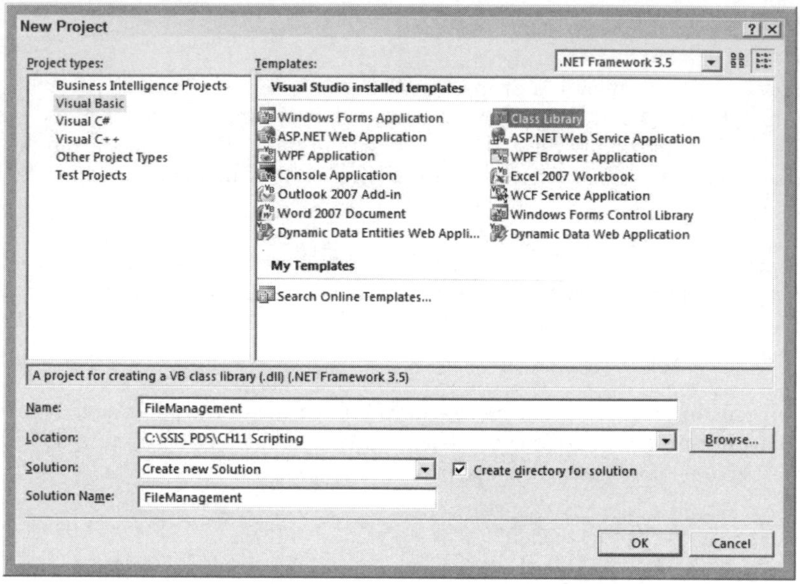

Figure 11-2

Name this assembly `FileManagement` and rename the class to the same. The following listing shows the full code that you can copy into the `FileManagement` class file:

```
Imports Microsoft.VisualBasic.FileSystem
Imports System.IO

Public Class FileManagement

    Public Sub ArchiveFiles(ByVal sourceDir As String, _
                            ByVal destDir As String)

        If Not Directory.Exists(sourceDir) Then
            Throw New DirectoryNotFoundException("Source directory does not exist")
        End If

        If Not Directory.Exists(destDir) Then
            Throw New DirectoryNotFoundException
                ("Destination directory does not exist")
        End If

        For Each sourceFile As String In Directory.GetFiles(sourceDir)
            Dim destFile As String = destDir + sourceFile.Replace(sourceDir, "")
```

```
          If IsFileArchivable(sourceFile) Then
              If File.Exists(destFile) Then
                  File.Delete(destFile)
              End If
              File.Move(sourceFile, destFile)
          End If
      Next

  End Sub

  Public Function IsFileArchivable(ByVal fileName As String) As Boolean
      If (File.GetAttributes(fileName) And FileAttributes.Archive) = _
              FileAttributes.Archive Then
          Return True
      Else
          Return False
      End If
  End Function

End Class
```

The class contains two methods to assist in the archiving process. The first subroutine accepts two variable arguments for the source and destination directories for the file. The logic then loops through all the files in the source directory and checks to see whether the archive attribute has been set. If so, the file is moved to the destination directory, overwriting any files that previously existed.

The second function checks the file attribute status, and returns true if is it archivable and false if it is not. In this example, you are using this function exclusively in the preceding method. This example leaves the Public modifier on this function, so that it could be called directly from your Script Task if the need arises.

Lastly, you must ensure that the assembly has been given a *strong name*. Signing an assembly with a strong name ensures that the assembly will be unique. An identical or updated assembly cannot be created by another person. This guarantees that the assembly came from the originator, and has not been modified by anyone else. The first thing to do when strong-naming an assembly is to create a cryptographic key pair that will be placed in a file.

You can sign an assembly with a strong name through the properties of the class library project. To do this, select Project ⇨ Properties from the toolbar. When the Properties window appears, select the Signing tab, and then select the "Sign the assembly" checkbox, as shown in Figure 11-3. Choose a strong-name key file by using the drop-down menu and selecting Browse to find the key file created. If the key has not been previously created, you can create it by selecting New instead of Browse from the drop-down list.

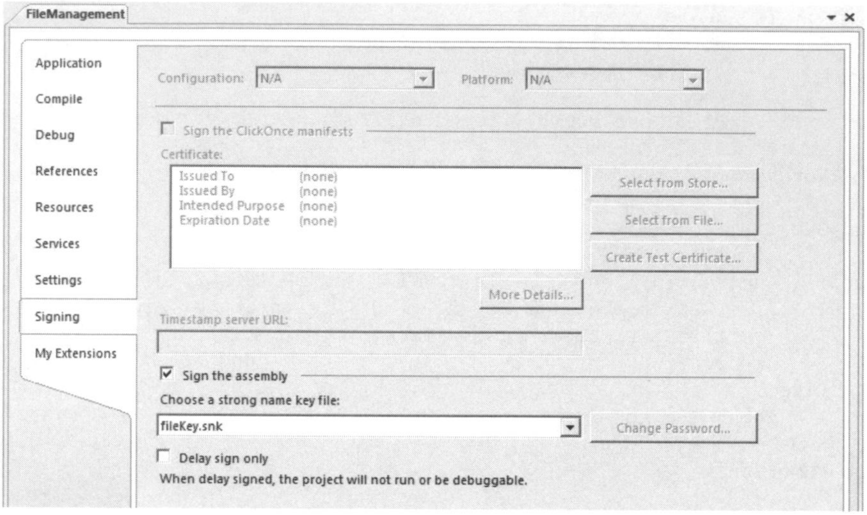

Figure 11-3

Build your solution, which results in a file named `FileManagement.dll`. Now, it's time to use the assembly you just created inside of your Script Task.

Access the External Assembly

Before you can use a custom assembly, you must make it known to SSIS. SSIS requires you place custom objects within the Global Assembly Cache (GAC) on the machine that is executing the package to maximize performance of the pipeline and tasks. The GAC is a code cache where you can place assemblies as a central repository.

The easiest way to add the assembly to the GAC is by copying the assembly to `C:\WINDOWS\assembly`. However, you can use the Global Assembly Cache Tool (`Gacutil.exe`), found in `C:\Program Files\ Microsoft SDKs\Windows\v6.0A\bin`, as well. At a command prompt, type **gacutil.exe /i "<assembly path>"** to start the utility, as shown in Figure 11-4.

Figure 11-4

On any development machines, you must also place the assembly in the `C:\Windows\Microsoft.NET\Framework\v2.0.50727` path. This is where Visual Studio Tools for Applications looks for references.

Archive the Files

Now that you've created the external assembly and properly placed it, you are ready to create and code your package. It will be a straightforward archiving package with just one Script Task. Figure 11-5 shows the final package.

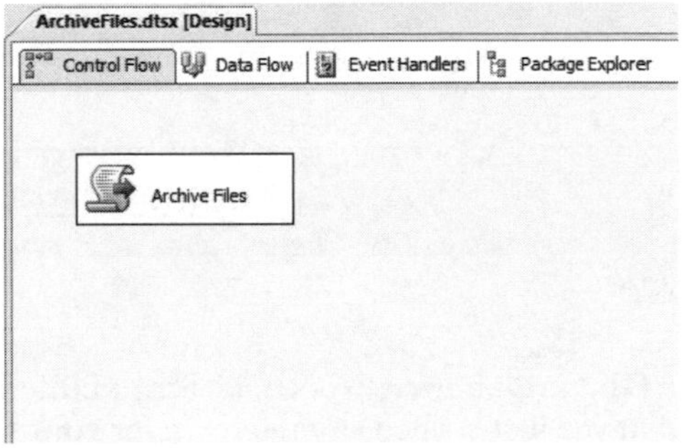

Figure 11-5

Add two variables to the package, scoped at the package level with the values shown in Table 11-1.

Table 11-1

Name	DataType	Value
destinationDirectory	String	C:\SSIS_PDS\CH11 Scripting\Archive
sourceDirectory	String	C:\SSIS_PDS\CH11 Scripting\Files

Double-clicking the Script Task allows you to edit the properties through the Script Task Editor. As previously discussed, set the `ScriptLanguage` property to Microsoft Visual Basic 2008. Using the ellipses button next to the `ReadOnlyVariables` property, open the Select Variables window and check both variables that you previously created, as shown in Figure 11-6.

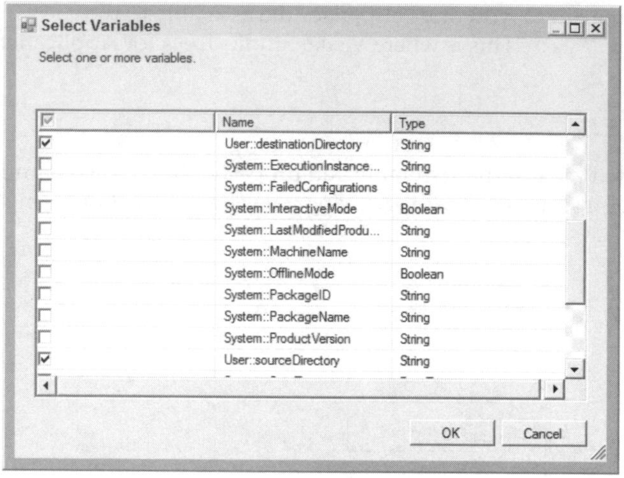

Figure 11-6

At this time, you can click the Edit Script button to open the Script Editor. You must add the `FileManagement` assembly that you just created as a reference for your script to use.

When you have the Script Task in design mode, you can reference the assembly by double-clicking the My Project icon within the Project Explorer pane, and then selecting the References tab and clicking the Add button. A list of available assemblies appears that you can reference. You can add the reference by selecting the assembly's name and clicking the Add button, as shown in Figure 11-7. The added assembly appears on the Add Reference window. Click OK to accept this addition and close the window.

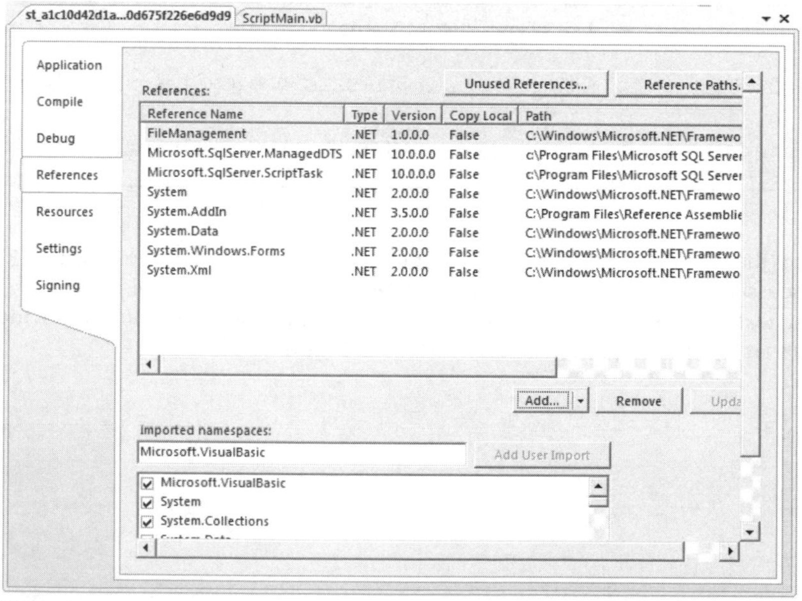

Figure 11-7

Now, modify the script in two ways. First add an `Imports` statement at the top of the code listing. Next, reference the `FileManagement` object and directly call the `ArchiveFiles` function with the variables from your package. You can see both of these steps in the following code listing:

```
' Microsoft SQL Server Integration Services Script Task
' Write scripts using Microsoft Visual Basic 2008.
' The ScriptMain is the entry point class of the script.

Imports System
Imports System.Data
Imports System.Math
Imports Microsoft.SqlServer.Dts.Runtime
Imports FileManagement

<System.AddIn.AddIn("ScriptMain", Version:="1.0", Publisher:="",
    Description:="")>
<System.CLSCompliantAttribute(False)> _
Partial Public Class ScriptMain
    Inherits Microsoft.SqlServer.Dts.Tasks.ScriptTask.VSTARTScriptObjectModelBase

    Enum ScriptResults
        Success = Microsoft.SqlServer.Dts.Runtime.DTSExecResult.Success
        Failure = Microsoft.SqlServer.Dts.Runtime.DTSExecResult.Failure
    End Enum

    Public Sub Main()
        Dts.TaskResult = ScriptResults.Success

        Dim fileMgmt As New FileManagement.FileManagement
        fileMgmt.ArchiveFiles(Dts.Variables("sourceDirectory").Value.ToString, _
                            Dts.Variables("destinationDirectory").Value.ToString)

    End Sub

End Class
```

Executing this package now moves all files from the `Files` directory to the `Archive` directory if the archive attribute has been set. Based on your configuration management schema, you may want to set those variables to be configurable from an outside system to allow you to modify those locations outside of the package.

Summary — Advanced File Management

This "Problem-Design-Solution" section showed an example of advanced file management by showing how to create a package to archive files. You saw how to reference an external assembly and reference SSIS objects from within a Script Task. You could expand the external assembly to return a list of archivable files, or make the attribute-checked dynamic based on an argument being turned in. You could also change the assembly to move/return files that have recently been modified as archivable files.

Now dig deeper into SSIS scripting by looking at the Script component next.

Problem — Call Center Fact ETL

The other side of the SSIS scripting coin is the Script component in the Data Flow Task. Even though the control flow and data flow look similar in the designer, they have very different purposes.

The control flow focuses on distinct units or processes of work, and the data flow is one complete pipeline that starts with data sources, manipulates and transforms the data, and ends by putting that data into a destination. When you drag a toolbox item onto the control flow, you are using a task, versus in the data flow, you are using a component. Likewise, the control flow and data flow contain precedence constraints and pipeline paths, respectively, in the form of arrows connecting the items.

Reasons to Use Scripting

SSIS contains many components out of the box to handle all aspects of the data flow. However, creating additional logic by scripting it directly is sometimes necessary. Following are a few reasons you would want to resort to scripting logic inside of the data flow:

❑ *No available standard component* — The primary reason for using a Script component is that there is just no other way. If the components that are provided with SSIS don't have the exact option or function that is available inside of the .NET framework, you can access it instead by using a Script component.

❑ *Reduce complex logic* — Data transformation can get quite complicated. If you are trying to perform a custom aggregation or a complex case statement, you may not be able to manipulate the data in just the way you want to. If you can come up with the logic, you should be able to script out the solution using a Script component.

❑ *Encapsulate business logic to one location* — There is often a set of business rules that must be applied repeatedly inside of a data load process. Some examples of these rules could be filtering out all rows with a specific code, or formatting a date in the exact same format each time. You can put this type of business logic into a Script component, where it can be called multiple times in the script.

Scenario

You may recall from Chapter 8 the snapshot fact table example, which loaded the call center fact table. To recap, the `AdventureWorksDW2008` database contains a fact table named `FactCallCenter`. For every shift of every day, this table contains snapshots of data, including the total counts of calls, issues, and orders. In an effort to make your life more difficult, the source data does not come from the `AdventureWorks2008` table, but from a flat file obtained from a legacy ticketing system that does not pre-aggregate the data for you. As such, it is up to the ETL process to aggregate the data by issues, operators, and then by day and shift.

Chapter 8 shows how to do this in the data flow using the standard components. But it is a messy package with some duplicated logic. Because you have hit upon two of the rules for using a Script component, this presents a prime example for modifying this package! In the following "Design" section, you learn about some of the properties you can use when writing a Script component, and decide on the ones to use to implement the call center fact ETL.

Design — Call Center Fact ETL

Most of the properties and information discussed previously concerning the Script Task are applicable to the Script component, including script language choice and accessing external assemblies. Following are a few additional choices you must make when working with the Script component:

❑   Which type of component should you use?

❑   Which type of output is needed?

❑   Which methods should you override?

For each category, this section goes over what the options are, how to make your choice, and which options make the most sense for the call center fact.

Component Type

As soon as you introduce a Script component to the data flow by dragging it from the toolbox, the Select Script Component Type dialog box (see Figure 11-8) appears, asking you what type of component you desire. You must choose to create either a Source, Destination, or Transformation before you can continue to configure the component.

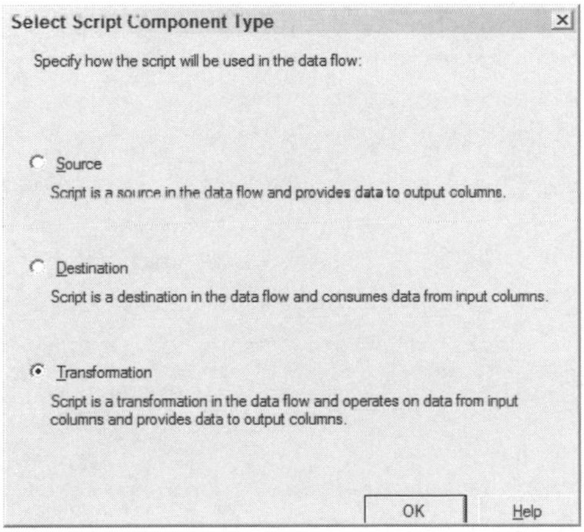

Figure 11-8

This decision affects the inputs and outputs that are created inside of the component. These inputs and outputs are the vehicles that accept and pass on rows of data to and from the component. You can have one input and multiple outputs for a component.

> **Carefully select the option that applies to your situation. After you have selected Source, Destination, or Transformation, you cannot change your mind without deleting and re-creating the entire Script component.**

If you select a *Source component*, one output will be created. The choice of a *Destination component* will result in one input. As you can expect, a *Transformation component* will have both an input and an output. The Add Output button enables you to add additional outputs, but it is only enabled in the Source and Transformation components.

For the call center fact table, use a transformation component. Doing so enables you to accept records from the flat-file connection, and pass aggregated data to an OLE DB Destination into the AdventureWorksDW2008 database.

Output Type

If you have selected a component type of Transformation, you then need to make a choice of what type of output you want to create in your component. Your two choices are *synchronous* and *asynchronous*.

Synchronous Outputs

A synchronous output will use the same set of rows, known as a *buffer*, that came from an input. As the buffer passes through the component, the data in the columns can be modified, or new columns can even be added. New rows cannot be generated, and you cannot rearrange the order of the rows in the buffer.

Each synchronous output must be mapped to its associated input. When you create a transformation, the SynchronousInputID of the output is automatically mapped to the ID of the input. Figure 11-9 shows the property having been set for a synchronous output.

Figure 11-9

Many of the standard SSIS components have synchronous outputs, and thinking of them when designing your own component may be helpful. For example, the Derived Column transformation uses a synchronous output. For each row that comes in, the expressions that you create either override the values in a column, or add a new column. The Lookup transformation also contains synchronous outputs. Although a lot of work is accomplished inside of the component to cache the reference table and make a match against that data, at the end of the day, the same rows are coming out of the component that went into it.

Asynchronous Outputs

On the other hand, an asynchronous output creates a new buffer to pass data to the next component. In a nutshell, an asynchronous transformation means that, inside the script, you actually copy each row from the input into the output. This copying would mean the operations would be slower, but the benefit is that the set of output columns could be quite different from the set of input columns in terms of number, type, and size.

You make this change on the "Inputs and Outputs" menu. One of the properties of the output is called `SynchronousInputID`. By changing this to `None`, you have created an asynchronous output. You then need to add columns to the output, so that you have something to populate in your script.

Other Component Types

Now you know about the synchronous and asynchronous outputs in terms of transformations, but what about the other types of components? You actually have no choice when dealing with either a Destination or Source component. A Destination component has no outputs, so it is neither synchronous nor asynchronous. A Source component is automatically asynchronous because it has no input to act synchronously with.

Design Choice

By the very nature of needing to aggregate data, the Script component needs to have an asynchronous output. The component loops through all rows to store values before it outputs the aggregated values onto a new output buffer.

Now that you understand the decisions you must make regarding the types of components and outputs, you can learn how to access external SSIS objects.

Overridable Methods

The Script Task contains one method to work with: the `Main` subroutine. Programming the Script component becomes more complicated because you are dealing with the inputs and outputs to pass data around. The Script component automatically calls different methods during its execution to handle this data. The scripting overrides these functions so that your logic is called during the script's execution.

Take a look at some of the methods that you can override and when it would be appropriate to use them:

❑   `CreateNewOutputRows` — This method is best used for Source components. You can use it to add new rows to the output, but it is called before any of the `ProcessInput` methods. Because you will not have access to the data from the inputs, transformations could only use this method to create an empty output row, or populate the output row with data independent of the input.

❑ PostExecute — This method is used for any post-processing tasks and is the only one where variables can be written to. This is for performance reasons to keep variables from being locked constantly as each row goes through the component. The PostExecute subroutine is only called after all rows have gone through, and you can write to a variable at that point to show how many rows you transformed.

❑ PreExecute — This method is used for preprocessing any objects or items needed for the component. These preprocessing tasks could include initializing variables or ensuring a location exists.

❑ <InputName>_ProcessInputRow — This method is called for every row in the input. You use this method if you need to process each row one at a time.

❑ <InputName>_ProcessInput — This method should be overridden if you need to perform some action after all rows have been processed. In the call center fact example, you will need to write the aggregated values to the output after all rows have been processed. This method is perfect for performing that function.

Solution — Call Center Fact ETL

Now that you understand the steps you must take to implement your logic with the Script component, you can put it all together in a package. Just so you can get an idea of where this example is headed, the final package is shown in Figure 11-10.

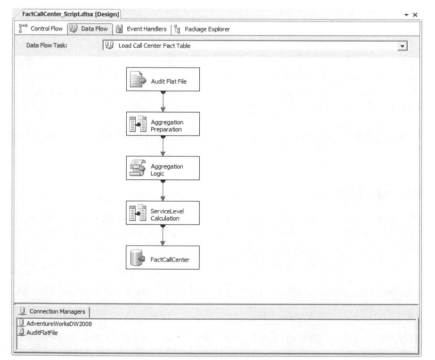

Figure 11-10

Package Setup

This package starts out looking similar to the package you created in Chapter 8. You use a flat-file connection manager and flat-file source to connect to the audit stream file. Figure 11-11 shows the columns for the flat-file connection manager.

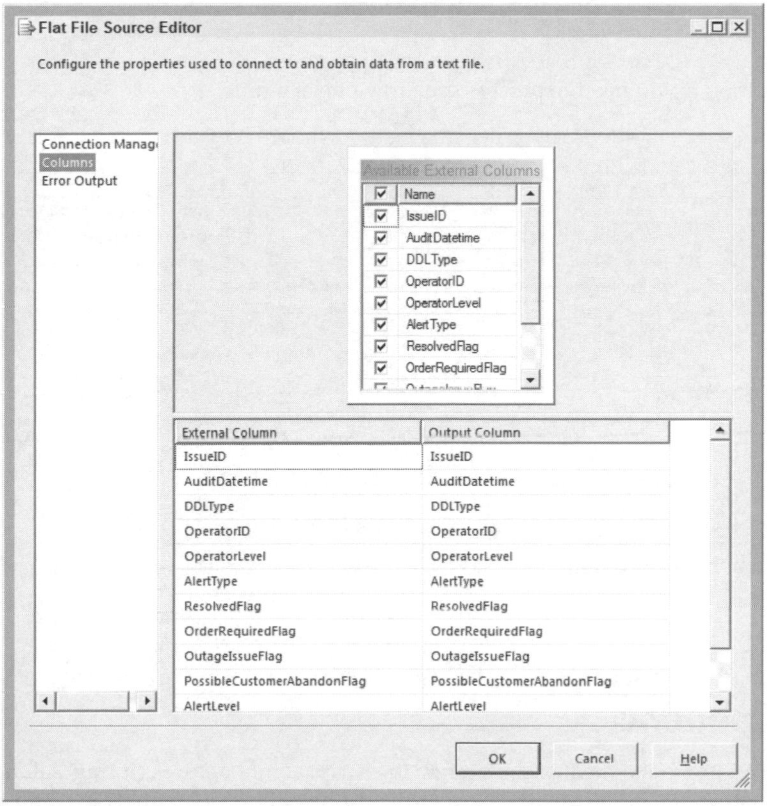

Figure 11-11

Next, you use a Derived Column transformation. The logic will vary slightly, in that you will remove two of the rows from this transform: the logic to create the `DateKey` column and the derivation of the `Shift` column. You use this logic again later in the data flow for another date, so move it to Script component, where it can be used multiple times. Figure 11-12 shows the final Derived Column Transformation Editor.

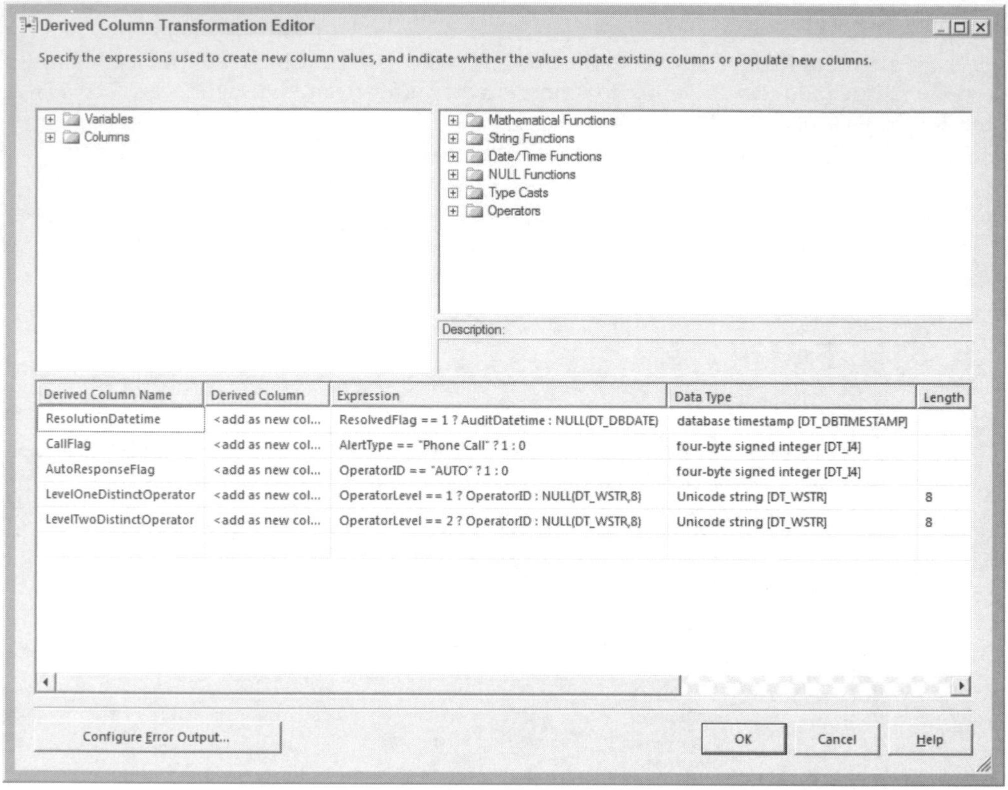

Figure 11-12

Script Component

In this section you get to the meat of the design: the Script component. Scripting will replace a majority of the transformations from the original package, including all Aggregation, Sort, and Merge Join transformations, and some of the Derived Column transformations. Because of the flexibility of the scripting, you can combine all of that logic into one component!

To begin, bring a Script component from the toolbox onto your designer. In the Select Script Component Type dialog window that appears, choose the Transformation option, which should be the default selected option. You want to use a transformation so that the component will create both an input and output path. This allows you to access the data coming into the transformation and pass information to succeeding transformations. Attach the Script transformation to the Derived Column transformation, and double-click the item to edit the properties.

Inside the Script Transformation Editor, select the Input Columns menu on the left side of the window. Selecting columns on the Input Columns menu tells the component which columns the script needs to access. Only select the columns that you need to reduce the code overhead that is created.

Next to each column, specify whether you need to read the column to use it in your own output, or overwrite the value by setting the Usage Type property to either ReadOnly or ReadWrite for each column, respectively. For this example, you need to access all columns in ReadOnly mode. Figure 11-13 shows the Script Transformation Editor with all columns selected.

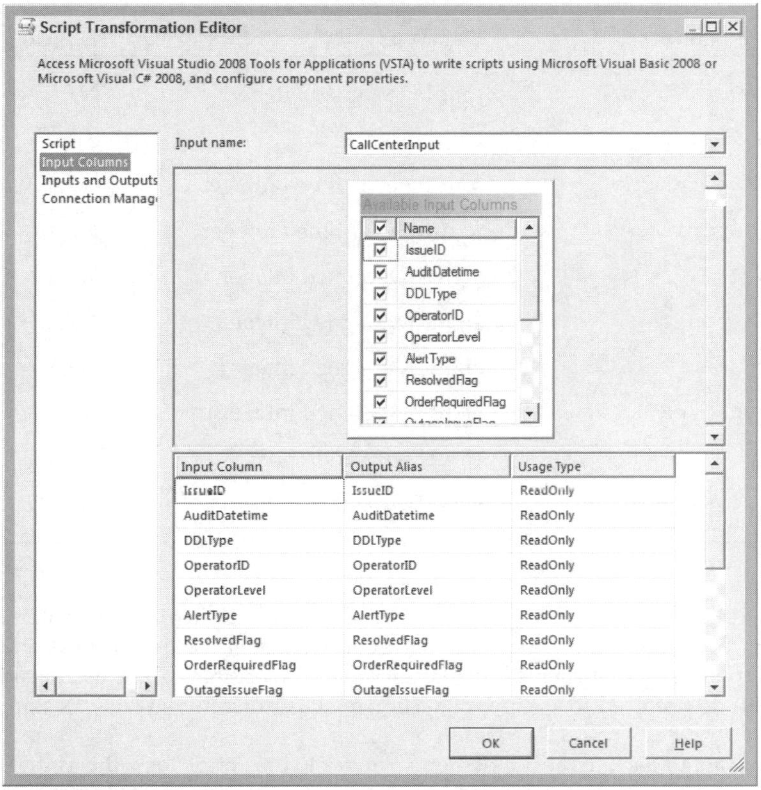

Figure 11-13

Next, you configure the "Inputs and Outputs" menu in the Script Transformation Editor. Note that Input 0 already contains the columns that you previously selected on the Input Columns menu. Rename Input 0 to CallCenterInput, because you will need to reference it inside of your script. Next, you move on to the output, which will need further modifications.

Rather than referring to the output as Output 0, rename it to CallCenterOutput. As discussed in the "Design" section, this output should be asynchronous because you will be aggregating the input rows and creating a new output buffer to pass data to the pipeline. To do this, change the SynchronousInputID to None.

Now, you must configure `CallCenterOutput`'s columns. When the output is created, there are no columns created yet. With your mouse focused on the `Output Columns` folder, click the Add Column button and configure ten columns, as shown in Table 11-2.

Table 11-2

Column Name	DataType	Length
DateKey	four-byte signed integer	N/A
Shift	Unicode string	8
Level1Operators	four-byte unsigned integer	N/A
Level2Operators	four-byte unsigned integer	N/A
Calls	eight-byte signed integer	N/A
AutoResponses	eight-byte signed integer	N/A
Orders	eight-byte signed integer	N/A
IssuesRaised	eight-byte signed integer	N/A
AverageTimePerIssue	Double-precision float	N/A
CustomerAbandons	eight-byte signed integer	N/A

The final menu, called Connection Managers, allows you to specify which connection managers you want to access in your script. Ensure that the connection manager has been created in your package, and use the Add button to add that connection manager to the object that can be used inside of the script. For this example, you do not need to use the connection manager directly, so you can skip this menu entirely.

At this time, you can go back to the Script menu. Similar to the Script Task, this is the place to add which variables you want to read or write. The call center fact ETL does not need to reference any variables, so leave those properties blank. You also specify what script language you want to use. You learned about making your language decision in the "Design" section of the earlier "Problem-Design-Solution" example, and, as such, use Visual Basic for this example as well. Figure 11-14 shows the parameters set up on this screen.

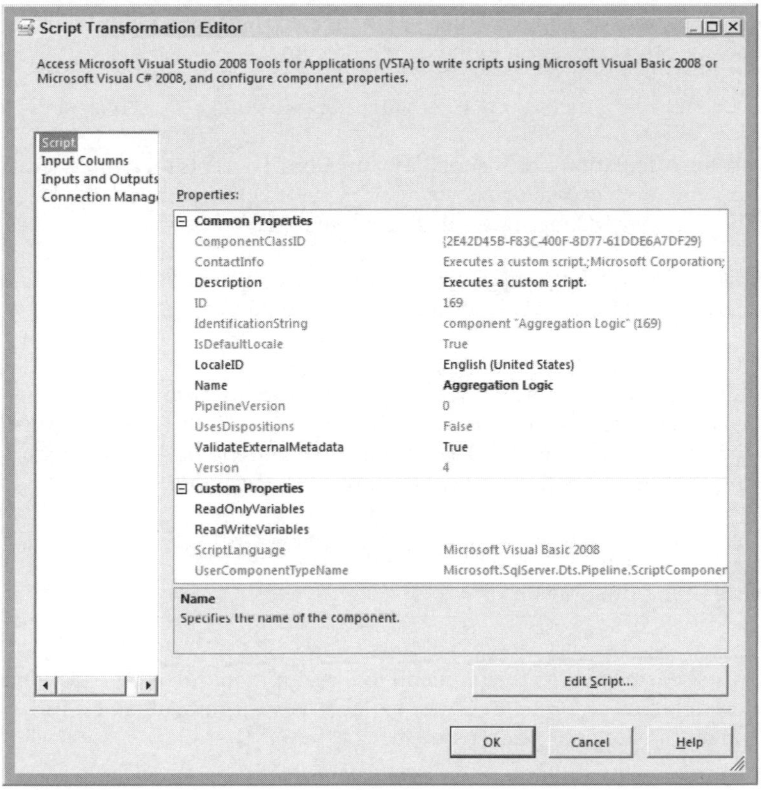

Figure 11-14

Now that you have all the parameters set up, you can click on the Edit Script button to open the scripting environment. The following sections offer a look at the code in three different stages:

❑ Reusable methods

❑ Row-by-row processing

❑ Process input

Reusable Methods

You removed two columns from the original package's initial derived column component, DateKey and Shift, with the intent of encapsulating that business logic into functions that can be used multiple times. You will use these methods in your processing methods, so now take a look at each of those columns and their corresponding methods.

For the DateKey calculation, you append the year to the two-digit month, and then to the two-digit day value. Following is the SSIS expression in the derived column:

```
YEAR(AuditDatetime) * 10000 + MONTH(AuditDatetime) * 100 + DAY(AuditDatetime)
```

When you convert the calculation to a Visual Basic function, it accepts a variable with a data type of DateTime. The function then uses a format string of "yyyyMMdd" to convert and return the date in the correct format. The following listing shows this function:

```
Private Function GetDateKey(ByVal inputDate As DateTime) As Integer
    Return CInt(inputDate.ToString("yyyyMMdd"))
End Function
```

The Shift column used the hour portion of a date to determine in what shift the issue occurred. If the hour was less than 6, the shift was midnight. If it was from 6 to 11, the shift was AM. The next grouping was PM1 with hours from 12 to 17, with the remaining hours falling under the category of PM2. Following is a listing showing the logic from the derived column SSIS expression:

```
DATEPART("Hh",AuditDatetime) < 6 ? "midnight"
  : DATEPART("Hh",AuditDatetime) < 12 ? "AM"
  : DATEPART("Hh",AuditDatetime) < 18 ? "PM1"
  : "PM2"
```

In contrast, the Visual Basic function that you add to the script looks like the following listing. This listing is a function call that accepts a DateTime variable as an argument, and returns the appropriate shift value based on the previously discussed logic.

```
Private Function GetShift(ByVal shiftDate As DateTime) As String
    Dim shift As String
    Select Case shiftDate.Hour
        Case 0 To 5
            shift = "midnight"
        Case 6 To 11
            shift = "AM"
        Case 12 To 17
            shift = "PM1"
        Case Else
            shift = "PM2"
    End Select
    Return shift
End Function
```

Row-By-Row Processing

The "Design" section for this example goes into detail about each of the methods that you can use inside of the Script component. For this example, you override two functions. The first function, CallCenterInput_ProcessInputRow, handles the row-by-row processing.

A buffer object named Row will get passed into this function for every row. The logic will then be performed on the current row of the buffer. The following listing shows the signature of the function:

```
Public Overrides Sub CallCenterInput_ProcessInputRow
    (ByVal Row As CallCenterInputBuffer)
```

There are then two separate pieces of logic to handle the operators' aggregation and the issue aggregation. The code uses three global variables to store values, and a custom object in the form of a structure. The declaration of these objects is as follows:

```
Private Structure IssueStruct
    Public InitialDateTime As DateTime
    Public ResolutionDateTime As DateTime
    Public ResolutionDateTime_IsNull As Boolean
    Public OrderCount As Int64
    Public IssueCount As Int64
    Public CustomerAbandonCount As Int64
    Public CallCount As Int64
    Public AutoResponseCount As Int64
End Structure

Private Level1OperatorHash As New Hashtable
Private Level2OperatorHash As New Hashtable
Private IssueHash As New Hashtable
```

The code for the operators' aggregation is as follows:

```
Dim OperatorKey As String = CStr(GetDateKey(Row.AuditDatetime)) _
            + GetShift(Row.AuditDatetime)

' Add new operators to the appropriate hashtable at the Date-Shift grain
If Not Level1OperatorHash.ContainsKey(OperatorKey) Then
    Dim Lvl1Operators As New ArrayList
    Level1OperatorHash.Add(OperatorKey, Lvl1Operators)
    Dim Lvl2Operators As New ArrayList
    Level2OperatorHash.Add(OperatorKey, Lvl2Operators)
End If

If Row.OperatorLevel = 1 Then
    If Not CType(Level1OperatorHash(OperatorKey), _
       ArrayList).Contains(Row.LevelOneDistinctOperator) Then
        If Not Row.LevelOneDistinctOperator_IsNull Then
            CType(Level1OperatorHash(OperatorKey), _
        ArrayList).Add(Row.LevelOneDistinctOperator)
        End If
    End If
ElseIf Row.OperatorLevel = 2 Then
    If Not CType(Level2OperatorHash(OperatorKey), _
       ArrayList).Contains(Row.LevelTwoDistinctOperator) Then
        If Not Row.LevelTwoDistinctOperator_IsNull Then
            CType(Level2OperatorHash(OperatorKey), _
                ArrayList).Add(Row.LevelTwoDistinctOperator)
        End If
    End If
End If
```

This code replaces the Aggregate transformation that gets a distinct count of level-one and level-two operators. Based on the `operatorLevel` column, an operator is added to the appropriate hash table if it does not already exist. This results in a list of distinct operators for every `DateKey` and `Shift` combination.

Following is the code for the issue aggregation:

```
' Update attributes for each issue
If Not IssueHash.ContainsKey(Row.IssueID) Then
    Dim issue As New IssueStruct
    issue.InitialDateTime = Row.AuditDatetime
    If Row.ResolutionDatetime_IsNull Then
        issue.ResolutionDateTime_IsNull = True
    Else
        issue.ResolutionDateTime_IsNull = False
        issue.ResolutionDateTime = Row.ResolutionDatetime
    End If
    issue.OrderCount = Row.OrderRequiredFlag
    issue.IssueCount = Row.OutageIssueFlag
    issue.CustomerAbandonCount = Row.PossibleCustomerAbandonFlag
    issue.CallCount = Row.CallFlag
    issue.AutoResponseCount = Row.AutoResponseFlag

    IssueHash.Add(Row.IssueID, issue)
Else
    Dim issue As IssueStruct = CType(IssueHash(Row.IssueID), IssueStruct)
    If Row.AuditDatetime < issue.InitialDateTime Then
        issue.InitialDateTime = Row.AuditDatetime
    End If
    If Not Row.ResolutionDatetime_IsNull Then
        If Row.ResolutionDatetime > issue.ResolutionDateTime Then
            issue.ResolutionDateTime_IsNull = False
            issue.ResolutionDateTime = Row.ResolutionDatetime
        End If
    End If
    If Row.OrderRequiredFlag > issue.OrderCount Then
        issue.OrderCount = Row.OrderRequiredFlag
    End If
    If Row.OutageIssueFlag > issue.IssueCount Then
        issue.IssueCount = Row.OutageIssueFlag
    End If
    If Row.PossibleCustomerAbandonFlag > issue.CustomerAbandonCount Then
        issue.CustomerAbandonCount = Row.PossibleCustomerAbandonFlag
    End If
    If Row.CallFlag > issue.CallCount Then
        issue.CallCount = Row.CallFlag
    End If
    If Row.AutoResponseFlag > issue.AutoResponseCount Then
        issue.AutoResponseCount = Row.AutoResponseFlag
    End If
    IssueHash(Row.IssueID) = issue
End If
```

This code replaces the first issue Aggregation transformation by populating the issue hash table with an issue structure instantiation for every issue. It takes the minimum value of all the audit dates in the rows, and takes the maximum value for all the other columns.

Process Input

The second function you override, `CallCenterInput_ProcessInput`, executes for each buffer of data that comes in. Take a look at the following code, and then look at the logic that is happening:

```
Public Overrides Sub CallCenterInput_ProcessInput
        (ByVal Buffer As CallCenterInputBuffer)
    While Buffer.NextRow
        CallCenterInput_ProcessInputRow(Buffer)
    End While

    If Buffer.EndOfRowset Then
        Dim dateKey As Integer
        Dim shift As String
        Dim level1Operators As Integer
        Dim level2Operators As Integer
        Dim calls As Int64
        Dim autoResponses As Int64
        Dim orders As Int64
        Dim issuesRaised As Int64
        Dim totalTimePerIssue As Int64
        Dim totalTimeCount As Int64
        Dim customerAbandons As Int64

        If Not IsNothing(level1Operators) Then
            For Each key As String In Level1OperatorHash.Keys
                dateKey = key.Substring(0, 8)
                shift = key.Substring(8, key.Length - 8)
                level1Operators = CType(Level1OperatorHash(key),
                    ArrayList).Count
                level2Operators = CType(Level2OperatorHash(key),
                    ArrayList).Count

                calls = 0
                autoResponses = 0
                orders = 0
                issuesRaised = 0
                totalTimePerIssue = 0
                totalTimeCount = 0
                customerAbandons = 0

                For Each issue As IssueStruct In IssueHash.Values
                    If GetDateKey(issue.InitialDateTime) = dateKey And _
                        GetShift(issue.InitialDateTime) = shift Then
                        calls = calls + issue.CallCount
                        autoResponses = autoResponses + issue.AutoResponseCount
                        orders = orders + issue.OrderCount
                        issuesRaised = issuesRaised + issue.IssueCount
                        If issue.ResolutionDateTime_IsNull = False Then
                            Dim initialDateNoMin As DateTime =
                                issue.InitialDateTime.Subtract
                                    (TimeSpan.FromSeconds
                                    (issue.InitialDateTime.Second))
```

```
                              Dim resolutionDateNoMin As DateTime =
                                  issue.ResolutionDateTime.Subtract
                                  (TimeSpan.FromSeconds
                                  (issue.ResolutionDateTime.Second))
                              totalTimePerIssue = totalTimePerIssue +
                                  DateDiff(DateInterval.Minute,
                                  initialDateNoMin, resolutionDateNoMin)
                              totalTimeCount = totalTimeCount + 1
                          End If
                          customerAbandons = customerAbandons +
                              issue.CustomerAbandonCount
                      End If
                  Next

                  CallCenterOutputBuffer.AddRow()
                  CallCenterOutputBuffer.DateKey = dateKey
                  CallCenterOutputBuffer.Shift = shift
                  CallCenterOutputBuffer.LevelOneOperators = level1Operators
                  CallCenterOutputBuffer.LevelTwoOperators = level2Operators
                  CallCenterOutputBuffer.Calls = calls
                  CallCenterOutputBuffer.AutoResponses = autoResponses
                  CallCenterOutputBuffer.Orders = orders
                  CallCenterOutputBuffer.IssuesRaised = issuesRaised
                  CallCenterOutputBuffer.AverageTimePerIssue =
                      totalTimePerIssue / totalTimeCount
                  CallCenterOutputBuffer.CustomerAbandons = customerAbandons
              Next
          End If
          CallCenterOutputBuffer.SetEndOfRowset()
      End If

   End Sub
```

This method starts out by looping through each of the rows in the buffer, setting each of them to the current row. This row is then passed to the `CallCenterInput_ProcessInputRow` function that has already been reviewed. After all rows have been consumed, the function checks to see whether this is the last buffer coming through. If so, it completes the final set of logic to send the data to the output path.

The final set of logic begins by getting the count from the operators' hash tables and setting the count values. For each `DateKey` and `Shift` combination in the hash table, it then iterates through all the issues to ascertain the summed values for all columns. Finally, a new row is created in the output buffer, and all values are assigned to be sent to the next transformation.

Entire Script

You can find the entire script in the correct order on this book's companion Web site (`www.wrox.com`), along with the script embedded into the `FactCallCenter` package.

Package Wrap-Up

Now wrap up the package using the same Derived Column transformation and destination as in Chapter 8. Configure the Service Level Calculation Derived Column transformation to add the columns as specified in Figure 11-15.

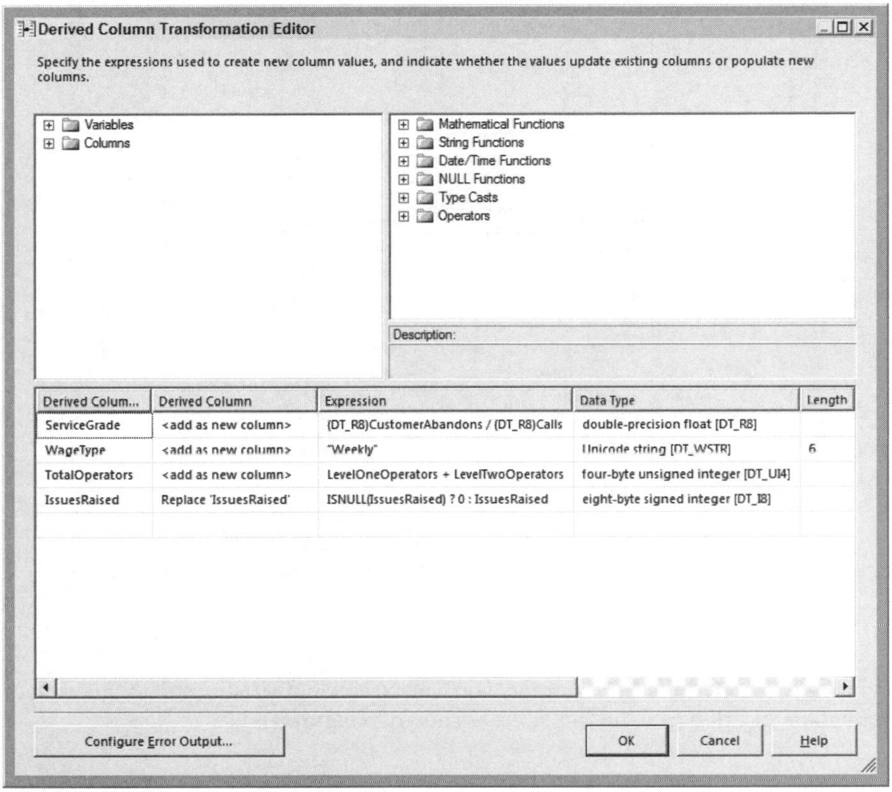

Figure 11-15

Finally, you use an OLE DB Destination to perform a fast load into the dbo.FactCallCenter table. Figure 11-16 shows the column mapping.

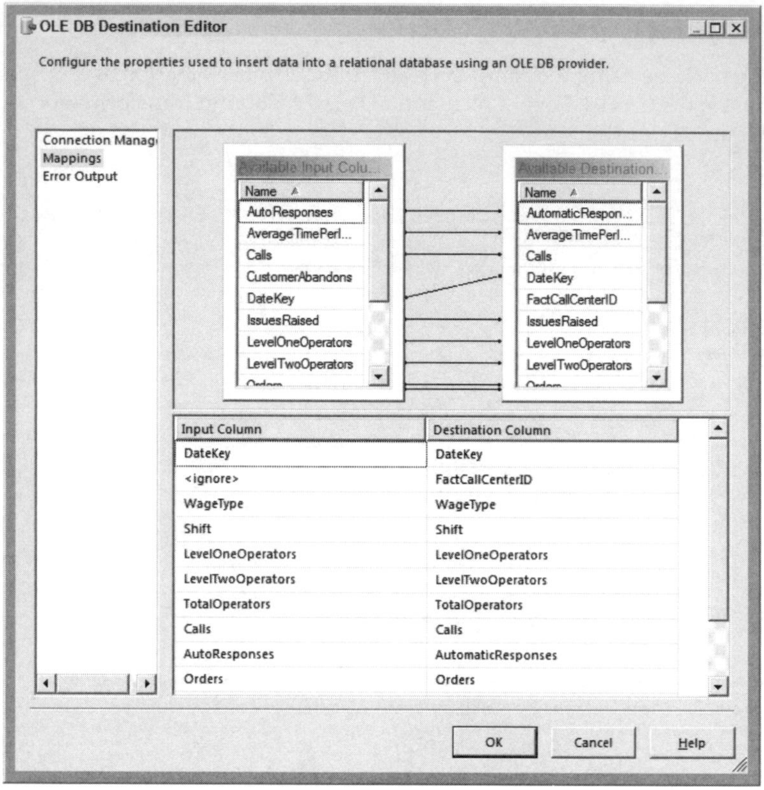

Figure 11-16

Now that you've completed the ETL package, you can execute it. By using a data viewer, you can see the records that will be inserted into the fact table, as shown in Figure 11-17.

Figure 11-17

Summary — Call Center Fact ETL

This part of the chapter rewrote the FactCallCenter package that you originally saw in Chapter 8. Using a Script component, you learned how to specify what type of Script component to use, how to modify the output type, and how to write a complex set of logic. The finished product took the original package that contained 12 components, and turned it into a slim-and-trim package of 5 components.

Summary

This chapter discussed two "Problem-Design-Solution" sections. By looking at the Script Task, you learned how important it is to create reusable code. You extended scripts by reusing custom functionality within assemblies to perform logic that could not otherwise have been accomplished in an SSIS package. By looking at the Script component, you were able to streamline the package. You should not use the Script Task and Script component lightly, but they can provide a great benefit when used correctly.

Chapter 12 delves into using SSIS to automate DBA maintenance tasks and plans.

SSIS Package Scaling

Have you ever asked the question, "Why is my SSIS package running so long?" Or, have you ever thought, "Did I design this in the best way possible?"

In this last chapter, you learn how to identify SSIS performance issues and understand how to resolve issues through proper design and tuning. This topic is not new, as ways to achieve scalability have been presented throughout the book (such as how to efficiently work with transactions and snapshots, and how to scale your dimension processing). But the difference is that this chapter hones the discussion of scalability to several key areas, including identifying bottlenecks, using SQL in the right places, dataflow tuning, and destination adapter optimization.

By now, you have the main approach to the Problem-Design-Solution series down pat. This chapter fits the same approach, with a slightly different focus in the "Problem" section. Because this chapter discusses scalability, the first section, "Problem," is about identifying the performance problems in SSIS. Here's what you can expect in this chapter:

❑ *"Problem"* — The "Problem" section answers the question, "Where's my bottleneck?" It dives into identifying long-running tasks, slow destinations, intensive transformations, and sluggish sources.

❑ *"Design"* — The "Design" section presents the best-practice design patterns for ETL problems, which include the balanced use of database features and the SSIS data flow.

❑ *"Solution"* — The "Solution" section delves into how to optimize your packages with tuning practices, and things to watch out for. You also learn how to optimize destinations, and work with partitioned tables.

Problem

When it comes to identifying bottlenecks in packages, over time, you will develop that innate ability to know where to look. Similarly, you will also start designing your packages with scalability in mind, which will come out of knowing what works best for different challenges.

Some of the basics for when you want to take your packages to the next level of scalability include knowing where your performance hits are, and choosing the right task to handle your data processing. When it comes to evaluating performance, the main objective is to identify the task or component that has the most impact, and also monitor memory utilization. This is not always easy (some situations are easier than others!), but the good news is that you can follow some steps to help you figure out what is going on.

The following steps are outlined in more detail in this section, but here's a brief overview:

1. *Monitor task durations* — Knowing how long each task takes goes a long way. If you've implemented a package framework, then you are already there.

2. *Identify destination issues* — Destination can pose problems, especially if you don't have much control over them. Identifying destination problems involves monitoring destination activity and calculating the impact.

3. *Identify memory issues* — In the data flow, memory management is critical for optimal transformation performance.

4. *Identify source issues* — Sources can also pose problems, especially if the source is based on a view or a query. But, usually there are ways to help optimize the extraction.

Identifying Task Durations

When you have a package that is taking a long time to run, the natural first step is to identify which tasks are taking the longest. If you are running a package in BIDS, you can pretty much see how long each task is taking. However, if your package is running via a command-line script or job, then identifying the long-running tasks will be more difficult than it sounds.

If you haven't implemented a package framework yet, then you will have some legwork to do in order to figure out the task durations. If so, be sure to review Chapter 2 on how to implement a package framework that will report package execution details, status, errors, durations, and so on. The upfront work will go a long way!

Without a package framework, you must first turn on package logging and capture the events to a SQL table (the sysssislog table). The events that are logged do not provide the task-duration information in a single line. Instead, the log events are sent out as the events happen. For example, the OnPreExecute event is sent out with a timestamp of its occurrence. Later, when the task finishes, the OnPostExecute is sent out. Therefore, to display the duration of tasks, you must capture the OnPreExecute and OnPostExecute events, and then compare the times.

You can run the following TSQL statement against the dbo.sysssislog table. It displays each execution of a package, and the tasks contained within that execution, as well as their execution times.

```
    WITH Task_Details_CTE (ID,Source,SourceID,ExecutionID,StartTime,EndTime)
      AS                                        --provides the task exec. detail
(
SELECT sys1.ID, sys1.Source, sys1.SourceID, sys1.ExecutionID
     , sys1.StartTime, sys2.EndTime
  FROM dbo.sysssislog sys1
 INNER JOIN dbo.sysssislog sys2
    ON sys1.Event = 'OnPreExecute'           --gets only the start time
   AND sys2.Event = 'OnPostExecute'          --gets only the completed time
   AND sys1.ExecutionID = sys2.ExecutionID   --groups package execution
   AND sys2.SourceID = sys1.SourceID         --associates identical tasks
)

   SELECT                                       --identifies the "package" tasks
     CASE WHEN sys.SourceID = CTE.SourceID
          THEN CTE.Source + ' (' + convert(varchar(30),sys.starttime,100) + ')'
          ELSE '    TASK: ' + CTE.Source
      END AS [Package|Task]                     --indents tasks to package execs
        , CTE.StartTime
        , CTE.EndTime
        , RIGHT('00' + CAST(DATEDIFF(SECOND,CTE.StartTime, CTE.EndTime)/60
                        AS VARCHAR(20)),3) + ' min.' +
          RIGHT('0'  + CAST(DATEDIFF(SECOND,CTE.StartTime, CTE.EndTime)%60
                        AS VARCHAR(20)),2) + ' sec.' AS TaskDuration
     FROM dbo.sysssislog sys
 INNER JOIN Task_Details_CTE CTE
       ON sys.Event = 'PackageStart'          --lists single row pkg exec.
      AND sys.ExecutionID = CTE.ExecutionID
   ORDER BY SYS.ID, CTE.ID, CTE.StartTime    --orders by package, task
```

This query uses a *common table expression (CTE)* to perform the task associations. It joins the CTE with the task details to the package executions themselves, and performs some simple datediffs to create a duration in minutes and seconds. You can write this, of course, in several different ways, or extend it to include error details. Table 12-1 shows the query output.

Table 12-1

Package	Start Time	End Time	Duration
SSIS_SQL_Design.dtsx	2009-06-28 22:14:17	2009-06-28 22:20:43	6 min 26 sec
TASK: Truncate Staging	2009-06-28 22:14:17	2009-06-28 22:14:18	0 min 01 sec
TASK: Extract to Staging	2009-06-28 22:14:18	2009-06-28 22:14:31	0 min 13 sec
TASK: Update Attributes	2009-06-28 22:14:31	2009-06-28 22:16:22	1 min 51 sec
TASK: Load Header	2009-06-28 22:16:22	2009-06-28 22:17:10	0 min 48 sec
TASK: Load Detail	2009-06-28 22:17:10	2009-06-28 22:20:43	3 min 33 sec

Although simplistic in its output, this query does show the duration of each control flow task, the first step in identifying areas that need attention for performance tuning.

The point of identifying the task durations is to figure out which are the longest-running tasks. If the task is *not* a Data Flow Task, then SSIS has little control over the task duration. Here are some examples:

❑   If your FTP Task is taking a long time, then the issue is likely related to the time it takes to transfer a file from the FTP server to a local drive.

❑   If the longest task is an Execute SQL Task, SSIS has no control over the duration of the query that is being executed. Check the relational database where the query is being run for optimization, and consider revising the query for optimization or tuning the database.

❑   If you have an Analysis Services Processing task that is running forever, then you must evaluate the queries that SSAS is running against the underlying database, or consider a change in the way you process your cubes (such as an incremental process).

In many situations, you will experience performance problems with one or more Data Flow Tasks. If this is the case, then you will need to peel the onion back a little further to figure out what is the cause.

Identifying Data Flow Destination Issues

Data flow destinations are a common performance bottleneck in SSIS, usually because of how SSIS is inserting rows, or how efficient the destination can handle the data.

To identify whether the destination is a problem, you should perform two steps:

1.   *Perform a trace on the destination system.* If your destination is a flat file, your destination is probably not a problem (but you can still perform Step 2). If your destination is a table, what you are looking for is a high number of INSERT statements when your destination is inserting data. Perform a trace on the destination database and look for how often an INSERT statement is sent to the table. Having hundreds, thousands, or millions of INSERTs indicates that the destination is inserting one row at a time, and is not batch-loading the data. Figure 12-1 shows a profiler trace of SQL Server during a data flow process that is inserting rows with a destination adapter.

EventClass	TextData	ApplicationName	NTUserName	LoginName	CPU	Reads
RPC:Completed	exec sp_cursor 180150005,4,0,N'[Ful...	SSIS-OLE DB ...	Adminis...	SOLIDQ...	0	1
RPC:Completed	exec sp_cursor 180150005,4,0,N'[Ful...	SSIS-OLE DB ...	Adminis...	SOLIDQ...	0	1
RPC:Completed	exec sp_cursor 180150005,4,0,N'[Ful...	SSIS-OLE DB ...	Adminis...	SOLIDQ...	0	1
RPC:Completed	exec sp_cursor 180150005,4,0,N'[Ful...	SSIS-OLE DB ...	Adminis...	SOLIDQ...	0	1
RPC:Completed	exec sp_cursor 180150005,4,0,N'[Ful...	SSIS-OLE DB ...	Adminis...	SOLIDQ...	0	1
RPC:Completed	exec sp_cursor 180150005,4,0,N'[Ful...	SSIS-OLE DB ...	Adminis...	SOLIDQ...	0	1
RPC:Completed	exec sp_cursor 180150005,4,0,N'[Ful...	SSIS-OLE DB ...	Adminis...	SOLIDQ...	0	1
RPC:Completed	exec sp_cursor 180150005,4,0,N'[Ful...	SSIS-OLE DB ...	Adminis...	SOLIDQ...	0	1
RPC:Completed	exec sp_cursor 180150005,4,0,N'[Ful...	SSIS-OLE DB ...	Adminis...	SOLIDQ...	0	1
RPC:Completed	exec sp_cursor 180150005,4,0,N'[Ful...	SSIS-OLE DB ...	Adminis...	SOLIDQ...	0	1
RPC:Completed	exec sp_cursor 180150005,4,0,N'[Ful...	SSIS-OLE DB ...	Adminis...	SOLIDQ...	0	1
RPC:Completed	exec sp_cursor 180150005,4,0,N'[Ful...	SSIS-OLE DB ...	Adminis...	SOLIDQ...	0	1
RPC:Completed	exec sp_cursor 180150005,4,0,N'[Ful...	SSIS-OLE DB ...	Adminis...	SOLIDQ...	0	1
RPC:Completed	exec sp_cursor 180150005,4,0,N'[Ful...	SSIS-OLE DB ...	Adminis...	SOLIDQ...	0	1
RPC:Completed	exec sp_cursor 180150005,4,0,N'[Ful...	SSIS-OLE DB ...	Adminis...	SOLIDQ...	0	1
RPC:Completed	exec sp_cursor 180150005,4,0,N'[Ful...	SSIS-OLE DB ...	Adminis...	SOLIDQ...	0	1
RPC:Completed	exec sp_cursor 180150005,4,0,N'[Ful...	SSIS-OLE DB ...	Adminis...	SOLIDQ...	0	1
RPC:Completed	exec sp_cursor 180150005,4,0,N'[Ful...	SSIS-OLE DB ...	Adminis...	SOLIDQ...	0	1
RPC:Completed	exec sp_cursor 180150005,4,0,N'[Ful...	SSIS-OLE DB ...	Adminis...	SOLIDQ...	0	1
RPC:Completed	exec sp_cursor 180150005,4,0,N'[Ful...	SSIS-OLE DB ...	Adminis...	SOLIDQ...	0	1
RPC:Completed	exec sp_cursor 180150005,4,0,N'[Ful...	SSIS-OLE DB ...	Adminis...	SOLIDQ...	0	1
RPC:Completed	exec sp_cursor 180150005,4,0,N'[Ful...	SSIS-OLE DB ...	Adminis...	SOLIDQ...	0	1
RPC:Completed	exec sp_cursor 180150005,4,0,N'[Ful...	SSIS-OLE DB ...	Adminis...	SOLIDQ...	0	1

```
exec sp_cursor 180150005,4,0,N'[FullSalesLoad]',@DATE='2001-03-28
00:00:00',@STORE_ID=3190,@WEIGHT=5.9099998474121094,@ITEM_ID=2423,@ITEM_COUNT=3,@DISCOUNT_FLAG=0,@EXPIRED_FLAG=0
```

Trace is running.   Ln 34319, Col 1   Rows: 34354   Connections: 1

Figure 12-1

The issue here is that the destination is not doing a fast load process, which can be debilitating to a data flow! The "Solution" section later in this chapter outlines how to optimize destinations through the destination adapter properties, and how to deal with indexes and partitioned tables.

2. *Identify the impact of the destination adapters.* You may not see a bunch of INSERT statements in Step 1, but you still may have destination problems. The next step is to quantify just how much impact the destination adapters are having on the data flow.

Essentially, run your data flow with the destination adapters, and capture the total data flow execution time. Next, replace the destination adapters with Multicast transformations (Multicast will just be used as a placeholder, and has no overhead because there is no output) and re-run the data flow. Compare the execution times. It's simple, but effective. Figure 12-2 shows the same data flow two times with this approach taken.

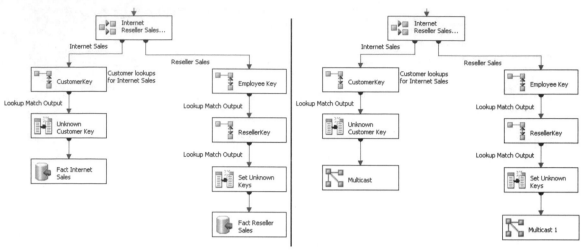

Figure 12-2

If your revised data flow performs a lot faster, then you know that you have a problem with your destination. Common problems include indexes or triggers on your destinations tables. The "Solution" section later in this chapter reviews how to optimize destinations.

Identifying Transformation and Memory Bottlenecks

Maybe you have tuned your data flow destinations, but you still must optimize the transformations. When it comes to transformations, the most important thing to be aware of is your system memory. Therefore, one big area of focus for data flow scalability is memory management — identifying when you exceed thresholds, and when you need more memory to leverage for performance.

> When identifying the bottleneck of a system, you can use the standard Performance Monitor (Perfmon) counters, such as memory usage and paging, disk throughput and queue lengths, and processor utilization. Although out of the scope of this discussion, they are the foundation to identifying which server resource is constraining the processes.

Within the transformation layer of an SSIS data flow, often you will see bottlenecks in the area of memory and disk input/output (I/O). If you are seeing both, and the only application running on your server is SSIS (and your destinations are on a different server), chances are that the disk I/O is being caused by the limited memory. Low memory causes the operating system to start using virtual memory and swapping files between the physical disk and the physical memory. Low memory also causes SSIS to start using temporary space on a drive to manage the size of the memory request. This is called *buffer spooling*, and it can quickly escalate to very poor SSIS package performance.

To identify transformation bottlenecks, you should use Perfmon, including a couple of the SSIS Pipeline counters. The most important SSIS counter is the SSIS "Pipeline: Buffers spooled" counter. Any time it goes over 0, you have a memory problem.

Now it's time for an illustration of how to use Perfmon to identify data flow memory issues. Figure 12-3 shows a package that is importing five identical flat files (each contain approximately two million records). They are first brought together through a Union All transformation, and then sent into a Sort transformation, which applies an order across the five columns in the file. They are being landed into a Row Count transformation for demonstration purposes.

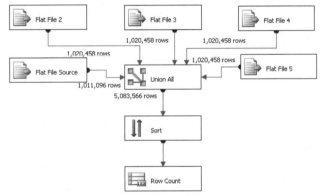

Figure 12-3

On a single processor machine with 1GB of memory (with about 300MB of memory free), the package ran into performance problems when the memory reached the 1GB limit of physical RAM. This package took just more than 20 minutes to execute. Visually, through the debugger, when the package reached about 10 million rows read, the package significantly slowed. Figure 12-4 shows Performance Monitor counters (of this execution), including "Memory: Available MBytes," "Physical Disk: Average Disk Queue Length," "SQL Server SSIS Pipeline 10: Rows read," and "SQL Server SSIS Pipeline 10: Buffers spooled."

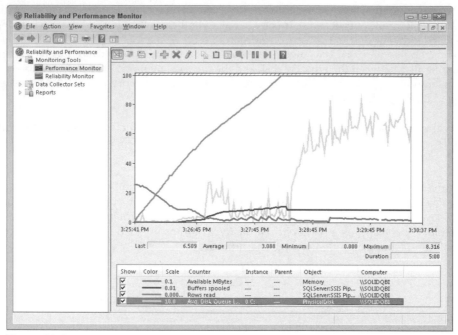

Figure 12-4

As you can see, as soon as "Memory: Available MBytes" neared 0, the number of rows read started to slow down, and the server started experiencing disk I/O issues (the "Physical Disk: Disk Queue Length" began spiking over 2). The package began to use temporary disk space to complete its operation, and you can see this because the "SSIS Pipeline: Buffers spooled" shows that SSIS needed to temporarily store more than 600 buffers to disk during this execution. With approximately 10,000 records per buffer, that is about 6 million rows temporarily stored to disk.

Second, after all the rows were pulled into the Sort transformation (when the Rows Read maxed at 1,000,000 — or 100 with the scale adjustment), then the Sort transformation began processing the data. At this point, the Disk Queue Length jumped to more than 6, which is two to three times an acceptable rate for a single disk drive. Clearly, this package was unable to run efficiently on this system.

When the same machine is upgraded to 2GB of RAM, and the package is run again, this time it completes in 2 minutes 38 seconds. Figure 12-5 shows the Performance Monitor counters during the second execution.

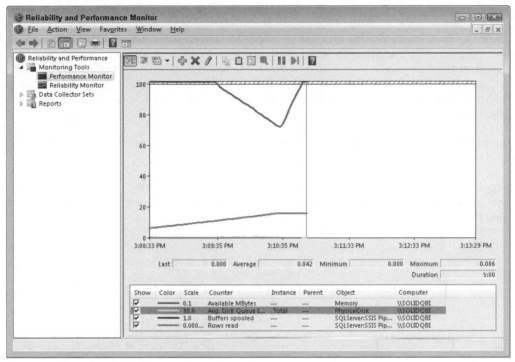

Figure 12-5

As you can see, during this execution, the "Memory: Available MBytes" counter never reached 0, showing the amount of physical RAM was sufficient. The "Physical Disk: Disk Queue Length" rarely increased over 0, showing the disk was sufficiently handling the I/O needs. And the "SSIS Pipeline: Buffers spooled" counter showed that SSIS never needed to spool buffers to disk.

The second execution ran almost ten times faster as the first test. After a review of the "Available MBytes" captured during the second execution, this simple package needed approximately 700MB of memory for efficient execution. Because the first execution started out at about 300MB of available memory, this means that the machine had a memory deficiency of approximately 400MB, which translated to a heavy performance hit.

This overall comparison demonstrates that a sufficient amount of system memory can keep your data flows leveraging the memory, eliminating the need to use temporary storage. Furthermore, when the data flow started spooling buffers to disk, it caused a disk bottleneck on the system, and the disk queue length jumped up well over 2, indicating that the disk I/O could not keep up with the I/O requests.

Memory management is key when it comes to SSIS performance, and several of the data flow optimization techniques reviewed in the "Design" and "Solution" sections later in this chapter show ways to manage the amount of memory that is needed in order to optimize the buffers and package execution.

Identifying Data Flow Source Performance Issues

Similar to destinations, sources can also impact data flow performance. And, just like you identified destination issues by tracing the database engine, you can also leverage the relational database query tools to identify when you have a problem with a source query. If you are extracting from a file, chances are the source adapter is not the problem, but it never hurts to test anyhow. Just like the destination tests, you can test the source extractions by themselves, and you can also use the database engine tools to determine how the query is executing.

The first test involves running the source adapters by themselves, and comparing the time the entire data flow takes to run against just extracting the data from the sources.

First capture the execution time for your entire data flow. Next, delete all your transformations and connect each source to a Multicast transformation. (This allows the rows to get consumed by the pipeline engine.) Figure 12-6 highlights a data flow with only the sources.

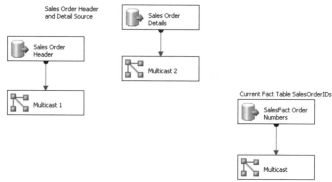

Figure 12-6

If the total time it takes to extract data from your source is about the same time for the entire data flow, then chances are you have a source bottleneck. The question is, what should you expect for data extraction performance? A good general rule is that you should at least see 250,000 rows per minute being extracted. That's pretty modest. If SQL Server is the source and the source is optimized, you could even see several million rows per minute.

The giveaway that you have a source query problem is if the time taken before the rows even start being consumed by the data flow is long. This situation means the source database can't optimize the query, because it doesn't have the right indexes, or the query is too complicated.

The second test is to take the source query and, using your favorite query management tool, run the query plan and observe the results.

As you are looking at the query plan, you want to look out for some telling signs. Look for table scans and index scans. They usually indicate problems. Of course, if you are pulling all the rows from a table, then you should expect to see scans. However, if you are targeting a portion of a table, then watch out for a scan that covers an entire table.

Because this is not a query-tuning book, you won't find detailed techniques on optimizing a query, but here are some quick principles:

❑ If your source query is very complicated, consider using the data flow transformations to handle some of the logic, and then reduce the complexity of the query (see the "Design" section).

❑ If you are seeing table scans, then you don't have a clustered index on the table, and possibly not a primary key. In most cases, both a clustered index and primary key can help optimize source queries.

❑ Also, review the data extraction principles in Chapter 5 on limiting the impact on source systems. You may want to consider staging the raw table data and moving the data transformation logic to the data flow.

The next section presents some principles on how to effectively leverage SSIS for data processing.

Design

SSIS is an application platform that focuses on processing data. And, like any platform, as you well know by now, there are good techniques and poor techniques. Design *is* important. In fact, design plays the biggest role in SSIS performance — good and bad. What this means is that you must pay attention to how you design your packages, as well as what features you use and how you use them.

This section starts out by addressing the most important design consideration — how to balance SQL operations with data flow operations. Later in this section is a review of the data flow engine, which leads into a design example of how to leverage the data flow.

Balancing SQL Operations with the Data Flow

This section provides the principles for knowing when to apply SQL functionality (leveraging the underlying database) versus the SSIS data flow. Comparing the data flow with SQL statements, indeed, is a matter of scalability, because the appropriate use of SQL code and the data flow enable your solutions to scale. In essence, this comparison is about choosing the right tool for the job.

Before diving into the details, take a look at Table 12-2, which provides a summary of the SQL disadvantages as compared to the SSIS data flow advantages. But don't fret if you are a SQL guru! There are also SQL advantages over and above SSIS.

Table 12-2

SQL Disadvantages	SSIS Data Flow Advantages
Load then transform (ELT)	Transform then load (ETL)
Sequential and serialized	Parallel/asynchronous
Disk I/O and RDBMS intensive	Memory intensive
All or nothing statements	Built in restartability
Error rows rollback statements	Error rows can be redirected
Limited data cleansing	Fuzzy matching and text mining
Complex query statements	Built-in common transformations
Auditing requires customization	Built-in logging features
1 to 1, source to destination	N to M, union/merge/split/duplicate
Join requires all data must be in SQL	Join across any source types
Large transactions	Batch-driven capabilities

As you can see, the SSIS pipeline engine for ETL operations offers some compelling advantages. The advantages are fully developed later in this discussion. But the SSIS data flow also has its drawbacks. Table 12-3 summarizes the limitations.

Table 12-3

SQL-Advantages	SSIS Disadvantages
SET-based updates	Row-based updates (cursor-like)
Sort performance (ORDER BY)	Sorting requires a lot of memory
Direct RDBMS integration	Requires data access providers
Limited data conversion overhead	Sources and destinations require data type checking overhead
Good performance with grouping	Grouping requires a lot of memory
Advanced queries (IE recursion)	Limited support for advanced queries

In the end, you will need to decide when to apply SQL logic verses data flow components. Of course, every situation is unique, but there are some principles to follow, outlined later in this discussion.

Data Flow Advantages as Compared with SQL

The goal of this discussion is to set the stage for making a determination of when to use each technology (using a SQL statement or the SSIS data flow) in your ETL process.

❑ *The data flow can perform true in-line transformation processing* — This means that, while data is being extracted into the data flow pipeline, business transformation logic can be performed on the data before it is loaded to the destination. SQL-based processing has a limited ELT-type architecture, meaning extraction, loading, and then transforming. When you are using SQL code to process data, the data must first be moved from one location to another, and then transformed. In-line transformations are not possible with Transact-SQL.

❑ *The data flow has the capability to perform transformations asynchronously or in parallel on the same data stream being brought into the pipeline* — This provides greater scalability by reducing the steps needed to transform your data. Contrastingly, SQL scripts are inherently synchronous processes, meaning that Step 1 must be fully complete before Step 2, and Step 2 before Step 3. If you have a source flat file that must be brought into your database, first the bulk copy (BCP) step must finish loading data to a staging table, then the update or transformation process must complete before the data is ready to be loaded, and then, finally, the data can be inserted into the destination. The SSIS data flow can be extracting the same data, transforming the data in-memory, and loading the data at the same time.

❑ *The SSIS pipeline engine leverages system memory to scale its operations, which can perform exponentially better than disk operations* — Memory I/O operations are much faster than disk I/O operations. Therefore, when your server has enough memory to handle the data flow process, your packages will perform tremendously well. SQL inherently causes disk I/O, which, for large operations, is very intensive and often the bottleneck for an ETL process. The disk I/O overhead comes from the underlying relational database dependency that any RDBMS has by the obligation of consistency and durability.

❑ *The SSIS data flow has the capability to handle data flow errors without affecting the entire data set* — For example, when a row is being processed through the data flow, and a conversion error happens on a particular value, that row can be redirected and handled separately. The row can either be brought back into the same pipeline, or sent out to an error row table. On the other hand, SQL code is an all-or-nothing proposition when processing data. For sure, SQL has error handling, but the error handling is at the batch level, not the row level. If one row being converted fails, the entire batch statement fails.

❑ *Within a single SSIS data flow, the source-to-destination transformation can involve many-to-many mappings* — This means that you are able to bring data together from many sources, perform transformations, do data correlation, multicast or conditionally split the data, and then land the data in multiple destinations simultaneously. A SQL INSERT statement, on the other hand, is fixed with one-to-one, source-to-destination mapping.

❑ *The SSIS data flow contains data cleansing, text mining, and data-mining capabilities, which provide advanced data transformation logic beyond the standard capabilities that SQL scripting can perform* — With a host of out-of-the-box basic and advanced transformations (including the Fuzzy Grouping, Fuzzy Lookup, Term Extraction, Term Lookup, and Data Mining Query transformations), the SSIS data flow can handle many unique and complicated scenarios not easily handled by SQL functionality.

❑ *When dealing with large data insert operations, the data flow can handle large data sets by batching inserts through the destination adapter's advanced properties* — A review of these features appears later in the "Solution" section of this chapter. SQL can also perform batching when doing bulk INSERT operations. For normal INSERT statements, the entire data set being loaded must be handled in one transaction, which often comes with long commit times.

In all, the data flow provides some nice benefits and features over and above what a SQL-based process can perform for many operations that are very common for ETL.

SQL Advantages when Compared with the Data Flow

SQL has several advantages when compared with data flow. SQL contains some significant value over and above the data flow for some ETL operations:

❏ *SQL inherently has the capability to perform set-based updates* — This concept has been discussed in several places in this book, but is important to highlight here because, when compared with how the data flow performs updates, SQL is able to significantly scale beyond the data flow. To perform an update natively in the data flow requires the use of the OLE DB Command transformation, which runs the UPDATE statement one row at a time. SQL can handle the update in a single operation by joining a temporary table with the table to be updated.

❏ *Relational database engines can perform sorting operations efficiently with appropriate indexing* — With large tables where scans are necessary, even though sorting with the ORDER BY statement may require inefficient query plans, the sort can often complete faster than leveraging the SSIS data flow Sort transformation. This will be true in cases where the SSIS server does not have enough memory to fit the sort set into the private buffer cache. When this happens, SSIS is forced to write temporary information to disk, severely impacting the performance of the transformation, as well as other packages and data flows being executed.

❏ *SQL operations perform natively in the database engine* — Because of this integration, code written in SQL has less conversion operations and, therefore, less chance for conversion failures with implicit conversions. The data flow requires data conversions into the pipeline engine and conversions out of the pipeline into the destination. The data flow also relies on data access providers to connect and import or export, whereas data coming from a SQL table into another SQL table is much more integrated with the database engine.

❏ *SQL (specifically TSQL) excels in performing advanced queries* — This includes recursive self-joins, correlated subqueries, multi-table joins, and more. Although the data flow can perform various data correlation operations in the data flow, some queries are too difficult to model with the available out-of-the-box transformations.

As you can see, SQL-based operations provide some valuable functionality that, when leveraged, can assist in providing scalability to your packages.

Applying SQL Code in Your SSIS Packages

In all, after comparing the data flow and SQL code, here are a few areas where SQL can effectively be used within SSIS:

❏ One area is where an UPDATE statement (as opposed to an INSERT statement) is required, and the number of records that need to be updated is more than several thousand. Leveraging SQL code for a set-based update scales your operation. If your current set-based operations are merely transformation logic not affecting existing destination rows, then look to integrate that transformation logic into the data flow.

❑ Storing auditing and logging information in a database enables easy querying and reporting. Therefore, SQL can provide the mechanism to integrate between a relational database and SSIS, through the Execute SQL Task. This use of SQL and the database applies to auditing tables (reviewed in Chapter 2) for capturing performance and status information; management tables for tracking metadata administration information (such as persisting incremental extraction information); and procedures and functions that drive the auditing and lineage.

❑ Within the data flow itself, custom SQL can enable faster performance and better scalability for source queries when used to filter data, order data (ORDER BY), or perform some join logic when the data is in the same database and indexes support the query.

❑ Managing indexes and partitioned tables requires SQL logic to drop indexes; create, split, or switch partitions; or rebuild indexes.

What is often the case is that SQL is overused within an SSIS package. Many solutions exist that simply run Execute SQL Tasks over and over. Although these TSQL-based solutions can still leverage the precedence and logging support in SSIS, there is really no use of the data flow engine, and the drawbacks of SQL as described earlier in this section become apparent.

SSIS Pipeline Architecture Concepts

Before demonstrating how to leverage the SSIS data flow engine, the following presents some general concepts to help you understand what is happening within the data flow engine.

First, the SSIS data flow engine uses data buffers (allocated blocks of memory) to manage data as it flows through the pipeline. As data is extracted from the sources, it is consumed into these reserved memory spaces, called *buffers*. Each buffer contains approximately 10,000 rows (although this number can be adjusted, as described later in the "Solution" section). These buffers are acted upon by the various transformations as the data flows through the transformations to the destination.

Here are some key points about the engine, which can help you understand how to design effective data flow solutions:

❑ When data is loaded into a buffer, the transformation logic is applied to the data in place (where possible). In a sense, the transformations pass over the buffers, giving SSIS the capability to handle high volumes of data in the pipeline. These inline buffer changes are cheap as compared to when the pipeline needs to copy data to new buffers. In some cases, the source data can be in the process of extraction while at the same time, data is being landed to a destination.

❑ Transformations can be categorized as blocking transformations, partially blocking, or streaming transformations (streaming transformations are sometimes called *row transformations*). *Blocking transformations* (such as the Aggregate or Sort transformations) hold all the rows up in the pipeline before they are allowed downstream. *Partially blocking transformations* hold up a portion of the data, and *streaming transformations* allow the data to be available to the next transformation immediately.

❑ Partially blocking and blocking transformations have asynchronous outputs, meaning that the output of the transformation is not synchronously connected to the inputs of the next transformation. The effect is that the data in the buffers is copied to a new buffer from the upstream transformation to the downstream transformation. Because of the creation of new buffers and the copy process, these transformations have some resource overhead.

❑ The Conditional Split and Multicast are examples of streaming components, even though they appear to copy data. Their outputs are synchronous and, therefore, their operations perform logical multicasting and splitting, not physical. This helps optimize the data flow by limiting the places that require data copies, which are expensive. The Union All transformation has an asynchronous output and is, therefore, a semi-blocking transformation, even though it appears to be streaming.

❑ Each data flow has *execution trees*, which are groupings of sources, transformations, and destinations based on whether data is copied to new buffers (asynchronous outputs).

❑ The maximum number of process threads that can work on the transformations in the data flow is controlled by the EngineThreads property for each data flow. For a complicated data flow, ensure that you set this property to at least the number of execution trees, and possibly more, depending on how complicated your data flow is, and how many cores you have in your server. Each execution tree can use more than one process thread (in SSIS 2008).

❑ Execution trees and engine thread mappings are viewable by logging the PipelineExecutionTrees and PipelineExecutionPlan events, which are available in the SSIS Logging at the data flow level.

Data Flow Design Example

To illustrate some of the concepts reviewed in this section, let's consider a very SQL-intensive SSIS package, and then see how it can be rewritten with the SSIS data flow.

SQL-Centric SSIS Process

This example package is fairly typical of an integration process that imports data from some flat files, performs some cleanup operations, and then inserts the data into a couple destination tables. Figure 12-7 shows the control flow design of the package with its various steps.

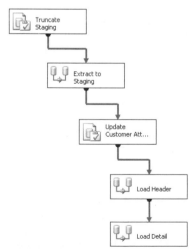

Figure 12-7

The package has several data flows, a couple Execute SQL Tasks, and several precedence constraints that control when things happen. Here are some of the detailed steps to explain what is going on in this package:

1. Truncation of two staging tables

2. Data extraction from two flat files into the staging tables, executed in parallel

3. An UPDATE statement run against the staging table to associate and update data in one of the staging tables

4. A data flow that performs some cleansing logic in the SQL Statement source, and inserts data into the header destination table

5. The insert table data flow process to load data into the detail destination table

The data flows in Steps 2, 4, and 5 are straightforward. No SSIS-based transformation logic is applied. They simply extract the data from the source, and insert the data into the destination. Figure 12-8 shows an example data flow task from Step 2, highlighting the import process.

Figure 12-8

This example package takes a few minutes to run and processes about 500,000 rows. In fact, here are the detailed execution times on a modest server.

❑ Step 1: 0 minutes 01 second

❑ Step 2: 0 minutes 13 seconds

❑ Step 3: 1 minute 51 seconds

❑ Step 4: 0 minutes 48 seconds

❑ Step 5: 3 minutes 33 seconds

❑ *Total: 6 minutes 26 seconds*

You may be thinking, "not bad." And, truth be told, this is a simple example with a small data set, and the execution time is reasonable for the volume. Even if the volume and execution time are ten times more, you may have plenty of time in your ETL window to handle this volume. But watch out. SSIS (like its predecessor DTS) has a tendency to sprawl. You may end up with dozens or hundreds of packages running during a nightly window, and every second and server resource all of a sudden become important.

This package has three primary shortcomings:

❑ There are too many steps for such a simple operation, and each Task must complete before the next Task can run. In the staging steps, the very last row must be landed before the next step can begin. This process is very synchronous, and mostly serial, and impacts your overall execution time.

❑ It uses SQL operations for simple transformations that can be handled in the data flow. Step 3 is the culprit here. Although it is doing a set-based update (which is often a good thing), the problem is that it's simply updating values to perform data cleansing. This can easily be done in the data flow (as the next example shows), and it adds another step in the middle of the process that is unnecessary.

❑ The disk I/O impact of this package is tremendous. Two staging tables and an unnecessary SQL operation will generate a high I/O hit on the system. Every staging table generates twice the I/O impact of the data because you are landing the data to a table, and then pulling the data immediately off the same table — writing the data to disk, then reading the data from disk. If you have several of these types of packages, you'll be spending a lot of money on an overly expensive storage area network (SAN).

Rather than leave it there, step back for a second and think about how you could create a more optimized and efficient design. Can you change the way some of the package is designed? How can you reduce the I/O? Are there certain steps that are still needed?

Now take a look at one redesign approach of the same package.

Rewritten Data Flow–Centric SSIS Process

The goal of this section is to demonstrate how you can fully utilize the SSIS engine to make a more efficient process, and reduce the overall execution time of the previous example.

To accomplish this goal, and to make a compelling case, the redesign removes all the steps except for a single data flow task. Figure 12-9 shows a data flow that handles the same process as the package highlighted in Figure 12-7, except that the staging tables are removed and the update statement is gone, and the destinations are handled at the same time.

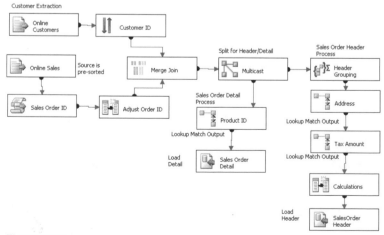

Figure 12-9

Here are some details around how this data flow handles the same process:

1. Two flat-file source adapters to import the text data

2. A Sort transformation to order the customer data

3. A Merge Join transformation that joins the customer and sales source data together

4. A Multicast transformation

5. Several Lookup transformations to associate related data from other tables and return values needed for the destination

6. A Derived Column transformation to calculate metrics

7. Two destination adapters to insert the data into the tables in parallel

When the package is run, the total execution time is 37 seconds. This is about ten times faster than the previous package with the same logic — small scale, but impressive.

Another hidden benefit is the I/O. The counters indicate that the total I/O was reduced from 2GB of I/O activity on the disk down to 120MB total. That's 16 times less I/O with the optimized package.

This package goes a little overboard in trying to fit everything into one data flow, but this design is deliberate to illustrate the point of how leveraging the data flow in many cases can yield performance gains. When the data volumes increase, this leverage becomes even more important. However, you must also be conscious of memory management, as discussed earlier in the "Problem" section of this chapter.

In summary, package design is the most important factor in performance and scalability. And, like many of you know, no substitute exists for getting the design right the first time. Trying to change an SSIS solution after it has been deployed always presents challenges (both political and process). So, be conscious as soon as you can, and put the right design in place. It will go a long way to an efficient, manageable, and scalable environment.

Solution

This final section presents many practical SSIS scalability practices. Use them in your package designs to build solutions that scale.

The section begins by looking at tuning techniques for your data flow, including data flow properties, and concludes by addressing destination-tuning practices, including how to efficiently insert data into a partitioned table.

Tuning Your Data Flow

Thus far, you have learned how to identify problem areas in your data flows, and how to design effective processes in SSIS. This section extends that discussion by considering the detailed implementation practices for an efficient data flow, beginning with data flow transformations, and concluding with destinations.

Use Blocking Transformations Sparingly

Blocking transformations (such as Sort, Aggregate, and Fuzzy Grouping) hold up all the data flow data in memory. They can especially impact performance when dealing with large data sets in the pipeline. If you do not have enough memory to handle these operations, then SSIS uses temporary disk space to store data, which increases I/O and processor impact.

Limit your use of these transformations and, when you use them, ensure that the server can handle the memory load.

Limit Row-by-Row Operations

A row-by-row (or *row-based*) operation requires that independent actions be taken, one at a time, for each row going through the particular transformation. The worst offender is the OLE DB Command transformation, because it calls an OLE DB command (such as an UPDATE statement or stored procedure) for every row that is sent through it. The non-cached Lookup, Fuzzy Lookup, Import and Export Column, and Slowly Changing Dimension transformations all exhibit similar characteristics. To be sure, these transformations provide valuable functionality in moderate to low volumes, or where expected package execution time is flexible.

Use row-based transformations in situations where your data flow record counts are in the thousands, and not hundreds of thousands, or millions. Consider set-based SQL statements as a replacement.

Manage Data Flow Backpressure

Backpressure is the situation when a transformation or destination is causing enough impact that the upstream data feed has to slow down because the transformation or destination cannot keep up. For example, blocking transformations and row-by-row transformations often cause backpressure in your data flow. For example, if an Aggregate transformation is being used, and there is either not enough RAM to handle all the buffers in memory, or not enough processor utilization to handle the Aggregate calculations, then the upstream source extraction or transformation will be slowed down. Another example is if you have an OLE DB Command transformation that is not using up memory, but the rows are going so slow through the transformation that the upstream transformations slow down. If you are trying to extract data from a source as quickly as possible, then you must resolve the backpressure.

Resolve backpressure by ensuring you have enough memory available, or limiting the use of blocking transformations or row-based transformations.

Pre-sort Sources as an Alternative to the Sort Transformation

You can tell a source adapter that the data is pre-sorted, and, therefore, limit the Sort transformation use (see the Fact Sales example in Chapter 8). As already mentioned in the "Design" section of this chapter, a relational database can effectively apply an ORDER BY statement to reduce or eliminate the need to use the Sort transformation. However, flat files may also be created in a physical sort order. Therefore, you can set up these and any source adapters to know that the data entering the pipeline is sorted. Other transformations such as Merge and Merge Join require that the inputs be sorted. You can preserve memory, and enhance performance, by eliminating the Sort. Pre-sorting requires the input source and column properties to be modified.

When you need to sort data in a data flow, check to see whether you can order the sources as they are coming into the data flow, and you will save overhead and memory.

Optimize the Lookup and Managing the Cache Size

When you have a large table required for a Lookup transformation reference table, you can use a few methods to optimize its performance. First, a non-cached lookup is a row-based operation, and when your input row count is large, then the cost of every source row causing a separate database query is expensive. Therefore, using a partial cache or full-cache Lookup transformation is better.

A *partial cache* builds the cache as the Lookup transformation is executing, and, therefore, also comes with high transaction impact. A partial cache approach is a viable solution if you have a large number of input rows, but the unique count of distinct values is low for the lookup key columns.

However, the best option is to use the *full-cache* feature of the Lookup transformation, and filter the reference table.

Following are two approaches that can filter the reference table cache:

❑ *Apply an 80/20 rule and load one Lookup transformation with 20 percent (or some smaller percentage) of the most common matching records, which will allow at least 80 percent matches in the full cache —* Then, for any row that does not match, redirect the row to a non-cached lookup which will catch the rest of non-matched rows. This approach would look like the data flow in Figure 12-10, and greatly reduce the memory requirement.

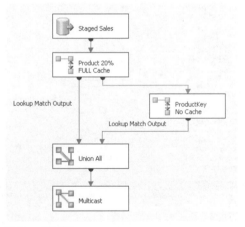

Figure 12-10

❑ *Filter the* Lookup transformation *to use a view or hard-coded SQL statement that only loads the rows that are needed in the Lookup transformation cache —* This assumes, however, that you know which rows need to be available in the Lookup transformation cache. To do this, you must have the matching key columns from the source in a staging table on the same server. If you already have a staging table, then you can simply perform an `INNER JOIN` with the primary Lookup transformation reference table (hard-coding the SQL statement or using a SQL view). If you don't already have a staging table, then you must add a new data flow to your package (before the data flow that contains the Lookup transformation cache) that creates a staging table with only the matching key columns.

The following code shows a SQL statement used in a lookup that filters the lookup cache by only data rows that are in a staging table:

```
SELECT ProductKey, DimProduct.ProductAlternateKey
  FROM dbo.DimProduct
 INNER JOIN SSIS_PDS.dbo.stgFactInternetAndResellerSales
    ON DimProduct.ProductAlternateKey
     = stgFactInternetAndResellerSales.ProductAlternateKey
```

You may be surprised, but this approach often produces a package that will run faster than not filtering the Lookup transformation (because of saved memory), even though there is an added data flow. And, in many cases, this approach will allow the use of the full-cache Lookup transformation, where before it was not possible.

However, when all else fails and you need to use a non-cached Lookup transformation, then you should at least be sure that the underlying reference table has an index with the matching key columns as the first column in the index, followed by the Lookup transformation return columns.

Remove Unused Columns from the Data Flow

An often unheeded warning in the execution results is that columns exist in the data flow that are not being used downstream in the pipeline. Figure 12-11 shows the common warning message.

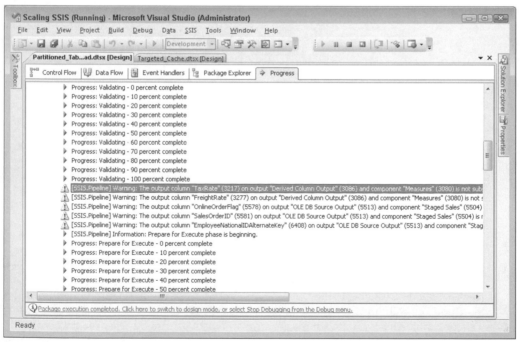

Figure 12-11

Sometimes this message is seen as an annoyance, but, in reality, it is a very important warning. What is happening is that the pipeline engine is reserving space in the buffers when columns are not being used downstream, which can cause significant memory overhead. With the extra columns, your data flow buffers take up more space than necessary. By removing the columns, you are making more memory available for other operations. To be sure, you can only remove columns between execution trees (after an asynchronous transformation output), such as within the Union All, Aggregate, Sort, Merge Join, and other transformations with asynchronous outputs,

Edit your transformations and only let the columns through if they are being used! (This technique is similar to the DBA tenet of never using SELECT * and, instead, always naming only the columns needed in a SQL SELECT statement so that the SQL engine can optimize the query.)

Be Mindful of the SSIS Logging Impact

SSIS logging certainly provides a valuable tool for monitoring and troubleshooting packages, but be aware of the overhead. Logging every event and having a complicated package produces a lot of overhead activity for the package. Furthermore, if the underlying connection that the logging is configured to use is a database connection (as opposed to a file), it can generate hundreds of database calls.

Limit the logging to only the OnPreExecute, OnPostExecute, OnWarning, OnError, *and* OnTaskFailed *events to reduce the possibility of your logging significantly impacting your package performance.*

Regulate Transactions

Be careful of the impact of transactions on your data flow. When you set the TransactionOption property of a package or task to "required," SSIS uses the Distributed Transaction Coordinator (DTC, a system service) to allow transaction association with various technologies. However, this service comes with overhead, and using native transactions in the database with which you are working may be better (depending on your situation). For example, for SQL Server, coordinating Execute SQL Tasks before and after your data flow with BEGIN TRAN and COMMIT TRAN allows you to use native transactions.

The bigger impact of transactions is rollback time. If you have large volumes in your data flow and get an error near the end of the large transaction, rolling back your transaction may take just as much time (if not more) as it did to process the data flow before the error! And, if you set a transaction on the entire package or parent package, this problem is exacerbated. Review the Chapter 10 discussion on reliability, which will help you design your restartability and ensure that your database is in a consistent state.

Apply transactions to manageable data sizes (based on what the task is doing), or consider using database snapshots to handle your rollback needs.

Setting Data Flow Properties

Each Data Flow Task has a series of properties and settings that are important to know and understand so that you can tune your data flows. Figure 12-12 highlights a simple data flow with the Properties window showing.

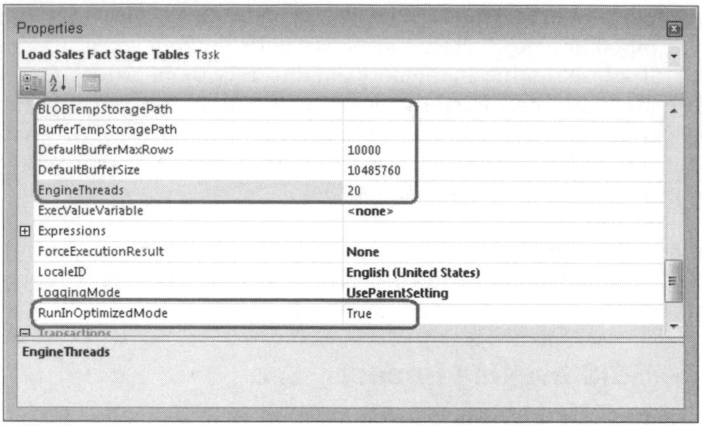

Figure 12-12

Highlighted in Figure 12-12 are six properties that each Data Flow Task has that can affect performance. Take the following into consideration when you are working with these properties.

Up the EngineThreads Value

The EngineThreads data flow property determines the most number of threads that a data flow can use. You should consider jumping up the value of the EngineThreads property from the default to 20 or 30, just to ensure that each execution tree has at least one thread it can use. Even if your server only has two or four processors, many process threads can be running efficiently in parallel, because each may not be working with the same level of intensity, or require code execution for every processor cycle. However, remember that this property is just a hint to the scheduler; there is no danger of creating a set of unused threads by setting this value too high.

Be sure to set the EngineThreads property on your data flow to at least the number of execution trees that the data flow contains.

Optimize the Temporary Storage Locations

The BufferTempStoragePath and BLOBTempStoragePath properties tell the data flow where to store temporary data to disk, if needed. By leaving these blank, SSIS will use the system-defined temp path in the server's system properties. If the data flow ever needs to use temporary space, be sure that it is pointing to a system volume or mount point that has higher I/O throughput. Setting this property is especially important when dealing with large object binary data (either flowing through your data flow or through the use of the Import or Export Column transformations) because binary large object (BLOB) data such as images takes up considerably more space than standard numeric or character data types.

Change the BufferTempStoragePath and BLOBTempStoragePath to drive locations that have been optimized, and ensure they are not using the system drive (the local C:\ drive) of the server.

Leave RunInOptimizedMode as True

RunInOptimizedMode helps performance by removing columns from execution trees with leaf components (such as destinations or other transformations that terminate a pipeline) where a column is not used in the leaf component. This does *not* mean that columns are removed from other execution trees if a column is no longer needed after already being used in an earlier transformation. You should still apply the principle mentioned earlier of removing columns from components that have asynchronous outputs not used downstream in a data flow.

Leave the RunInOptimizedMode value set at True.

Tune Buffers

Two advanced properties of the data flow enable you to tune the size and number of rows that are in the allocated buffers. These settings, DefaultBufferMaxRows and DefaultBufferSize, apply to all the different buffers in a data flow, not just a single buffer type for one of the execution trees.

Essentially, the DefaultBufferMaxRows is defaulted to 10,000, which means that no single buffer can have more than 10,000 rows. However, this setting may not be optimal if your average row width is very small, because the buffers will be small, and in total there will be many more buffers for the execution trees to manage. So, in these cases, consider revising this number upward and testing performance.

The DefaultBufferSize is also a threshold setting specifying the number of bytes that a single buffer cannot exceed. If the maximum row setting multiplied by the width of a single row is greater than this value, then the number of rows used in the buffer will be reduced to be under this limitation. For example, if the DefaultBufferMaxRows is set to 10,000 and the DefaultBufferSize is set to 10,485,760 and a single row is 1,200 bytes, then the calculation of max rows (10,000) times row width (1,200) equates to 12,000,000, which is greater than the DefaultBufferSize (10,485,760). So, the pipeline engine would scale back the count of rows in the buffers so that this threshold would not be exceeded.

No magical formula exists for determining how to set and balance these properties. It is a matter of testing, because each transformation that is used in a data flow is affected differently by the size and row count in the buffers. Buffer size and row counts do have an effect on batching rows into a destination, which is discussed in the next section.

Database and Destination Optimization

One of the more important factors in scaling a package is ensuring that you have optimized the destination inserts. This topic has been partly addressed in other chapters (such as Chapter 8), but this concluding section covers several advanced considerations, such as destination properties and partitioned tables.

Limiting Database Growth

With SQL Server, when the underlying database files reach a certain saturation point, the server will pause operations and grow the files. This is a problem if you or your DBA are not performing file-management operations to ensure that the file growth does not happen during peak hours, or during ETL operations. Because ETL and other data processing operations perform bulk data inserting, database growth is more possible during these times. If you see your destinations chugging along, and all of a sudden they pause for a long period of time, then it may be caused by a database growth process (or a locking/blocking condition).

For SQL Server, be sure to set your destination database Auto Shrink setting to False; otherwise, the files will shrink, and then more space will have to be reallocated, which takes time. Also, pre-allocate enough space in your files so that you will not experience a database growth situation during your ETL.

Consider Dropping and Re-creating Indexes on Destination Tables

When records are inserted into a relational table (or updated) and the table has indexes, the engine must reorganize the underlying indexes before the commit process is complete, which can add significant overhead to your data flow destinations.

To understand the overall impact of the indexes, in your test environment, drop all the indexes on the destination table and rerun the data flow, which will show you the delta of change and impact of the indexes.

A very common optimization technique for bulk operations is to first drop the indexes on the destination, run the data load, and then re-create the indexes. Dropping and re-creating the indexes is more often than not faster than inserting the records with the indexes in place, and forcing the relational engine to manage the changes.

Using the OLE DB Destination Adapter

The most common destination adapter used to insert data into a relational database is the OLE DB Destination adapter. This is because the ADO.NET Destination adapter often doesn't perform as well as the OLE DB Destination. To be sure, the ADO.NET adapter is fine to use, but it is based on an underlying data provider intended more for application use and not for ETL. However, you should test the performance in your situation, because there may be other factors that give an advantage to the ADO. NET Destination adapter.

The SQL Destination adapter can also be used, and is quite fast for bulk data inserts, but it requires that the SSIS package be running on the same machine as the destination database (SQL Server) to take advantage of the performance. If your data flow has some lag, you may experience timeout issues with the SQL Destination adapter. The OLE DB Destination, however, is the most stable adapter.

Another benefit of the OLE DB Destination adapter is in its features that control what tables to insert the data into and how that data is being inserted. Figure 12-13 shows the OLE DB Destination Editor.

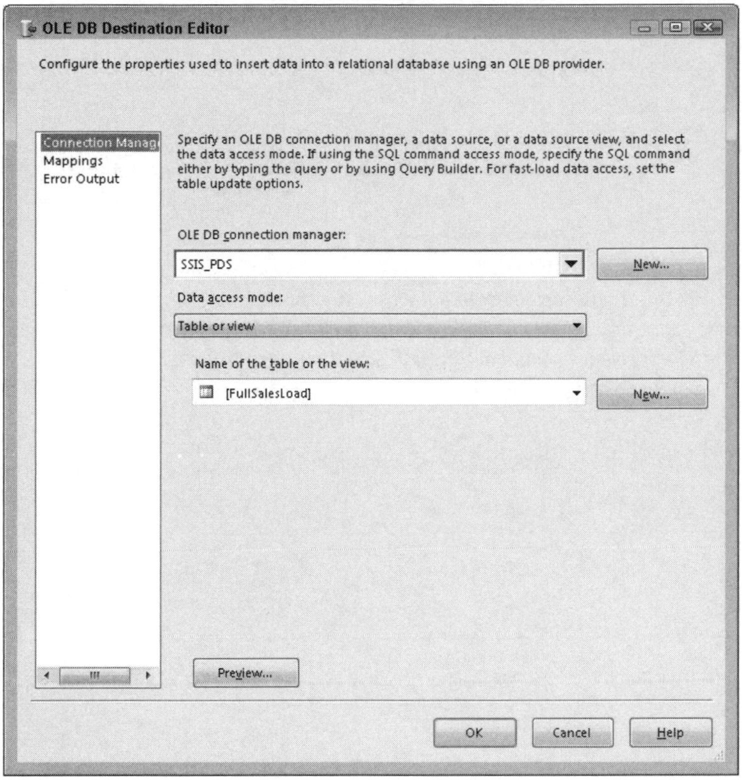

Figure 12-13

The OLE DB Destination settings shown in Figure 12-13 has the Data access mode set to the "Table or view" option, and a table is selected. This adapter is configured to land data into a table called FullSalesLoad in the SSIS_PDS database. The data flow in this example contains a single source file with two million rows, which is directly connected to the OLE DB Destination adapter referenced earlier.

The problem with this destination is that each row is inserted separately into the table. Earlier in this chapter, Figure 12-1 showed a SQL Server Profile trace on the database while this destination is being landed. This profiler session reveals that the INSERT statement would have run two million individual times, and would have taken a couple hours if the package had not been stopped prematurely. Therefore, when dealing with large volumes and scalability, using the "Table or view" option for the "Data access mode" is not the right approach to take with the OLE DB Destination.

If you are using SQL Server as a destination, a better approach when configuring the OLE DB Destination adapter is to use the "Table or view — fast load" option of the "Data access mode." This option allows the rows to be bulk-inserted into a single batch or multiple batches. Figure 12-14 shows the options available when using the fast load feature.

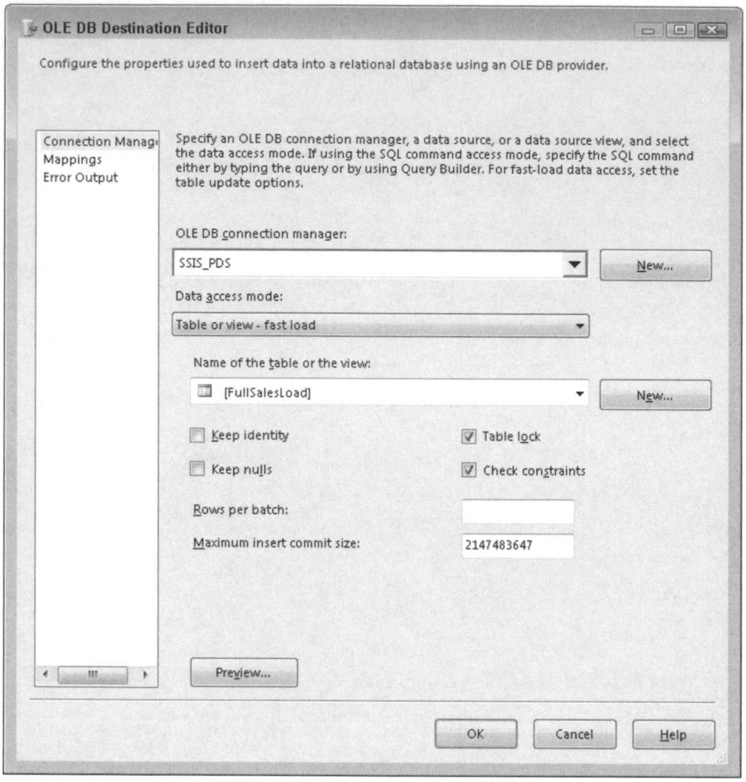

Figure 12-14

By choosing the fast load support, you are given several more advanced features to configure for the destination. These options align directly with the BULK INSERT statement in SQL Server, the mechanism actually used for the inserts. Following is a summary of the options:

❑ *Keep identity* — By selecting this option, you are able to insert explicit values into an IDENTITY column. This is identical to the IDENTITY INSERT function within TSQL.

❑ *Keep nulls* — Check this option to have SQL ignore DEFAULT assignments in the destination table if a NULL value is inserted, which has the effect of helping performance, although negligible. However, this setting may adversely affect data integrity if default values were meant to avoid NULL values being present in certain columns.

❑ *Table lock* — Enable this option to put an exclusive lock on the destination table so that the insert process can optimize the inserts. However, this option could cause locking or blocking problems if other processes are trying to update the same table simultaneously.

❑ *Check constraints* — With check constraints enabled, the insert will still go through the process of checking the constraints on the destination table. De-selecting this option will increase performance if you are handling the value checks in the data flow. However, the constraints will be marked as not-trusted.

❑ *Rows per batch* — This entry simply provides an estimated source row count to help the bulk insert optimize the insert.

❑ *Maximum insert commit size* — The insert commit size drives the size of the batches that are inserted. When set to 0, the entire batch will be inserted; otherwise, this will dictate how many rows should be committed to a destination at one time. More details are provided later in this chapter, as this can help to optimize your destination insert by committing rows in smaller batches than the entire statement.

You must test the bottom-line impact of these settings in your environment with your data and destination table. However, if you are looking to achieve the best scalability, begin by selecting the "Keep nulls" and "Table lock options," and clearing the "Check constraints" option. Of course, you must evaluate these options with the business rules behind your process. If at all possible, handle the constraints and NULL values in your data flow, and allow the table to have an exclusive lock. The "Maximum insert commit size" setting can also have a profound impact on your inserts, and is discussed next.

Maximum Insert Commit Size

With large data volume processing in the multimillions of records, you can control the insert transaction batch sizes with the "Maximum insert commit size" entry setting (referenced in the prior section). Here are some considerations to make when setting this option and testing various values for optimization:

❑ Any insert failures within a batch commit group causes that entire batch to be unsuccessfully inserted.

❑ Leaving the maximum commit size at 0 requires the entire data set to be batched in one commit. This has a couple drawbacks. First, *if there is a failure, the entire data set will be rolled back* and no rows will be committed. Second, if you have indexes and foreign key relationships, the commit time can be very lengthy in a single large volume insert, because the database must reorganize the indexes and check the foreign keys.

❑ A setting greater than 0 will not necessarily mean that the engine will batch that exact number of rows. *The commit size will be the lesser of the number of rows in this setting or the number of rows in the data flow being inserted.* For example, if you set the maximum commit size to 50,000, but your pipeline buffers only contain 9,000 rows, then only 9,000 rows will be committed at a time. Similarly, if you set the commit size to 7,000, and you have 9,000 rows in your buffers, the first batch for every buffer will be 7,000 rows and the second will only be 2,000 rows.

❑ For every commit batch, the database engine will perform the index reorganization and check any foreign keys, therefore reducing the overall performance impact if this all happened at once.

❑ If your destination table doesn't have indexes, foreign keys, or constraints, the commit time will be very rapid and negligible, no matter what you set the commit size to be. The only difference is that a 0 setting will be an all-or-nothing insert.

Consider the following two situations when evaluating this setting:

❑ If you set the maximum commit size, but do not want to lose all the rows in the batch for one row that fails, you can redirect the batch, and then do a second OLE DB Destination that inserts the data one row at a time. Figure 12-15 shows how this would look.

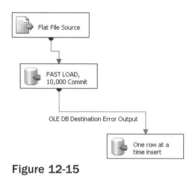

Figure 12-15

❑ To achieve much larger commit batches, you need to modify the `DefaultBufferMaxRows` and `DefaultBufferSize` settings. See the "Design" section earlier in this chapter for a review of these settings. Simple data flows that have limited row widths can greatly benefit by increasing the number of rows in a data flow buffer, which enables you to set the insert commit size higher.

Use Advanced Oracle and Teradata Destination Adapters

Microsoft purchased the use of an advanced set of adapters for Oracle and Teradata that provides optimized sources and destinations. You can download these adapters from Microsoft's download site, `download.microsoft.com`, by searching for "Attunity." After you've installed and configured them, you will have additional adapters in your data flow toolbox.

The Oracle Attunity destination, for example, includes the capability to perform a Fast Load into an Oracle table, which is not available in the out-of-the-box OLE DB Destination adapter if you choose an Oracle OLE DB provider. Figure 12-16 shows the Attunity Oracle Destination editor.

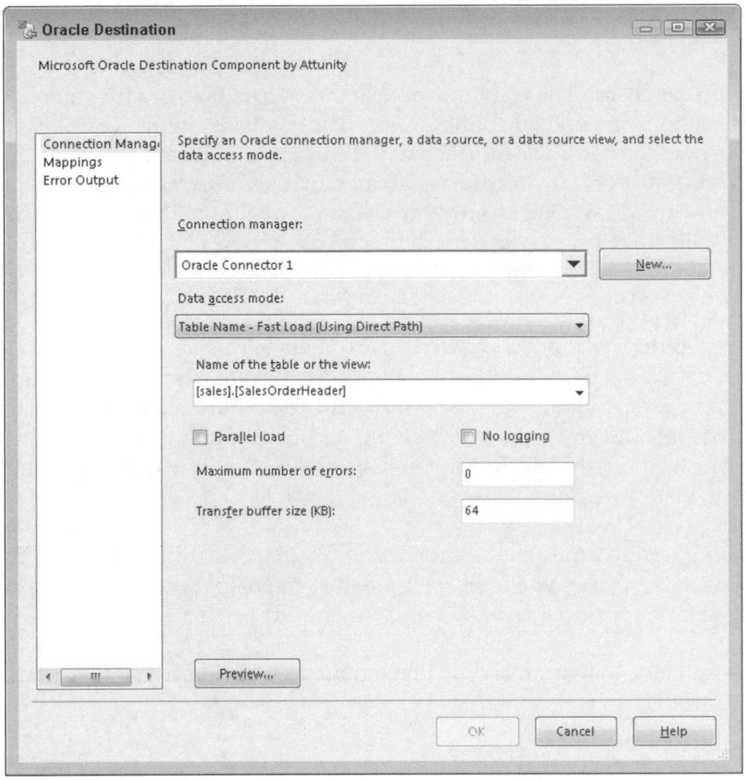

Figure 12-16

The adapter allows parallelized loading, the capability to turn off logging for the insert, and you can set the number of errors before the adapter stops with an error. Further details are available in the help file that comes with the installation.

Handling Partitioned Tables

Partitioned tables are used in enterprise environments for many reasons, including the following:

❑   Allowing tables to scale to the hundreds of millions to tens of billions of rows

❑   Performance for queries by physically partitioning data and allowing parallelization

❑   Physically separating a single table across multiple volumes

❑   Easier management of data archiving

For large tables, partitions are usually based on date ranges, such as weeks, months, quarters, or years. More often than not, when you are loading data into a partitioned table, you are adding rows to the last partition in the table, because the date column is often the most recent data being added. This is not always the case, but if it is, it will allow you to use SSIS to optimize the inserts.

Before looking at a solution, let's step back and talk about working with partitions. Inserting data into partitioned tables can be either easy or difficult:

❑   *Easy* — You can insert data right into a table that is partitioned with any of the SSIS destination adapters without any special configuration. The database engine determines which partition each row should go in. The drawback with this approach is that you can't drop indexes beforehand, and every row must be evaluated to determine to which partition it needs to be added. This can add 20–30 percent overhead and even more if you have indexes (which you probably will). Take the easy approach if you either have a lot of time to run your ETL, or you have a small to moderate number of rows to insert!

❑   *Difficult* — For performance reasons, inserting data into specific partitions by itself after you have dropped the partitions indexes would be better. This task may sound easy, but to do it you must remove the partition from the partitioned table into a temporary table, and then drop the index. After the data load, you must reindex the temporary table, and then add it back into the partitioned table. As you can see, managing partitions and indexes can be a very complex process, but well worth the effort if you have high volumes to deal with, and a narrow window in which to load the data.

The following example shows the general process in SSIS to work with partitioned tables. This approach is not the only way, as there are some tools out there that can help. But it provides you with the framework and general process as you evaluate your specific needs.

Figure 12-17 highlights the SSIS control flow that handles the partition management steps using Execute SQL Tasks.

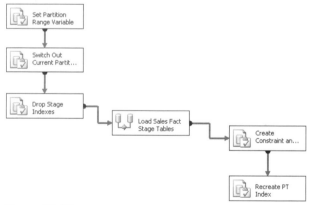

Figure 12-17

In this example, the table is partitioned on the DATETIME COL with partitions on a yearly basis. The package is run on a daily basis and the new data is always for the current day's data and, therefore, must be added to the latest year partition. The overall process involves six distinct steps. (The complete package and code is available with the chapter's examples at www.wrox.com.)

1. An SSIS variable, called PartitionRangeDateKey, is used in this example for the lower bound of the last partition in the table, and is used in the other statements to identify and switch the partition in and out of the table.

2. The second step drops the table index, and then switches the last partition out to a temporary table. (This is a metadata operation, and happens quickly if the temporary table is on the same file group as the partitioned table.) The following dynamic code performs the switch:

```
'ALTER TABLE [dbo].[FactInternetSalesPartitioned]
SWITCH PARTITION ' + CONVERT(VARCHAR(8),@BoundaryID)+
    'TO [dbo].[FactInternetSalesPartitioned_STG]'
```

3. Next, the indexes and constraint are dropped on the staging table so that the data load can be as efficient as possible.

4. The data flow performs the transformation logic, and then loads the staging table with the new data.

5. In the fifth step, the identical indexes and the constraint are re-created on the table, and the table is switched back into the partitioned table. The indexes and constraints are required for the temporary table to be added back to the partitioned table. The following snippet of code performs the switch:

```
'ALTER TABLE [dbo].[FactInternetSalesPartitioned_STG]
SWITCH TO [FactInternetSalesPartitioned] PARTITION ' +
        CONVERT(VARCHAR(8),@BoundaryID)
```

6. In the final step, the complete table index is re-created on the partitioned table. (This index spans all the partitions in the table.)

The complete solution is provided in the chapter's example code found on the Wrox Web site (www.wrox.com), which includes setting up the partitioned table. Your situation may have slightly different requirements, and you should adjust accordingly. For example, if most of your rows go in the latest partition, but some of the data goes into an historical partition, you could use a Conditional Split in your data flow and direct current rows to the temporary table, and the rest of the rows directly into the partitioned table. Figure 12-18 shows what this would look like.

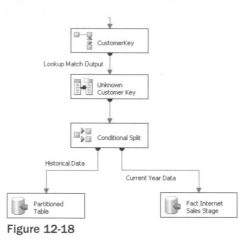

Figure 12-18

In the end, you must closely evaluate your situation and work with your DBA (unless you do that role as well!) to effectively handle the partitioned table.

Summary

When it comes to SSIS scalability, there is no silver bullet. However, you have several ways to identify performance problems and many practical tuning techniques for your packages. Because SSIS is a platform, many ways exist for implementing a design for the same requirements. This makes package design important in achieving scalability. Know when and where to use SQL code, and when to employ the data flow.

The critical aspect of SSIS in terms of scalability is optimizing the data flow, which boils down to memory management and destination optimization. Ensure that your designs are leveraging the features and functionality of SSIS in the right creative ways that limit common bottlenecks such as blocking transformations and large Lookup caches.

Finally, choose a package architecture that considers your source and destination servers, as well as the impact that the data flow will have on those, and, if needed, create a distributed or scaled-out execution architecture. Applying these principles and the others found in this book can take you on the way to designing and implementing stable and scalable SSIS solutions that meet the demanding business requirements for your data processing.

Index

Symbols

F

V

W

X